New Orleans Sports

SPORT, CULTURE & SOCIETY

DAVID K. WIGGINS, SERIES EDITOR

Other Titles in This Series

Moving Boarders:
Skateboarding and the Changing Landscape of Urban Youth Sports

Defending the American Way of Life: Sport, Culture, and the Cold War

New York Sports: Glamour and Grit in the Empire City

LA Sports: Play, Games, and Community in the City of Angels

Making March Madness: The Early Years of the NCAA, NIT,
and College Basketball Championships, 1922–1951

San Francisco Bay Area Sports:
Golden Gate Athletics, Recreation, and Community

Separate Games: African American Sport behind the Walls of Segregation

Baltimore Sports: Stories from Charm City

Philly Sports: Teams, Games, and Athletes from Rocky's Town

DC Sports: The Nation's Capital at Play

Frank Merriwell and the Fiction of All-American Boyhood:
The Progressive Era Creation of the Schoolboy Sports Story

Democratic Sports:
Men's and Women's College Athletics during the Great Depression

Sport and the Law: Historical and Cultural Intersections

Beyond C. L. R. James: Shifting Boundaries of Race and Ethnicity in Sports

A Spectacular Leap: Black Women Athletes in Twentieth-Century America

Hoop Crazy: The Lives of Clair Bee and Chip Hilton

New Orleans Sports

Playing Hard in the Big Easy

Edited by Thomas Aiello

THE UNIVERSITY OF ARKANSAS PRESS
FAYETTEVILLE
2019

Manufactured in the United States of America

ISBN: 978-1-68226-100-2
eISBN: 978-1-61075-670-9

23 22 21 20 19 5 4 3 2 1

∞ The paper used in this publication meets the minimum requirements of the American National Standard for Permanence of Paper for Printed Library Materials Z39.48–1984.

Library of Congress Cataloging-in-Publication Data
Names: Aiello, Thomas, 1977– editor.
Title: New Orleans sports : playing hard in the Big Easy / edited by Thomas Aiello.
Description: Fayetteville : The University of Arkansas Press, 2019. |
Includes bibliographical references and index. |
Identifiers: LCCN 2018054039 (print) | LCCN 2019002184 (ebook) | ISBN 9781610756709 (electronic) | ISBN 9781682261002 (pbk. : alk. paper)
Subjects: LCSH: Sports—Louisiana—New Orleans—History. | Sports—Economic aspects—Louisiana—New Orleans. | Sports—Political aspects—Louisiana—New Orleans. | Sports—Social aspects—Louisiana—New Orleans. | Discrimination in sports—Louisiana—New Orleans.
Classification: LCC GV584.5.N38 (ebook) | LCC GV584.5.N38 N48 2019 (print) | DDC 796.09763/35—dc23
LC record available at https://lccn.loc.gov/2018054039

The forlorn condition of the South will in all probability surrender the majority of the old racing grounds to the weeds and grass, but with New Orleans the case is different. It matters not what comes to pass—whether sugar cane flourishes or the cotton plant blossoms—New Orleans will be the rendezvous of gaiety for all America.

—New Orleans Picayune, *December 1866*

Contents

Series Editor's Preface

Sport is an extraordinarily important phenomenon that pervades the lives of many people and has enormous impact on society in an assortment of ways. At its most fundamental level, sport has the power to bring people great joy and satisfy their competitive urges while at once allowing them to form bonds and a sense of community with others from diverse backgrounds and interests and various walks of life. Sport also makes clear, especially at the highest levels of competition, the lengths that people will go to achieve victory, and it is closely connected to business, education, politics, economics, religion, law, family, and other societal institutions. Sport is, moreover, partly about identity development and how individuals and groups, irrespective of race, gender, ethnicity, or socio-economic class, have sought to elevate their status and realize material success and social mobility.

Sport, Culture, and Society seeks to promote a greater understanding of the aforementioned issues and many others. Recognizing sport's powerful influence and ability to change people's lives in significant and important ways, the series focuses on topics ranging from urbanization and community development to biographies and intercollegiate athletics. It includes both monographs and anthologies that are characterized by excellent scholarship, accessibility to a wide audience, and interesting and thoughtful design and interpretation. Singular features of the series are authors and editors representing a variety of disciplinary areas and who adopt different methodological approaches. The series also includes works by individuals at various stages of their careers, both sport studies scholars of outstanding talent just beginning to make their mark on the field and more experienced scholars of sport with established reputations.

New Orleans Sports: Playing Hard in the Big Easy provides a fascinating look at the pattern and development of sport in the famous city founded in 1718 as La Nouvelle Orleans. Thomas Aiello, the editor of the volume, has compiled a number of very interesting and thoughtful essays that explore the connection between sport and a city that has always fascinated people and drawn much attention for its distinct culture, Mardi Gras celebrations, and exciting Bourbon Street nightlife. Appropriately, Aiello begins the book with a chapter from Dale A. Somers' *The Rise of Sports in New Orleans, 1850–1900*—the classic 1972 text on sport in the city during the late nineteenth century that remains as fresh and insightful as it was when originally published. Following Somers' chapter are twelve others that cover topics ranging from tennis and the New Orleans Athletic Club to horse racing and the New Orleans Saints. In the process, the book provides much insight on sport and its interconnection with race, class, education, technology, gender, economics, politics, and the media in a city that has, fittingly, always been obsessed with its own history.

David K. Wiggins

Introduction

On September 25, 2006, Michael Koenen was preparing to punt the football. He had come to the Atlanta Falcons after signing a free-agent contract out of small Western Washington University, an unlikely path to the NFL, to be sure. Koenen had bested veteran Toby Gowin the previous season to earn the job. But now it was fourth down after three brief plays, and Koenen was called in to punt the ball back to the New Orleans Saints. The crowd was deafening. It was the team's first game back in the Superdome after Hurricane Katrina had ravaged the building and the city it represented. People had died in that building, its crumbling infrastructure a hulking, burly stand-in for the crumbling infrastructure of the city it represented. It was a symbol of the ravages of weather, of the failures of the Federal Emergency Management Agency. But now there was football, and the Falcons were punting to the Saints. It was a routine play, but nothing seemed routine on this night that meant so much to so many. When the center sent the ball back to Koenen, Steve Gleason moved through the middle of the Atlanta line. Gleason, too, was from Washington, a graduate of larger Washington State University, but still, like Koenen, had come to the NFL undrafted, signing a free-agent contract first with the Indianapolis Colts, then, after being released, with the New Orleans Saints. He ran through the line, dived, and blocked Koenen's punt, sending the ball into the end zone, where his teammate Curtis Deloatch fell on it and scored for the home team.

It was the penultimate moment in New Orleans sports, bested only, perhaps, by Tracy Porter's interception of Peyton Manning in Super Bowl XLIV, giving the Saints and their city the team's only professional football championship in February 2010. At the same time, however, the event raised legitimate questions about the city's civic priorities that would lead it to spend $200 million renovating a football stadium while people were, more than a year after the storm, still suffering in homelessness and poverty. In so doing, it stood as a culmination not only of the city's recovery, but also its fraught relationship with sports and the intersecting lines of class, race, and civic development that served as the boundaries for its place in the city. This volume seeks to evaluate those boundary lines in the centuries and decades leading up to such twenty-first century moments.

The historiography of those fraught moments has long been dominated by the one monograph on the subject, Dale A. Somers's *The Rise of Sports in New Orleans, 1850–1900*. The book is an institution unto itself in New Orleans sports historiography, but it leaves much for expansion. Somers's work was published in 1972, and its coverage stopped at the end of the nineteenth century. This volume will provide an expanded, modern examination of sports in the city. It will pay homage to Somers while expanding on his work and developing an understanding of sports in twentieth century New Orleans.

Such an understanding is vital, as New Orleans was and is a city obsessed with its own history and culture, where that history and culture are so palpable that they have become the city's principal economic vehicle. Founded in 1718 by the French, transferred to the Spanish in the Treaty of Paris in 1763, and sold to the United States in 1803, the city's culture, law, architecture, food, music, language, and sports evinced a rude conglomeration of the influence of all three countries. The history of New Orleans, then, bore down on residents in every game that was played. It was, befitting that French heritage, *un métissage culturel*, a culture of blended ancestries and memories that coalesced into one collective history. Because of that cultural mélange and the realities of southern urban life, race would become another dominant factor in the development of the city's athletic contests.

In a setting like New Orleans, it couldn't be otherwise. It was the New Orleans of Homer Plessy, recruited by a group of concerned black business leaders in the city to challenge segregation on local train cars. It was a response to the legislature's Separate Car Act that ultimately ended in the Supreme Court's *Plessy v. Ferguson* (1896) decision that validated segregation in public facilities. It was the New Orleans of Robert Charles, a black laborer who got into an argument with a white police officer in summer 1900 when he tried to beat him with a nightstick. They shot each other, and Charles fled to a rooming house. When a white mob came to find him, he shot twenty-seven of them, killing seven. Charles was finally shot, his corpse stomped beyond recognition. Four days of rioting ensued, killing at least a dozen and injuring many more. It was later the New Orleans of the Greater New Orleans White Citizens Council, led by Plaquemines Parish lawyer and staunch segregationist Leander Perez. It was the New Orleans of the New Orleans Public Service Company, which responded to NAACP pressure in 1958 by ending segregation on public buses and streetcars. It was the New Orleans of the interminable fight to integrate the city's public schools, a fight led by activist lawyer Alexander Tureaud, and one that ultimately led to race riots fueled by disgruntled whites after desegregation.

It was also a city divided by class. It was the New Orleans of the 1892 Triple Alliance general strike, an integrated fight against the economic policies of the New Orleans Board of Trade. It was the New Orleans of the 1907 dockworkers' strike against city shipping companies for better wages and working conditions. It was the New Orleans of political machines like, in the nineteenth century, The Ring, and in the twentieth, the Old Regulars, led by mayor Martin Behrman, the city's mayor for much of the Progressive era, then the Crescent City Democratic Association, led by DeLesseps Morrison. It was the New Orleans of Storyville, the city's vice district that lasted from 1897–1917, a region that regularly suffered from epidemics of yellow fever, malaria, and rickets, not fully implementing a modern sewage and drainage system until 1910. It was a New Orleans whose wealth grew unevenly throughout the twentieth century, much of that growth coming from oil and natural gas production, exacerbating the gap between rich and poor.

That gap would become more and more significant when a new imperative, that of Sunbelt civic and business development, drove New Orleans to a new kind of growth that was impossible prior to integration. The city joined many of its fellow southern counterparts to rehabilitate its image after the civil rights movement, using economic subsidies, low tax rates, and good weather to woo corporations to relocate in the South. New Orleans's historic role as one of the nation's most vital port cities at the mouth of its largest river only helped that pitch. Still, growth in aid of cultural legitimacy required the trappings of other American metropolitan areas, including major league professional sports, seen as fostering further growth, aiding gentrification, and standing as symbols of civic success.

Sports, however, had always been part of the city's growth, had run parallel to and played a vital role in shaping the political and social machinations that gave New Orleans is particular distinction as both southern and beyond the South. Professional football, for example, first came to New Orleans in 1925. It was a young and struggling game, but first achieved national notoriety when University of Illinois superstar Harold "Red" Grange turned pro, agreeing to play a nineteen-game barnstorming tour with the NFL's Chicago Bears. The trip took Grange and the Bears to Miami, Tampa, and Jacksonville before arriving in New Orleans. There, the team scrimmaged against a group of local college all-stars at the city's Heineman Park. Professional football had arrived in the nation. And it had, however briefly, arrived in Louisiana.[1]

The city's effort to secure a professional football team of its own began in the late 1950s. Under the leadership of mayor and all-around civic booster DeLesseps Morrison, New Orleans made overtures to the NFL before attempting to cast its lot as a new member of the inaugural American Football League. But the plan failed, largely because a new stadium plan had not been put in place. Tulane Stadium, home to the city's Green Wave and the annual Sugar Bowl, was legendary in its own right, but it was a college stadium. The gravity that professional football had achieved by the 1960s required of its member institutions that they play in signature stadiums designed for league members first and foremost. In 1964, Dave Dixon combined with other local leaders to create New Orleans Professional Football, Inc., and through that organization sought to include New Orleans in an early, failed attempt to create a third United States Football League.

Meanwhile, the NFL was feeling the heat from its upstart AFL competitor. The resulting competition threatened to bankrupt both groups, and the two decided that a merger would be the best way to remain solvent. They announced the decision in June 1966. A merger, however, wouldn't be that easy. The only hope to overcome antitrust laws was a Congressional exemption. To grease the wheels, Louisiana Senator Russell Long—a football fan and no stranger to backroom deals—met with Pete Rozelle for a quid pro quo. He would ensure its passage through the Senate. New Orleans congressman Hale Boggs would ensure its passage through the House. When the Football Merger Act of 1966 became law, New Orleans would receive the league's first expansion franchise.[2]

A month after the announced merger, in July 1966, the Louisiana legislature, anticipating the possible team and worried about potential competition from rival cities, passed a constitutional measure to support the funding of a new domed stadium, scheduled to go on the ballot in November. On November 1, Rozelle made his announcement. "Today, I'd like to announce that a professional franchise has been awarded to the State of Louisiana and the City of New Orleans." The timing was no coincidence. "This announcement is coming the week before the election because there's no question about the importance of next week's vote. A permanent facility is vital." With the prospect of an NFL franchise on the line, the stadium measure passed overwhelmingly.[3] Eventually, that team would become the Saints, that stadium the Superdome, and that setting the site of the city's redemption when Steve Gleason blocked Michael Koenen's punt.

The Saints will appear often in these pages, but many other athletic exemplars of the intersection between race, class, and civic development will not, as collections such as this provide representative studies rather than comprehensive coverage of any particular subject. New Orleans, for example, was a hub of gambling throughout its long life. Gambling had always been a creature of both the New Orleans vice trade and state political bosses in early Louisiana. In 1868, the legislature chartered the Louisiana State Lottery Company, which became incredibly powerful in the state after allying itself with the principal political machine in New Orleans. Its blatant corruption led to declamations of vice and scandal that ultimately brought the original Lottery to an end in the early 1890s, but Storyville provided all the gambling that New Orleans would need. After the Progressive era, however, gambling would continue. When Earl Long took the reins of power in the late 1940s and 1950s, he consolidated that power by, among other things, renewing state ties with the mafia, allowing organized crime to operate a number of casinos and horseracing gambling throughout the state, particularly in New Orleans and south Louisiana. A lottery then returned in 1990, approved in a statewide referendum. In September 1991, the first million-dollar jackpot was announced. Because of Lottery corruption that had plagued the state in earlier incarnations, regulation was severe, ensuring fairness and keeping the lottery relatively trustworthy and popular. But the lottery soon led to riverboat casinos, which led to other land-based casinos in June 1992. And these more traditional forms of gambling have not been so free from controversy. Not only have corruption and legislative favoritism been rampant, but the payoff has been far less than originally advertised in the early 1990s. Even more significantly, those of the lowest incomes have proven particularly susceptible to the incursion. It has made the poor even poorer in a region already known for its poverty.

There were so many other intersections. Like when Algiers became an early nineteenth century bullfighting hub. Like when German immigrants brought gymnastics to the city in the nineteenth and early twentieth centuries. Like the development of a variety of Negro League baseball teams, from the Algiers Giants to the New Orleans Black Pelicans, that brought together disparate communities in a stifling Jim Crow environment. Like Tulane University's trip to the Rose Bowl on January 1, 1932, a close loss to local USC, or the arrival to New Orleans later in the century of the Bayou Classic, the showcase game of the state's two prominent public black colleges. Or like the time in February 1965, four days after the assassination of Malcolm X, when the basketball team of New Orleans's white Jesuit High School played the Purple Knights of St. Augustine High School in the first organized, integrated team game in the history of the city and state. Such examples, among many others, are for another volume.[4]

No such intersections, however, were as important to the development of New Orleans sports as those of race, class, and civic boosterism. In an attempt to dissect those intersections, then, *New Orleans Sports* is divided into three sections providing an approximate temporal progression while emphasizing, first, class, then civic institutions, followed finally by an emphasis on race. Of course, the connections between the three run throughout the volume, as does the imprimatur of masculinity and gender, but the volume tracks the development of sports in the city by organizing sections by points of differentiation that have long dominated the experience of athletics in New Orleans.

The first of those sections, Victorian Sensibilities, emphasizes the class dynamic of sports in the city, beginning with a selection from the dean of New Orleans sports historians, Dale Somers. His *The Rise of Sports in New Orleans, 1850–1900*, published in 1972, has a singular place in the historiography of New Orleans sports, the one acknowledged authority on athletics in the city's Gilded Age. The book's first chapter is an example of that work. Of the sports that attracted nineteenth-century Americans, none enjoyed a greater popularity than cycling. For the athletically inclined, the bicycle was a pleasurable exercise, a passport to the tonic freshness of the open countryside, a speedy racing machine, and a low-cost, convenient mode of transportation. During the height of the cycling craze in the 1890's, *Munsey's Magazine* explained, "Today, in reckoning the achievements of the nineteenth century, to such epoch-making discoveries as the railroad, the steamship, the telegraph, and the telephone, we can hardly refuse to add, as the latest item on the list, the bicycle." Residents of New Orleans first evinced a desire for two-wheeled transportation during the velocipede mania that swept the country during the late 1860s, even witnessing the creation of organizations like the League of American Wheelmen. By the 1920s, however, the League had collapsed, marking the end of the city's Gilded Age obsession with the vehicle. Although the craze was short-lived, cycling accustomed people to individual transportation and a higher degree of mobility than they had ever known. As an agent of social change, this middle-class pastime occupied an important position in the history of the latter nineteenth century.

Bicycling was one of the city's first mass-participation sports. But horse racing was America's first mass-audience sport, as histories of American athletics generally acknowledge, with nods to the crowds at Jerome Park and Sheepshead Bay in the 1870s and 1880s. But long before that, racing fans knew that the richest, fastest track in America was New Orleans's Metairie Course. The Metairie hosted the 1854 Great Post Stakes, one of the first great sports spectacles in American history, in which states sent their best runners to duel for turf supremacy. The race produced the rivalry between Lexington and Lecomte, a feud that would grip the nation, draw American horses into international competition, and produce two sires whose blood still runs in American Thoroughbreds. The first argument of Chapter 2 is thus that New Orleans racing played a critical role not only in the history of equine competition in the United States but in the rise of big-time sports as a financial and emotional touchstone of American life.

But the track at New Orleans was also one of the first places black men became national celebrities because of their prowess in athletic competition. When Abe Hawkins, the enslaved black man who rode Lecomte, stepped aboard his mount, newspapers all the way to New York noted it. Antebellum New Orleans was a place where black men who trained and rode Thoroughbreds could clearly see demonstrated the contrast between their reputation in their sport and their legal status as human property. But New Orleans was also where black men from around the country got to know each other on the backstretch and laid the foundations of professional networks that would thrive after emancipation and propel former slaves and their sons and apprentices to fame and fortune after 1865. New Orleans was the site of a significant challenge to segregation in the 1870s, as black fans demanded equal access to seating at the racetrack, where they could watch black men compete across the color line and win. And it was in New Orleans that one of the last black stars of racing, Jimmy Lee, grabbed a white jockey by the collar and railed against the violence that drove him off the track. Chapter 2 thus also traces the long and painful history of New Orleans's role as a site of contestation over black men's right to compete as athletes and the significance of their success.

Boxing had its own painful history of class and race, and New Orleans was most certainly a boxing hub in the late nineteenth century. In September 1892, the city's Olympic Club staged a three-day boxing spectacular that included George "Little Chocolate" Dixon defeating white fighter Jack Skelly, as well as Gentleman Jim Corbett beating John L. Sullivan for the heavyweight championship, widely considered to be one of the most important contests in boxing's history. As Chapter 3 demonstrates, the success of the event only bolstered the city's interest in the sport, leading in 1893 to a fight between mulatto Andy Bowen and "Texas" Jack Burke for the Lightweight Championship of the South. It was to be a "fight to the finish" without a round limitation, and ultimately lasted more than seven hours, 110 rounds, the longest boxing match in history.

At the other end of the economic Gilded Age spectrum, tennis in New Orleans was, as it was in other urban areas, a vehicle of restrictive exclusivity, but that exclusivity worked in myriad ways across lines of class and race, beginning with the founding of the New Orleans Lawn Tennis Club in 1876 and moving through a century beset by racial and economic turmoil. Post-Reconstruction New Orleans tennis looked much like antebellum Louisiana writ large, with a small exclusive upper class, an also-small upper-middle class with slightly less exclusivity but seeking as much as they could muster, then the majority of white players below who were left to use playing ability rather than social or financial status to gain access. Then there was the black population that was excluded from all of that competition, middle and upper-class players participating in a separate world until pioneers came along to push back against that closed system. Black tennis in New Orleans, then, democratized from the top down, those with access working to open doors for themselves, then leading the way for their social and economic inferiors who otherwise would not have access. White tennis, meanwhile, democratized from the bottom up, with players originally priced or classed out of the NOLTC making new opportunities to play the game and creating new access for a new group of players.

The book's second part, Institutions of the City, describes and evaluates legendary institutions of New Orleans and their relation to the city's infrastructure and civic development. In 1872, for example, fourteen young men founded the Independent Gymnastic Club, which later became the Young Men's Gymnastic Club (YMGC), then later the New Orleans Athletic Club (NOAC). Chapter 5 describes the NOAC, which included a gymnasium, running tracks, handball/squash courts, bowling lanes, a shooting range, steam baths, a marble-lined swimming pool, and at one time, a cycling track and boat house. Social events and entertainments utilized a magnificent ballroom and the gym, and members enjoyed a bar, library, and barber shop. In 1889 the club began sponsoring professional boxing matches, and John L. Sullivan trained at the YMGC for several of his fights. In 1893 the YMGC cofounded the Southern Amateur Athletic Union and supplied its first president. Supreme Court Chief Justice Edward D. White was a member, as were the Longs and several New Orleans mayors. Jack Dempsey, Primo Carnera, Clark Gable, Frankie Laine, Tennessee Williams, Johnny Weissmuller, and others were visitors. Girls and women participated in social activities but black people were only permitted to be present as employees.

Other institutions of the city, however, developed their civic importance less from developing a venue to play sports and more from creating a venue to watch them. It was in 1917 when Tulane decided to build a new football stadium with funding from private donors from the city of New Orleans and Tulane students. Such a prompt to build a new and larger stadium emerged from the popularity of Tulane football and the continual growth of the sport in general, as well as a desire to keep pace with peer institutions in the East and Midwest. Chapter 6 describes the erection, modernization, and ultimately the demolition of Tulane Stadium from 1926–1975, emphasizing the impact of New Orleans residents, the Sugar Bowl, and innovation with respect to the construction and razing of the facility. Tulane Stadium embodied modernization, with several stadium improvements ranging from seat expansions to the arrival of artificial turf and lights. Aiding in the modernization of Tulane Stadium was the birth and development of the Sugar Bowl, an annual holiday event supported by the New Orleans Mid-Winter Sports Association. As the Sugar Bowl gained momentum, Tulane Stadium adapted through renovation efforts, which created more space for spectators and fan amenities, ultimately confirming the importance of college athletics for the university and the Sugar Bowl as a permanent holiday tradition for New Orleans.

Tulane Stadium would also eventually become the temporary home of the city's first major league professional team, the New Orleans Saints. As Chapter 7 explains, the genesis of the team was borne from the political trouble surrounding the potential merger of the National and American Football Leagues. It was Representative Hale Boggs and Senator Russell Long, two federal legislators from Louisiana, who helped steer the anti-trust legislation through Congress. The quo for the quid of the state's congressional delegation was an expansion team for New Orleans, ultimately giving birth to the Saints and the city's newfound New South legitimacy.

Four decades later, the team was temporarily forced from its home after Hurricane Katrina. Katrina devastated the city of New Orleans in late August 2005, resulting in damage to much of the city's sports infrastructure and the temporary departure of both of New Orleans's major league professional sports teams, the National Football League Saints and the National Basketball Association Hornets. As Chapter 8 explains, the city spent over $500 million restoring the sports infrastructure in New Orleans, and both teams subsequently returned to the city. In addition, the city has since hosted numerous mega-sporting events including the Super Bowl, the NCAA Men's Basketball Final Four, and several college football national championships. This chapter examines the economic impact of Hurricane Katrina on professional sports in New Orleans and traces the recovery of the city in conjunction with spectator sports.

The book's third section, Race and Respectability, focuses on the most consummate form of differentiation in New Orleans and in almost all southern sports, one that seeps through all of the previous chapters: the racial line that formed the contour of life's shape in the twentieth-century South. The section begins by returning to the Sugar Bowl, as Chapter 9 explores changing views of manhood, race, and the southern woman in New Orleans and the larger Gulf Coast region from 1935 to the present using the football game as a magnifying lens. The Sugar Bowl is the only major bowl game staged in the Deep South. (The Rose Bowl is held on the West Coast and the Cotton and Orange bowls on the periphery of the South.) The chapter examines college football's highly important role in southern life and culture, and the sport's commercialism and corruption. It also emphasizes the carnival activities associated with the Sugar Bowl, including the selection of Sugar Bowl Queens and their Courts. The pageants, parades, and balls—central features of Sugar Bowl week—provide insight into southern views of female beauty and identity. The Sugar Bowl, which regularly drew 70,000 spectators, second only to the Rose Bowl, often took the form of symbolic confrontations between North and South, with press accounts of the games invoking images of Civil War battles. This remained a significant feature of the game at least through the 1973 Notre Dame-Alabama contest. Intersectional rivalry assumed particular significance during the period of civil rights conflict from the late 1940s through the 1960s.

The symbolic battles taken on by the Sugar Bowl and the slow racial progress that developed over the twentieth century can also be seen in other scheduled grand events in the city, even when those events never actually took place. As

Chapter 10 explains, New Orleans had managed to host the Amateur Athletic Union's national track and field championship once before, in 1910, a lily-white affair that went off without real controversy. In 1926, with an expanded media presence driving an increased interest in sports and a local desire to showcase New Orleans as a pre-Sunbelt example of southern civic development, the city made a bid to host the 1927 championship, winning the honor in November. The games had not been lily white for a number of years, but leaders assumed that the presence of the games in the Deep South would act as its own warning to keep black athletes from the competition. Those assumptions would be wrong, and the games would be defined by racial controversy, the AAU ultimately canceling the event. The Southern Association of the Amateur Athletic Union (SAAAU) would continue to fight for white supremacy well into the next decade.

Racial positioning was the most difficult aspect of New Orleans's attempt to transition to the Sunbelt model, but the roots of that racial positioning came in the generations prior. The SAAAU, for example, made its home in New Orleans, and its racial politics in the first half of the twentieth century demonstrated a willingness to hue to Jim Crow over and against championship level events in the city, a policy that would have to evolve if New Orleans was ever to participate in Sunbelt prosperity. This chapter examines the Southern Association's relationship with race and amateur sport in New Orleans, Mark Dyreson arguing, "In American track and field from the 1890s through the 1960s, the SAAAU, led by a heterogeneous cabal of New Orleans elites from the Crescent City's Irish, Italian, and Jewish communities, policed the color line between white and black with an unrivalled ferocity." The policy that rejected racial integration would not end as a result of a moral awakening, but instead because Sunbelt financial politics required it for metropolitan progress.

Sunbelt financial politics would continue to shape New Orleans civic decisions in other sports, as well. In the 1960s, after Lamar Hunt and others unsuccessfully attempted to acquire an interest in the National Football League's Chicago Cardinals and after NFL Commissioner Bert Bell's refusal to grant them an expansion team, the men gathered in 1959 and formed the American Football League. The league began with six charter franchises, many in competing NFL markets. The young AFL had to overcome numerous obstacles in its early days, but through innovative acts such as early network television revenue sharing and a later acquisition of an enormous television contract with the National Broadcasting Corporation, the league had sufficient revenue to compete with the NFL. The league also broke the norms of the NFL clubs at the time by welcoming African American players, especially those from historically black colleges and universities who were rejected by clubs in the National Football League. As Chapter 11 explains, this would later cause problems during the 1965 AFL All-Star Game, scheduled to be played in New Orleans at Tulane Stadium. The city of New Orleans did not welcome black players at all, in their taverns or their hotels. A majority of all AFL athletes suggested the league boycott New Orleans as the host city for the game. It was eventually moved to Houston.

Thus, racial integration was slow in coming to the city. But racial integration did not mean the birth of equality in New Orleans. As Chapter 12 explains, an important accomplishment of the American women's rights movement was the passage and implementation of Title IX, and an important accomplishment of the civil rights movement was the passage of Title VI. The timing of the passage and execution of these laws facilitated the establishment of racially integrated women's professional sports leagues across the nation, though backlashes kept them short-lived. In many ways New Orleans served as an economic, political, and a social exception to the South and the nation as a whole. The fight to regulate women's bodies and vice along with the historically racial and ethnic diversity of the city are but a few things that help explain the residents' historically unique experience. Utilizing feminist theories of sport, feminist theories of the body, critical race theory, and by integrating a textual analysis of archival sources, Chapter 12 examines the factors that led to the establishment and dissolution of the New Orleans Pride (1979–1981), a basketball team that existed in this abbreviated period of popularity in women's professional sports leagues. The New Orleans Women's Professional Basketball League (WPBL) team, the Pride, did not serve as an exception to the national trends in women's sports. It too suffered from the scale back of women's sports that occurred during the 1980s cultural backlash. Even in this racially and ethnically diverse climate, the franchise failed to challenge the national trend to feminize women's sports, a movement that focused on the maintenance of white, heterosexual femininity.

That kind of social identity also manifested across a broad spectrum of city residents. Chapter 13 focuses on the New Orleans Saints and the team's effect on citizens of its host city, as well as on fans from the surrounding region. While a large body of research shows little evidence that new stadiums and professional sports teams make a significant economic impact on the region, some findings have shown that sports teams can provide intangible benefits. These intangible benefits are often related to the positive associations fans of the team have by considering themselves a part of that particular in-group. This final chapter applies social identity theory to the New Orleans Saints' fan base and discusses the reactions of the team's fans during the 2009 Super Bowl–winning season as reported in national, regional, and local publications.

Taken together, these chapters represent the various contours of sport in New Orleans, developing as they have along the fault lines of race, class, and civic development. They do not, of course, represent the whole of New Orleans sports. They are instead an attempt to represent that greater whole. The chapters that follow do not evaluate, for example, the fact that New Orleans introduced fencing to the United States, or that it was the home of Pete Herman, the first boxing champion of the South, or that its first major professional basketball team, the ABA's New Orleans Buccaneers, was the inheritor and brainchild of later New York provocateur Morton Downey, Jr.[5]

The chapters do, however, demonstrate the reasons for the popularity of sports in the city, its role as a tie that bound (civically and culturally), even as it sometimes divided (racially and economically). It is only within that historical nexus that the seminal moment provided by Steve Gleason and Michael Koenen can be understood, a moment remembered with wistful fondness by everyone in the city, even though many of them surely would have benefited from a portion of the $200 million spent on the Superdome's renovation. In many ways, such could be taken as at least relatively inevitable. "It matters not what comes to pass," the *New Orleans Picayune* explained in 1866, "whether sugar cane flourishes or the cotton plant blossoms—New Orleans will be the rendezvous of gaiety for all America."

I

Victorian Sensibilities

CHAPTER ONE

A City on Wheels

The Bicycle Era in New Orleans[1]

DALE A. SOMERS

Sports have played an interesting role in the American search for recreation since colonial days when Virginia gentlemen rode to the hounds or wagered on their favorite thoroughbreds and a few atypical New Englanders frolicked around the Maypole. But it was not until the latter half of the nineteenth century

A New Orleans girl rides a bicycle in the early twentieth century. Photo courtesy of The Historic New Orleans Collection, Williams Research Center, New Orleans, Louisiana.

that sports developed the characteristics and importance associated with this prominent social institution today. Before the Industrial Revolution, American sports were mainly rural, out-of-doors activities. Hunting, fishing, horse racing, cockfighting, and animal-baiting were the chief sporting diversions of agrarian America. The dearth of athletic amusements led one observer to write in 1901 (with some exaggeration), "Until the middle of the century just closed we were practically without sports."[2]

When industrialization caused violent shifts in the basic structure of society, sports reflected the transformation. As thousands and then millions of Americans made the pilgrimage from farm to city, they felt a more pressing need for organized recreation than they had experienced in the sylvan environment of their pre-industrial society. To ease and to escape the pressures of urbanization and industrialization, Americans fashioned what historian Frederic Logan Paxson termed the "safety valve of sport."[3] Its rate of growth was phenomenal. At the turn of the century a contemporary could in all honesty designate the period as the "era of sport. Practically every man and boy, every woman and girl, takes part, or wishes to take part, in some branch of it," he explained. "And it is fortunate that the field is broad enough for all."[4]

This rage for competitive sports developed like a rising tide, reaching flood proportions in the 1890s, when an interest in sports permeated every level of society. Professor John Higham has suggested that this intensified interest in sports, with a corresponding enthusiasm for nature cults and martial music, reflected a desire "to break out of the frustrations, the routine, and the sheer dullness of an urban-industrial culture." While Higham doubtless exaggerates the docility with which Americans submitted to "the gathering restrictions of a highly industrialized society," there is no denying the spectacular growth of sports at the *fin-de-siècle,* particularly those activities that emphasized speed, strength, and rugged exercise.[5]

Of the sports that attracted nineteenth-century Americans, none enjoyed a greater popularity than cycling. For the athletically inclined, the bicycle was a pleasurable type of exercise, a passport to the tonic freshness of the open countryside, a speedy racing machine, and a low-cost, convenient mode of transportation. In the age of the automobile the bicycle's appeal seems limited and remote, but during the height of the cycling craze in the 1890s, a *Munsey's Magazine* writer assigned this conveyance a high position on his century's honor roll: "Today, in reckoning the achievements of the nineteenth century, to such epoch making discoveries as the railroad, the steamship, the telegraph, and the telephone, we can hardly refuse to add, as the latest item on the list, the bicycle."[6]

The bicycle of the 1890s was the result of almost a century of experimentation. In 1816, Baron Karl von Drais of Germany invented a wooden velocipede shaped something like a modern bicycle without pedals. Although the *draisine,* as it was known, enjoyed only a brief vogue, the concept of self-propelled transportation fired the imagination of inventors, who continued to tinker with the contraption. In the 1850s two Frenchmen, Ernest Michaux and Pierre Lallement, developed a wooden velocipede with pedals attached to the front wheels. Introduced in this country, the velocipede attracted ardent devotees in 1868 and 1869. Interest in the machine subsided when velocipedists found the machine ill-suited to outdoor rambles. British inventors perfected the high-wheeled bicycle, which Americans first observed at Philadelphia's Centennial Exposition in 1876. Since the front wheel had a much greater diameter than the rear one, this bicycle was difficult to mount and not entirely comfortable to ride. Nevertheless, the high-wheeler established a taste for cycling that was to be universally gratified after further technical improvements. By the mid-1880s British enthusiasts had developed the "Rover," a chain-driven vehicle with wheels of equal size known as the "safety." In 1887 the Overman Wheel Company began to produce "Victor" safeties in this country and other manufacturers soon followed. After the introduction of the pneumatic tire in 1889, the bicycle had practically assumed its modern form.[7]

Safety bicycles made cycling less a sport for specialists and more a general pastime. Soon men and women of all ages were pedaling the highways of the country to the tune of "Daisy Bell," "My Love's a Cyclist," "A Merry Cyclist," and countless other period tunes that reflected mass interest in the sport. In 1892, Luther H. Porter, a national authority on the wheel, said, "Within the last five years cycling has attained the dignity of being the most popular form of outdoor recreation indulged in by Americans as well as by Englishmen."[8] Technical improvements and mass production gave the country a sporting pastime as well as a utilitarian mode of transportation that amused millions of people until it fell victim to a new craze—the automobile.

Residents of New Orleans first evinced a desire for two-wheeled transportation during the velocipede mania that swept the country during the late 1860s. Several months after the craze conquered New York, it struck the Crescent City. In February 1869, a local paper reported that officials proposed to buy twenty-five velocipedes for each of the city's fire companies.[9] In the following month a few daring young men imported several of the novelties and opened a school to give indoor exhibitions and to instruct anyone interested in mastering the new art. "The school," said the *Picayune,* "is the resort of our most elegant and fashionable young men, and each evening numbers of ladies assemble to witness the performance." Following demonstrations of "fancy riding," riders and spectators devoted the evening to the safer pastime of dancing. More intrepid enthusiasts ventured outdoors with their machines. Riders frequently labored along outlying roads, and it was reported that some could "make their mile in four minutes on the Shell Road, if not in faster time." During the summer, firemen featured velocipede races at their Sunday outings.[10]

Pedaling over dirt and oyster-shell roads soon disclosed the deficiencies of the velocipede. Known as the "boneshaker," this forerunner of the modern bicycle was often painful to ride and always difficult to maneuver. As velocipedists discovered the shortcomings of their toys, they quickly abandoned the sport. Benevolent societies sponsored races as late as 1871, but these infrequent contests did not reflect widespread interest in the velocipede.[11]

Residents returned to cycling only after the introduction of the high wheeler. Even then interest mounted slowly. While cyclists in the East enthusiastically embraced the ordinary in the latter part of the 1870s, New Orleanians showed no interest in the sport as late as 1880. In May of that year, at about the time eastern sportsmen were organizing the League of American Wheelmen, the *Picayune* lamented the indifference of local athletes: "It is remarkable that the exercise has not found favor in New Orleans, as the various shellroads offer rare advantages for bicycle practice."[12]

Shortly after the *Picayune*'s appeal, "a few gentlemen who were considered cranks on the subject" organized the New Orleans Bicycle Club (NOBC).[13] This association was an elite social group that included many professional men and merchants who were "men of affairs of relatively high standing." In a period when bicycles cost from one to two hundred dollars, a club spokesman said, "The fundamental principle, that personal ownership of a wheel is a requisite for membership, acts in itself as a sort of check against indiscriminate applications for admission." Moreover, the club had a "rigid rule" making "two black balls sufficient cause for the indefinite rejection of a candidate."[14] Toward the end of the high-wheel era, a group of independent cyclists organized the Louisiana Cycling Club, a society that became important after the introduction of safety bicycles.[15]

For several years after its founding the NOBC sponsored only a few organized activities. Members devoted much of their riding time to individual jaunts around the city or to nearby amusement places such as Milneburg.[16] Among the more popular events sanctioned by the club were those involving visiting cyclists. In 1882 the NOBC brought Elsa Von Blumen, the "White Fawn," to the city for a race against a trotter and a pacer. Elsa, who was the champion female cyclist of the ordinary era, won two of three heats held at the fairgrounds.[17] Early in 1885 the Cotton Centennial and Industrial Exposition cooperated with the NOBC to bring John Prince, "champion bicyclist of America," to town for a match with W.M. Woodside, "the Irish champion." After defeating Woodside, Prince claimed the title of "World's champion."[18]

Cycling received a great boost in the mid-1880s when members of the NOBC decided to join the League of American Wheelmen (LAW). As stated in the constitution, the League's purposes were "to promote the general interests of bicycling, to ascertain, defend and protect the rights of wheelmen, and to encourage and facilitate touring." When the NOBC joined its ranks, the LAW had more than thirty-five hundred members, representing about ten per cent of the cyclists in America."[19] After joining the League, local cyclists showed a marked increase in devotion to their sport. In December 1884, E.W. Hunter and Charles Genslinger, former president of the NOBC, began publication of the monthly *Bicycle South*. By 1886 this paper reportedly had eighteen hundred subscribers. As the official organ of the Louisiana Division of the LAW, the *Bicycle South* kept members abreast of national developments by publishing news about cycling in cities throughout the country.[20]

Like all League affiliates, the Louisiana Division held annual races for local championships. During the high-wheel period, members of the LAW (most of whom also belonged to the New Orleans Bicycle Club) sponsored three meetings to determine divisional supremacy. In 1887 the Louisiana Cycling Club also participated, but its members made a poor showing against the more experienced riders of the NOBC. Cyclists practiced strenuously for these meets wherever they could find level ground—in the yards of cotton presses, on shell roads, or on the city's few asphalt streets.[21] The paucity of paved thoroughfares prompted the *Picayune* to observe: "It is a sad commentary on the administration of this city that the bicyclists can find no fit road upon which to have their races."[22] But in spite of the discouraging conditions under which the races were held, as many as thirty-five hundred spectators assembled for the championship contests.[23]

Interest in League activities subsided suddenly in the early 1890s as southern wheelmen confronted the spectre of Negro membership in the LAW. In the 1880s many members of the NOBC had opposed the club's affiliation with the League because they objected to the stringency of national regulations. But despite occasional rumblings, the number of members in the Louisiana Division had slowly mounted to a peak of about one hundred and fifty in 1892.[24] In the summer of that year, however, the chief consul of the Louisiana Division, W.C. Grivot, sent the national organization a vigorous protest against "forcing obnoxious company upon southern wheelmen" by admitting Negro members and threatened to dissolve the state organization unless the LAW changed its admission policies. H.E. Raymond, chairman of the LAW's racing board, sent a lengthy reply fully explaining the position of the League:

> While I am a thorough Northerner I can still appreciate the feelings of the southern wheelmen on the negro question, and . . . with the class distinction so arbitrary in your section, it would be most unwise for the league to accept applications of negroes for members in any of the southern states.
>
> It is at the same time more or less unfair to ask us to cut out the negro up here, where he is not so obnoxious and does not rub up against us as frequently as he does in the south.
>
> . . .
>
> There is no question of our accepting the negro in preference to the white wheelmen of the south. If it should be narrowed down to a question such as that, we should undoubtedly decide that we want our southern brothers in the league in preference to the negroes of the country.
>
> . . .
>
> We, all of us, both north and south, have a feeling of antipathy towards the colored brother, but he is not so prominent or so likely to apply for membership in the L.A.W. in the north as he is in the south.[25]

While the League debated the Negro question, southern wheelmen began to resign from the association. By June 1893, only fifty-one members remained in the Louisiana Division, and in November only nine in the once-thriving state organization.[26] Alarmed by dwindling support in the South, the LAW sought to improve conditions by expelling its few Negro members. At a national convention in 1893, anti-Negro delegates fell only a few votes short of securing the two-thirds majority necessary to revise membership requirements. But at the next quarterly meeting, in February of 1894, the Negrophobes successfully inserted the word "white" in the section of the constitution outlining qualifications for membership.[27] This decision made possible the revival of the Louisiana Division.

Although enthusiasm for the LAW waned for several years after 1890, cycling attracted scores of enthusiasts in this period. As the safety bicycle came into universal usage and as the price of cycles declined, many persons who had formerly disdained the sport now manifested a sudden desire for wheels. Ordinary bicycles had discouraged participation in the sport, not only because they were difficult to ride but also because they were regarded as physically dangerous. As one doctor said, "We have pressure where pressure should never be made, . . . aggravated by the jolting motion, causing a series of rapid concussions."[28] Opposition to cycling on these grounds gradually evaporated although cyclists occasionally complained about "old fat-heads who . . . prate about bow legs and crook-spines." And as late as 1895 the *Picayune* cited a "medical man" as its authority in observing, "Now that bicycle riding has become so universal it is feared that the result of the craze will be a race of hunchbacks."[29] Despite such dire predictions, cycling continued to fascinate people of both sexes and all ages.

The growing appeal of cycling was reflected by a flurry of activity among enthusiasts. Novices emulated veteran riders and organized several new clubs to encourage racing, pleasure riding, and social gatherings.[30] In 1891 a cycling school for men and women was established. Bert Spring, founder and instructor, taught riding and took his pupils on tours around the city. Reporting one of Spring's excursions, the *Picayune* said, "Soda water and chewing gum was the menu of a feast after the ride."[31] By far the most popular activities were the races arranged by the older clubs. Both the New Orleans Bicycle Club and the Louisiana Cycling Club sponsored frequent contests for special prizes donated by club members.[32]

Clubs often encouraged tours to various watering places and other retreats in the vicinity of New Orleans. During the high-wheel era, cyclists usually journeyed only as far as the lakefront resorts, but as they mounted safety bicycles, they pedaled longer distances.[33] In 1888 a local correspondent for the *Bicycling World* reported: "Club runs to the sugar plantations above and below the city are all the go now, and many a pleasant Sunday has been spent among the immense fields of sugar cane and in the sugar houses of the hospitable planters."[34] Bicycle clubs also began to sponsor expeditions to Gulf cities such as Mobile and Biloxi. On one such excursion three local cyclists were lost for two days with only corn bread, fat meat, and creek water to sustain them until they returned to civilization.[35]

Venturing beyond the confines of the city occasionally presented more serious problems. Nonparticipants throughout the country complained that bicycles frightened livestock, cluttered the roads, and endangered the lives of pedestrians. City councils and state legislatures listened attentively to grievances and often passed laws to drive bicycles from the public thoroughfares.[36] Local riders encountered their share of hostility, but in 1887, Harry Hodgson reported: "There is a better feeling now towards wheelmen than ever before" as citizens "who formerly regarded the wheel as a toy, or child's sport . . . have begun to realize that the wheel as practical mode of travelling is a fixed fact." In 1890 the state legislature recognized cycling's status by awarding riders "the same rights upon the public highways of this state as are prescribed by law in the cases of persons using carriages drawn by horses."[37] City officials also gave cyclists "a fair and impartial show" when they clashed with the ubiquitous "Road Hog." In 1896 the city council adopted a code of traffic regulations for bicycle riders requiring wheelmen to carry lanterns after dark, to keep one hand on the handle bars, to stay on the right side of the street, to abjure riding on sidewalks, and to go no more than ten miles per hour in town."[38]

Statutes alone could not entirely solve the problems that confronted cyclists. Although city and state officials accorded riders full legal rights, private citizens rendered riding a difficult and often dangerous pastime. "The bicycling population is up in arms against two very disagreeable forms of men who ought to be put down with all possible speed," the *Picayune* announced in 1891. "The first and worst is known as the 'road hog', a class of drivers who are unwilling to give a wheelman sufficient room to pass them on a public thoroughfare."[39] The second type of offender was the person who acted maliciously by attacking cyclists or setting dogs loose on riders. In August 1891, while New Orleans cyclists were riding in Mississippi, Charles Cox of Biloxi "attempted to bite off the finger" of one of the excursionists. Cox was convicted of assault, a decision the *Picayune* believed would serve as an object lesson to the "few inhospitable residents still in Biloxi."[40]

For many cyclists, the social aspects of club membership were as attractive as participating in the sport. In 1889 the New Orleans Bicycle Club constructed a spacious clubhouse on the corner of Prytania and Valence streets. Equipped with bowling alleys and a large lawn for croquet and tennis, the meeting place was described as "the nicest and coziest house they have ever had." Members of both the NOBC and Louisiana Cycling Club held "stag smokers" as well as social gatherings for both sexes. When Colonel Albert A. Pope came to New Orleans in December of 1890, all cyclists in the city pooled their efforts to entertain the "Father of the American Bicycle."[41]

Although cycling seemed to be progressing from a young man's fad to a universal mania, interest waned suddenly in the autumn of 1892. As one resident explained, New Orleans had as many bicycles as any city of comparable size, but "riders seem to be contented to pedal them to and from their place of business. Such a thing as getting up a race meet . . . is seldom thought of."[42] Another resident strenuously denied this report, but the decline of cycling news in the local press told a graphic story.[43] In March 1893, the *Picayune* lamented, "The sport has almost ceased to exist in this city."[44]

For the next two years cycling enthusiasm continued at low ebb. Wheel owners used their conveyances almost exclusively for necessary transportation, taking part in few races or pleasure excursions. But in 1895 a cycling revival occurred, inspired by a surging interest throughout the country and by a handful of local enthusiasts who had organized the Crescent Wheelmen in 1894 to infuse new life into the pastime.[45] The *Picayune* marveled at the "sudden craze for wheels" as hundreds of residents, both male and female, organized new cycling clubs and reactivated older ones.[46]

Interest in cycling surpassed anything the city had witnessed before. Earlier clubs had been fortunate to attract a hundred members; the new associations admitted as many as seven hundred cyclists.[47] In 1895, as cycling enthusiasm grew, William E. Meyers and G. Abbott Waterman began publication of the *Southern Cyclist,* a periodical issued weekly "in the interest of the Sport and Trade."[48] Amazed by the sudden preoccupation with two-wheeled vehicles, a writer for the *Picayune* observed that "within a little year the bicycle, from a modest institution in the community, has become one of the powers of progress. It has become a factor for pleasure as well as business and is here to stay."[49]

During the next few years it appeared that the *Picayune*'s analysis might prove correct as cycling clubs sponsored scores of races which attracted thousands of spectators. The most active of these associations was the Southern Wheelmen, a stock company capitalized at $20,000. Charles H. Fourton initiated this club to finance construction of a race track in New Orleans. Since cyclists had complained for years about the poor roads available for racing, the

Southern Wheelmen proposed to remedy the situation by building a concrete oval. In October of 1895 members opened their track at the corner of Carrollton Avenue and Common Street (later Tulane Avenue).[50]

During the remainder of the decade this concrete track was the site of the city's most important races. Local cyclists vied there frequently and often attracted more than a thousand spectators. Track managers also induced professional and amateur riders from other cities to come south. In December of 1895, Peter J. Berlo, a touring professional, raced in the city and set three world records, thus proving "the local race course was the fastest in the union." During the following year, a group of promoters persuaded the LAW to hold one of its meets in the city. The League sanctioned a series of professional and amateur races from coast to coast, and New Orleans was one stop on the circuit in June 1896. Two of the traveling professionals, Otto Ziegler and Arthur Gardiner, once again demonstrated the advantages of the local track by setting world records.[51]

Cooperation between the League of American Wheelmen and local cyclists terminated abruptly in July 1896, when the League suspended eight riders for racing on Sunday, a violation of its rules.[52] Sunday recreation had been a feature of New Orleans' social life for a century; when the LAW, dominated by Eastern members who had yet to shed their puritanical notions about merrymaking on the Sabbath, refused to allow local option on this question, Crescent City cyclists ceased to follow national rules. Managers of the concrete track continued to sponsor Sunday races, and in May 1897, local wheelmen organized the Southern Cyclists' Association to control racing in the city. The SCA soon extended its influence beyond New Orleans by admitting clubs from adjacent states.[53] European wheel associations expressed sympathy for the cause of Sunday racing, and in October 1897, the German Cycling Association recognized the Southern Cyclists' Association "as a contemporary cycling government."[54] Faced with similar rebellions throughout the country, the LAW gradually relinquished control of racing, and in 1900 decided to devote its full attention to the campaign for good roads.[55]

While racing cyclists struggled with League regulations, the majority of riders who participated in the sport amused themselves with pleasure riding and social gatherings. Members of the New Louisiana Jockey Club organized the Country Club, an exclusive society that frequently went on "bicycle runs."[56] Another group of cyclists formed the Sunday Riding League, a club "devoted solely to Sunday riding and recreation."[57] The Louisiana Road Club sponsored numerous excursions to Baton Rouge, Abita Springs, Bay St. Louis, and other towns in Louisiana and Mississippi. This club also arranged dances and other evening amusements.[58]

As scores of cyclists pedaled city streets and country roads, complaints about the condition of public thoroughfares inevitably developed. In the 1880s local cyclists had shown some interest in the national movement to improve the country's highways. The Louisiana Division of the League of American Wheelmen had a standing committee on Roads and Road Improvements, and all cyclists supported attempts to pass drainage and paving taxes.[59] But neither city nor state officials followed a systematic program of road betterment, and when the cycling craze reached its zenith, riders once again attacked the problem. The Louisiana Road Club was formed in 1896 expressly "for the purpose of improving the roads of this state."[60] When the Louisiana Division of the LAW was reactivated, members devoted much of their attention to the crusade for paved streets. In August of 1896, for example, Chief Consul Harry Hodgson distributed three hundred aprons for horses which bore the inscription, "I Want Good Roads." By September the Louisiana Division had attracted more than two hundred members, who, said Hodgson, "have begun to understand that nothing of importance can be secured without organization."[61] Although it would be a gross exaggeration to maintain that cyclists singlehandedly brought about macadamized streets and highways, they nevertheless launched a crusade that quite literally paved the way for the automobile.

During its heyday, cycling had a far-reaching impact upon American life. Like many popular pastimes, the sport had its detractors as well as its advocates. Carriage makers and horse traders complained that the sale of bicycles ruined their businesses; and ministers, alarmed by declining church attendance, warned that Sunday riders were pedaling straight to perdition. But even the staunchest critic could not fail to perceive some of the benefits derived from cycling.

Economically, cycling gave the country a booming industry. If the carriage trade suffered the loss of thousands of dollars in trade, bicycle manufacturers more than compensated for this reduction by selling equipment which cost buyers millions of dollars. By the mid-1890s the manufacturing of bicycles reportedly represented an investment of a $100 million.[62] In 1895 the *Picayune,* in a summary of the cycle industry, estimated that each year Americans spent $50 million for bicycles and related equipment: "Besides making millionaires of the manufacturers, this sum supports an industry which gives employment to thousands of bread-winners."[63]

In New Orleans, retail outlets for bicycles were among the first businesses to exploit fully the demand for sporting equipment. Before the rise of cycling, agents for billiard, baseball, and aquatic equipment had found the sale of sporting goods a lucrative enterprise, but these dealers fell far short of the net sales now registered by firms supplying the middle class with a new device for travel and pleasure. In the mid-1890s the city had more than a dozen dealers acting as agents for national manufacturing companies. During the peak of the bicycle craze, the *Southern Cyclist* reported that residents had purchased five thousand bicycles in a three-month period, and "there would be twice as many sold if the agent received any assistance from the manufacturer" in the form of advertising.[64]

Although manufacturers advertised only in national periodicals such as *Bicycling World,* local agents hawked their wares extensively in newspapers, trade journals, and club magazines. Hodgin's Riding Academy on St. Charles Avenue offered bicycles for both sexes—the Napoleon for men and the Josephine for women. The Jackson Cycle Company, agent for Stern's Bicycles, told prospective clients, "The only way to do it is to do it on a Stern's." This company also offered a bicycle with yellow rims, and advertisements clearly indicated that the company was courting female riders: "Golden Tresses, Girls so Neat; Yellow Rims on Wheels that Beat."[65]

Agents frequently utilized promotional gimmicks to gain support for their wheels. H. & D. Folsom Arms Company advertised new bicycles "at cut prices." Another dealer offered a $300 prize for the rider who registered the most mileage on a Rambler bicycle between April 1 and December 1, 1896, and $200 for the most miles ridden on any type bicycle with Gormully and Jeffery pneumatic tires. In February 1896, all agents in the city cooperated to sponsor a cycle show at Washington Artillery Hall. With exhibits illuminated by electric lights, salesmen showed residents the latest in bicycling equipment, including ball-bearing shoes guaranteed to make pedaling easier.[66]

Dealers derived most of their income from the sale of bicycles, but many businessmen also relied heavily upon the sale of related goods and services. Most agents advertised lamps, bells, and other gadgets for safety-conscious riders. Folsom Arms Company sold all the "latest Bicycle Novelties," including women's skirt holders and ladies' stocking leggings—"The Latest Parisian Novelty." Dry-goods merchant Leon Godchaux found it profitable to act as the official tailor for the Louisiana Division of the LAW, because all members bought special uniforms. Edward G. Stoddard, an agent for Pope Manufacturing

Company, made money by renting bicycles to those unwilling or unable to buy a machine. He was also, according to his advertisements, the "only repair man with factory experience in the City."[67] While it is impossible to give a detailed accounting of the importance of the cycling industry in New Orleans, the proliferation of dealers and the variety of bicycles and related equipment available indicate that the city's economy profited substantially from the growing appeal of wheeling.

Socially, cycling also exerted a tremendous influence. In a period when most sports made spectators of the masses, cycling encouraged universal participation. Sedentary businessmen and bored juveniles found cycling an attractive pastime offering both exercise and recreation. Perhaps the best indication of the social impact of cycling was its appeal to women. The American woman, trying to free herself from the confining aspects of Victorian society, saw participation in sports as a convenient method of vivifying her struggle for equality with men. Cycling was one of the few activities that offered women an opportunity to disport as actively as men. Few women ventured to the lofty perch of a high wheeler, but with the introduction of safety wheels and the drop frame, the bicycle attracted droves of skirted riders. Conservative elements at first questioned the propriety of a woman on wheels, but this opposition faded as people recognized the healthfulness of cycling. "The bicycle," asserted one free spirit, "is one of the few out-of-door sports open to the average woman by reason of its convenience, comparative inexpensiveness, and pleasure."[68] On the open road astride her wheels, the athletic female became the symbol of emancipated womanhood.

Women in New Orleans turned to cycling soon after the invention of the drop-frame safety. "The ladies' safety is commencing to loom up," a correspondent told the editor of *Bicycling World* in 1889. "Two months ago there wasn't a rider, now there are three . . . . They are all delighted, too, with their wheels, though that mount does worry 'em considerably."[69] Easily shocked residents blanched as Southern belles embraced what many prudent citizens regarded as an essentially unladylike sport, but a local girl who rode frequently devised a formula to ward off adverse comments: "Sit straight, ride slowly, have the saddle high enough, use short cranks, never, never chew gum, conduct yourself altogether in a ladylike manner and sensible people will not shake their heads in dis-approval when you ride."[70] When the bicycle craze gripped the city in the mid-'90's, the *Picayune* reported that "hundreds of women" could be seen riding daily. Girls from Newcomb College joined the movement, and those who did not own bicycles said they intended to "torment their papas to death until they had one."[71] Teachers rode bicycles to school to save carfare. Ida Barrow, who taught at Girls' High School, declared, "I don't think anything is so beneficial to a woman's health and nerves as a long spin in the open air."[72] Another female cyclist simply stated that women were "better and happier for the wheel."[73]

Male riders accepted female cyclists reluctantly at first, but as they discovered the pleasures of mixed cycling parties, their reservations vanished. Both the New Orleans Bicycle and Louisiana Cycling clubs sponsored "ladies' nights" at their club houses "to reward the ladies for the great interest they have taken" in the clubs.[74] Moreover, the NOBC even considered the formation of a "ladies' auxiliary to assimilate with the organization."[75] When the cycling fad reached its peak in 1895 and 1896, both the Southern Wheelmen and the Crescent City Cycling Club agreed to admit ladies to full membership, a feature of these organizations which the *Picayune* described as "especially adroit."[76] The Crescent City Club had two undeniably sound reasons for opening the association to both sexes. Members first conceded "that man had never created anything great without the assistance of his natural helpmate in life" and then added that "if it be desirous that a club should be made known to the world there was no advertising medium in the world to rival the tongue that forever wags."[77] Those ladies who failed to secure a position in one of these predominantly male clubs could join the Olympic Club, a cycling association composed exclusively of women.[78]

Besides giving women an opportunity to participate in sports, the bicycle mania aided in the reform of women's dress. As women everywhere fell prey to the wheel, it became obvious that fashion changes were in order; the bulky skirts so long favored by the American woman were palpably ill-suited to cycling. When women began to abandon trailing skirts and tightly corseted waists, the bicycle was recognized as the catalyst of change. Said a writer for *Puck*: "The bicycle makers have accomplished more for dress reform in two years than the preachers of that cult have accomplished since clothes began to be the fashion. Today, thanks to the bicycle, there is every prospect that woman will soon be able to dress sensibly, comfortably, and modestly, all at the same time."[79] Thus the bicycle, which at first attracted women because it symbolized their desire for freedom, also assisted in the struggle; the bicycle's appeal to women was both a reflection of, and a stimulus to, the cause of female emancipation.

Like their counterparts in other cities, female cyclists in New Orleans found bulky skirts an acute problem. In 1891 the *Picayune* reported, "Ladies are puzzling their brains to know what to wear on a wheel. . . . If any lady can suggest a becoming and suitable costume for the southern wheelwoman, she will confer a great favor upon many of her sex who ride the wheel, and also many more who are very anxious to ride, but find the question of skirts a burden to manage."[80] Although conservative elements scorned the bloomers adopted by girls in the East, local women soon capitulated. Within a few years numerous female cyclists were seen wearing bloomers, divided skirts, or other garments that resembled men's pants. The discriminating woman at first covered herself with a cloak because "she looks queer in her divided skirt or knicks," but as the novelty of bloomers wore off, false modesty also disappeared.[81] By 1897 the *Picayune,* which at first opposed what it regarded as immodest clothing, conceded that the style made famous by Amelia Bloomer in the 1850s had at last gained public acceptance. In its fashion column of February 27, the paper included a pattern for bloomers accompanied by the observation that "if bloomers are to be, then this pattern is certainly preferable to immodishly scant ones."[82]

As the electric streetcar came into wide usage and the automobile made its appearance, the bicycle era was rapidly drawing to a close when America entered the twentieth century. By the 1920s the League of American Wheelmen had collapsed, cycle racing had all but disappeared, and riding had become a source of amusement primarily for young boys. Although the craze was short-lived, cycling accustomed people to individual transportation and a higher degree of mobility than they had ever known. As an agent of social change, this middle-class pastime occupied an important position in the history of the latter nineteenth century.

CHAPTER TWO

"He's a good rider because of where he comes from"

Horseracing, Slavery, and Haunting

KATHERINE C. MOONEY

In the spring of 1855, he "st[ood] proudly before the world as the best race horse ever produced on the turf."[1] He had defeated the only horse ever to beat him, and he had lowered the record for four miles by more than six seconds. His name was Lecomte. Louisiana Creoles probably gave the word its proper French inflection, but Kentuckians drawled it "Lee Count."[2] He ran with his legs pulled up under him, his powerful hindquarters driving him relentlessly forward. The American racing correspondent who wrote under the pseudonym Larkin complained that even the most highly regarded portraits failed to capture the horse's essence, because they did not show him in motion. "Lecomte is the very impersonification of action and grace . . . and should be taken—flying."[3]

Larkin reminds us that we will never see Lecomte at a gallop and thus never truly grasp the reasons for his admirers' visceral response to him. It is difficult to do more than merely report their words. But we have to try if the history of horse racing is to be more than an antiquarian pursuit, a mildly interesting amalgamation of statistics and names in blurred and often intricately abbreviated type. To grasp both how people in the past felt and thought about Thoroughbreds and how those feelings touched the rest of their lives, we have to cross geographical boundaries, leaving the racetrack to see how far its reach extended beyond its fences. It certainly extended to the public rooms of the St. Charles Hotel, the prime gathering place for New Orleans politicians and turfmen, where they practiced the track's customs, abided by its assumptions, and applied them to other aspects of their world. Like many New Orleans stories, then, this one is often set in a bar.

Jimmy Lee, legendary African American jockey who in 1907 swept a full racing card at Churchill Downs. The following year he would win the Travers Stakes at Saratoga. Photo courtesy of John C. Hemment Photograph Collection, Keeneland Library, Lexington, Kentucky.

The St. Charles was situated in what is now the Central Business District. In the antebellum period, the hotel was surrounded by the pens and yards that made the city one of the most lucrative slave markets in human history. To truly understand the significance of racing in New Orleans, we have to recognize how tightly tied it was to the history of human bondage. In the world of racing, we can see the inner workings of slavery and the tendrils its legacies have wound into our most intimate places and intangible understandings. In Toni Morrison's *Beloved,* Sethe cautions her daughter never to return to where their family was held in slavery, because places and experiences together make something that will never go away. "I mean, even if I don't think it, even if I die, the picture of what I did, or knew, or saw is still out there. Right in the place where it happened . . . . The picture is still there and what's more, if you go there—you who never was there—if you go there and stand in the place where it was, it will happen again; it will be there for you, waiting for you."[4] The racetrack and the St. Charles were places where slaves and former slaves knew that they would find such pictures. Sometimes those pictures promised only the danger and consuming despair about which Sethe warns her daughter. Sometimes they offered the prospect of building on what had come before to make a new future. Always they revealed how desperately slavery clung to life and how painfully impossible it was and is to draw sharp lines that mark an end to its power. Thus, like many other New Orleans stories, this is a story about haunting, a ghost story.

To begin with, how did Lecomte become the king of the track at New Orleans in 1855, and what did that mean to the men who loved him? By the 1850s, everyone acknowledged that New Orleans was the horse racing capital of the United States. Local sugar and cotton planters had begun racing on an informal track on Wade Hampton's plantation outside New Orleans shortly after Louisiana statehood. Throughout the 1820s, the city hosted race meetings at tracks in town.[5] But in the late 1830s racing blossomed as never before in the Crescent City, with the rise of the Eclipse Course in 1837 at the site of what is now Audubon Park and the opening of both the Metairie Course and the Louisiana Course in 1838.[6] New Orleans racing was decidedly a paying proposition, lucrative enough to appeal to men like the New Yorker Richard Ten Broeck, who managed tracks professionally.[7] Ten Broeck had a particularly sharp eye for profit, which had led him across the South until he made his way to New Orleans and to the most elegant and richest track of all, the Metairie.[8] Drawn by extravagant purses, racing men from all over the South converged on the Metairie to make it not only the city's premiere racetrack but the region's and even the nation's.[9] One regular magazine correspondent rated the best tracks in the South and concluded, "Presto—New Orleans. Here we have *racing.*"[10] Here was where the pluperfect form of the sport was to be found, with all its accompanying loyalties, convictions, and dreams.

The St. Charles Hotel was one of the showplaces of New Orleans, famous as a destination for tourists and locals alike and the headquarters of the city's prominent turfmen during race meetings.[11] The life of the backstretch and life at the hotel bar were deeply entwined. It was in that bar and its surrounding parlors that New Orleans's racing men met to administer the jockey clubs that ran the city's tracks.[12] The hotel sponsored a stakes race, with an appropriately lavish trophy, in recognition of the "numerous and highly respectable racing gentlemen, who throng that splendid Hotel during our fall and spring meetings."[13] Turfmen returned the compliment, recommending the St. Charles, in the language of racing, as "the crack hotel of the South" and particularly lauding "the extent and splendor of the Bar-room, which is, perhaps, without a parallel in the world."[14] The new bar, remodeled in 1853, had small windows that let in little natural light; instead, the glare from thirty-one gas burners flickered off eight massive columns and nine bronze chandeliers.[15] It was such a success that when two owners set up a match race between their horses, one announced confidently, "that if the St. Charles Hotel belonged to him, he would bet it all off (barring the bar-room) at the same odds."[16]

Bars are full of people's projections of self, of their feelings about who they are and who they wish to be. And the bar at the St. Charles, where cotton brokers, planters, the striving, and the established rubbed shoulders, would have been a hotbed of men's attempts to measure themselves against one another. Walter Johnson has argued persuasively that the slave market was built on the dreams of white people, that the traders' yards that densely encircled the St. Charles were places where consumer capitalism was carried to its ultimate and ugliest point. White people literally purchased other human beings to embody and enable all their most intangible desires and assuage their deepest insecurities.[17] And those transactions didn't stay outside. The St. Charles set up auction blocks at each end of the marble bar on Saturday nights.[18] In that bar, New Orleans's powerful and aspiring men made and recounted the purchases they believed could turn them into the men of their dreams. And when they gathered to establish and maintain the governing bodies of local racetracks, they imagined those ovals as another controlled space where they would succeed as competitors, as masters, as men who could shape the nation and the world. At New Orleans, white men built a racing scene of unsurpassed scale and glamor, designed to display the power of those like themselves. "No where," declared the *Spirit of the Times,* "are such sums of money laid out in matches."[19]

It was that kind of money and hunger for acclaim that fueled the aspirations of New Orleans racing men when they extended invitations for the Great Post Stakes to be run in the spring of 1854, with horsemen from ten states instructed to handpick entrants to run for a purse swelled by a $5000 entry fee. While only Kentucky, Mississippi, Alabama, and Louisiana took up the challenge, the field was stacked with highly-regarded runners. A consortium of Kentucky turfmen, headed by Metairie shareholder Richard Ten Broeck, had purchased the promising young Lexington to run for the state. Alabama entered the experienced Highlander, and turfman Duncan Kenner sent his Arrow into battle for Louisiana. Rapides Parish planter Thomas Jefferson Wells was so eager to enter Lecomte, his beloved homebred, undefeated in five starts, that he consented to allow the horse to represent Mississippi.[20] Fans across America couldn't wait. "Come and see it in April next, for the campaign that follows will be terrible; and as the best blood of the Union will be in New Orleans, all the lovers of the sport should meet here to enjoy the best racing they will ever have an opportunity of seeing."[21] Journalists speculated that a million dollars might be wagered on a race they expansively predicted had "never been equaled by any sporting event of the age."[22]

Spring rain pelted the track the morning of the race, but the weather cleared before post time, to the joy of the 20,000 fans in attendance. Many of the planters and politicians of the South and other national figures, like former president Millard Fillmore, gathered, as downtown New Orleans emptied.[23] "Business seemed . . . to be suspended; everybody who was anybody, or wanted to be deemed anybody, had gone to the race. Dinner hours were postponed, engagements were forgotten. . . ."[24] The rain, however, had turned the track into a muddy mess. Lexington took the first heat without much difficulty. In the second, Lecomte took the lead, and, by the end, only Lexington was left to challenge him. The two "swung into the home stretch side by side, the excitement running high amongst the anxious thousands and cheers rending the air. Down they came home, rushing forward like a torrent, each at the top of his speed, as if life depended upon every jump," until Lexington was able to wrestle the lead away, coming home to finish the final mile faster than any other in the race.[25]

T.J. Wells, inspired by his horse's courage, demanded a rematch and got it from Ten Broeck, who bought out his partners to enter Lexington in the Jockey Club Purse the following week, despite the fact that the horse had been out of training, with his shoes pulled off and his dietary restrictions loosened. This time, Lecomte turned the tables, defeating Lexington in back-to-back four-mile heats and smashing the American record for the distance by more than six seconds, as well as the record for the average time for consecutive heats. His jockey brought him to the finish riding with one hand and waving at the ecstatically shrieking crowd with the other.[26]

Ten Broeck immediately challenged Wells to a rematch. Wells refused, and months of challenges, counter-challenges, complaints, and disputes of honor and etiquette followed in the columns of the sporting press.[27] As summer turned to fall and then to winter, everyone still waited, hoping to hear that the two giants would clash once again. One racing writer announced, "I know several who intend visiting Orleans this spring, who are so desirous of seeing a race between them, that they intend *taking the chances*."[28] In April 1855, Lexington again set foot on the track at New Orleans, this time to run against the clock, and he bested Lecomte's record by more than six seconds. The telegraph wires sang with the news, which was immediately posted on the bulletin board in the lobby of the Astor House in New York as an event of national significance. Now, the sporting press exulted, the two horses would have to meet in a tiebreaker to prove ultimate supremacy.[29] And meet they did two weeks later in the annual installment of the Jockey Club Purse, the same fixture where Lecomte had set his record the previous year. "Lexington and Lecomte were the great lions of the day; and bulletins from their respective stables were waited for and read with the same interest and avidity as though they announced the possible change of a dynasty, or the probable fate of a nation."[30]

Lexington met all his supporters' expectations, sailing to the lead and once again beating Lecomte's record for the distance in the first heat. Lecomte, however, had to be eased two miles into the race, and Wells withdrew him from competition, forfeiting the victory to Lexington.[31] It was an ignominious end to racing's golden age in New Orleans and to one of the great rivalries of American sports.

The Post Stakes was the pinnacle of racing in New Orleans and one of the most exciting and significant contests in the history of Thoroughbred racing in America. But fans regarded it as more than that. Southern turfmen had long experience entangling and equating their on-track and off-track lives. Henry Clay, an enthusiastic racing man, was a beloved figure at racetracks all over the South. When he came to New Orleans, he put up at the St. Charles Hotel with his friends and used it as his base to promote his American System, the political program he believed would power a new United States, built on cutting-edge infrastructure, complementary support of industry and agriculture, and the enthusiastic embrace of anything that evoked modernity.[32] Racing men saw in Lexington and Lecomte the two greatest runners in American history, embodiments of their confidence in the future they would make. The horses' successive record-breaking performances, argued the *New Orleans Picayune,* were reassuring evidence. "Truly, we live in a progressive age, and what we are coming to, who can tell?" A few weeks later, the *Spirit of the Times* echoed the sentiment, trumpeting, "Here is feasible proof that this is an age of progress."[33]

For southerners, in particular Clay's Whig adherents, this progress was their pride and their operating assumption. Their immensely lucrative plantation society, which paid for their racehorses, and their ruthlessly calibrated reliance on human bondage, which inflected the whole of their lives, could be the engine of American prosperity and power.[34] And racing, which displayed and celebrated their society's accomplishments, could be a means of ascension to global prominence. As southerners warily watched Cuba in the early 1840s, they pursued diplomatic and military avenues to maintain both slavery and American influence on the island. Logically, for men who believed that racing had the power to crystallize ideologies and consolidate allegiances, they turned also to the track.[35] Southern turfmen made an ultimately failed effort to invest in a track in Cuba and fashion a racing circuit in the circum-Caribbean, with hubs at Havana, Kingston, and New Orleans. The project promised to bring the United States and its Caribbean neighbors "into more intimate relations, and that, too, through gentlemen. A free intercourse between the wealthy classes, who alone have the principal control over the sports of the turf, will go farther than the most frequent commercial transactions to promote good fellowship and friendly feeling," the newspapers promised.[36] While the transnational racing circuit never became a reality, the allure of racing as a form of cultural diplomacy, an unassailable assertion of worthiness instantly recognizable to international elites, remained.

Indeed, the success of Lexington and Lecomte bolstered racing's status as a potential tool of statesmanship. William J. Minor was certainly convinced that it was a reflection of American prowess like other notable examples of national character and innovation. "The success of . . . McCormick's Reaping Machine has doubtless increased the respect the English previously felt for us, and in a disproportionate degree increase[d] the good feeling growing up between the two nations. To make the English our fast friends for a century to come, we must go over and win the Goodwood Cup with an American-bred horse; and then beat all England, heats of four miles, weight for age."[37] The Goodwood Cup was one of the premier fixtures of the British racing calendar, and it had in this period been carried off on a few occasions by challengers from the Continent, so Minor was essentially calling for Americans to prove their right to be counted among the world's great nations, a status he equated with the capacity to produce a fast, durable Thoroughbred. These kinds of calls were what sent Lecomte and his sister Prioress to England in 1856, in company with other American animals and horsemen, including J.B. Pryor, who had trained Lexington for his clashes with Lecomte.[38] Racing at New Orleans was to be the proving ground for the qualities that would bring the United States and, in particular, the South to the forefront of the world. For men who made the decisions and deals that shaped their destinies on the backstretch and in bars, this strategy seemed not only practicable but pragmatic.

But of course this confidence was always bound up in the imperatives and understandings of a slave society. The search for international connections and legitimacy was in part a function of needing markets for slaves and slave-grown products and wanting guarantees that the United States would be able to continue carving out those markets with impunity. The success of racing was a marker of the overwhelming power of slavery itself and the demand that the world acknowledge and bow before it. A piece about the Lexington and Lecomte duels in the *Spirit of the Times* suggested just how comfortable New Orleans turfmen were with slavery. The writer had returned home with T.J. Wells after Lecomte's great victory in the spring of 1854. When they arrived at the Wells plantation, slaves gathered around to hear about the race and announced that they would give a party in celebration of the horse's win. "The ball was accordingly given, and it would have made an abolishionist blush to have been a witness to their joy; the scene would have laughed to scorn their slandering tales of injury. . . ." During the party, a slave woman named Airy gave birth to twins, and Wells immediately announced they would be named Lexington and Lecomte. "[W]hich is to be called Lecomte and which Lexington is hereafter to be determined when which shall prove the 'fastest boy' in his 3 yr. old form . . . . I have seen these twins by George, out of Airy; they are of good size, rather pony built, but remarkably fine in the barrel."[39] The *Spirit* presented the letter as straight reporting, though we do not know if everything in the article is exactly true. It sounds, though, like the kind of story that would have been greeted with tipsy, back-pounding laughter in the bar of the St. Charles Hotel, a story that reinforced everything the drinkers wanted to believe. Abolitionists were wrongheaded and contemptible, because slaves were happy extensions of their owner's will and emotions. The equation of slaves with horses, human beings with animals, was almost but not quite complete. The horses, at least, were entitled to their own names from birth.

Slaves dared to imagine that they were more than livestock or embodiments of other people's ideas. Occasionally, owners caught glimpses of those imaginings, even as they remained as willfully ignorant of them as possible. The St. Charles was not only a base for slave buyers from New Orleans and the surrounding plantations. It was a stop in a large city, where slaves could hope to disappear out the back door into the crowds, never to be seen again. The newspapers reported that people like Mary Lewis and Wilson Crane had seized that very chance, only a few months away from Lexington and Lecomte's first meeting.[40] In a nerve center of white dreams, they had their own. And the same was true at the racetrack, where white southern racing men depended for the realization of their hopes on black southern racing men who had their own hopes. Slaves were not just spectators to the glorious triumphs of slave owners. They were, more often than not, the grooms, stable foremen, jockeys, and trainers who supervised, rode, and schooled the champions of the New Orleans track. It was generally acknowledged that the notoriously perfectionist William J. Minor did not employ a white professional trainer. He managed all aspects of his equine operation "entirely with his slaves."[41] And the kind of skill such labor demanded was highly prized and rendered the men who possessed it valuable commodities. They were investments, publicized and managed as such. The *Spirit of the Times* reported gleefully that the Post Stakes at New Orleans had aroused such a frenzy of interest that "the price of blood stock" had skyrocketed. The story included a table of the prices paid for some of the horses entered. At the bottom of the list was the name Abe, a jockey for whom Duncan Kenner had, the table indicated, laid down $2350, an immense sum for any slave, even at the inflated prices of the 1850s.[42] A year later, T.J. Wells wanted Abe, who had been aboard Lecomte in his victorious rematch with Lexington, to take the reins again if he agreed to a third contest. But he grumbled at the hundreds of dollars Kenner wanted for Abe's services. W.J. Minor, serving as a go-between, offered Wells a lesson on the basic economics of the situation. "K. paid a large price for 'Abe' and will never get the interest on his money, unless he hires him out as a jockey—if he was mine, I would not hesitate to do it," he reminded Wells.[43] Now was no time for gracious favors between gentlemen; it was ridiculous to expect a shrewd man to forego the chance of recouping his expensive investment. Like all slaves, Abe was both a valuable commodity, a literal embodiment of invested capital, and a tool for generating more cash. But the men who worked with Thoroughbreds were also very much unlike other slaves.

The contests between Lexington and Lecomte, a proud manifestation of the power and reach that southern turfmen claimed, would have been impossible without the highly skilled labor of slaves. Lexington's first trainer was the former slave known as Burbridge's or Viley's Harry, who conditioned the horse for his maiden victory, where he caught the eye of the racing consortium that entered him in the Post Stakes for Kentucky.[44] Minor's assistant trainer, Anthony Hall, was well known for his particular skill at getting a horse from the barn to the track in good order; he would have Lecomte's head for his final match with Lexington.[45] Supervising this process was Lecomte's trainer Hark, a long experienced professional, well known throughout the South, whom Wells had hired from his Virginia owners. Hark had been at the top of his profession for more than a decade by the time he worked Lecomte; the *Spirit of the Times* had included him in an interracial list of the most competent and respectable of the rising generation of trainers as early as 1848.[46] The inclusion of a slave in such a list suggests the unusual status of Hark and men like him.

Wells would later acknowledge, speaking before a crowd of dignitaries, that, "To Hark, the world is indebted for the renown Lecomte enjoys." It was also Hark, Wells explained, who had insisted after the Post Stakes that the horse needed a better jockey to take on Lexington again. He needed Duncan Kenner's Abe.[47] Hark was not the only one who recognized the jockey's talent; anyone who read a newspaper in America could have known about Abe.[48] When Kenner bought Abe, he bought a known quantity, an athlete already named specifically in racing write-ups at a time when jockeys' names virtually never appeared in print.[49] Hark and other shrewd observers like him trusted Abe's skill enough to convince T.J. Wells to give Abe the mount on Lecomte despite the jockey's exceeding the required handicap weight by three pounds. It was a choice that testified implicitly to what racing men believed Abe could do for a horse's performance.[50] But they also spoke openly of his skill. Even William J. Minor conceded that Abe possessed "great coolness and judgment."[51] Other newspaper authors described Abe as "unconquerable," "a prudent, skillful horseman."[52] Turf writers rated him as the equal of the nationally preeminent white jockey of the moment, Gilpatrick.[53] William J. Minor called him "the famous Abe"; less than a year later, he became "the world-renowned Abe."[54] When he rode a close race, the crowds at the rail screamed his name.[55]

The turfmen who frequented the bar of the St. Charles Hotel would have spoken his name as well—toasting the winnings he earned them, retelling his exploits. Abe's success was theirs, his celebrity an index of the resilient character of slavery, its capacity to meet highly specific technical demands. The horses, the horsemen, and the crowds at the Metairie proved slavery's power and southern confidence, displayed for everyone to see during the races at the track and its surroundings. It is thus unsurprising that Jefferson Davis gathered with a number of his partisan colleagues in one of the parlors at the St. Charles and agreed that they would walk out of the Democratic Convention of 1860 if they did not receive explicit guarantees of protection for slavery, a decision that splintered the remaining national party and allowed the election of Abraham Lincoln with less than forty percent of the popular vote.[56]

The confidence that Davis and his friends took with them to Charleston, their assumption that they could shape the destiny of the United States to their will, propelled the South into secession. In the spring of 1861, as the nation fissured, the Metairie Course staged its regular meeting, with entries from Duncan Kenner, W.J. Minor, T.J. Wells, and a variety of other local stalwarts, the proceeds to be donated to the fighting men of the South and their families at home.[57] They believed they were invincible. After all, that day Abe brought home a longshot with style.[58] Louis Bringier wrote to his sister that the crowd seemed as big as it had "in the days of Lecompte and Lexington" and hoped that Deep South horses would trounce Virginia entries, to punish them for the state's faltering progress toward secession. "They deserve something of the sort, for nothing else than hailing from such a miserable subservient state as Old Virginia."[59]

The realities of war, however, soon came to the track, as racing was suspended and the equine prizes of Louisiana and Mississippi turfmen were confiscated and sold at auction in New Orleans.[60] Along with the horses, Union forces sometimes brought black horsemen away from the plantations, despite southern turfmen's desperate attempts to keep them in their stables.[61] Tracks lay abandoned or repurposed for military use. But some things were too important to let lapse. The "clang of war has scarcely died away," reported *Turf, Field and Farm* in the autumn of 1865, and the magazine had already received reports of efforts to rebuild racing in the South, particularly in New Orleans.[62] The Metairie had been used as a campground for an occupying force of Union soldiers and suffered significant damage, but, by the end of 1865, it was on the path to revival, with the enthusiastic support of citizens who believed it to be an economic pillar and a marker of national prestige for the city.[63] In the same parlor at the St. Charles that Jefferson Davis and his fellow Democrats had used to plot their convention strategy, hopeful members of the Metairie Jockey Club convened to plan a gala winter event for 1866, the revival of the Great Post Stakes, the perfect signal of New Orleans's intent to resume its status at the top of the American racing world.[64] The turf was to be the ultimate site of reconciliation, as both northern and southern voices gladly insisted. The *New Orleans Times* cheerfully told its readers, "It is a well known fact the sympathy and fraternal feeling which exists among lovers of the turf, are stronger and more enduring than any political or emotional prejudices."[65] The New York-based and staunchly Republican *Wilkes's Spirit of the Times* agreed, opining that racetracks were better than political parties in building and maintaining sectional and partisan consensus.[66] The day of the revived Post Stakes seemed to bear out all their greatest hopes, as William T. Sherman and Philip Sheridan, two of the most famously destructive Union commanders, were honored guests at the Metairie.[67]

The revival of New Orleans racing never quite fulfilled the expectations sparked that day. New York had seized national supremacy with the construction of Saratoga and Jerome Park. And divides among the elites of New Orleans based on the sources of their wealth and the currents of their politics meant that the Metairie Course and the Metairie Jockey Club never secured the sort of overwhelming power they had wielded before the war. Competing clubs and tracks blossomed, and finally, in 1872, Charles Howard, previously snubbed by the Metairie, purchased the track and demolished it in order to use the land as a cemetery.[68]

But racing had always stood as a marker of the power of Southern slaveholders, and in many ways it continued to do so, even in the face of emancipation and Reconstruction. T.J. Wells's brother James Madison was serving as Louisiana's governor during the disputed election of 1876 and was widely accused of taking bribes from both sides to award the state's electoral votes. A Congressional investigating committee headquartered itself in the jockey club's usual meeting room at the St. Charles to take testimony on the subject.[69] Duncan Kenner found himself having to explain that he and Wells, while not close personal friends, had a long acquaintance through both men's being "on the turf."[70] Kenner admitted that he had obliquely solicited bribery funds from former cotton planter and Democrat D.D. Withers, though he did not note that Withers was also a racetrack friend.[71] Nor did he acknowledge what the Wells family later claimed—that he had actually presented a check to Wells from John Morrissey, New York Democratic Congressman and operator of the Saratoga racetrack.[72] In the end, Louisiana's electoral votes went to Rutherford B. Hayes, and the Republicans took the presidency in exchange for the end of Reconstruction in the South. Whatever the specifics of Kenner's dealings with Wells on this occasion, they reveal that racing continued to do what New Orleans turfmen had always meant it to do—give them a comfortable place to build networks of influence, to create mutual interests and sympathies, to demonstrate their authority and exert it to political ends. Slavery might have ended. But didn't the St. Charles Hotel still fly a flag each day there would be racing in the city, to alert eager fans to the condition of the track?[73] When the New Orleans papers reported the racing results, they described the victorious jockey as "a dwarf in size, but well formed, and 'knows the ropes like a book.' We make these remarks for the benefit of strangers, for all frequenters of the Southern turf know Abe."[74] Surely the track could do its part to remake the world so that racial subordination remained omnipresent and omnipotent, so that black men's skill could continue to bolster white men's power.

These were the terms of the battle for the South during and after Reconstruction—how much of the world of slavery could be revived, and how much could never be resurrected? What would freedom actually mean: would it entail equality, and what did equality really look like? One practical manifestation of this question in daily life was the issue of racial integration in public space. The Metairie and Louisiana Jockey Clubs of the 1870s reversed decades of track custom, prohibiting black spectators. Black New Orleanians sued, because they knew that access to places of amusement—in particular access to places that had been politically weighted for generations of white men—meant much more than the enjoyable chance to watch horses compete. The *Louisianian,* which touted itself on its masthead as "Republican At All Times, and Under All Circumstances," reminded its readers, "It should be remembered that cases of this kind are not mere personal issues, but, that in a correct solution of them lies the settlement of the vexed question of Civil Rights, which is a matter of vital importance to every colored man in the State of Louisiana."[75]

Black spectators, who raised dangerous questions about whether freedom entailed equality and what that equality might mean in practice, could be shut out. But black athletes were already established on the track. Whites might behave as though those men's continued prominence proved the continuation of the world they had known, but almost immediately it was clear that their work could prove exactly the opposite. Men who had read about Abe in the papers before the war could now see him ride on the palatial new tracks of the East. And they recorded their awe at his exploits with verve. They called him a "natural artist" and "the king of riders," a "dark master of the equestrian art," "a mighty man" and a "little necromancer," whose "sagacity is greatly relied on by the gentlemen who know him."[76] Abe had been a celebrity before emancipation, and white racing men had never seen anything to concern them in that; indeed, their very silence in the midst of white-knuckled tension over threats to bondage suggests how much they regarded his success as a marker of their society's stability and power. But Abe embodied a dangerous change, as men famous in slavery became men honored in freedom, men who would demonstrate what it might mean to be free when every moment of social interaction, previously scripted by the constraints of slavery, was a potentially revolutionary one.

New Orleans sought to revive the Post Stakes in 1866, but New Jersey had already inaugurated the Jersey Derby in 1864, a race intended to operate on the model of the English Derby as a truly national contest. The 1866 running drew turfmen from all over America, including the racing men of the South. Abe had the mount on the winner that year, and one of the turf reporters lauded his skill in riding a tough but not especially talented horse to victory. But the writer also devoted a good deal of space to a breathless description of the celebrities in attendance, including John M. Clay, Henry Clay's son and successor on the turf, and the planter Keene Richards, who had frequently sent his horses to the track at New Orleans. In the crowd, the reporter also encountered Abe and reported casually that he had shaken hands with the jockey.[77] Abe had been a celebrity before the war, but he had never been a man with whom white men shook hands. A few months later, the letter column of the *Spirit of the Times,* for so long the reading of enthusiastic southern racing men, published a query about allowing black men to participate in harness racing. The writer thought it was wrong and contrary to "custom." The paper scoffed. Not only was it entirely ordinary for black men to participate in all forms of horse racing, it pointed out, but no man "with a pennyweight of brains" looked down on white men who competed against black ones. The paper reeled off a list of black riders, beginning with Abe, who were equal competitors with the top white riders.[78] To best them, it implied, was a hard-fought honor. And to associate with them in competition was no disgrace. These were the questions and the possibilities that freedom opened up. What would it mean for black men to be fully recognized as competitors, as men worthy of the forms and benefits of respect? What would it mean, more broadly, for them to be citizens?

New Orleans did not escape these questions. Indeed, it saw them raised clearly and constantly for more than thirty years after the Civil War. While the city never regained its antebellum prestige on the turf, it remained a hub of racing in the South and Midwest, like Chicago, Louisville, and Lexington. And on those tracks African-American riders reigned supreme.[79] Pike Barnes, Monk Overton, and Tom Britton, all African-American riders of great skill and reputation, rode regularly at New Orleans, as did black Kentucky Derby winners Lonnie Clayton and James "Soup" Perkins.[80] Isaac Murphy, still the rider with the all-time highest winning percentage, rode at New Orleans as well, with his usual combination of impeccable technique and reserved style. It was Murphy who most often drew comparisons to the great black men of the past. Gilpatrick himself, who had ridden Lexington against Lecomte, was said to see in him "the shades of Abe and many of the old school."[81]

Murphy, often the flashpoint for conflict over the success and significance of black jockeys, brought all the questions they raised with him to New Orleans. When one reporter encountered him in the local train station, he happened to notice Murphy's valet traveling with him and was moved to muse, "And this reminds me that I have seen men with valets—white men at that—who could hardly claim more gentlemanly pretensions than this same Isaac Murphy."[82] Murphy, like Abe before him, called for an accounting of the changes emancipation had wrought. And Murphy had been born during the war; he had no reassuring, well-known past as a slave to soften the implicit demand. He confronted men who held dear their own sense of themselves as gentlemen with what it meant for a black man to have the resources, poise, and charisma to carry that label as well. Murphy regarded New Orleans as a place where these confrontations were more likely to be resolved in his favor than they might be elsewhere. In 1890, Murphy suffered a notorious collapse on the track at Monmouth, an episode sometimes reported sympathetically as a tragic physical breakdown and sometimes derisively as the consequence of drinking on the job. Murphy seems to have looked to the city as a potential haven. After his premature death in 1896, a reporter recalled him saying so in the midst of the controversy. "'I think I will go down to New Orleans,' he said, 'and maybe I can make a reputation once more. I am disappointed with the way they treated me in the East. . . . When I won it was all right, but when I lost, and when not on the best horse, they would say, 'there, that nigger is drunk again.'"[83]

Murphy had experienced how quickly black men could fall from the pinnacle of success at the track, how eagerly white fans and employers turned to racially charged disdain to defuse the threat of black men's celebrity when it dramatized the possibilities of equality. He may have hoped that in New Orleans, where the first nationally famous black jockey had ridden, older assumptions would hold sway and protect him to some degree. Paradoxically, it may have been both the deeply-rooted passion for racing and the well-worn and comfortable association of racing's pageantry with white authority that made New Orleans a potentially safer place for the expression of black success.

Indeed, sometimes, in New Orleans, the past merged seamlessly with the present. In 1903, a young man named Wallace Hicks made his debut as a jockey, quickly rising to success first at New Orleans and then at the most prestigious New York tracks. He rode for Alphonse Plicque, the owner of the plantation on Bayou Lafourche where Hicks had spent his childhood. Hicks ended up in the courts when it turned out that his illiterate father had made his mark on two different agreements of apprenticeship, one with Plicque and one with a man named Hamilton Wright, that signed away both his parental rights over his son and his rights to control the boy's labor and earnings.[84] Plicque's attorney accused Wright of violating the thirteenth amendment, but both sides were obviously engaged in stretching it to the breaking point, in a way that would have been familiar to many black children pressed into apprenticeships on Louisiana plantations after the Civil War.

Hicks and Jimmy Lee were contemporaries and may have been neighbors. Accounts of Lee's family differ, but the most substantive places him at the track in New Orleans as a child. Lee's mother, like Hicks's father, supposedly saw the racetrack as his best opportunity and made an arrangement with a "wealthy merchant" named Godchaux, perhaps the proprietor of the elite men's clothing emporium to which visitors at the St. Charles Hotel were directed. Godchaux took charge of him and "raised the boy to the care of his horses," just as generations of children in slavery had been raised. From this background familiar to New Orleans turfmen, Lee climbed the ladder as a jockey at New Orleans.[85] But it was at Churchill Downs that he would skyrocket to fame. In June of 1907, Lee rode six straight winners in one afternoon at Churchill, sweeping to victory in every race on the card. Only one of his mounts, experienced punters pointed out, had been a favorite, rendering the afternoon a virtuoso performance of jockeyship.[86] Crowds roared, headlines screamed, and racing, it seemed, had a new black hero.

But there were to be no more such heroes. Less than two miles from the St. Charles Hotel, less than five miles from the old Metairie Course, Homer Plessy had been arrested for violating Louisiana's segregation laws by riding in a whites-only train car. In 1896, the Supreme Court had upheld Plessy's conviction, judging segregation constitutional and refuting African Americans' claims to a freedom that entailed equality. The ease of custom, the possibility of using modified structures of subordination like the ones that bound Wallace Hicks, had kept black men on the track a decade after Jim Crow was the law of the land. But the continuing consequences of black success had become too much, particularly for white jockeys trying to compete against rising black stars like Lee. In the spring of 1908, rumors began to surface that white jockeys were conspiring to stop Lee's domination by ganging up on him, making sure his mounts couldn't win and trying to get him thrown or pushed into the fence.[87] The violence had occurred at multiple tracks, but it was in New Orleans that it had begun, the *New York Sun* informed its readers. Lee, fresh off his rise to the elite level of his profession, suddenly found himself in danger of losing his new status if he simply couldn't get his horses to the front or if wary owners denied him mounts. Worse than that, he faced the very real possibility of being killed or maimed.

When he ran into one of the white jockeys believed to be involved in the plot on the steps of the St. Charles Hotel, Lee grabbed him by the collar and told the man "that he would stand for no nonsense." The white jockey evidently insisted that Lee had made a mistake, that there was no conspiracy against him. His colleagues shrugged and told reporters openly that Lee was probably the best jockey they had ever seen but that they "did not like to have the negro riding in the same races with them."[88]

Jimmy Lee had confessed publicly to one ambition. "His sole goal," the *Louisville Times* reported, "is to be a greater jockey than was Isaac Murphy."[89] He knew the history of men like him in his profession. We do not know if, when Lee put his hands on his tormentors, he was conscious that he was doing so in a place where Murphy and Abe and others had been bought and sold, admired and toasted. Whether he knew how close to them he was or not, the picture, as Toni Morrison would say, was there anyway. The long history of celebrity and commodification, of freedom and subordination, of standing proudly on the thresholds of doors that had only been opened because there seemed no risk to white authority in doing so—it was all waiting for him. He was the one there when the doors closed, and he was on the wrong side. Now whites saw no comfort in his success. Now skill did not matter, because men like him had threatened to make it mean too much. Now all that mattered was color.

Lee would find himself struggling to get mounts, battling injuries caused by his embattled position, and ultimately riding on Canadian tracks for the brief period before he disappeared from racing records.[90] The racing press marked his decline with bemusement. "There is no doubt that when easy in his mind Lee is a skillful jockey but he too frequently gets an idea into his head that the white riders are conspiring to injure him," the *Daily Racing Form* explained.[91] In a nation where *Plessy v. Ferguson* was the law, Lee was accused of imagining the reality of racial prejudice and violence. Jimmy Lee was living with the consequences of the past; he was haunted by the dead who had come before and by the history of white people's attempts to stave off the consequences of their successes. But like many people who claim to see ghosts, he was branded delusional.

The ghosts are still there to be seen, if we look. But so are the men who have followed Jimmy Lee and Isaac Murphy and Abe. Marlon St. Julien, who came to prominence at New Orleans, became the first black man to ride in a Kentucky Derby for almost a century when he stepped aboard Carule for Godolphin Racing in 2000. St. Julien found himself recounting the history of black horsemen, patiently reminding those surprised by his presence, "We've been around for a long time."[92] The young rider C.J. McMahon, who first rode against high-class competition at New Orleans, is the son of a jockey, well aware of the long history that stands behind him, and has begun snagging riding titles at tracks in the West. McMahon has ridden successfully for NFL veteran Vince Wilfork, a black jockey riding for a black owner, in a fulfillment of emancipation's promises.[93]

Kendrick Carmouche is the son of noted jockey Sylvester Carmouche, the longtime pilot of Louisiana star Hallowed Dreams, the winner of sixteen straight races. The younger jockey has ridden successfully at mid-Atlantic tracks since his parents sent him north when he was sixteen. They believed a black man could not achieve the kind of career he wanted in Louisiana, because of the continuing legacies of slavery and Jim Crow. Carmouche now rides at Saratoga, Belmont, and Aqueduct, the powerhouse New York tracks, following the path of generations of black men going back to Abe, after he rode Lecomte in New Orleans. And that history, both its pain and its possibility, his father firmly believes, has given his son a legacy. "I told him he can go anywhere," Sylvester Carmouche summed up. "He's a good rider because of where he comes from."[94]

CHAPTER THREE

Fighting to the Finish

The Ill-Fated Andy Bowen and the Longest Boxing Match in History[1]

RANDY ROBERTS

They said that Andy Bowen was a mulatto. And even in late-19th century New Orleans such fine distinctions of race meant something. The language of racial mixing, with such designations as quadroon, octoroon and quintroon, salt-and-peppered the novels of Harriet Beecher Stowe, Kate Chopin and George Washington Cable as well as the poetry of Walt Whitman and Henry Wadsworth Longfellow. Bowen was one of them, one of those mixed-blood offspring who writers insisted on labeling "tragic."

Light complexioned, he claimed to be of Irish-Spanish extraction and passed as white. By trade he was a laborer, earning day wages with the strength of his hands and back. He pounded metal on anvils, hauled bales in cotton yards and unloaded banana boats in from Honduras. Anything, really, that needed done by an unskilled laborer in the port of New Orleans.

By choice he was a prizefighter. Not much more than 5 feet 5 inches and 135 pounds, he cut his hair short in the style of the great John L. Sullivan and stood ready to fight anyone if the price was right, though as a small man Andy's price was never very high. In the early 1890s, when New Orleans occupied the vital center of a world boxing map that stretched from Great Britain and South Africa to Australia and New Zealand, Andy Bowen plied his trade and made a name for himself. He's largely forgotten now but back then he demonstrated the real meaning of "fighting to the finish."

New Orleans was America's original Sin City. During the Gilded Age it was as gilded as it got. Scratch its thin veneer, walk through the right door, and you might find anything—a bordello, opium den, ratting pit or illegal prizefight. At the time, prizefighting was universally regarded as a "relic of barbarism," a

The boxer Jack Burke, featured on a 1910 boxing card. Picture courtesy of The Ring Magazine.

bane and a stain on the very notion of civilization. Outlawed by state legislators, punished by judges and condemned by journalists, it was virtually a sporting activity without a home.

Except in free-wheeling New Orleans. There, against the law, it existed. And in 1882, when Sullivan stopped Paddy Ryan to win the heavyweight title in a contest staged in Mississippi City (a short train ride from the Crescent City), pugilism began to prosper. By the late 1880s, New Orleans hosted scores of matches. Then in 1889 the Young Men's Gymnastic Club and Southern Athletic Club, organizations of lofty social standing and "silk stocking" membership, entered the mix, promoting gloved contests that conformed to the Marquess of Queensberry rules. Regarding these matches as "exhibitions," city and state authorities generally overlooked laws against prizefighting and permitted these quasi-respectable matches.

The pugilistic gold rush was on. The best professional boxers in America boarded trains bound for New Orleans. James J. Corbett fought Jake Kilrain, Bob Fitzsimmons battled Arthur Upham and such other highly regarded men as Peter Maher, Charlie Mitchell and Frank Slavin made appearances. They came from all corners of the prizefighting world, but one, Andy Bowen, was home grown. Recognized by the *National Police Gazette,* the *RING Magazine* of the day, as the lightweight champion of the South, Bowen fought regularly.

The finest moments in the history of New Orleans prizefighting occurred in September 1892. Out on Royal Street, in a swank arena equipped with electric lights, the Olympic Club staged a prizefighting Triple Event for the ages. Three days, three championship contests.

Journalists scrambled to New Orleans from the major cities of the nation. A *National Police Gazette* writer asserted that "the whole civilized world" was giddy with anticipation for the results of "the greatest pugilistic carnival in the history of the world." The matches were so closely followed that news about the upcoming presidential election between Benjamin Harrison and Grover Cleveland all but disappeared from the press.

On September 5, Jack McAuliffe knocked out Billy Myer to retain the lightweight title. On September 6, George "Little Chocolate" Dixon took out Jack Skelly to retain the featherweight championship. Then on the following night, in the fistic carnival's spectacular finale, James "Gentleman Jim" Corbett pounded John L. Sullivan into submission to win the heavyweight crown. The last bout ranks among the greatest contests in the history of the sport. It also demonstrated that professional boxing could be a lucrative commercial enterprise. After expenses, the Olympic Club cleared more than $50,000.

The money and the attention encouraged the city's athletic clubs to promote more events. Local battler Andy Bowen suddenly found himself in demand. Although his ring skills were minimal, patrons applauded his unusual stamina and fighter's heart. By Spring 1893, the prestigious Olympic Club backed Bowen, matching him for the Lightweight Championship of the South against "Texas" Jack Burke of Galveston, a fighter who, the New Orleans *Daily Picayune* announced, had "unlimited confidence in himself." The boxing writer for the *Daily Picayune* thought that the contest was a crossroad match for both fighters and predicted it would be "a fast and furious battle while it lasts."

"While it lasts" were the operative three words in the phrase. Similar to the other major contests of the period, the Bowen-Burke match would be fought according to the Queensberry rules but would not have a set round limit. A "fight to the finish," it would end only when one of the men was knocked out or could not continue.

Bowen trained to go the unspecified distance. He worked out daily on the Gulf Coast, lifting dumbbells, handling Indian clubs, sparring, and running between 1.5 and 20 miles a day. "Brown as a bronze statue," he had trained to a fine edge. "Burke can bet every dollar on me," he said, "for I will whip him certainly."

By April 6, the day of the fight, New Orleans was alive with "Texas sports" and other out-of-town visitors. More people attended the match than any of the period. Not even for the great Fistic Carnival of 1892 had so many spectators crammed into the Olympic Club, and carriages and pedestrians lined Royal Street. Inside, the incandescent whiteness of electric lights lent an otherworldly atmosphere of excitement to the evening and confirmed the drawing power of prizefighting.

Bowen began the fight like he expected to make another appointment before the end of the night. Time and again in the opening round he rushed Burke, making up for his inferior technique with his superior strength. Occasionally he landed a punch, but by the end of the round Burke caught on to his opponent's primitive strategy and avoided the furious rushes.

In the second round, Burke took the offensive, landing "clever jabs on Bowen's nose" but causing no meaningful damage. In response, Bowen attacked Burke with vicious body blows until the Texan's torso was "red and swollen."

Bowen's strength was undeniable. The punches hurt, and Burke responded by clinching. To the dismay of the spectators, the contest turned boringly predictable: Bowen plowed forward, swinging for all he was worth, and Burke grabbed and held, looking more like he wanted a bit of close dancing than championship fighting. Thirty rounds came and went. Spectators yawned. Some began whistling "Home, Sweet Home." The serenade stirred Bowen, and he responded with a flurry of activity. The accumulation of his punches finally knocked—or pushed—Burke to the floor, and he would have been down for the count if the "gong" signaling the end of the round had not sounded.

Soon both boxers weakened. Their arms hung leaden at their sides, their flailing swings resembled mere shadows of punches. Bowen tried to force the action, but Burke refused to do anything but hold. In the 51st round, referee "Professor" John Duffy, the city's most respected official, heard Bowen ask Burke, "Why don't you fight?" "I cannot, both of my hands are gone," replied the Texan boxer. Taking a close look at Burke, Duffy observed, "I saw that his wrist above the glove and the forearm were swollen to twice their natural size." Refusing to quit, he told Duffy, "If Bowen whipped him, it was all right."

The three-minute rounds tumbled by one after another. At 3 a.m., they struggled out of their corners for the 89th round. Rumors circulated that Burke had broken his wrist; it was the only way to account for his refusal to punch. But he fought—or at least slogged—on. Some hungry spectators went out for breakfast. Others departed for some sleep or caught a nap in their seats. But most grimly stayed put, sensing that they were witnessing something unique.

About 45 minutes later the fight went into the 101st round. That made it the longest gloved contest in history, surpassing the 100-round, 6-hour, 39-minute match between Dan Needham and Patsy Kerrigan in San Francisco in 1890. By then it had also exceeded the longest bare-knuckle contest, a 6-hour, 15-minute match that had taken place in Australia.

At the end of 108 rounds "Professor" Duffy decided that he was the only one who could end the fight. Shortly before sunrise he told the fighters they had two more rounds to win the fight, or he was going to call it a "no decision." Burke said he was doing the best he could with two broken wrists. Bowen was too exhausted to say much of anything.

Two actionless rounds later, Duffy ended the fight. It had lasted 7 hours, 20 minutes, a full, dull 110 rounds.

Burke's seconds examined him in the dressing room. His stomach and ribs were swollen and his eyes and ears puffy, but he was uncut. It was his hands and wrists that were most damaged. "It was my misfortune that the fight did not end differently," he told reporters. "I did not try to hit Bowen at first, and when I did I broke the bones in both my hands . . . . You see how swollen they are now, and they pain me fearfully now and did throughout the fight."

Bowen's face was unmarked. "I am feeling as well as when I went into the fight, and I got no punishment worth talking about; but I am sore over the result," he said. Under the rules of the Olympic Club, a no-decision verdict meant that neither fighter received any part of the purse—that, in fact, they had fought 110 rounds for free.

The day after the fight the leaders of the Olympic Club generously split the purse of $2500 and paid each fighter half. Bowen chirped at the decision. As far as he was concerned, he had carried the fight, delivered all the heavy punches and deserved the lion's share of the purse. But with the onset of the depression of 1893 and growing hard times, he took what was offered and looked for other paydays.

Boxing in New Orleans was close to the end of its golden age. Financial problems hit the Olympic Club, the Crescent City Athletic Club and several other organizations that promoted matches. Then legal decisions reversed the cozy relationship prizefighting enjoyed with the police. But, oddly, Andy Bowen dealt the coup de grace of boxing in New Orleans.

After the Burke match, Bowen continued to fight, but friends and associates said his heart was no longer in the sport. In 1893 he engaged in another marathon match, defeating Jack Everhardt in 85 rounds, and then in 1894 he accepted a match against George "Kid" Lavigne, one of the greatest lightweight boxers of the era. It was an obvious mismatch. Compared to the master craftsman from Michigan, Bowen was not much more than a determined club fighter with a solid punch. Making matters worse, he was losing interest in the sport and the "Kid" was improving with every fight.

Before the contest, referee John Duffy noticed a difference in Bowen, some slight indication of disinterest. He had seen it in Andy's dressing room. Something was wrong with the little fighter, he thought. "(H)e looked as though he had something on his mind. He seemed troubled and did not look himself."

The fighters met in the ring at the Auditorium Athletic Club on December 14 for a purse of $3,000. In the early rounds, a reporter observed, Bowen "did some very clever work, especially in ducking." But any boxer whose best efforts involve ducking out of danger usually ends up not ducking quite as often as necessary. This was the case of Andy Bowen. Before long, Lavigne was having his way with the New Orleans boxer.

As the fight progressed, Bowen audibly registered the beating he was taking. "He had a habit of grunting pretty loud," a *Daily Picayune* boxing scribe noted, when Lavigne landed a body punch, "which he did pretty often." Soon, spectators began to laugh, some even anticipating and imitating Bowen's yelps. It rattled him, and at times he appeared confused, like he was caught in trap with no way to escape. It was as if Bowen had too much heart and stamina to get taken out, and too little talent to protect himself.

Duffy observed Bowen's painful predicament. He could have stopped the contest, but he didn't. That wasn't his job, he thought. "(T)he seconds should have thrown up the sponge when they saw that the poor fellow was gone, but of course, as referee, I could not tell them to do so."

So the fight continued. Unlike the long but oddly nonviolent Bowen-Burke contest, this match witnessed too many hard punches landed, almost all by

Lavigne. After a series of clean blows early in the 18th round, Bowen "staggered around like a drunken man." Near his corner, he grabbed Lavigne, wrapping an arm around his opponent's neck and holding on to avoid more punishment. Finally, Duffy stepped between the fighters and separated them, suspecting that a couple more punches would finish Bowen.

Free from Andy's clutches, Lavigne went to work, landing repeated blows. The last combination demonstrated the "Kid's" skill. He feinted with his right, and then, as Bowen attempted to duck, shot out an elbow which caught Andy under the chin. As Bowen raised his head, Lavigne threw a right to his jaw.

Bowen fell hard. Although stretched canvas covered the ring floor, it was unpadded and afforded no protection for a fighter. As a result, an observer wrote, Bowen's "head hit the wooden floor with a thud which could have been heard a block away." Some spectators feared that he had broken his neck, but after his seconds and a doctor had worked on him for five minutes, he began to breathe. Yet that was all he did. Other than breathing on his own, he was out cold and his seconds had to carry him from the ring.

According to the accumulated and accepted lure of prizefighting—little more than superstitions passed down from one generation to the next—there were signs of hope. Although unconscious in his dressing room, Bowen's hands continued to move as if he were fending off Lavigne's punches. That was a "favorable omen," said an authority, as was the fact that he vomited. It was enough to convince his supporters that there was no need to take him to the hospital, and instead they transported him to his tiny home on Thalia Street.

There his wife Mathilde kept vigil. With Victorian pathos, a New Orleans *Daily Picayune* journalist wrote, "Through the long hours of the night . . . and through the gray dawn until the first rays of yester sun streamed forth to herald the approach of another day, a close and anxious watch was kept at the side of the bed whereon Andy Bowen, once the inconquerable champion light weight of the south, but now defeated, unconscious and fast being wrapt in the embrace of death, who the mightiest of pugilists cannot withstand, lay." At 6:43 a.m., "he passed into eternity."

"Andy Bowen is dead, and professional pugilism in New Orleans will more than likely fill the same grave," predicted a journalist. An editorialist for the *Daily Picayune* seconded the opinion. The fatality, he wrote, "should sound the death knell of that bloody brutality misnamed 'sport.'" And so it happened. Soon after the end of Andy Bowen, the Louisiana Supreme Court eliminated the legal fiction that "boxing exhibitions" in exclusive athletic clubs was not actually "prize fighting." Even in the most gilded of cities, there were limits to the toleration of the courts. The golden age of the New Orleans ring had passed.

After mourning his death, little more was written about Andy Bowen, though one court record referred to him as a "mulatto." His was another "mulatto's tragic end," remembered today only as a footnote to the history of boxing.

CHAPTER FOUR

In the Land of Dreamy Dreams

Tennis and the Nexus of Class and Race in New Orleans, 1876–1976

THOMAS AIELLO

Perhaps the most famous match played at the New Orleans Lawn Tennis Club (NOLTC) never actually happened. LaGrande McGruder only agreed to play a match against Roxanne Miller after continued prodding, not wanting to because Miller was, in her conception, "a cripple," and because Miller and her husband were new members, Jews, only admitted because the club had just moved to a new location and needed an infusion of cash. McGruder, whose father had once been president of the United States Lawn Tennis Association, had played at the club her entire life, and was confident that she could easily throttle the crippled, Jewish newcomer. But the newcomer was good. She surprised McGruder with shot after improbable shot, until finally a frustrated McGruder called a ball out that was clearly not out, hoping to gain an advantage. She did, and after that momentum swing, she was able to defeat the interloper, but it was a Rubicon of sorts for McGruder. She was so frustrated with herself that she drove to the Huey P. Long Bridge and dumped her tennis equipment into the Mississippi River.[1]

The McGruder-Miller match occurred in Ellen Gilchrist's short story, "In the Land of Dreamy Dreams." McGruder's abandonment of tennis after failure in the face of moral crisis mirrored the crisis of faith in her mentor, Claiborne Redding, who lamented the infusion of new-money members, Jewish members, and their breach of protocol. Coffee was being served in styrofoam cups with powdered creamer, for example, whereas at the old club waiters had formerly

A group of late-nineteenth century tennis players in New Orleans. Photo courtesy of the New Orleans Lawn Tennis Club and the Louisiana Research Collection, Tulane University, New Orleans.

brought café au lait in silver serving. Nailor, the black groundskeeper, was equally wistful about the bygone era. Gilchrist's story, published in 1981 but taking place in 1977, used the coffee cups and the violation of honor to symbolize the passing away of upper-class insulation that was part and parcel of the competitive tennis culture at the club. The old standards of class and culture that had dominated from 1876 to 1976 had seemingly dissolved in a styrofoam cup of stale coffee.

Tennis in New Orleans was, as it was in other urban areas, a vehicle of restrictive exclusivity, but that exclusivity worked in myriad ways across lines of class and race, beginning with the founding of Gilchrist's New Orleans Lawn Tennis Club in 1876 and moving through a century beset by racial and economic turmoil. Post-Reconstruction New Orleans tennis looked much like antebellum Louisiana writ large, with a small exclusive upper class, an also-small upper-middle class with slightly less exclusivity but seeking as much as they could muster, then the majority of white players below who were left to use playing ability rather than social or financial status to gain access. Then there was the black population who was excluded from all of that competition, middle and upper-class players participating in a separate world until pioneers came along to push back against that closed system. Black tennis in New Orleans, then, democratized from the top down, those with access working to open doors for themselves, then lead the way for their social and economic inferiors who otherwise would not have access. White tennis, meanwhile, democratized from the bottom up, with players originally priced or classed out of the NOLTC making new opportunities to play the game and creating new access for a new group of players.

The modern version of tennis came about in England in 1873, and the following year, American Mary Ewing Outerbridge brought the game to Staten Island. In 1877, formal rules for the game would be established by the All-England Croquet and Lawn Tennis Club, Wimbledon. Even before Wimbledon's rules, however, the United States had first developed its own club for the sport in December 1876, the New Orleans Lawn Tennis Club, still the nation's oldest.[2]

December 1876 was an inauspicious time to begin such an endeavor, after the contested presidential election of 1876 and before the Compromise of 1877 two months later that would eventually withdraw the remaining federal troops from New Orleans and restore home rule. The NOLTC was founded at the tail end of a violent Reconstruction process that began with a bloody race riot where mobs of angry whites murdered 44 black victims and wounded 150 more outside of the city's Mechanics Institute. As the NOLTC formed, the city was still reeling from a September 1874 coup known locally as the Battle of Liberty Place, wherein a band of roughly five thousand members of the White League, a paramilitary terrorist organization affiliated with the far-right wing of the Democratic Party, attacked the police and held the statehouse for three days before fleeing to escape the arrival of federal troops. If that wasn't enough, just a year after the club formed and home rule was restored, a yellow fever outbreak killed thousands in the city and even more throughout the lower Mississippi Valley in 1878. Despite political, social, and environmental turmoil, however, the NOLTC forged ahead.[3]

The development of an upper-class tennis culture in New Orleans also came at an inauspicious economic time in the city's history. The NOLTC was founded in between the Panic of 1873, which decimated the city's economy, and the yellow fever epidemic that decimated a portion of its population. Understandably, the city's economic growth rate was not as pronounced as it was in its antebellum heyday, but its economic growth in products traveling by rail and products traveling from the Gulf both more than doubled over the course of the Gilded Age, keeping New Orleans the country's second largest port, though the economic distance between it and New York continued to grow. Throughout the late nineteenth century, according to historian Joy Jackson, both capital and labor "had organized and centralized their efforts," and despite the interracial cooperation of some of the city's trade unions, the rich continued to get richer.[4]

As Eric Arnesen has demonstrated, the 1880s were a legitimately successful decade for the labor movement in the city, as biracial unions and segregated black and white unions of waterfront workers acting in tandem helped cotton workers and stevedores earn more control over the conditions of their employment, aided by a "Democratic party machine" that helped unions "confront employers in an unfettered way." The 1890s saw that movement decline as racism rose in the wake of Jim Crow and the economy fell in the wake of the Panic of 1893. But it didn't disappear. Strikes littered the New Orleans waterfront in the first decade of the twentieth century, facilitated by interracial unionism that was blamed for all of the unrest. In the decades that followed, the employers, many of whom were members of the NOLTC, would consolidate their control, creating labor stability and less control for workers, which only further highlighted the differentiation between social and economic classes, even after the city's red-light district had largely disappeared.[5]

The club's first president was Gustaf Westfeldt, of the city's Westfeldt Brothers Coffee empire. He was joined by founding members like Atwood Violett, who was president of the Southern Mineral and Land Improvement Company, the Standard Fireless Engine Company, and the New Orleans Telephone Company, along with several other powerful city businesses. Gilbert Green was a prominent banker. N.D. Wallace was a powerful cotton factor who owned several other companies. They were joined by leaders like Henry Charnock, an import-export magnate who had come to New Orleans from England, bringing his passion for the new game with him, and several other English immigrants. It was an elite group, and their intent was to create an elite club, an organization that catered to those of similar breeding.[6]

The club's location bounced around in the late nineteenth century from the corner of Jackson and Prytania streets to another Prytania location to the corner of Dryades and Amelia until it finally settled in February 1898 on Saratoga Street, where it would stay until 1973. To secure its Saratoga Street location, members formed a private stock company. Selling stock in the new company facilitated the land purchase and building of its first clubhouse, with a broad viewing gallery that overlooked the playing space. Because of the club's English influence, the gallery always featured afternoon tea. The club's groundskeeper, John Irwin, rolled and graded an area for twelve Bermuda grass courts. With many British immigrants among the membership, space was also set aside for a cricket crease. On its initial founding, women were only allowed to play on Wednesday afternoons, designated Ladies' Day, but upon the purchase of its new space formal ladies' memberships were opened to women (though full "stockholder" memberships would not be open to women until 1998).[7]

Tennis made sense as a southern entity, a region dominated by a wealthy oligarchy who had kept millions of its black citizens enslaved and recently carried the bulk of its poorer white citizens into a costly and devastating war to protect an investment in which those poor fighters would never participate. "The remarkable interest displayed in lawn tennis throughout the North, and the increasing popularity of the game, as shown each year by the multitude of new players and new clubs, have been fully equaled in the South during the past two seasons," one commentator concluded in 1889. "The Southern interest is an awakening one. The athletes of that section have become aware, only during the last few years, that lawn tennis is a game which fully develops every muscle, and at the same time possesses the elements of excitement and competition which render any athletic game more attractive."[8]

As Larry R. Youngs explains in his study of the intersection of sports and tourism in wintertime Florida in the Gilded Age and Progressive Era, "Having acquired the necessary time and disposable wealth, certain affluent men and women put increasing value on the quality and meaning of their time away from work and home." Youngs is interested in those from northern cities spending winters in Florida and the broader Southeast, but his analysis is fitting for many in New Orleans as well. "Such people increasingly embraced the idea that participating in outdoor recreation, including certain competitive sports, helped to immunize against the unhealthy aspects—both mental and physical—of modern urban life, especially life in an industrial and capitalistic society."[9]

Steven Reiss agrees with Youngs. "As widening income levels, substantial differences in discretionary time, and diverse social values resulted in different leisure options for different social classes" in the late nineteenth and early twentieth centuries, "sport came to mark social boundaries and to define status communities."[10] That was certainly true in New Orleans, but in a place where "diverse social values" and "discretionary time" had always been part of the definition of the city itself, those boundary markers were going to be far more populous and far more intricate, particularly when a game like tennis, which already had its own social and economic boundary lines built into it, came to a city with its own pre-established boundaries.

As Alecia Long has noted in her study of post-Civil War New Orleans concert saloons, social class and respectability were deeply intertwined among the city's citizens. They bore a particular weight on African Americans and immigrants, most of whom appeared at the mouth of the Mississippi with far fewer privileges than the English immigrants who helped found the NOLTC. And respectability could easily be shaped by the places one chose to spend his time. Long evaluates an 1893 lawsuit brought against a local concert saloon by its neighboring businesses, each worried that the saloon was a nuisance to the neighborhood and that its presence would decrease property values. Lawyers emphasized that "people of the very lowest class and very lowest order" made up the bulk of the saloon's clientele. "Of course, there are occasions where gentlemen go there, but those are exceptions." One witness openly admitted not attending concert saloons because of the risk to his "good reputation." When one of the plaintiffs admitted that the shows at concert saloons were at least similar to the "ballet at the French Opera House," the lawyer questioning him asked, "One is the rich man's opera, and the other a poor man's opera, is that it?" The plaintiff rejected that comparison, but the implication was clear. Respectability was not alone built on ideology and bank account. It was also a creature of the buildings one frequented and the social codings for what went on inside them.[11]

Inherent in such endeavors was also a celebration of masculinity, as men frequented concert saloons to experience the hospitality of its female employees. While New Orleans was unique in some of its methods of excess, it was not unique in excess, as a working-class rejection of Victorian moral idealism in the postwar nineteenth century led to a new emphasis on toughness as a better biological standard on which to judge people, in lieu of more culturally constructed and unfair categories like social standing and wealth. Thus developed the saloon blood-sport culture across the country, which also dominated in New Orleans and fed the city's ever-expanding bar scene. Concert saloons themselves served a different purpose, but bar culture, animal bloodsports, and the working-class reaction against Victorianism would give way to a boxing culture that absolutely dominated in New Orleans, a reputation solidified at the city's Olympic Club in September 1892, when Jim Corbett knocked out John L. Sullivan in twenty-one rounds to win the heavyweight championship. Boxing was the living embodiment of the social Darwinian ideal, as the strongest survived despite privilege of birth or breeding, and thus leveled the social playing field. It created, in what Elliott Gorn has described, explaining the draw of the *Police Gazette,* proud progenitor of such amusements, "a democracy of pleasure denied by Victorian culture."[12]

It was hard to argue biology, and so Victorians, in turn, sought to develop their own athletic ethic. Already shunning physical brutality as they had done prostitution and concert saloons, the middle and upper classes sought to cordon off a place for uplifting, beneficial sports. They celebrated amateurism as the ultimate sports experience to counter the pay and professionalization in boxing (and, increasingly, in team sports like baseball). In 1888, for example, the Amateur Athletic Union developed under the original auspices of the New York Athletic Club as an umbrella organization to organize amateur athletic contests—to celebrate pure competition devoid of the professionalism that brought ruin to players and fans.[13] Amateur sports like tennis, golf, and polo generally required a club membership of one kind or another. Thus, they solved every Victorian problem in one fell swoop. They taught amateur values, shunned the violence of lower class sports, and had a built-in system for ensuring that only those of a certain class and breeding would be able to participate. The NOLTC was far different than a concert saloon, but it worked the same way socially.

In the 1890s, YMCA leader Luther Halsey Gulick emphasized the organization's athletic offerings, arguing for what he called "muscular Christianity." Spiritual life rests on the equal development of the mind and the body, he argued, so not developing the body was against the will of God. Gulick became a leader in the Boy Scouts movement and the Playground Association of America, among other similar endeavors. He also teamed with sociologist G. Stanley Hall of Clark University to develop a pseudo-biological response to the "survival of the fittest" mantra of boxing enthusiasts. Their evolutionary theory of play became incredibly influential in the early twentieth century, arguing in a roundabout way that humans had developed an impulse to play during evolution and that everyone mimicked the broader stages of human evolution in every phase of their lives. With each person recapitulating the history of humanity through sports, those games were necessarily essential to proper physical, moral, and neural growth. Gulick and Hall used their paradigm to argue for the benefit of team sports in particular, but it also provided a greater emphasis on physical activity for those not attending boxing matches and concert saloons.[14]

The bind in which upper class tennis enthusiasts found themselves, however, is that precisely because of its association with wealth and leisure, tennis was not placed on par with other, more democratic physical activities. At the national level, its reputation for effete dandyism even developed among the privileged at times. In 1878, several Harvard men deserted crew for tennis, and the school newspaper was indignant. "Is it not a pity that serious athletics should be set aside by able-bodied men for a game that is at best intended for a seaside pastime?" asked *The Crimson*. "The game is well enough for lazy or weak man, but men who have rowed or taken part in a nobler sport should blush to be seen playing Lawn Tennis."[15]

Still, it was a Harvard man who contributed to the game's rise in national popularity, when in 1900, Dwight F. Davis established the International Lawn Tennis Challenge Cup to foster international rivalries. A generation later, superstars like Big Bill Tilden and Suzanne Lenglen drove an even greater national obsession with the game.[16] What they were unable to do, particularly in places like New Orleans where class and respectability politics were so intertwined, and where the NOLTC was the symbol of both tennis and restrictive exclusivity, was to disassociate the game from its privileged image.

American tennis had always been a decidedly upper-class endeavor. The first United States tennis championship took place in August and early September 1881, in Newport, Rhode Island. Held at the Casino Club, an institution so exclusive that it denied membership to president Chester Arthur because he did not have what the club considered to be the proper social standing.[17]

That being the case, tennis clubs like NOLTC created social cues for those who wanted to identify themselves as having become part of the city's elite. In New Orleans, the game's upper-class status was cemented not just by club exclusivity, but by the corresponding disinterest of everyone not included in the club. "Why lawn tennis, one of the most fascinating of out door amusements open to both sexes, has not attained to a more extended popularity in this city, is a mystery," wondered the city's *Times-Picayune* newspaper in 1879. The game's required supplies were relatively inexpensive, costing less "than that of a cheap croquet set." And yet croquet was still more popular, though it was less skillful, athletic, and exciting.[18] What the paper failed to take into account was that in those early days, tennis was associated almost solely with the NOLTC, with wealth, making it anathema to so many without such means.

As if to highlight that disconnect, the paper ran an anonymous piece of fiction in 1880 that told of an idle young wealthy man who still maintained some work at the city's cotton exchange. When asked why, he explained that "it helps me along wonderfully in society, when I talk about my 'June deliveries,' and all the other contracts I have on hand. Really, a fellow can't be playing lawn tennis all the time, you know—really he can't." Another editorial comment that year referred to lawn tennis mockingly as "Presbyterian base ball."[19]

Adding another hindrance and making the rise of New Orleans tennis all the more improbable, the tennis players of early New Orleans entered a climate that was relatively averse to sports. "Exercise for health reasons was not stressed or considered worth promoting," writes historian Joy Jackson. "Most men preferred to spend their hours after work or on Sunday afternoons at their social clubs, or at saloons and beer gardens." By the 1890s, however, that attitude had changed. Baseball and bicycling gained an incredible popularity, along with tennis, golf, crew, and yachting. And their popularity was growing, even among those not of advantageous breeding. In 1880, for example, Seebold's on Canal Street, a store typically dedicated to books, stationery, and art supplies, began advertising the sale of tennis equipment, along with supplies for archery and croquet.[20]

That democratizing trend would exist at the top of the social hierarchy as well. The NOLTC's club championship tournament began in 1890, won twice in its first seven years by plantation owner and sugar magnate C. C. Krumbhaar. In 1901, after substantial debate, the club began an annual interclub tournament. It was not the sort of event that aided restrictive exclusivity, but because of that exclusivity, in the words of the *Times-Picayune,* the club was "comparatively a stranger to the tennis world at large, and must necessarily win its own recognition by the excellence of its tournaments and the skill of its members." Much of the benefit of exclusivity, in other words, came from others knowing what they were missing. That first event included teams from the Tulane Tennis Club and Alameda Tennis Club, along with a delegation from Georgia's Atlanta Athletic Club. The Atlantans had only played on clay and came to the NOLTC to test their skills on grass. Still, the club had not become a democracy overnight. No spectators were admitted without a special card that certified them as worthy of watching the tournament.[21]

It was, however, a first step. The following year the club took a second step, aligning officially with the United States Lawn Tennis Association and hosting the Gulf States Championship, which the venue would continue to host annually from 1902 to 1914. The Gulf States awarded prizes in men's and ladies' singles and men's doubles. After winners were declared in the men's divisions, winners played the champions from the previous year for a challenge cup. All matches were decided by two of three sets, with the exception of the men's finals and challenge matches, which were best three of five. The club was also part of the Southern Lawn Tennis Association (SLTA), organized in 1887 and by the early 1900s comprised of clubs in Atlanta, Memphis, Knoxville, Macon, Montgomery, Mobile, and Greenville, South Carolina. The SLTA's founding document included the express dictum, "No club which is situated north of Wilmington, Delaware, should be admitted to membership in the Association."[22]

Beginning in 1914, the NOLTC graduated to hosting the Southern Championship, a larger event than the Gulf States with the same divisions and rules. To make the club more accommodating to visiting tournament players, in 1925 the NOLTC added four clay courts and a concrete court to complement its grass offerings.[23]

This emphasis on tournament play may at first seem to cut against the bent toward restrictive exclusivity, but within the cloister of class-restricted tennis, where everyone was white and everyone had basically equal pocketbooks, winning became the arbiter of prestige, a way to find the first among equals. Even the athletic contest itself, then, became part of the social contest outside of its fault lines.[24]

The club's place as a venue for the Southern Championship lasted into the 1950s, a tournament that would come to be dominated in the 1930s, 40s, and 50s by the diminutive Bryan "Bitsy" Grant, who won the championship eleven times. Grant was the South's best player, despite being 5'4" and only 120 pounds. The Atlantan had grown up playing on that city's clay courts and translated that experience into three National Clay Court Championships titles. He defeated Ellsworth Vines and Don Budge and played on three Davis Cup teams. Despite the lack of clay, New Orleans was a second home for the southerner, who demonstrated to his fellow players that southern tennis could be a vehicle to global renown in the game.[25]

The success of the club and its tournament would certainly redound to Grant, but it would also have more local beneficiaries, as Tulane's tennis team became a dominant force, winning seventeen SEC championships in the 1940s and 1950s. One of its most prominent stars was two-time NCAA singles champion Hamilton "Ham" Richardson, who would supplant Grant as one the dominant southern players in the 1950s and 60s.[26]

Tulane's success was orchestrated by a different kind of migrant. Emmet Paré was from Chicago, a professional who had toured with Bill Tilden before coming to New Orleans in 1934 to coach the Tulane tennis team and serve as the teaching pro for the NOLTC. Along with his team's SEC championships, he also led them to the 1959 NCAA national championship. Ham Richardson was not his only singles champion. Under Paré's watch, Tulane also produced Jack Tuero, Jose Aguero, and Ron Holmberg, all of whom won NCAA titles and became legends of New Orleans tennis at the NOLTC. The club and the university were near one another, and that proximity combined with the dual influence of Paré kept them in a symbiotic relationship.[27]

So too did the devotion of female players. Interest in tennis had been developing among the city's women since its inception. Though tennis had early been pilloried as a "ladies game," and men had pushed back against the accusation, others saw the game more positively as "a game in which the elements of exercise and competition are combined." For a woman, "lawn tennis seems to be her only refuge. It is the one athletic game which women may enjoy without being subjected to sundry insinuations of rompishness." Such sentiments drove female interest in tennis, leading, for example, to the NOLTC's "Ladies' Day" and other opportunities to play, the one cardinal rule for women being "no heeled shoes."[28]

With the game's popularity continuing to grow, the city's Audubon Park installed its own lawn tennis court in 1901, as did City Park, and the following year a group of players formed an early version of the City Park Tennis Club (CPTC). It didn't last, but the city's interest in tennis did begin growing, and in 1922 City Park expanded to include seventeen public tennis courts for white players. In March 1928, a group of thirteen players formed a new version of the CPTC. They were a group of far more modest means, including the park's tennis pro, William Macassin—a white middle-class coterie of tennis enthusiasts with no possibility of entering the NOLTC. That did not mean that the group was without means. In the heart of the Depression, the now-larger group offered the park $1000 annual rent for the exclusive use of six courts, and for three additional courts if the city would agree to build more. The city did, building nine more courts at a cost of $9,000 and reserving six of the new additions for the CPTC.[29] There was in the endeavor a clear understanding that while the club could not be as restrictive as that of its betters, it was still seeking validation through exclusivity and was willing to pay a substantial amount of Depression-era money to create it. Unlike the NOLTC, which began as an upper-class endeavor, the CPTC evolved from play at a public park over the course of a generation, demonstrating that even when starting from a relatively democratic base, the arc of tennis bent toward class exclusivity.

To mimic its social betters, the club soon started its own championship tournament, dominated in the 1930s by Paul Goosman. Goosman was not a planter or a banking magnate. He was a lower-middle class man who rented a small house on Annunciation Street in the Fourteenth Ward, a factory clerk who had only completed his second year of high school. His place on the city's social arc was earned not through his accomplishments but through his play.[30]

The obsession with appearance can be seen in two separate debates in the fall of 1937. The first was the use of shorts, a utilitarian new style that had dominated among many of the city's players, allowing for easier movement and a break from New Orleans's stifling heat. Some, however, were resistant, desiring to preserve the game's respectability over and against ease of play.[31]

The second came in a scandal involving Anna Koll, the city's best female player throughout much of the 1930s. In May, she was ruled ineligible to play in the public parks tournament in June and the city open tournament in September after being charged with professionalism by the USLTA. It was a scandal among the city's tennis players, as amateurism was upheld as the ultimate value in the sport, and Koll was accused only after local testimony essentially outed her as charging for tennis lessons. The reality that Koll had been accused by some of her own only added to the scandal, and she vigorously fought the charges. Her lawyer produced receipts that demonstrated the costs she incurred for balls, court rentals, and trophies for her students exceeded the payments she received. Koll, a school teacher by trade, produced a litany of witnesses to testify on her behalf, including the superintendent of athletics for New Orleans public schools. Even after the legal push, Koll's reinstatement in November happened not because the city open tennis committee or the USLTA admitted mistakes in judgment, but instead because the national body ruled that her suspension through the full run of the summer season was a substantial enough punishment. It was the kind of ruling that ended the controversy but kept the scarlet letter upon Koll, who never regained her championship form. And so, whether through the more trivial collision between traditional fashion and improved performance or the more substantive clash between amateurism and professionalization, New Orleans tennis courts became a discursive theater for the politics of respectability.[32]

Making the controversy even more illustrative of the evident crosscurrents in national tennis and New Orleans society, earlier that year the city's newfound passion for the game brought the biggest names in professional tennis to town. American Ellsworth Vines and Englishman Fred Perry played an exhibition at the Tulane gym. The two major champions played each other on both American and British tours, finally making it to New Orleans, where Vines defeated an ailing Perry in straight sets. It was a contest attended by all of the city's tennis fans, the two players celebrated on their professional tour, just months before Koll was barred from city play after a false reading of a technicality branded her a professional with much different connotations than those of Vines and Perry.[33]

In a February 1938 exhibition, Vines played Perry in a repeat of the pair's earlier contest at the Tulane gym, part of another national professional tour. A decade later, on March 22, 1948, Bobby Riggs, Jack Kramer, Pancho Segura, and Dinny Pails played exhibition matches at the Tulane gym. At the end of March, Charles E. Hart, former British Davis Cup captain, conducted a weekend clinic at City Park, Audubon Park, and the NOLTC. The event was a temporary postwar stay of the NOLTC's exclusivity, as the event was free and open to the public, putting many on the grounds who would not normally have a chance to do so.[34]

To provide a sense of ownership to those who were normally left out of such events, the city had created a public parks tournament—the same tournament from which Koll was originally barred—to build a measure of exclusivity going the other way. Established in 1923, the tournament, taking place at Audubon Park and City Park, barred those belonging to any club that had its own courts. It charged a twenty-five cent entry fee and required the loser of the match to pay for the balls. It was the people's tournament, and to demonstrate its popularity, the 1938 event had almost two hundred entrants.[35]

Over the first half of the twentieth century, there were plenty of other clubs that began their own tennis programs, all with varying degrees of exclusivity. After the NOLTC, the West End Tennis Club organized in 1890, then the New Orleans Country Club, the Aurora Country Club, the Timberlane Country Club, the Audubon Tennis Club, the Lakewood Country Club, the Orleans Women's Tennis Club, and the Metairie Country Club all fielded players in the city's various tournaments. The New Orleans Bicycle Club and the Metropolitan Athletic Club drew court boundaries on croquet lawns to allow their members to play. Even more social organizations like the Elks and Linwood clubs began playing in the 1890s, all demonstrating that even those unable to join a club were interested in the game. Several wealthier citizens built their own private courts. One local commentator suggested approvingly that "the laying out of the 'garden district'" in the city "makes possible many more private courts than in most large cities." Some tennis clubs, like Timberlane and Audubon, maintained teams in a Metropolitan New Orleans League, pitting clubs against one another in the years following World War II. The rivalries between the groups were friendly ones. In 1930, for example, when rain slowed play at the New Orleans Country Club's annual men's invitational tournament, the NOLTC offered use of its courts to speed up play. In January 1967, when rain slowed the annual Sugar Bowl tournament, the championship match was moved to the NOLTC because the club had artificial light that facilitated nighttime play.[36]

City Park and Audubon Park remained the most influential early venues, though the grass of "lawn tennis" would prove too costly and labor-intensive to maintain. Audubon switched to clay and asphalt courts and City Park to clay, but clay too had its problems, particularly for an area as water-logged as New Orleans. Clay retained water, keeping players off the courts long after a rain. In 1937, Audubon resurfaced its asphalt courts with concrete and its clay courts with brickdust, followed shortly by City Park, as brickdust was just as easy as clay to maintain but drained water far more rapidly.[37]

The new courts were part of a democratizing trend for white tennis in New Orleans, with players passionate about playing creating opportunities for themselves. Those opportunities would then generate greater expansion. From the early 1930s until World War II, Howard Jacobs's "Men in White" column in the New Orleans *Times-Picayune,* the city's largest daily newspaper, became the public voice of New Orleans tennis, reporting on local tournaments and players and showing citizens otherwise barred from the city's various clubs how and where they could participate. From the 1940s to the 1960s, the *Times-Picayune*'s Jimmie Powers served much the same purpose with his long-running "Over the Net" column.[38] The opportunities of new courts and columns in white newspapers, however, were not available to the white players' black counterparts.

African American tennis was almost as old as American tennis itself. The first black tennis clubs on the East Coast began in the 1890s, the Chautauqua Club in Philadelphia in 1890, the Monumental City Tennis Club in Baltimore in 1895, and others forming during the decade in New York and Washington. Black tennis in the South also had its beginnings in the 1890s when Tuskegee built faculty courts on campus. Such foundings occurred in the era of Jim Crow retrenchment. They were necessary because early private tennis clubs like the NOLTC "were not just for the elites," notes historian Sundiata Djata, "but for white elites." The black clubs that rose in response to that segregation began organizing tournaments as early as 1898, and at one such tournament in 1916, the idea for the American Tennis Association (ATA) was conceived. The ATA was founded later that year to be the chief organizing body of black tennis, led for its first twelve years by Dr. H. Stanton McCard of Baltimore's Monumental City club. The organization held national championships and supported the game throughout metropolitan areas, particularly on the East Coast.[39]

Of course, New Orleans had a prosperous black community even prior to the outbreak of the Civil War, and in the two decades after the conflict, that prosperity—or that prosperity's proximity to its white counterpart—continued to grow. Along with it grew the cultural life that accompanied privilege. "Negro social life in New Orleans was varied, rich, and in many ways a reflection of activities in the white community," explains John Blassingame. "This social life united the black community while at the same time accentuating class divisions." As the NOLTC was being formed, black New Orleans had its own symphony orchestra. It engaged in crew contests at the Saratoga Rowing Association and the Antoine Rowing Club. Upper-class endeavors like rifle matches or horse races also dominated, though tennis, as a game comparatively new compared to equestrian events, crew, and shooting, took longer to make an imprint.[40]

Such is not to say a nascent black interest did not exist. As early as 1881, five years after the founding of the NOLTC, the black *Weekly Louisianian* mentioned tennis as a distinctly British game. "*Nous connsiasons deja le cricket, le croquet, le lawn tennis, le polo et antres jeux d'importation anglaise,*" the *Louisianian* explained, lumping it with other games that black New Orleans did not play, like polo and cricket. Still, while the paper grouped the games together as English imports, they were also games that served as signposts of social advancement and institutional wealth. They were foreign games, but they were also goals.[41]

In December 1886, the *Weekly Pelican,* a later Gilded Age New Orleans black newspaper, ran a *New York Tribune* advertisement for *The Tribune Book of Open Air Sports,* a volume "especially for the young men of the United States" that would include chapters on both "Court Tennis" and "Lawn Tennis." The

Tribune assured black New Orleans readers that "no book of this character has ever been put into print in America."[42] The same edition of the *Pelican* featured a short story, "A Fir Pillow," about a relationship on a summer retreat between a man in his twenties and a woman in her fifties. The man, Jack, was "an active young fellow so devoted to tennis and baseball," which made the woman all the more curious as to why he would sit and sew with her, or as to "what tender, loving thoughts he was working into those great clumsy arms when I saw that peculiar far off look come into his beautiful brown eyes."[43]

The *Pelican* was devoted to creating a cultured black middle class, reprinting articles from white papers throughout the country and world designed to aid such an end. Tennis was a symbol of social respectability, and so made it into the paper, despite a lack of any real play from black New Orleanians. In January 1887, for example, an article about the frustration of Parisians about the dress of Englishmen at French opera houses reported that one French newspaper suggested that "the unmannerly English will shortly look on at the play in their flannels 'du lawn tennis,' leaving their racquets in the cloak room."[44] Later that year, the *Pelican* reproduced an *American Magazine* article about "care in taking exercise." Mountain climbing "is to be avoided," as was most rowing and swimming, which could be "dangerous to any one whose heart is weak." It was, the article reasoned, an unnecessary risk. But "tennis is different. Although it requires agility and considerable exertion, there are intervals of rest that make it one of the safest of games. It is only necessary to slip on a light coat or shawl when a set is finished to avoid sudden chill."[45]

An 1889 *Pelican* reprint, told in the voice of a rural upstate New York farmer who had seen his life transformed by cosmopolitans from the city vacationing on his farm, described experiencing the game for the first time. "Lucy's feller and the college dudes was playin' what they call lawn tennis out in the cow pastur one day," explained the narrator. "The boys was waltzin' around the pastur' with their white coats and panties on." He had never seen a game that "looked more thrillin'. Me and the hired man just stood there and watched." Tennis, the article implied, was a cosmopolitan, elite game. Those who didn't play it were rubes. Black New Orleans residents were not yet playing the game in any sustained way, but they were receiving messages equating the game with Victorian respectability standards from an aspirational newspaper devoted to touting those standards.[46]

The *Louisiana Weekly,* founded in September 1925, first mentioned tennis in an Associated Negro Press article about the American Tennis Association

1926 national tournament in St. Louis. While the president of the St. Louis Tennis Association's statement that tennis fans in the city had "organized to secure the backing of the tournament by the entire Colored population" surely rankled the black upper class of New Orleans, forever in a rivalry with their Mississippi River neighbor to the north, tennis was only a developing interest of the city's black social set in the early 1920s.[47] The African-American clubs of New Orleans focused their early attention on dinners, dancing, and whist, a seventeenth century trick-taking card game popular in New Orleans and throughout south Louisiana. The Phyllis Wheatley Club, the Twentieth Century Whist Club, the Entre Nous Club, the Autocrat Club, the Marble Heart Whist Club, the Marechal Neil Aid and Pleasure Club, the Young Men Twenty Club, the Housewives Industrial Sewing Club, and dozens of other organized secular groups held meetings, parties, dances, teas, suppers, and "whists," but did not early entertain tennis as part of the social hierarchy.[48] Neither did the Iroquois Club, the oldest and most prominent black social club in the city.[49]

Though it wasn't as accessible as dancing, dinners, and whist, however, there was a small but prominent early black tennis presence in New Orleans. The St. Katherine Tennis Club served as the early home of the game's enthusiasts. Unlike the NOLTC, membership was not based on social exclusivity and instead on a passion to play. In August 1926, the club announced that Edna Cordier, a local school teacher, and William Mitchell, the executive director of the Dryades Street YMCA, would represent the club at the ATA's St. Louis event. "Much interest is being manifested in tennis in New Orleans," St. Katherine's announced confidently, "with the result that there are several exceptional players." So much so that the group was helping to organize a Gulf States' Tennis Association that would have its headquarters in New Orleans.[50]

The Dryades Street YMCA was an important hub for such activity. In 1927, it sponsored the Colored Public School Athletic League to give boys and girls access to sports that school budgets couldn't give them. The Y's Young Men's Division paid particular attention to developing male youth. Other programs targeted boys and girls of various ages and interests. Such programs were necessary in 1920s New Orleans, when the Jim Crow line was starker than ever. The Amateur Athletic Union had scheduled its annual track meet for New Orleans in July 1927, for example, but pulled the event in April of that year after city officials and local leadership refused to include black athletes in an integrated meet. A city willing to sacrifice that much revenue and reputation to uphold the racial line in athletics made the mission of the Y that much more substantial. One of its chief projects was an annual summer camp in nearby Waveland, Mississippi at the Gulfside Chautauqua and Camp Meeting Grounds, a resort of more than six-hundred acres maintained entirely by black leaders for the recreation of the black population. The boys who made the trip camped in tents, they swam, hiked, did craft projects, and played tennis on the facility's new courts.[51]

In July 1927, Xavier University installed three tennis courts and began forming a tennis club. Xavier was a relatively new institution, founded in 1914, the same year that Southern University, originally a New Orleans school founded in 1880, moved to Scotlandville, just outside of Baton Rouge. Straight College was much older, established as Straight University in 1868 by the American Missionary Association. As such, it had already installed tennis courts and hosted an annual tournament in July for the city's black players. There were also courts for black players on the playground of the Thomy Lafon School, a public primary and secondary school associated with Straight, founded in honor of one of its principal donors, the Creole abolitionist and philanthropist Thomy Lafon. The school had been around since 1897, though the first iteration of the institution was destroyed in the New Orleans Race Riot of 1900. Its tennis courts did not appear until the 1920s. Additionally, black players could find a place to play on the Willow St. courts of the relatively new Lusher Elementary School, founded in 1917, where the YMCA would sometimes hold boys' tournaments, or the John W. Hoffman Junior High School on South Prieur Street, where tennis courts were also part of the playground facilities. There were also courts at Daniel Hand School, a black preparatory school funded by the American Missionary Association and aligned with Straight.[52] Finally, there were courts available to black players at Gaudet House on Gentilly Road, the former rehabilitation compound of black social worker Frances Joseph-Gaudet, who used the several buildings on what became a wide campus for a school and orphanage before donating it to the Episcopal Diocese of Louisiana. The tennis courts on the property, then, became open to interested black Episcopalians who wanted to play.[53]

Late in July, the city's black newspaper, the *Louisiana Weekly*, began publishing a tennis column. "Yes, sir, tennis is here to stay," began the column's opening effort, devoted to celebrating Xavier's new courts. They would "become among the finest in the city if the plans for developing and maintaining them do not miscarry." The courts were clay and would drain well. "There is one thing sure and that is organization can do things. Xavier is organized. Tennis there will go." Everyone was invited, and yearly dues were one dollar. "This is a splendid opportunity for beginners to get a chance to play," the column encouraged. And they could even play on Sundays, "as tennis is considered as pure, wholesome recreation."[54]

The author of that and future efforts was E. Belfield Spriggins, a teacher at McDonogh #35 High and Normal School who also wrote for the *Weekly* about his other passion, jazz. In his second tennis column, Spriggins lamented that "tennis is a great game and deserves to be played and studied by more of our group, both young and old." To that end, the column began in the proceeding weeks explaining how to choose a racket, where to buy supplies, the rules and various methods for play.[55] It was a demonstration in microcosm of the differences between the sporting tendencies of white and black New Orleans. White players began immediately by coding the game with exclusivity, while black players pushed for democracy. Courts at the private Catholic college would be open to everyone with a small membership fee. Columns in the newspaper encouraged people to play and gave them advice for making that possible. Again, it was a democratization of the game from those in power, from the top down, those with access instinctively opening the door to those who otherwise would not have access. Meanwhile, though a measure of democracy came to white tennis in New Orleans, it developed from the bottom up, players seeking access outside the cloister of the NOLTC making new opportunities to play the game.

That year, 1927, the ATA held its annual national tournament in Hampton, Virginia, on the campus of Hampton Institute. Spriggins was disheartened to note that no one from New Orleans would be representing the city at the event but hoped that continued development of the game would grow national success and participation. At the national tournament, Ted Thompson of Washington defeated Everest Saitch of New York, Thompson avenging a finals loss to Saitch from the previous year. The women's final was also a return engagement, Lulu Ballard defeating Isadora Channels for the second year in a row. Thompson and Saitch, Ballard and Channels, along with Ora Washington, Edgar Brown, and Reginald Weir were the powerhouses of black tennis, the precipice of where columnists like Spriggins wanted New Orleans to be.[56]

In an effort to get there, Xavier held its now-annual tournament in September. Thirty-six entries marked a record for a black New Orleans event. The men's winner, Olando Moss, "the diminutive but explosive tennis flash, finally settled all disputes as to his local tennis supremacy by blazing his way from the first round to the undisputed local championship." The women's winner was Jeanne Victor, "little school girl southpaw from Xavier College," who "duplicated the feat of Mr. Moss and went him one better by winning all of her matches in straight sets."[57]

Tennis was growing steadily among black New Orleanians. The following June, the Xavier Athletic Club and the Dryades Street YMCA both held tournaments for their respective members, the Y staging its tournament at Hoffman School. At the same time, the Sylvania F. Williams Community Center, connected to the Thomy Lafon School, held its own junior tennis tournament at the Lafon School courts. At the end of the month, a dance and celebration was hosted for the city's tennis champions at Piron's House of Joy, a dance hall established in 1927 in the Pythian Temple at the corner of Loyola and Gravier Streets. Two local players even played an exhibition match during the party on a court marked off on Piron's dance floor.[58]

One of the city's premiere early black players was Woody I. McCann, an elementary school teacher who won several tournaments, most of them in the doubles division with his partner, Henry Jones. Spriggins himself was an accomplished player, as was Castro Haroldson, Carle E. Smith, and mail carrier Edward Dejoie Burbridge.[59] The best male singles player of the period was Moss, a local barber who dominated much of the early competition. His female counterpart was Victor, a young mulatto college student.[60] Jeanne Victor's sister Lydia was an accomplished player as well, as were Pearl Cahn, Maude Johnson, and Edna M. Cordier, all public-school teachers.[61]

Despite this apparent democracy of tennis access, however, historian Lee Sartain has produced a more problematic analysis. Thomy Lafon was "situated in one of the rougher neighborhoods of New Orleans." The Williams Community Center was incredibly active in creating outreach projects for youth and for adults, "yet such projects were often restricted within the confines of dominant middle-class gender expectations." Sartain noted handicraft clubs and calisthenics classes for girls, athletic clubs and the Boy Scouts for boys. That imposition of middle class values and expectations, however, was not limited to restrictive gendered norms. Tennis was open to both boys and girls in the community center's junior tournament, but the effort was clearly designed to expose black children of the working poor to a more upscale game as a paternalistic civilizing force. Tennis offered the juniors amazing competition and did valuable things for those playing, but such lessons could be taught with myriad sports. Tennis was different precisely because of its class-based reputation.[62]

Such efforts, whatever their intent, did grow the game. In the summer of 1928, a new club formed, the Northside Tennis Club, associated with the American Tennis Association, and built its own courts near Canal Street. Leaders promised that the club would be "one of the classiest and most up-to-date tennis clubs seen in this neck of the woods," a club that would "send representatives to the national tournament every year." Edward Dejoie Burbridge was president of the new group; Straight athlete James Cherault was vice president. Earl M. Wright, *Louisiana Weekly* sports editor, was named secretary, along with assistant secretary Agnes Adams and treasurer Ezell Farrell, also a student at Straight. Until their private courts were complete, the new club would play at Straight's Daniel Hand School. The new group quickly realized, however, the costs involved with building its own courts, and thus subsumed a ladies' club, the St. James AME Church Usherettes, in an effort to secure space on the church grounds to build and equip a court. Another group, the Optimo Tennis Club, which played at the Gaudet Home on Gentilly Road, had been languishing, leading many to assume they too would be combining with Northside. The Northside group was now a larger and wealthier aggregation, but in an effort to stay young, it capped membership to those 25 years old and younger, angering many who tried to join. This was a different kind of exclusivity, an ageist exclusivity, only adding to the nexus of cultural codes and limits associated with the game in New Orleans.[63]

A 1928 *Louisiana Weekly* editorial was pleased with the growth of new clubs and interest in tennis, but lamented the various restrictive exclusivities that placed a ceiling on that growth. In particular, the paper argued that "many more people would be converted into the various clubs if the officials and learned players would devote more time to the novice." It was the kind of exclusivity that was inherent in all sports, but had particularly dire repercussions for those playing a game that measured respectability. "Most of our clubs fail to exercise the slogan 'Join and Learn.' If they did, their membership would be much larger, the number of class 'A' performers greater." The respectability that redounded to the race, the paper seemed to argue, was not measured by a handful of quality players, but instead by the broad spread of competence and interest in exclusive sports like tennis. Experience restrictions only diminished the broader communal benefits of the game.[64]

Another substantial hindrance to tennis's growth among the black population was the Great Depression, followed by the upheaval of World War II. After those conflagrations, however, black tennis in New Orleans was led into the civil rights era by one man, Nehemiah Atkinson.

In 1945, Atkinson founded the Crescent City Hard Court Tennis Club to teach tennis and garner interest in the sport among black students in New Orleans. He and the club used the two courts at the Dryades Street YMCA and the two cement courts at Xavier, charging eight dollars an hour for lessons. "We helped to develop many young black tennis players when there was little interest in the schools," he later remembered, adding that "many went on and won scholarships at Southern and Grambling Universities." While in the city, the Crescent City club held its annual tournament at Xavier and the Dryades Y. Atkinson was originally from Biloxi, but had moved to New Orleans as a child, growing up on Saratoga Street in the neighborhood of the New Orleans Lawn Tennis Club. He later described himself as the only one of his friends who followed tennis, which was not popular among black residents of the city. When he returned to the city in 1945 after service in World War II and created the Crescent City Club, however, he attempted to change that with the help of the NOLTC, which, while clearly observing the restrictions of the racial line, did sell Atkinson tennis balls three for a dollar. "They always tried to look out for me there," remembered Atkinson, contextualizing "looking out" through the prism of the restrictive Jim Crow standard of the day. (Still, while such talk seems to romanticize a wholly unequal situation, his access was legitimately rare, and it is hard to imagine leadership of the NOLTC opening its doors to sell balls to poor white players without the contacts Atkinson had at the club.)[65]

The Crescent City Hard Court Tennis Club, like its forerunners, was affiliated with the American Tennis Association. The group would organize tournaments and national championships every year. Because of the South's Jim Crow restrictions, the ATA held its national events at HBCUs, which provided not only the courts but also residential space to accommodate players who would not be welcomed at most southern hotels. School administrators, for their parts, welcomed the events, hungry to make the acquaintance of the black upper class, who they saw as potential donors to their schools. The group would also be a part of ending the segregated state of tennis. In 1940, grand slam champion Don Budge played at the ATA-affiliated Cosmopolitan Tennis Club in New York. Eight years later, Dr. Reginald Weir played in the formerly all-white US Indoor Lawn Tennis Championship, also in New York. Two years after that, in 1950, Althea Gibson became the first black athlete to compete at the United States Lawn Tennis Association's national championship at Forest Hills, beginning what would become her dominance of women's tennis through much of the 1950s. In 1952, Weir would become the first black male to compete at Forest Hills.[66]

The one thing such milestones had in common was that they all came in New York, far from the Gulf Coast and Atkinson's Crescent City club. For years after Gibson's pioneering efforts, New Orleans tennis kept its race bar as sternly fixed as its class bar. From 1956 to 1958, however, Gibson won five major titles, demonstrating that quality tennis required the best players, not the wealthiest or most socially acceptable. And so in 1960, Atkinson played in the state closed tennis tournament, an annual event held only for residents of the state. He was only the second black player to participate in the event, ultimately losing to Paul DeCamp, a surgeon at Ochsner Medical Center in New Orleans and a member of the NOLTC. Again, the restricted club was on the fringe of positive racial contact. The tournament was held at the City Park courts, not at the NOLTC, but members played against those in their draw.[67]

That year, however, was known less for bridging the color line in local tennis and more for bridging it in New Orleans public schools, and the resulting desegregation crisis would become international news, cripple the city, and provide a new intensity for seemingly smaller acts like participating in a formerly white tennis tournament. New Orleans's public-school desegregation was more controversial. The case had been instigated by the NAACP's Legal Defense Fund and headed by Louisiana lawyer and civil rights activist Alexander Pierre Tureaud. Largely because of his effort, the US District Court ordered the Orleans Parish School Board to come up with a desegregation plan, but they stalled, leading to controversy that enveloped the population throughout much of 1960.[68]

In November 1960, two New Orleans public schools desegregated. By the end of the week, white parents had pulled their children from the schools and enrolled them in private schools (or kept them out all together). On November 15, the White Citizens Council held a massive rally, with infamous Plaquemines Parish race-baiter Leander Perez and others whipping the crowd into such a frenzy that the next day a white mob began marching to the school board. The police turned the water hoses on the protesters, which kept them from the school board, but only made them angrier. They turned their attention to black bystanders, injuring almost twenty. After New Orleans mayor DeLesseps Morrison tried to calm the white rebels by assuring them that the police department was not going to enforce the integration order, an angry black population took to the streets, too. Though no one died in the protests, there were more than one hundred casualties and more than 250 arrests, and almost all of those arrested were black. Two years later, the Archdiocese of New Orleans desegregated the city's 153 Catholic elementary and high schools to much less violence and national fanfare.[69]

Just like the efforts of the city's black children attempting to desegregate local public education, Atkinson's early endeavors in integrated tennis were not easy, despite his success, winning tournaments in Baton Rouge, Lafayette, and elsewhere. He suffered indignities at tournaments outside of New Orleans that ran the gamut from urine-filled tennis balls from a taunting crowd to racist umpires calling rogue foot faults against him. As the 1960s progressed, however, relations—particularly in the city—began to improve. "Although there are savage segregationists who have caused trouble from time to time, many New Orleans whites seem to live amicably alongside New Orleans Negroes, in closer proximity than in any other southern or northern city," explained *Sports Illustrated* in 1966. "Golf courses, tennis courts and baseball fields are fully integrated with no resulting difficulty." The magazine explained that the New Orleans Recreation Department had integrated programs for boys and girls in a variety of sports, save swimming, and the organization was hopeful that even its swimming pools would soon be open and integrated. As if to validate the optimism of *Sports Illustrated* and NORD, one of Atkinson's students, Sharon Pettis, became the first black competitor at the national junior Sugar Bowl tournament, originally founded in 1934, at Tulane. Atkinson became a member of the formerly all-white City Park Tennis Club. He was sponsored for membership by a Jewish geologist for Esso, Harry Anisgard, who was temporarily expelled for his effort. When he returned in a few months, Atkinson actually sponsored his membership. He also wrote a column, "Hard Court Tennis Notes," for the *Louisiana Weekly,* doing for the city's black population of the 1950s and 1960s what Spriggins had done in the 1920s.[70]

The standard for New Orleans tennis, however, would always be the New Orleans Lawn Tennis Club, which did not integrate its membership until approximately 1986. The NOLTC was the oldest tennis club in the nation. The New Orleans Fair Grounds, founded in 1872, was the nation's third oldest racetrack, and the Southern Yacht Club, founded in 1849, was the country's second oldest yacht club. Such milestones were celebrated by the city's white elite, as they not only demonstrated wealth and prestige, but a currency even more valuable in southern social standing—longevity.[71]

And social standing was the thing. Tennis in New Orleans used restrictive exclusivity to define the contours of race and class in the Crescent City. White players went first, beginning with the most exclusive NOLTC. Then other players had to draw new boundaries and create new clubs to carve a place for themselves in that hierarchy from the bottom up to create the landscape of white tennis. Black players began differently, developing early exclusivity as markers of class distinction within the community, but, partially because there was a racial ceiling on the heights such markers could reach, the black tennis community shared its knowledge and access to generate a more democratic game from the top-down. When the sport's standard-bearer would not desegregate until the mid-1980s, there was little other opportunity.

In December 1970, Vice President Spiro Agnew, in town for a fundraising dinner at the Jung Hotel, managed to make time to venture over to the NOLTC to play a private game of tennis. But reporters seeking a glimpse of the vice president's play soon discovered that the club's exclusivity applied to the press, as well. His visit, however, was not celebrated by club members who were incredulous and visibly frustrated when Secret Service agents, for example, forced them to park in different spaces because of Agnew's pending arrival. It was a frustration borne of the class intersections tied to tennis since its American birth. If Rhode Island's Casino Club was not good enough for Chester Arthur in the 1880s, members of the NOLTC felt that their club was not good enough for the sitting vice president if it meant disrupting their normal routine.[72]

One can only imagine that LaGrande McGruder from Gilchrist's land of dreamy dreams would have been one of those most perturbed by Agnew's imposition on the pace of club life. For those who loved it, tennis was a passion, an outlet, an obsession. But it was also a symbol—a signpost of social, economic, or athletic achievement that built its meaning depending on where a given player found himself or herself in the nexus of those forces. For those like McGruder, sitting comfortably at the top of each of tennis's myriad semiotic hierarchies, Agnew would have been just another new money interloper who probably didn't belong in tennis, and certainly didn't belong in New Orleans.

II

Institutions of the City

CHAPTER FIVE

The New Orleans Athletic Club

Pantheon of Sport and Society on Rampart Street[1]

RICHARD V. MCGEHEE

New Orleans already had a rich sport heritage when the Young Men's Gymnastic Club was founded in 1872. The Crescent City was at times during the nineteenth century the horse racing and boxing capital of the United States. Horse racing was the first big sport in the city, with three tracks being built in the late 1830s. The most important was the Metairie Course, located where the Metairie Cemetery is today. Famous thoroughbreds and trotters ran before huge crowds during the 1850s, the heyday of New Orleans racing. Sailing was another of the city's earliest organized sport activities. The Southern Yacht Club, with a mostly New Orleans membership, was founded at Pass Christian, Mississippi in 1849, the second yacht club established in the United States. Rowing, cricket, and baseball were other New Orleans sports that thrived before the Civil War.[2]

Boxing matches and animal fights were attended mainly by the poorer social classes, and these activities were prohibited at times by city ordinances. Teams of eighty or more on a side played a rough game based on lacrosse that they called raquette. Socially and racially mixed crowds of several thousand spectators turned out for the Sunday raquette games of the two principal black teams, the Bayous and the LaVilles. The first New Orleans Turnverein was established in 1850, and the Turners became effective promoters of gymnastics in the city. (The Turners were a gymnastics, sport and social organization brought to the US by German immigrants around the middle of the nineteenth century.) As occurred in other parts of the United States, their activities spurred the growth of physical education in the city's schools. The New Orleans YMCA was organized in 1852, and although its members participated during the post-Civil

A view of the New Orleans Athletic Club in 1929. Photo courtesy of The Historic New Orleans Collection, Williams Research Center, New Orleans, Louisiana.

War years in rowing races on Lake Pontchartrain, bicycle races on the levee, and track and field meets, it was not until 1879 that the organization had its first gymnasium.[3]

The New Orleans Athletic Club, which claims to be the second oldest athletic club in the United States, was founded by fourteen "young gentlemen" in New Orleans in 1872. The young men began their activities in the backyard of their first president, Jacinto C. Aleix, on Esplanade Avenue, using some crudely built parallel bars. The club's constitution specified the following points: (1) the club's objective was to develop the members' bodies through gymnastic exercises, including fencing and boxing; (2) the members were to be between 16 and 35 years old, of good moral character and gentlemanly deportment and have no deformity; (3) there was to be no congregating on the sidewalk in front of the club; (4) ladies were not to be admitted except on special occasions; and (5) members would not be admitted without coat and tie. Dues were 50 cents per month, with Aleix authorized to levy assessments when needed.[4]

The club was first known as the Independent Gymnastic Club, and a by-law provided that the membership should never exceed fourteen members. This rule was soon modified, and the club grew to fifty members within two years. In 1874 those members moved to a new location, renting an old stable at the corner of Rampart and Bienville near the west end of the French Quarter. At this time the name was changed to the Young Men's Gymnastic Club (YMGC). Members adopted their motto, black and gold colors, and a diamond-shaped emblem. To pay the 30-dollar rent on the new quarters, the club raised monthly dues to 75 cents. The new facility was not the most elegant in the world. In the early years, if a member wanted to take a shower he had to haul water in buckets from two blocks away, then carry it up a ladder so that the water could be released to fall on him. In 1876 the club installed five tubs and piped in cold water from the Mississippi River.[5]

Members of the New Orleans Turnverein helped the YMGC set up its gym, which was equipped with second-hand weights and pulleys, dumbbells and Indian clubs. During the 1870s the YMGC and the Turners put on gymnastics exhibitions in their clubhouses and at weekend outings.[6] By 1884 membership had grown to 350, and the old structure the club had rented since the 1870s was in great need of repair or replacement. The owner of the property refused to let members rebuild it and also threatened to raise the rent to 40 dollars, so the club decided to suspend activities until it could make other arrangements. That same year, members bought an old high school building on Burgundy Street, directly behind where their building fronts today. In 1889 they also bought an old family mansion at 44 North Rampart Street (the present site of the club).[7]

In 1890 the school was torn down in order to build the club's athletic facilities, which included one of the "costliest and best-equipped gymnasiums in the country," a rubber and felt indoor running track, a workout area and cinder track on the roof, bowling alleys, rifle and pistol shooting range, Russian and Turkish baths, and a marble-lined pool, where the members enjoyed salt-water swimming (after 1911, without wearing swimming trunks). The existence of the salt-water pool resulted from the fact that there was no running water available east of Canal Street in 1898 when the pool was installed, and the well the club drilled encountered salt water.[8] Another salt water well was drilled in 1925. At one time the club also operated a hotel and apartments, with its own YMGC-monogrammed stationery.

In addition to gymnastics the YMGC provided a varied program of athletic[9] and social activities for members and sponsored sporting events for community and regional participation. In the late 1880s and 1890s the bicycling craze was in full swing in New Orleans as elsewhere in the country. Races were held at the Fair Grounds and on a track in Audubon Park, and the YMGC built its own track "far out" on Tulane Avenue. The club also gave cycling classes.[10]

In the 1890s the YMGC, along with the Southern and American Athletic Clubs, was sponsoring annual track and field meets at Audubon Park or the Fair Grounds, and in 1893 these three clubs combined to found the Southern Amateur Athletic Union.[11] Its first president was W.A. Briant of the YMGC. The first Southern AAU spring track and field meet was held in 1893, and this annual meet was an important athletic event for the region until 1900. The spring meet program for 1895, held on Saturday, May 11, listed as participants the YMGC, Southern AC, American AC, Crescent Wheelmen, and Catholic Club from New Orleans, the Birmingham (Alabama) AC, Pensacola (Florida) AC, and the Mission Athletic Club of San Antonio, Texas. Serving with Briant as president, the other three officers were from the American Athletic Club.[12] Several thousand spectators commonly turned out for these spring meets.[13]

In 1898 New Orleans was the site of the national AAU spring meet. There were around 8,000 spectators, and participating clubs were listed as including the Boston Athletic Association, Chicago Athletic Association, Eagle Pass Athletic Association, Nashville Athletic Club, New York Athletic Club, YMGC, Southern AC, and Birmingham AC.[14] More northern clubs might have come to New Orleans, but the AAU final championships were scheduled for that summer in Chicago. In addition, there was perhaps a fear of the yellow fever epidemics, which caused sport participation to fall off generally in the city in the late 1890s.[15]

Boxing was especially popular in New Orleans in the late 1800s, and the YMGC hired professionals to train their members. In 1889 the YMGC moved from purely amateur bouts between members to sponsoring professional boxing matches. When the Southern AC and the YMGC held these bouts, they called them "glove contests." Although "prize fights" were prohibited by state law and a city ordinance, "glove contests" were permitted.[16] John L. Sullivan trained at the YMGC for his illegal bare-knuckle fight with Jake Kilrain that was held at Richburg, Mississippi, in 1889, with a mainly New Orleans crowd of spectators. Sullivan also trained at the YMGC for his fight with "Gentleman Jim" Corbett in 1892, held at the Olympic Club of New Orleans. A cast of Sullivan's right arm was on display at the NOAC for many years. In the last years of the century, much of the remains of boxing occurred in the YMGC's weekly Saturday night "stags."[17]

As was true in athletic clubs elsewhere in the country before the turn of the century, football was also played by the YMGC, its first team being formed in 1895, although the Southern Athletic Club was the real New Orleans leader in football. College football was not highly developed in southern Louisiana and the surrounding region at that time, so the restricted schedules of teams like Louisiana State and Tulane often included athletic clubs.[18]

There was other competition as well. In 1896 a YMGC member placed in two weight throws in the national AAU championships in New York. One club member won places in national single sculls in 1901, 1902, and 1906, and another won a junior singles title.[19] The YMGC Rowing Club was formed in 1905, had a two-story, elegant boathouse on the New Basin Canal, and was very active and successful in competition until disbanding in 1915.[20] In 1899 and 1900 the YMGC also competed in "telegraphic shoots" against northern teams. Each team shot on its own range and telegraphed the results to the other. In the 1890s the YMGC and Southern AC held monthly track and field exhibitions, including "high kicking contests."[21]

In 1900 the YMGC sent Otto Schoenfeldt to represent the club in the "Paris games." He was apparently a physical instructor at the club at that time because he is referred to as "Prof. Schoenfeldt." He already had cleared six feet in the running high jump and twelve feet, seven inches with the pole, and also planned to enter other events, such as the "broad sword and foil."[22]

At the close of the nineteenth century, the YMGC had around 2,000 members.[23] The Club provided class instruction, practice, and competition for members in many individual and team sports, promoted sport activity in the city and region, and also served important social functions. In 1898 the Club was headquarters for all military companies of Louisiana who went through New Orleans on the way to Cuba in the war with Spain.[24] In the 1890s, the Southern AC and the YMGC even had an official journal called the *Spirit of the South*.[25]

An outstanding example of the YMGC's role in helping develop athletes was Harry Gamble. His father enrolled him in the club around 1916 when he was a student at New Orleans' Boys' High. Harry went on to a four-year distinguished football career at Tulane, including the Green Wave's 1925 undefeated season. Later he coached in New Orleans high schools and helped found the New Orleans Junior Sports Association, a forerunner of the New Orleans Recreation Department.[26]

In 1924 the YMGC began publishing a monthly magazine called *The Punch.* Irwin Poche, Sr., athletic director of the club, was its editor from 1924 to 1966, when J.C. Williams took over. Under Mr. Williams' editorship in 1972 *The Punch* published its NOAC centennial issue which included historical information and old photographs related to the club. In 1929 the Rampart Street mansion, which had served as the clubhouse part of their facility, was torn down and the present building constructed (now 222 N. Rampart). At that time the new name of New Orleans Athletic Club (NOAC) was adopted.

Much of the club's life was based on the existence of "inner clubs." In the late 1930s Irwin Poche, Sr., began formally organizing the inner clubs as centers for each sport and other activities within the NOAC. For example, there were inner clubs for softball, indoor baseball, billiards, golf, handball, boxing, card playing, running, volleyball, and squash, as well as two dinner clubs and an American Legion Post. In addition to the athletic facilities, members enjoyed the use of a library, club rooms, ballroom, dining room, barber shop, bar, and cigar and candy counter. There were around 2000 members in 1930, and the initiation fee was 50 dollars at that time.

During the 1920s and in later years the club sponsored internal and external sport competitions and provided class instruction for adult, juvenile, and junior members. Club teams and individual members competed in a variety of sports at all levels, including national meets. Much of the competition involved AAU events, but there were also games against local clubs, including the YMCA and Young Men's Hebrew Association (YMHA), as well as local and more distant colleges.

Lieutenant Orest Meykar, formerly of the Russian White Army, was fencing instructor at the club in 1935. A *Punch* article designed to promote interest in fencing included the statement, "In our old Saint Louis cemetery, here in our beloved city, reposes many a man that had to back his principles or actions with a sword blade."[27] Bernard Dahlen was NOAC shooting instructor in 1935, when weekly rifle and revolver matches were held at the club's range.[28]

In the 1930s the Business Men's Class met for 30-minute exercise and games workouts at noon and 5:30 PM. Their program began with a physical exam, and there was continuing physical testing, such as blood pressure, lung capacity and strength tests. The club regularly sponsored a five-mile Thanksgiving Day handicap road race for general New Orleans participation. For Thanksgiving 1931, an additional half-mile event was added for NOAC business and professional men. Poche started a "100-Mile Club" as an inner club to encourage members to run regularly for health purposes rather than competition, and in 1932 a few of its members got carried away and tried to complete a thousand miles in twelve months.[29]

Indoor baseball was played as early as 1905 and was included in Southern AAU competition. Indoor baseball (also called "indoor ball") is basically an indoor version of softball. It is still a popular game in New Orleans, and is played under a variety of rules, indoors and out, using a cabbage ball (16-inch softball). In one local variety of the game the pitch is overhand. Swimming, basketball, handball, squash, weight-lifting, badminton, and volleyball were other sport activities conducted at the club in the 1930s and later. An NOAC gymnast won sixth place in all-around competition at the National AAU Gymnastics Meet in Los Angeles in 1930, and other club gymnasts became professional hand-balancers and acrobats.

During World War II NOAC members were involved in patriotic activities, such as War Bond drives, and in 1944 a bomber was named in honor of the club.[30] Several members were killed while serving in the armed forces.

Outstanding Louisiana athletes were sponsored by the club in order to enable them to compete in national events. For example, in 1933, shortly after LSU won the NCAA national track and field meet, the NOAC paid the expenses of pole vaulter Matt Gordy and other members of the team to represent the club at the national AAU meet.[31] In 1949 the club began sponsoring an annual award for the outstanding athlete of Greater New Orleans. A few women have received the award, the first in 1952. All area residents were eligible, even though their athletic accomplishments may actually have occurred at a distant location, such as out-of-state universities.[32]

The club hosted or sponsored many sport events with participation of athletes of the southern region. For example, in 1930 the NOAC hosted the Southern AAU handball, gymnastics, wrestling, indoor swimming, and basketball championships, and also sponsored the outdoor swimming competition on the New Basin.[33] In addition to the Thanksgiving Day race, other events attracting out-of-town participants included the club's Jackson Day Road Race and two golf tournaments.

There was at the club a category of "athletic membership" that had an age limit of 17–21 and required attendance at the gymnasium twice a week throughout the year. A note from a 1930 edition of *Punch* says, "Only the deserving boy is given an athletic membership in this club . . . . You may have a job open for a young man, if so, give our boys a chance."[34] This seems to indicate that the athletic memberships were awarded on the basis of athletic ability, which permitted the club to field more competitive teams for outside events. In 1930 the basketball players of the athletic membership category were to be organized into one or two teams for junior leagues and two teams of seniors, one for a schedule of college and out-of-town games and the other for AAU Senior competition. Games were being planned with Vanderbilt, Tulane and Loyola.[35]

Under coaches like Tad Gormley,[36] Otto Schoenfeldt, and Claude Simons, the club produced high-achieving athletes such as Buddy Smith, national swimming champion; Walter Imahara, who won four national weightlifting titles and a gold medal in the Pan-American games; sprinter Emmett Toppino, who was a member of the US 400-meter relay team in the 1932 Olympics; Lloyd Bourgeois, who also participated in the 1932 Olympics; and Joey Hero, national handball champion.[37]

Although the club was originally restricted by its charter to a male-only membership, women participated in many of its activities. The bowling alley once had a weekly ladies night,[38] and there were parties, boxing and wrestling nights, monthly formal dances, and Sunday afternoon tea-dances for wives and dates. Jazz bands and singers such as the Boswell Sisters (in the mid-1920s) performed at the club. One of the entertainments held at the club in 1933 was a concert by a New Orleans Grand Opera Ensemble,[39] and at a 1933 party, which was the largest that had ever been held, over one thousand members and friends celebrated the "return of good beer." In the 1920s the club's entertainments included a cruise to the Caribbean on a large cruise ship for YMGC members and guests.[40]

Monthly stag parties were popular in the 1930s, the entertainment being relatively innocent by today's standards. One show consisted of several dance acts, including a fan dancer and a hula dancer, songs by a couple of male singers, and a gymnastic act. Another stag night program, attended by over 500 members, featured boxing and wrestling matches, a "Battle Royal in which some ten colored boys battled toe to toe," and the entire show from a nearby nightclub.[41] Sometimes athletic activities were accompanied by social events, as in the 1933 Senior AAU Gymnastics championships, which were to be followed by a dance in the gymnasium.[42]

Mardi Gras was celebrated at the club and prizes were awarded for the best costumes. In the 1970s an annual beauty contest was held, the title of "Miss NOAC" being awarded to "the most beautiful girl in New Orleans" at the July 4

Club picnic.[43] The picnic was also the setting for selection of a bodybuilding champion, "Mr. NOAC."

In 1897 a waltz was written about the YMGC to commemorate its twenty-fifth anniversary, and in the 1930s another song was written about the NOAC and was sung by the NOAC Glee Club at all the dinner club luncheons and the club shows.[44]

Many prominent business, professional, and political figures, including New Orleans mayors and Louisiana governors, have been NOAC members, and celebrities such as movie stars, writers, and athletes have used the club's facilities. During the 1930s Irwin Poche, Sr., the athletic director and editor of *The Punch,* was a great promoter of the club. He watched the papers for arrivals of celebrities and went to their hotels and invited them to visit and use the services of the club. Some of the better known visitors included Jack Dempsey, Primo Carnera, Clark Gable, Frankie Laine, Phil Harris, Associate Supreme Court Justice Tom C. Clark, Art Linkletter, Johnny Weissmuller, and the comedy team of Olsen and Johnson, who entertained at the club. Gene Tunney trained at the club for his 1925 bout with Martin Burke.

Famous members of the NOAC included Edward D. White, who wrote the YMGC's charter when it was incorporated in 1883, and later became Chief Justice of the US Supreme Court; the Louisiana Longs: Huey, Earl, and Russell; Sam Zemurray, head of a powerful fruit producing company in Central America; F. Edward Hebert, Louisiana Congressman from 1941 to 1977; Tennessee Williams;[45] boxer Pete Herman; many kings of Carnival and New Orleans mayors, from B.F. Flanders in the 1870s to Moon Landrieu in the 1970s, and more recently, mayors Dutch Morial and Sidney Barthelemy.[46]

The NOAC had 2,583 members in 1972. However, the question of racial discrimination by the club led to greatly diminished membership from the mid 1970s until recently. A 1984 headline in the *Times-Picayune* read: "NOAC Votes to Continue Barring Blacks."[47] The article reported a 161–124 vote taken after two hours of debate the night before. This was the first time that the race question had come up officially before the club since 1976, although it had been an important issue, and disagreements over it had diminished the club membership by about half from around 940 members in 1976.

That year the club canceled its reciprocal privileges with other clubs all over the country and began to lose membership after a resounding vote against accepting black members.[48] It was a vote precipitated by events that began on July 10, 1974. That day Thomas Perkins, a young black resident of New Orleans, entered the club, went to the bar and ordered a drink. The bartender served him, but the members who were using the bar cleared out, and the manager came and told him he would have to leave. At the time, Mr. Perkins was a student at Harvard University and a member of the Harvard Club of Boston, which had a reciprocal agreement with the NOAC, and accordingly was eligible to use the club's facilities and services.[49] The NOAC had a lifelong tradition of white-male-only membership, and although women had participated in many club activities as guests, the club was not prepared to accept the presence of blacks as anything other than employees.[50]

The lawsuit that arose from this incident resulted in an award of $1000 in damages to Perkins and the ruling that, as a private organization, the club was not required to admit non-white members. Its public functions and its meeting rooms and grand ballroom, however, which were available for rental to the public, were required to be open to all.[51]

Many changes have happened at the NOAC since 1984, including the admission of black members in 1986, and women in 1989, when the membership was around 600. Coeducational activities, aerobics classes, and modern exercise equipment were added, and less emphasis was placed on outside sport competition. Old traditions continued, but with some new twists. For example, interest in boxing remained, with a boxing ring and punching bags in an area overlooking the pool, and boxing trainers remained available, but several women also began participating. The marble salt-water swimming pool is still popular, although nude swimming is no longer acceptable. The ownership of the club changed from a stockholders' association to private ownership in 1991, with Bill More, a former president of the board, becoming the owner.[52] In 1993 there were nearly 1300 members, around a third of them women, and the club seemed to be on the road to regaining its position of prestige in the world of New Orleans physical education and sport activity.

However, in recent years the NOAC has largely discontinued its traditional sport activities and become for many of its members just another health and fitness club—with personal trainers and yoga, Zumba, and other classes—distinguished from similar commercial operations in the city mainly by its elegant physical plant (and high membership fees).[53] Given the directions that United States society is moving in the twenty-first century (and the special circumstances of New Orleans), it is unlikely that the NOAC will ever aspire to regain the position it held for over 100 years as a leader in sport, physical education, and social life in the Crescent City.[54]

The NOAC's prominence through so many years was due largely to its membership appeal to a wide range of ages and social statuses, the variety of sport and social activities available to members, its magnificent facilities on the edge of the French Quarter and within walking distance of the downtown business district, and the promotional activities of the club's leaders. Although some of the club's many functions were available in scholastic and collegiate sport programs, the YMCA and YMHA, country clubs, and business and social clubs, such institutions did not provide the full range of activities available at the NOAC, nor could they match the fraternal feelings engendered at the club. The NOAC survived when all other early athletic clubs of the city and region disappeared, often in response to the city's residential areas for professional and business classes moving ever farther from downtown. In the Crescent City, whose prominence and appeal depend heavily on historic tradition, the NOAC survives precisely because of the power of its tradition.

CHAPTER SIX

The Development of Tulane Stadium

From Rise to Raze

CHAD SEIFRIED, KASEY BRITT, SAMANTHA GONZALES, AND ALEXA WEBB

With generous donations from alumni, Harvard University constructed the first reinforced steel and concrete stadium in the United States, Harvard Stadium, during 1903, setting the tone for future permanent football facilities.[1] In support, *The American Architect* encouraged future stadia to be built similarly throughout the United States due to the durability and adaptability of concrete and

A view from the stands of Tulane Stadium at the end of the university's 1939 season. Photo courtesy of The Historic New Orleans Collection, Williams Research Center, New Orleans, Louisiana.

steel.[2] Such prompting resulted from developing consumerism and technological advances that allowed not only college football to become a "cultural spectacle," but college sport to become a permanent industry through the addition of "athletic departments, constructing concrete stadiums, and hiring a corps of professional experts."[3] Thus it was in the early twentieth century that universities and their associated communities gradually recognized the utility that sport, and permanent football facilities in particular, provided them to engage alumni, students, and the media. Further, they progressively thought football could help universities secure alumni donations, increase revenue (e.g., gate receipts), enhance "brand awareness" to increase prospective student enrollments, and create additional economic impacts (taxes, hotel, restaurant, and retail sales).[4] Evidence of this point is strong, as college football historian Raymond Schmidt noted that college football revenue reached nearly $50 million a year by 1929 through strong attendance, significant media interest, and improved alumni, student, and community support.[5]

The city of New Orleans and Tulane University, like other cities and universities in the early twentieth century, were interested in building football stadia to promote alumni involvement, create revenue, enhance interest in local businesses, and serve as an iconic social anchor of the university and community.[6] The *Times-Picayune* published several articles and promoted campaigns that called on businesses and private citizens of New Orleans, including Tulane students and alumni, to help raise the money needed to build new on-campus stadia in 1910, 1916, and 1925, and to renovate the third Tulane Stadium in 1937, 1939, and 1947.[7] The present chapter will focus on the development of Tulane stadia from 1893 thru 1975 to highlight the impact of the Sugar Bowl, technology, community and university officials, and consumer expectations on various expansions and subsequent demolitions.

Tulane football stadia provide excellent examples of how college football grew into a complex consumer activity that developed through cultural evolution and technological innovations. Like other campus cathedrals of concrete and steel, Tulane stadia confirmed the importance of college athletics both as a permanent university activity and a tool to exploit consumerist desires. The construction of massive stadium structures, like those at Tulane University, and their ability to accommodate local and later remote communities created an air of "institutional supremacy" for those schools and communities who built them, as they attempted to distinguish themselves from their competition for student enrollment, as well as business, political, and community support.[8]

On the first of January in 1890, roughly 700 spectators gathered in New Orleans Sportsman's Park to watch the game of football for the first time. Brothers Thomas L. and Hugh A. Bayne, working as attorneys in their father's New Orleans-based law firm of Denègre & Bayne, organized the 1890 event to introduce football, a game they enjoyed as students at Yale, to the city and to assist a local Ambulance Fund through prospective gate receipts collected. Recruiting players primarily from Tulane University and "Louisiana students from eastern schools who were home for the holidays," the Baynes arranged for a later contest against the Birmingham Athletic Club in 1892 that attracted nearly 2,000 spectators. The *Times-Picayune* suggested the contests created significant enthusiasm for the sport that "had been slow to gain acceptance" among community elites. The success and subsequent attention generated interest in developing football on both the Tulane and Louisiana State University (LSU) campuses in 1893. Mainly through the efforts of Thomas L. Bayne, who provided guidance on field layouts at local parks, built goal posts, organized ticket sales, refereed, and coached, football captured the attention of both schools, enough for each to appoint him as head coach during their first match-up.[9]

In 1895, Tulane joined the Southern Intercollegiate Athletic Association (SIAA), the first athletic conference in the South. The SIAA was constructed to help with "the development and purification of college athletics throughout the South." Within the drafted constitution, definitions were established for officer duties, the annual convention, officiating, eligibility, and rules enforcement. Participation in the SIAA also facilitated the scheduling of opponents. In 1895, Tulane finished 3–2 under the guidance of Bayne, with a schedule that featured other SIAA peers such as LSU, Alabama, Mississippi, and Texas.[10] Coaching stability, however, was not an outcome of SIAA participation. Subsequent seasons, including the undefeated (i.e., 5–0) SIAA championship team of 1900 and a 7–1 campaign in 1908, accompanied eleven coaching changes from 1895 through 1909. The university did not provide any real measurable financial support to these early teams; thus, coaches often committed their time to Tulane and other schools throughout the South for free, or they depended on meager gate receipts from schedules they arranged with small local facilities, like the aforementioned Sportsman's Park, a wooden facility absent concession stands, bathrooms, and suitable grandstand seating. Inadequate equipment, poor on-campus facilities for training, and the fact that coaches of this era were not motivated by possible earnings, as they typically had well-paying jobs, set conditions for active coaching turnover and erratic performances.[11]

In 1905, Arthur Moreno, representing the student body at Tulane, suggested that some "boys would be attracted to college by its athletic interests who would not come otherwise."[12] The university, searching to increase enrollments and responding to calls by their alumni to field a more stable athletic program, decided in 1909 to establish a Committee on Athletics to oversee the collection and use of a three dollar athletic fee for the establishment of an athletic grounds to cover six acres. Tulane professors made up a majority of the Committee that worked with the Tulane Athletic Association, a group composed of alumni and students, to enhance the production of athletics for the school, which included a goal to help erect the school's first on-campus athletic grounds.[13]

The city of New Orleans (i.e., businessmen, primarily of the Progressive Union, and municipal leaders) was also interested in helping Tulane because it sought to host the 1910 Amateur Athletic Union national championships for track & field. The AAU championships were attractive because community leaders thought the event would be "one of the best drawing cards that New Orleans has been given" and capable of bringing in many people that could benefit the city from a "commercial standpoint." With the city ultimately committing about $5,000 to the Tulane Stadium project, a new wooden facility was modeled after the track & field complex built in 1904 for the St. Louis Exposition and subsequent Olympic Games. Mayor Martin Behrman recruited architects DeBuys, Churchill, and Labouisse, Ltd., to build one of the finest wooden facilities in the South. Progressive Union president Phillip Werlein initially suggested the community recruit the games by promising "assistance of all its organized machinery." He also suggested that securing the AAU championships and developing a large wooden facility would allow Tulane to be viewed as "a legitimate and great university."[14]

By 1912, the enrollment at Tulane grew to approximately 2,536 across nine departments. Further, the university was "well equipped" with buildings through the generous donations of individuals like Mrs. Josephine L. Newcomb, Mrs. Ida A. Richardson, Alexander C. Hutchinson, and Mrs. Caroline Tilton, who gave to help construct and support projects related to the young women's program, medical school, and library. Local companies like United Fruit Company and other anonymous donors also gave money to endow scholarships and to help support programs like athletics.[15] Football continued to be a priority to help promote the school and recruit continued or new donations to academic programs but recruiting and promotion generally did not include Tulane Stadium after 1912 because the facility was designed primarily to host track & field and baseball games. Tulane's biggest football games were moved to the larger 2,000-seat Sportsman's Park, where seats in poor condition and very high grass were problems. Other games against more prestigious opponents were played at the still larger 6,000-seat Heinemann Park, another venue offering low-quality seating.[16]

An investigation by the Department of Public Property in February 1915 ultimately identified the facility as dangerous and ordered the Board of Administrators of the Tulane Educational Fund to close it. Further, the department recommended that a new "modern and up-to-date" facility capable of accommodating "several thousand persons" replace the venue.[17] Tulane Stadium was commercially abandoned because it was unsafe from a lack of maintenance and overuse by university students, local clubs, and high schools playing football, baseball, and competing in track & field.[18] The decay of Tulane Stadium was further exacerbated by its location, situated as it was in area known for standing water.[19]

Shortly after the Department of Public Property report, Tulane hired Clark D. Shaughnessy as head football coach and athletic director to improve the performance and attractiveness of football and to lead the effort to build a new permanent on-campus stadium. At the end of September 1915, New Orleans experienced a Category 4 hurricane that thoroughly destroyed what remained of Tulane Stadium, making any renovation of the original facility impractical.[20] The university acknowledged a need for concrete stands to withstand inclement weather and potential fires. A permanent facility was attractive to the school because carpenters would no longer be needed, thus saving on maintenance costs.[21] Finally, the university believed a new permanent stadium was necessary because it would enhance recruiting, suggesting the lack of a quality stadium prevented the school from getting the likes of Jim Thorpe to attend Tulane.[22]

Taking the destruction of Tulane Stadium as an opportunity to assist Shaughnessy's stadium building effort, administrators of Tulane committed resources for a new Tulane Stadium before the start of the 1917 football season. Tulane Athletic Association president Nugent B. Valrin selected an architect and purposely sought out former Tulane graduates and assistance from College of Engineering Professor Donald Derickson to estimate the cost of the new facility. Tulane Board of Administrators member John Dymond, Jr. assumed responsibility for legal matters and contracts regarding land acquisition. On campus, a burgeoning campaign for the new facility emerged and received resounding support from President Dr. Robert Sharp and notable faculty members like Deans Albert B. Dinwiddle (Professor of Mathematics and Astronomy) and Wallace Wood (Professor of Operative Dentistry).[23] Tulane Professor Douglas Anderson (Electrical Engineering) also approved of a suggestion that asked alumni to donate a day's salary to help the cause, an idea that became the precursor to an event eventually known as "Realization Day."[24]

Student enthusiasm for the project was strong as they not only assisted the construction effort through physical labor but also offered to donate a day's wages to the stadium.[25] Chaired by Paul F. Jahncke, what was deemed "Realization Day" emerged on March 31, 1916, when the *Times-Picayune* offered to facilitate opportunities for "businessmen, students, alumni, and even faculty members" to participate in a "citywide fundraiser." The university declared "a full holiday so students could work that day and turn their earnings over to a grandstand fund."[26] Local businesses that offered to hire students for the day to help the construction effort included the New Orleans Railway and Light Company, the Triangle Theatre, Parcel Transfer, H. Well Baking Company, Cotton Exchange, Fuert & Kramer, Katz & Besthoff, Maison Blancho, and D.H. Holmes Company.[27] Male students "worked as bootblacks, baggage smashers, advertising solicitors, salesmen, ditch diggers, reporters, mechanics, sandwich men, carpenters, gardeners, organ-grinders, jitney drives, messenger boys, bank clerks, musicians, dish washers, culinary assistants, and in every other capacity imaginable." Female students "served as clerks, saleswomen, soda dispensers, manicurists, waitresses, dancers, singers, seamstresses, and in numerous other occupations."[28] The overall event helped raise $35,000, which also included straight cash gifts, like the $10,000 provided by lumber and plant capitalist Frank B. Williams.[29]

Frank G. Churchill, one of the leading architects in New Orleans, designed the 3,000-seat structure that Lionel F. Favret was contracted to build. Like its predecessor, the second Tulane Stadium supported both football and track-and-field events. Harry Fitzpatrick, President of the Amateur Athletic Union, and Lawrence Di Benedetto of the Southern Amateur Athletic Union helped rally support for Realization Day by recruiting multiple business leaders in New Orleans and Baton Rouge to help the fund. LSU envisioned using the stadium for games and track-and-field events too. Thus, LSU promoted Realization Day and they pushed for Baton Rouge to help, as well.[30]

Churchill designed the facility after touring other stadia at the Universities of Wisconsin, Michigan, and Chicago and interviewing their patrons and employees. The 2,000-seat grandstand was 183-feet long by 61-feet wide by 38-feet tall and made from reinforced steel and concrete. The grandstand included cypress seats that had numbers branded into each. The facility incorporated four ticket booths and three immense double-iron gates to avoid entry and exit panics. The facility was suggested to be "close to perfection in the matter of ingress and egress" because of ample individual space and stairways. Churchill's interviews of patrons and employees suggested this should be a major focus of his design. Further, he valued the incorporation of a spacious concourse capable of protecting attendees when inclement weather surfaced. Addressing the needs of attendees, the second Tulane Stadium also housed several refreshment booths, which the university recognized as a potential source of revenue, and floodlights for the short fall afternoons. For the players and coaches, special entrances were provided, separate from those for the spectators. Offices for coaches and lounge, locker, and training rooms for players also emerged. Promoted as an innovation, "hot rooms" also surfaced featuring steam heating to help players mend injuries more quickly. Overall, the facility cost $32,932.01 and was argued to be one of the most "modern, comfortable, and attractive" in the South.[31]

Unfortunately, for all of its virtues, the second Tulane Stadium was small and not built with expansion in mind. For instance, the $18,344.14 wooden-seat expansion to 10,000 seats in 1921 could not accommodate the football craze growing in New Orleans. The gradual improvement of Tulane football teams under Shaughnessy saw the program rise into a regional football power, accumulating two conference championships (i.e., 1920 SIAA and 1925 Southern Conference) and a 56–23–6 record (1915 through 1925). Tulane President Albert B. Dinwiddie suggested:

> "Tulane University has reached the point where, in the opinion of not only the administrative and athletic authorities of the university but of practically the entire population of New Orleans, it is imperative that Tulane should have a new stadium sufficiently large enough to accommodate all who desire to witness its athletic contests."

As a point of emphasis, the second Tulane Stadium was regularly recognized as overflowing with sitting or standing people. As an example, approximately 12,000 showed up for the 1925 Suwannee game and additional accounts show several thousand people loitered outside the facility during many games. The box office was also regularly inundated by telegrams and telephone calls, many long distance, to reserve "blocks of seats."[32] Dinwiddie argued that university football required significant investment to remain competitive and that the future quality of Tulane football, as compared to other Southern Conference peers, depended on collecting all the gate receipts it could. He worried that the school was losing opportunities to generate important revenue streams; guarantees to opponents, for example, consumed 30–50% of game revenues. Without greater profits available from a larger gate, locals would have to watch games elsewhere, because future games would be staged away from campus.[33] The *Times-Picayune* advocated for the venue through stories that suggested a new stadium would prompt "national attraction and admiration" for the university and city of New Orleans. Further, a new stadium would represent "a hugely impressive proof of community esteem, graduate and undergraduate loyalty."[34] Other perspectives argued that a new stadium was also necessary to schedule big name opponents.[35]

To begin the process of building a new stadium, Tulane established the Committee of Ways and Means for Financing a New Stadium. In its report, the committee stated that it was necessary to raise $300,000 to build the new venue, provide new equipment, and to increase the salaries of the head coach and assistants, athletic director and his assistant, athletic trainer, publicity worker, and stenographer, all of whom would work in the building. The committee argued that the new facility, equipment and salary increases would help produce a profitable football program that could support other sports at Tulane. Next, the committee suggested it possessed confidence that this investment would help assure football's success in the South. To fund the facility, the committee supported a three-part funding model that would not allow the university to accept any debt. The three parts included: 1) a bond issue, 2) a bank loan from Indemnity Agreements, and 3) public donations.[36] Before work began, Dinwiddie also consulted Tulane's Dean of Engineering, Douglas Andrews, for suggestions on the construction of the stadium. Andrews suggested that the construction should be completed before the end of the 1926 football season, and that Tulane should be protected in the contract through late penalties.[37]

In support of the third Tulane Stadium, the *Times-Picayune* rallied public assistance for the "Greenbacks" campaign that followed the end of the 1925 season, one which saw Tulane go undefeated (9–0–1). Under the headline of "Citizens to Help Raise Tulane's Stadium Money," the *Times-Picayune* proposed to the city of New Orleans that they should "undertake to raise $300,000 between November 30 and December 5 in a campaign for funds with which to build the new stadium at Tulane University." The paper explained that evidence provided by "the athletic council in the past ten or fifteen years" suggested that Tulane would continue their winning ways with a new stadium. Letters of correspondence between Dinwiddie and University of Arkansas President John C. Futrall show that the university was already losing home games because of the inadequacy of the second Tulane Stadium.[38]

The construction of the new stadium involved support from Tulane professors and students, local architects and construction companies, and multiple New Orleans businesses and citizens, among many other contributors. New Orleans Mayor Martin Behrman served as an important voice lending support to the stadium campaign effort. In a December 1925 proclamation, Behrman recognized that the recent success of the Tulane football team has "done much to focus the public eye upon New Orleans and its products, to earn New Orleans favorable publicity and attention and to convince the world that New Orleans is among its leaders." Behrman further argued the "Tulane team has put New Orleans on the front page of every great newspaper in the country and the boys made New Orleans famous." He added that supporting a stadium was necessary to maintain the quality of Tulane football, as many other communities and colleges were building their own major facilities. Moreover, failure to build a new facility would "retard and offset the notable forward step made through the splendid publicity secured to New Orleans and Tulane."[39]

Behrman helped organize a fundraising campaign committee that included the Honorable Thomas Killeen (Chairman), S.P. Cassagne, A.C. Martinez, Sr., W.S. Daly, and Maurice J. Hartsen. Other major supporters of the campaign, recognized by his successor, Mayor Arthur J. O'Keefe, were J. Blanc Monroe (Field Marshall of the campaign), Paul Jahncke, Esmond Phelps, Herbert Flowers, and Judge Rufus Foster.[40] Both mayors articulated that the stadium was a "worthy goal" and could be realized by citizens of New Orleans who appreciated the place of Tulane and its ability to produce future leaders.[41] Further, they both explained that local businesses would benefit significantly from the presence of a new facility, and businesses responded. Local companies like New Orleans Public Service, Inc. and Bagur's Department Store contributed to the stadium fund.[42] Overall, a sum of $287,289.80 was raised during the six-day campaign (November 30 to December 5, 1925) to begin construction.

Designed by architect Emile Weil as a comfortable oval which offered seating primarily between the 20-yard lines, the third Tulane Stadium contained modern amenities such as a large 125-person press box and multiple women's restrooms, telephones, and one electronic scoreboard.[43] The facility also provided ample storage for expansion and other specialized equipment for protecting the field. New tarpaulins, for example, protected the ground from excessive rainfall. Professor Frederick H. Fox (Civil Engineering) supervised construction of the field and served as designer of the playing surface, which was considered to be high-quality.[44]

Weil and the university were well aware of Harvard Stadium and the University of Pennsylvania's Franklin Field and the praise the *American Architect* bestowed upon them regarding seat comfort. Further, they were aware of the high number of restrooms Franklin Field supported and the positive press Penn received in response to that demand.[45] Weil and the university were also conscious of the opportunity to potentially expand the stadium. The oval facility shaped like "two parentheses" provided open end-zones for potential expansion and emerged on Willow Street near Calhoun Street and Audubon Boulevard for this reason. The location provided ample parking for over 1,000 cars and was "accessible from several streetcar lines." Specifically, the Freret Street car passed "three blocks from the stadium" while the Broadway car line passed "two blocks from the stadium." The Claiborne Street car stopped at Audubon Boulevard and additional stops provided by the St. Charles/Tulane Belt provided additional access points to the new Tulane Stadium.[46]

Like the previous Tulane Stadium, other architects were contacted to secure advice and information to help design the new facility. A letter on June 18, 1925, from Frederick Mann, chief architect of the University of Minnesota's Memorial Stadium, shows he responded to a request from Dinwiddie to learn more about the expectations for a modern stadium. Mann stated that he "examined personally the most important stadium, including those on the Pacific coast and gathered much data and many suggest and I believe we not only avoided mistakes but incorporated improvements." Some costs shared about Memorial Stadium helped create estimates on heating, plumbing, and ventilation, electric wiring and equipment, and architect and engineering fees.[47] Work began on the third Tulane Stadium in January 1926 by the O.M. Gwinn Construction Company with the "hope to speed up the construction so the first games of next season may be played on the field."[48] To assist, students helped "a number of assistant engineers employed from the engineering college during the summer" as "carpenters' helpers and on other jobs."[49] The 28,000-seat stadium opened on October 23, 1926 with Tulane facing Auburn University.[50]

Shortly after Tulane football moved into its new stadium, the idea of a New Year's Day bowl game in New Orleans came to the mind of *New Orleans Item* publisher James M. Thomson and sports editor Fred Digby. In 1927, the duo introduced the idea of the Sugar Bowl following a trip they made to the 1926 Rose Bowl in Pasadena, CA.[51] Digby tried to get Tulane University an invitation to that same Rose Bowl following their successful 1925 season, but his interest was declined. A subsequent conversation between Digby and Thomson concerning the $375 spent with long-distance phone calls to Pasadena led Thomson to ask: "Why can't we have a postseason game in New Orleans?"[52]

Listening to subsequent conversations of Thomson, Digby, and others, Mayor Semmes Walmsley sent a delegation to the Southern Conference in 1929 to solicit support for a New Year's Day game at Tulane Stadium as a result of improvement to the facility and the continued success of Tulane.[53] In 1928, Tulane Athletic Director Wilbur C. Smith announced that the university was ready to put $30,000 more into the facility to further its modernization for 1929. Architect Emile Weil designed the new additions to the stadium, which included more west stands, new locker rooms, showers, training areas, and athletics offices, "a boiler plant to furnish heat to these additions," and "a Vorclone dryer, which alone . . . cost in the neighborhood of $3,000."[54] The added heaters, stands, and offices matched the trends of the times when "servicing spectator and guest needs frequently appeared as the major structural additions."[55]

The additions could not come soon enough as under head coach and former Shaughnessy protégé Bernard W. "Bernie" Bierman, Tulane finished the 1929 season undefeated (9–0) and won the Southern Conference. Despite the improvements, a strong performance by Tulane, and a strong presentation that suggested "the romance of the city and the Mississippi River, the walkability of the Vieux Carré, and the town's very sporting legacy" that "made New Orleans an ideal place for a showcase football game," the conference refused to support a New Year's Day bowl game in New Orleans.[56] Notably, a postseason event promoted by Thomson for Loyola University New Orleans against Loyola University Chicago in 1929 and the University of Detroit in 1930 was organized to support the *Times-Picayune* Doll & Toy Fund elsewhere in the city. The Doll & Toy Fund offered children from poor families gifts during the holiday season.[57] The success of these games and a recognition that football was effectively used throughout the country to improve the quality of life and local economies during the Depression added fuel to recruit more support for an annual New Year's Day game in New Orleans.

Benefit games surfaced during the 1920s and continued in the 1930s across the United States, which helped legitimize postseason bowl games after regular seasons and classes finished. Benefit games provided "relief to the homeless, poor, and unemployed," and many communities modified the benefit game to start their own bowl game in order to boost morale and promote economic growth.[58] By January 1, 1934, seven postseason games existed in the United States for this reason: Rose Bowl (Pasadena, CA), Dixie Classic (Dallas, TX), Festival of Palms in Miami (i.e., Orange Bowl), East-West Shrine (San Francisco, CA), Los Angeles Christmas (Los Angeles, CA), New Year's Classic (Honolulu, HI), and East-West All-Star Game (San Francisco, CA).[59] A growing sporting legacy regarding Tulane football paired with the obsession of local citizens led to the creation of the New Orleans Mid-Winter Sports Association and subsequent Sugar Bowl as tools to improve "the hopeless days of the Depression."[60]

The New Orleans Mid-Winter Sports Association was created on January 8, 1934, when a number of notable New Orleans newsmen such as Digby, Bill Keefe (*Times-Picayune*), and Henry Martinez (*States Item*), and businessman like Joseph M. Cousins, Dr. Fred Wolfe, Dr. M.P. Boebinger, Francis Reilly, Ralph Barry, Warren V. Miller, and T. Semmes Rantlett organized to add New Orleans to the postseason football event calendar. A charter approved on February 15, 1934, articulated that the Association was "a voluntary non-profit civic organization whose members serve without remuneration, there would be no connection with commercial interest or professional sports, there would be no private profit and any surplus above the required operating expenses or reserve fund must be devoted to 'charitable, religious, or educational purposes.'"[61]

Planning of the inaugural Sugar Bowl intensified during the latter part of 1934 after Tulane University's new conference, the Southeastern Conference, provided a soft 'maybe' in support of the bowl game. To spur interest with potential grid fans, the Association invited individuals to name the contest, with the lucky winner receiving a private box for the first game.[62] On July 25, 1934, the Association announced the official name of "The New Year's Day game to be . . . the 'National Sugar Bowl Classic'."[63] The Sugar Bowl fit well with the economy of the area at this time; New Orleans was "near the heart of Louisiana's mammoth sugar cane industry and Tulane Stadium [was] situated on the site of Etienne de Bore's sugar plantation."[64]

In December of 1934, Warren V. Miller reminded New Orleanians that the "midwinter sports program is not being launched with one event only." While the program would feature a New Year's Day football game for January 1, 1935, there would also be "a tennis tournament the rest of the week . . . . On Sunday, there will be a regatta, and on January 12, there will be a Jackson Day run."[65] The inaugural Sugar Bowl featured a Tulane team that was the SEC's co-champion against the undefeated (7–0–2) Temple Owls coached by nationally renowned Glenn "Pop" Warner. The *Times-Picayune* assured their readers that this team selection was "well matched" and that the first Sugar Bowl would "prove one of the finest football spectacles."[66] Tulane University contributed to the Sugar Bowl by providing "rent-free use of its stadium for one day a year by the Mid-Winter Sports Association."[67]

Tickets for the 1:30 PM kickoff were $3 for reserve tickets and $1.50 for general admission.[68] Spectators unable to attend the inaugural game could listen on the radio starting at 1:15 PM. Radio broadcasts of the game could be heard "over a network of 16 stations stretching from Philadelphia to San Antonio and from Tulsa, Okla. to Miami, Fla."[69] It should be noted that radio broadcasts served as an important technology to embrace during the Depression, as "schools attempted to enhance revenues with commercial radio broadcast contracts" and newspapers offered fewer sports articles than the previous decade.[70] Radio broadcasting required special equipment and space in the third Tulane Stadium because the university and Sugar Bowl could package them as something to be "negotiated, bundled, bought, and sold like any other commodity."[71] For Tulane, the SEC negotiated a contract with the A.J. Norris Hill Company in 1934 to sponsor radio broadcasts for an SEC Game of the Week to add important revenues during the Depression.[72]

The first Sugar Bowl ended with a victory for Tulane, and the Association was praised for the success of the game.[73] Two days after the first Sugar Bowl, New Orleans already wanted a bigger and better stadium for the next game. On January 3, 1935, sportswriter William Keefe provided his opinion in the *Times-Picayune* that "Tulane Stadium should be completed, not only for the Sugar Bowl but for Tulane's other big games." Further, the general public should be accommodated, and "thousands of new football fans would be created and encouraged if there were thousands of reasonably priced seats for them" in a new stadium.[74]

In the January 10, 1937, edition of the *Times-Picayune*, multiple issues were brought up concerning a major enlargement of Tulane Stadium. Pointing out that "Tulane University has contributed the Tulane Stadium to this cause [Sugar Bowl] without one cent of charge for the use of the stadium," the *Times-Picayune* cited the stadium's central location, convenient parking facilities, easy access from streetcars and buses to ask the public why the city of New Orleans, the Association of Commerce, and the Sugar Bowl committee could not help enlarge the stadium.[75] By May 1937, plans were being drawn up for the impending renovation at a cost of $100,000, which would include areas for permanent outdoor gatherings and space for 55,000 spectators. Joe M. Cousins, president of the New Orleans Mid-Winter Sports Association assured the public that construction would be complete before the 1938 Sugar Bowl. Further, he noted the construction would be funded by Tulane University upfront, with the Association repaying the university "at a rate of $20,000 per year and interest . . . . Fund[s] for this reimbursement of course [came] from proceeds of the Sugar Bowl game."[76]

Work began on the 1937 additions on July 30, and new steel stands surfaced with a seating capacity of 15,000. Supplementing the existing reinforced concrete stands that fit 25,000 and another 15,000 temporary seats, the next Sugar Bowl would be the biggest to date.[77] Less than two months into 1939, the citizens of New Orleans, fans of the Sugar Bowl, and members of the New Orleans Mid-Winter Sports Association were again dissatisfied with the Sugar Bowl's capacity despite the fact that the year started with the *Times-Picayune* reporting that there were no plans for expansion.[78] Tulane University's football program continued to be a strong performer in the region, producing a 7–2–1 record in 1938 and an undefeated regular season record in 1939 (8–0–1) which resulted in an SEC co-championship, record regular season attendance, and another Sugar Bowl appearance under Head Coach Lowell P. "Red" Dawson. By March, $391,700 was pledged to the cause of enlarging Tulane Stadium and a "cleanup squad" was created to "obtain the remainder of the $550,000 goal."[79] The money was raised and construction was set to start on June 8, 1939, for an expansion that was to include "the erection of stands at the South end of Tulane Stadium and double-decking the East and West side stands." This would transform Tulane Stadium and elevate the Sugar Bowl's capacity to 70,000, making the venue totally enclosed, "the largest in the South and second only to Pasadena's Rose Bowl."[80] Along with the seating expansion, additional construction featured "new ramps, entrances, gates, and other facilities," including a new the scoreboard near Barrett Street. As with the construction of other sport facilities, collegiate football at Tulane University also recognized the need to "provide enough room for the press."[81] Thus, a press box was "constructed under the overhang of the double-deck stand on the west side, [offering] . . . facilities for several hundred writers."[82]

The excitement for the updated stadium influenced the entire New Orleans winter sports schedule, causing an expansion of the program to over six days in 1940. The festivities included a basketball game between University of Kentucky and The Ohio State University on December 27, a tennis tournament at New Orleans Country Club going from December 28 to December 31, amateur boxing matches on December 29, the annual regatta and an annual rowing race on December 30, an annual track meet on December 31, and finally the Sugar Bowl on January 1. This particular Sugar Bowl would "make history because of the new attendance record for the deep South."[83] The Sugar Bowl of 1940 featured a matchup between the Associated Press's number one ranked Texas A&M University and fifth-ranked Tulane and produced an over-capacity crowd of 73,000. The following year, fifth-ranked Boston College and number four Tennessee met in the Sugar Bowl, producing an impressive crowd of 68,486. Days after the 1941 Sugar Bowl Game, Keefe of the *Times-Picayune* called for yet another expansion of Tulane Stadium. He stated "most of the visiting newspapermen asked, before going back to their bases, one question: 'when are they going to enlarge and double deck the end zone and give the Sugar Bowl a perfect bowl that will seat 100,000?'" similar to the Rose Bowl in Pasadena.[84]

The Sugar Bowl and its popularity played a vital "role in Tulane being able to continue competing with a major college football program years afterward."[85] The American de-emphasis on sports during World War II, however, "took the steam out of a lot of college programs, and Tulane was no exception."[86] Crowds reduced by as much as 25 percent, and there was less money for coaches and equipment from regular season contests.[87] The Sugar Bowl, however, remained significant, an example of an "observance of established traditions [that] helped prevent the thread of the American fabric from fraying during the days of economic and social tumult."[88]

The Sugar Bowl continued to draw top ten matchups in 1942 and 1943. For instance, sixth-ranked Fordham defeated seventh-ranked Missouri in front of 66,154 spectators during 1942 and seventh-ranked Tennessee upset fourth-ranked Tulsa in front of 58,361 the year after. Despite only having the thirteenth and fifteenth ranked teams in 1944, a large crowd of 69,134 attended the tenth annual Sugar Bowl to watch Georgia Tech beat Tulsa. Between 1945 and 1947, attendance at the Sugar Bowl remained over 68,000, proving that maybe an expansion should be seriously considered.

On July 6, 1947, Keefe wrote in the *Times-Picayune* that there was speculation of an announcement to enlarge Tulane stadium by 13,000 to 20,000 seats. This plan for expansion came shortly after reports that the Oil Bowl in Houston and the Orange Bowl in Miami were both going to expand their capacities to seat 60,000. Though competition for the best bowl game was high, the New Orleans Mid-Winter Athletic Association was "undaunted" and had "full confidence in New Orleans supporting the famous January 1 football classic."[89] No less than a week later, Sam Corenswet of the Association announced that the Sugar Bowl enlargement debenture bond issue sale would open on July 21 and close on August 9. The goal was to raise $500,000 through the purchase of $100 bonds that would carry a privilege to buy two annual tickets to the Sugar bowl beginning with the 1948 game. Additions increased "the capacity of the Sugar Bowl to more than 80,000 permanent reserved and box seats" and gave New Orleans one of the "five largest football stadiums in the nation." The expansion would include 12,000 additional seats by double-decking the north side stands, creating permanent and portable box seats, including new electronic scoreboards, and making other additions.[90] Other additions included a renovated press box, complete with an elevator, after construction was underway in 1948.[91]

Following completion of the Sugar Bowl enlargement, Tulane Stadium was dubbed "the perfect stadium" by Keefe.[92] The 1949 Sugar Bowl featured a matchup between fifth-ranked Oklahoma and third-ranked North Carolina and produced a crowd of 80,383. This was an increase of over 7,000 from the previous year, when an over-capacity crowd of 73,000 watched fifth-ranked Texas overwhelm sixth-ranked Alabama. Between 1950 and 1956, more than 80,000 spectators attended the Sugar Bowl five of those seven games.

Other changes, however, were underway. Rufus C. Harris introduced the topic of "reforming Tulane football in 1939, the same year that his former Yale Law School classmate Robert M. Hutchings abolished the University of Chicago's football program." Although he did not organize any formal action to curtail football, World War II reduced athletic expenditures, schedules, and the "importance attached to football," giving "Harris hope that once peace was restored, Tulane and other southern schools could avoid a return to past excesses." Harris encouraged his university and others to reduce the number of athletic scholarships and the level of financial support for each athletic scholarship. Further, Harris suggested to his peers that they collectively decide to "hire coaches whose vocabularies and literary interests extended beyond the content of 'sport pages and comic strips.'"[93]

Harris was not alone in his thoughts about the growing attention and excesses provided to intercollegiate sport. For example, Vanderbilt Chancellor Harvie Branscomb also supported de-emphasizing athletics by suggesting that national reform failures made it difficult to bring "southern football under control. Both Tulane and Vanderbilt belonged to the SEC where policies were shaped by major state universities and land grant schools with powerful athletic constituencies. The environment was not a congenial one for would-be reformers."[94] Southern schools regularly avoided or defied nationally established rules like the Sanity Code (1948–1951), which sought to regulate athletic scholarships and financial aid, recruiting, and academic standards.[95] "At a December 1951 meeting of SEC delegates in New Orleans, Harris presented an 'eight-point plan for the restraint of intercollegiate athletics' which represented 'largely what will be undertaken at Tulane.'" Specifics of the plan recommended limiting football scholarships to 75 and travel squads to 38 players, restricting recruiting activities to on-campus visits only, allowing only thirty calendars for spring practice, reducing football coaching staffs to one head coach and four assistants, eliminating two-platoon football to reduce roster size and specialists, lowering participation in bowl games, and abolishing special degree programs for athletes.[96]

Controlling expenses on football became a growing concern for Tulane by 1950. Supplements provided by the federal government to returning soldiers (Servicemen's Readjustment Act of 1944) boosted Tulane football in the 1940s. This G.I. Bill granted returning soldiers, many of whom played intercollegiate football, complete coverage on tuition and living expenses. Tulane and other smaller private schools, like Southern Methodist and Texas Christian, flourished as a result, because tuition, room, and board money could be spent on other activities within the universities and their athletics programs.[97] As this pool of money dried up, so did enrollments, and the "Athletic Advisory Committee estimated that at the cost levels which had prevailed in 1949, Tulane might soon face annual loss of $100,000 per year on football alone.[98]

Tulane Head Coach Henry Frnka sought 125 grant-in-aids for the 1950 season, twenty-seven more than awarded in 1949. "Harris approved 112 awards for 1950–1951 and advised the coach that further reductions were likely." In May 1950, "the Athletic Advisory Committee recommended that both football scholarships and coaching salaries be cut back to the levels of 1948.[99] Despite implementation, the austerity measures still produced a deficit of $46,000 for 1951.[100] In March 1952, Harris formally imposed the aforementioned limits to Tulane football on scholarships (75) and scouting while decreasing the size of the coaching staff and eliminating an approved-but-suspect academic program (Bachelor of Education in Physical Education). The "program of modernization," as it was known, also included several administrative and policy changes "intended to underscore the subordinate role of athletics in the university's overall mission." Frnka resigned almost immediately after the program was affirmed.[101]

Tulane football understandably struggled as a result, managing only two winning seasons in the next decade; their SEC brethren did not follow the same path of austerity. In a letter written to Associate Arts & Sciences Dean Russel M. Geer in May 1955, Athletic Director Richard O. Baumbach argued, "If Tulane could not attract football players who were able to do reputable work, it was time to give up Conference football." Baumbach underscored the competitive handicap resulting from Tulane's annual limit of 75 scholarships at a time when several SEC schools routinely awarded 100–120 or more grants per year.[102] Additional records show the debate regarding the place of football at the university and within the greater New Orleans community continued through the late 1950s and early 1960s. As an example, Joseph Jones, Chairman of the Board of Administrators, suggested along with his colleagues that "Tulane owes an obligation to the community, which has furnished an 82,000-capacity stadium to maintain a representative Southeastern Conference team." However, the university could "give up Southeastern Conference football."[103] During a meeting of the Board of Administrators in 1964, Darwin Fenner stated that he "would like to recommend to you that we withdraw in good standing," in similar fashion to how Georgia Tech left the SEC.[104] "On June 1, 1966, Tulane University officially departed the SEC. Citing an 0–10 season in 1962, Rix Yard, Tulane's Athletic Director, suggested, "The purpose was to lighten the schedule. We had to have some relief on the field. Those were tough days."[105] Interestingly, the Budget Review Committee also supported the move. Annual deficits associated with intercollegiate athletics threatened to explode once the Superdome was completed and the temporary infusion of revenue from the Sugar Bowl and the New Orleans Saints' rental of the Tulane Stadium came to an end."[106]

Serious talk of a professional team coming to New Orleans started in the early 1960s when the National Football League's (NFL) Green Bay Packers and the Chicago Cardinals met in front of 63,000 for an exhibition game at Tulane

Stadium. Buddy DiLiberto of the *Times-Picayune* reported that even though professional football may not have been ready for New Orleans, New Orleans was certainly ready for professional football. The owner of the Cardinals, Charles Bidwell, was impressed with the turnout, stating "a crowd this size for this time of year is a big plus for New Orleans."[107] Getting a professional team to New Orleans would not be an easy feat. At the time, the Southeastern Conference was concerned about professional football entering the South, and there was speculation that the SEC would prohibit its member schools from leasing their stadiums to professional football teams. The chance of New Orleans getting a professional team was "heavily dependent on the availability of Tulane Stadium."[108] Despite the conference pushback, New Orleans went ahead with is attempts to secure a professional football team, as Tulane made its thoughts about leaving the SEC open to the public. New Orleans followed the model of Atlanta, who was attempting to get a professional football team for the 1966 season. Expansion of the NFL would require two new cities.[109]

"N.O. Goes Pro!" was the headline of the *Times-Picayune* on November 1, 1966, when Peter Finney reported that an NFL franchise was acquired.[110] The official announcement came from NFL commissioner Pete Rozelle on November 2, coincidentally on All Saints Day. Tulane granted the team initial use of Tulane Stadium for three years.[111] Although the presence of Tulane Stadium played an important part in New Orleans' bid for a professional team, plans for a domed stadium were part of the NFL's interest in the city. On November 8, 1966, the city voted on Amendment No. 10, deciding whether or not they would support the establishment of the Louisiana Sports & Entertainment District that would host a domed stadium.[112] Governor John J. McKeithen argued that "when properly explained, (the amendment) is acceptable to almost everyone." McKeithen rationalized that dollars spent in Texas could be spent in Louisiana, thus creating taxes that would offset the cost of building the domed stadium, ultimately costing Louisiana nothing in the long run.[113]

Improvements were made to Tulane Stadium towards the end of the 1950s to set up the opportunity for professional football to be discussed in New Orleans. For instance, with the Sugar Bowl growing in attendance and popularity, the *Times-Picayune* reported that steps were being taken to install lights for the upcoming 1956 season. Tulane athletic director Richard Baumbach announced, "Tulane will install lights in Tulane Sugar Bowl Stadium and play some night football games there this fall, if the cost is found to be within the budget and if construction can be obtained in time."[114] In January 1957, Baumbach reported,

"Revised plans for the proposed lighting system at Tulane are being worked on." The budget for the job was $168,000.[115] The lights debuted against Virginia Tech in the 1957 season opener.[116] With the addition of lights, tickets sales increased slightly, as fans were relieved from the "discomforts of a hot sun shining in the faces of the east side." Night games also gave "thousands of folks who work Saturday afternoons . . . a chance to see the Greenies in action."[117]

The addition of lights to Tulane Stadium did not go unnoticed by the NFL while visiting New Orleans in October 1966. Specifically, the aforementioned weather relief was recognized by the NFL Expansion Committee during a facility tour of Tulane Stadium. Commissioner Rozelle and the Committee also importantly recognized the previous success the city enjoyed hosting the Sugar Bowl and its enthusiasm about football in general, prompting them to conclude New Orleans was an impressive "sports city." However, they also identified Tulane Stadium as an "interim facility" for any NFL expansion franchise and suggested a new stadium would be expected since so many other cities were building new facilities to host professional sport. Rozelle explained that Tulane Stadium had "basic problems such as parking" (or lack thereof, particularly during all the renovations) and offered a limited number of amenities (e.g., restrooms, concession stands, luxury boxes, and club seats) expected of professional sport stadia.[118] Similar to other facilities built during the 1920s, Tulane Stadium was criticized for a lack of production facilities, camera locations, and scoreboard space that used video/television. Professional football embraced television because it "made every team a potential 'home team' for football fans everywhere, enabling the National Football League to transcend geography."[119]

Despite the limitations of Tulane Stadium, the success of various Sugar Bowls over the years and significant spectator interest shown in the Saints franchise prompted New Orleans to make a bid to host the Super Bowl. Losing its bid to host the game in 1969, the city reworked its proposal and presented it on March 19, 1969, asking for Super Bowl IV. The Super Bowl would not only be "a feather in our town's sports cap," it would also mean "lots of American dollars in the city's cash registers." The NFL was impressed by the presentation, and, with Tulane's permission, Tulane Stadium was selected as the site for Super Bowl IV.[120]

January 1970 was busy for New Orleans and Tulane Stadium. On January 1, third-ranked Arkansas played number thirteen Ole Miss in the 36th annual

Sugar Bowl, drawing a crowd of 80,096. Ten days later, New Orleans successfully hosted Super Bowl IV, which featured a game between the Kansas City Chiefs and Minnesota in front of 80,562. The desire to host a second Super Bowl emerged shortly thereafter. In March 1971, Mayor Maurice "Moon" Landrieu helped facilitate that bid by approving city funding for artificial turf to be installed in Tulane Stadium because it seemed "necessary to bring the Super Bowl to New Orleans again."[121] Days later, New Orleans was awarded the 1972 Super Bowl. Rozelle gave three reasons for bringing the Super Bowl back to New Orleans: 1) the success of the 1970 Super Bowl, 2) the "pledge to install artificial turf," and 3) the weather.[122]

Artificial turf (i.e., Astroturf) surfaced in 1966 at the Houston Astrodome when grass could not grow under the venue's painted glass ceiling. By 1970, synthetic or artificial turf was widely accepted throughout the South. As an example, many SEC and Southwest Conference schools played their home games on newly installed surfaces.[123] Athletic directors and municipal directors raved about the benefits of artificial turf.[124] In a survey published by the *Journal of Health, Physical Education, & Recreation,* for instance, 91.7% of athletic directors overwhelmingly believed the surface to be more weather resistant, easy and less costly to maintain, and capable of reducing injury. Of most interest to New Orleans and Tulane was the reduction of maintenance costs, potentially saving between 30–50 percent. Three-quarters of athletic directors also suggested artificial grass was "instrumental in the recruitment of athletes."[125] Another campaign promoted to the people of New Orleans asked them to make a donation from which they would receive a certificate validating that they "helped make New Orleans 'Super City, USA.'"[126] The turf installation drive also included a telethon and a charity ball game between Mayor Landrieu's team and members of the press.[127] Installation of the turf started in mid-April and the citywide drive showed success, raising $96,000 in just a couple weeks.[128] Installation costs were $225,000 and Tulane, the Saints, and the Sugar Bowl made up the remaining difference.[129] Supporting artificial turf, the Sugar Bowl continued to produce 80,000 to 85,000-seat crowds. For example, 84,031 fans watched third-ranked Oklahoma beat fifth-ranked Auburn on January 1, 1972. Second-ranked Oklahoma beat fifth-ranked Penn State in front of 80,123 after the 1972 season. On December 31, 1973, another large crowd (85,161) attended the Sugar Bowl, which featured third-ranked Notre Dame against number one Alabama. Despite the large capacity, lights, successful hosting of prestigious events, and now artificial turf, however, the Association and NFL would look toward the emerging Superdome to support the Sugar Bowl, Saints, and potential Super Bowls.

Although Tulane Stadium reached a record attendance of 86,598 in 1973 when Tulane faced LSU, there was a newer stadium on the horizon waiting to replace the venue: The Louisiana Superdome. Tulane Stadium began to show its age and needed some costly repairs to make it adequate for future spectators. The lack of modern conveniences such as improved parking, restrooms, concession stands, luxury boxes, and club seats ultimately prompted Tulane to move its home games to the Superdome beginning in 1975.[130] Tulane football played its final game in Tulane Stadium on November 30, 1974, and one month later the last Sugar Bowl matchup occurred in the stadium. In 1975, Super Bowl IX was supposed to be played at the Superdome, but the new venue was not complete, so Tulane Stadium had one last moment in the spotlight.[131]

The Louisiana Superdome stood 273 feet tall and opened on August 3, 1975 as the new location for Tulane and Saints football games, the Sugar Bowl, and the Bayou Classic, annually played between Southern University and Grambling University. The 73,000-seat Superdome featured parking for over 5,000 cars and an air conditioning system that weighed about 9,000 tons that helped to maintain a comfortable 72-degree temperature. Other technology showcased in the facility included escalators (nearly thirty), elevators (approximately ten), and interactive scoreboards. Television was also incorporated into the Superdome with multiple camera locations, large production space, and multiple giant screens that hung from the 9.7-acre stadium roof. The television screens were 56 feet long by 36 feet tall and gave all seats the equivalent of a forty-inch television experience. The Superdome also supported 64 private luxury boxes, 22 concession stands, 30 beer bars, and over 50 restrooms. A club section capable of seating 1,000 and three restaurants were other locations offered in the new venue. Tulane Stadium, by contrast, offered no luxury or club seating, significantly fewer restrooms and concessions, and offered antiquated electronic scoreboards, low volume elevators, and no air-conditioning.[132] Tulane Stadium remained standing until 1979 as a facility for practices and high school football games but by 1980, the facility was officially closed, "the steel had been sold and the bricks were being hauled away, and that was all that was left of Tulane Stadium."[133]

The history and evolution of Tulane football stadia provide an excellent example of how new construction and various renovations that sought to expand capacities embraced technology that focused on consumerism (i.e., providing enhanced products and services for consumption). First made from wood, subsequent facilities grew larger and more complex through permanent building materials such as concrete, brick, and steel. These facilities also enabled the creation of new specialists to help with the production of events and the performance of teams. Both the temporary and permanent stadia of Tulane also allowed the university to brand itself as permanent and allowed football to achieve high status as an important activity in New Orleans. Tulane University notably used the various stadia on-campus to help recruit students, increase alumni engagement, and offer entertainment for a growing metropolitan area also simultaneously looking to enhance its national image.

The great success of sport in New Orleans ultimately influenced the production of a bowl game to improve the local economy, prompted interest and subsequent acceptance of a professional football team, and generated confidence that the city could host the NFL's most prestigious event, the Super Bowl. Eventually stadium decay and the emergence of the amenity-filled Louisiana Superdome caused the university to move out of Tulane Stadium. In the move to the Superdome, Tulane lost its original iconic facility and status. However, in response to public opinion there was a push for a new Tulane Stadium to emerge. In 2014, Tulane football moved back to an on-campus home named Yulman Stadium. Time will tell if it brings about the same attention and impact that the Tulane Stadium(s) provided.[134]

CHAPTER SEVEN

New Orleans Becomes a Big League City

The NFL-AFL Merger and the Creation of the New Orleans Saints[1]

MICHAEL S. MARTIN

On September 17, 1967, almost 81,000 fans packed into Tulane University's football stadium to watch the New Orleans Saints square off against the Los Angeles Rams. The Saints' first game of their inaugural season began auspiciously enough. The opening kick-off sailed into the outstretched arms of John Gilliam, who tucked the ball into his elbow, dodged would-be tacklers, and raced ninety-four yards to the Rams' end zone. From such glorious opening-minute heroics, the Saints promptly collapsed. Indeed, the final fifty-nine minutes of that first game foreshadowed the team's future—both for the 1967 season and for much of the succeeding thirty-five years—with much greater precision than Gilliam's return. The Saints stumbled, bumbled, and fumbled their way to a 14–10 loss.[2]

The game played that day marked a culmination of events that brought a National Football League (NFL) team to the Crescent City. Professional football awarded New Orleans its franchise after political maneuvers in the US Congress granted an anti-trust exemption allowing a merger for the NFL and its rival, the American Football League (AFL). Two Louisiana politicians, Senator Russell Long and Congressman Hale Boggs, were instrumental in the exemption's passage, and the granting of a New Orleans franchise was largely an act of gratitude for their actions. But the new franchise also reflected a long-developing trend: following World War II, professional sports leagues,

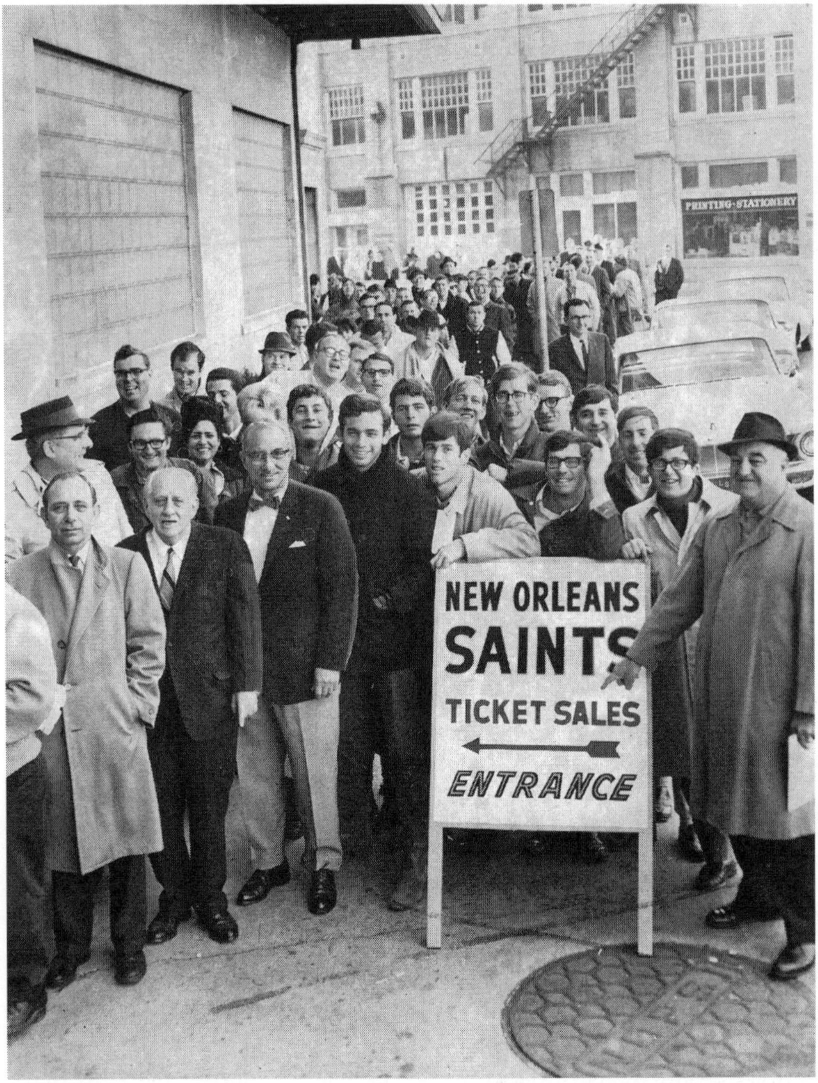

Eager fans queue up for tickets to see the Saints play in the team's inaugural season. Photo courtesy of *New Orleans Times-Picayune* and Barcroft Media.

led by Major League Baseball, spread out of northeastern and mid-western Rustbelt cities and into western and southern areas, where population and economic changes created demand for high profile entertainment. By receiving a franchise, many New Orleanians believed that their city reached the ranks of "big-league" cities.

Led by local businessman Dave Dixon, New Orleans entrepreneurial and political leaders had sought the "big league" badge via professional football since the late 1950s. Although Charles Erdmann, aide to Mayor DeLesseps "Chep" Morrison, had written in 1957 to the creators of one NFL rival that "we in the city were unable to come up with sponsors to get [a] franchise going . . . ,"[3] by 1959 Dixon and Houston businessman Bud Adams were corresponding about the possibility of New Orleans becoming a charter member of the American Football League.[4] In August 1959, Dixon wrote to Mayor Morrison, seeking support in putting together a group of Crescent City professional football promoters. "Professional football would bring millions of dollars into New Orleans," Dixon wrote. "Not only would our city prosper economically but added prestige would be worth additional millions."[5] Mayor Morrison, sounding more like a football coach than his usual urbane self, replied that he supported Dixon "1000%."[6]

New Orleans did not receive an AFL team, probably because the city lacked plans for a new stadium, but the city did host NFL exhibition games over the first few years of the 1960s. By early 1961, Mayor Morrison had been impressed enough by the success of Bud Adams's Houston Oilers that he wrote "after Houston's success in their initial venture, we are 'raring to go' here in New Orleans."[7] In 1962, rumors swirled that either the Dallas Texans or the Oakland Raiders might move to New Orleans. "Neither situation came to pass—tragically for New Orleans," Dixon later wrote.[8]

By 1964, Dixon and other football boosters in New Orleans had created New Orleans Professional Football, Incorporated, with the slogan "Bringing Professional Football to the South's Greatest City."[9] The next year, Dixon wrote to Mayor Victor Schiro that, "We believe that our efforts to obtain major league sports for this great major league city of ours are about to bear fruit . . ."[10] Early in 1965, New Orleans Professional Football, Inc. had entered into negotiations with "affluent and nationally prominent . . ." individuals in Anaheim, Atlanta, Houston, Jacksonville, Los Angeles, Miami, New York, Oakland, Phoenix, and San Francisco to create a United States Football League. This was the fruit Dixon foresaw, but the league never materialized.[11] Instead, by late 1965, the biggest of the big football leagues, the NFL, had entered into negotiations with New Orleans. Dixon and Governor John McKeithen met with NFL Commissioner Pete Rozelle to discuss the matter on December 2.[12]

During the summer and fall of 1966, NFL owners debated where to award an expansion franchise. The decision had been narrowed to three possibilities:

Seattle, Cincinnati, and New Orleans. On May 18, Governor McKeithen, Mayor Schiro, and the members of the Louisiana Congressional delegation met with NFL owners in Washington, DC.[13] At first, New Orleans had no clear advantage, other than meeting one of the league's prerequisites: the city already had a large stadium on Tulane University's campus that could be used until a new home was built. Other than that, the race for the expansion team looked to be a dead heat. That would be the case until Senator Russell Long worked a behind-the-scenes deal with NFL Commissioner Pete Rozelle.[14]

The NFL had encountered a growing problem during the 1960s: competition in the form of the fledgling American Football League. NFL owners traditionally tried to keep franchises scarce in order to control the supply-demand relationship and to foster competition between potential expansion sites. Additionally, due to the NFL's shared revenue system, expanding the league would, initially at least, decrease profits for team owners; bringing new franchises in would lessen the share received by each team owner until the newer teams produced profits. In other words, the profit pie at first would remain the same size, while more and smaller slices would be cut out of it. Rival leagues undermined such "monopoly profit considerations" by forcing the NFL to expand more rapidly and into different areas than might have been expected, usually through mergers with the rivals.[15]

Wealthy individuals such as Houston's Bud Adams and Dallas's Lamar Hunt had formed the AFL in 1960. The common denominator among the new leagues owners was that all originally had wanted NFL teams but could not get them. During the late 1950s, even many NFL owners had wanted to expand the league into new cities—Houston, Dallas, Miami, Minneapolis, and Buffalo were among the top candidates—but one or two owners exercised their veto power to stop this from happening. In reaction, the potential owners formed their own league. At first, the AFL of the 1960s sought to recreate the impact of earlier rival leagues—simply survive and the NFL would eventually merge with it. These previous competitors, including the American Football League I (1926), AFL II (1936–1937), AFL III (1940–1941), and the All-America Football Conference (1946–1949), had forced the dominant NFL to expand into new markets such as Cleveland, Baltimore, and San Francisco by absorbing successful teams.[16]

New technology, however, provided a key difference between the 1960s-era AFL and earlier rivals. Cross-country air travel allowed for a nationwide league, and television revenues offered the ability to actually compete, at least economically, with the NFL. Additionally, Congress passed the Sports Broadcasting

Act of 1961, which allowed professional sports organizations to collectively negotiate national broadcast rights—a boon to NFL owners, certainly, but also good for the AFL. In 1964, the AFL and NBC signed a $42 million, five-year deal. It brought about $850,000 annually for each AFL team.[17]

Armed with a weapon the earlier rival leagues never had—a guaranteed source of revenue—the AFL competed with the NFL on a much leveler playing field. The influx of television revenue did not guarantee the new league's survival, however. AFL owners realized that, in order to put fans in stadiums, they had to put the best athletes on the field. This need for top-notch talents created a bidding war between the AFL and NFL for marquee college players. Joe Namath became the first player to benefit from the new circumstances. The former University of Alabama star quarterback signed a long-term, $400,000 deal with the AFL's New York Jets, a move that offered immediate benefits for the franchise, including increased season ticket sales. Over the next few years, the NFL and AFL offered increasingly higher wages to the top newcomers to the professional fold. The money issue peaked in 1966 when the salary wars shifted from rookies to veterans. Although certainly beneficial for the star players, the increasingly upward movement of the salary structure threatened the profits and control of both NFL and AFL owners.[18]

A merger presented the best option for owners from both leagues. However, bringing together the AFL and NFL would require an exemption from anti-trust laws. Although major league baseball had been granted an exemption, no other professional sports leagues had one. In fact, the courts had explicitly ruled in the 1957 case *Radovich* v. *National Football League* that the NFL did not possess immunity from anti-trust laws. The only way around such laws was to get a Congressional exemption.[19]

To prod Congress into action, the two leagues announced a proposed merger on June 8, 1966. The league would be known simply as the National Football League, with National and American conferences. Details of the fusion included a play-off system, an inter-league championship game, and, most important for the owners, a common draft. Although these aspects of the combination would be instituted almost immediately, the complete merger into a unified league would not come until 1970. In the meantime, the new unified league's hopes rested on Congressional approval; without it, the courts undoubtedly would rule the merger illegal.[20]

In early October, the merger came before New York Representative Emanuel Celler's House Judiciary Committee. Celler looked disdainfully upon the new league, and he delayed any action on the anti-trust exemption. He hoped to hold out until Congress adjourned on October 22. Some sportswriters declared that Celler, still fuming over the relocation of baseball's Dodgers from his native Brooklyn, simply disliked sports owners. More likely, Celler, who, in his own words, had crafted the antitrust legislation as "the product of 10 years of blood, sweat and tears with [Senator] Estes Kefauver," had a deep-rooted suspicion of any antitrust exemption, especially one which had been brought to him with little debate beforehand: "They're asking me to rush through a bill that the Senate didn't even have hearings on or a debate. I don't know what it would do, and I intend to find out." By October 14, the New Orleans *Times-Picayune* noted, "there appears little chance the House will get to act on the bill." Four days later, on October 18, Celler said that the exemption would allow "a group of employers virtually unlimited power over a group of employees. At the same time, no safeguard is given to protect the employees against abuse . . . it is a shameful thing to do to any group of employees."[21]

At this point, Russell Long entered the scene. As an enthusiastic sports fan and, more important, as a US Senator, Long had been keeping up with the attempted merger. On June 30 he noted that "plans for expansion are widely reported to include the city of New Orleans . . ." and he commended "the owners and league officials for developing a constructive plan which will serve our country well . . ." When the antitrust legislation became bogged down in Celler's committee, Long contacted NFL Commissioner Pete Rozelle and arranged a meeting. Over dinner at a Washington, DC restaurant, and then later at Long's Watergate apartment, the two men struck a deal. Long proposed creating a tax bill, with the antitrust measures tucked into it, which would not be routed through Celler's Judiciary Committee. While in the Senate, Long would control the bill from his chair of the Finance Committee; once it reached the House, a supporter of the merger would control it in the Ways and Means Committee. Upon passage of the antitrust legislation, New Orleans would be awarded the NFL franchise.[22]

Long asked for and received from the Johnson administration a request to clarify admission and entertainment taxation. He used the request as a cover under which to craft the antitrust bill. He did not, however, include the antitrust language in the original bill. Instead, Commissioner Rozelle asked Senator Everett Dirksen, Republican of Illinois, to submit the antitrust amendment after the taxation bill came out of Long's committee. Dirksen agreed to do so because adding the amendment would benefit several franchises then encountering financial difficulties by allowing them "to receive income from charity games with special tax treatment."[23] The bill and amendment passed with little opposition. It then traveled to the House, where Democratic whip Hale Boggs of New Orleans guided it through the Ways and Means Committee. Celler protested that the football leagues were "poor labor negotiators . . . asking Congress to rescue them from their own ineptitude and folly"[24] and said on the House floor that an "end run was made around the public, who now have no way of knowing the whys and wherefores and results that may flow from this football merger."[25] The resulting Football Merger Act of 1966 exempted the National Football League from antitrust action and protected it from prosecution in the federal courts.[26]

Long's skill at manipulating the Congressional machinery to get the antitrust exemption passed should not be construed as sneaky, underhanded, or unethical. Neither he nor Boggs tried to cover up their involvement in the matter. Long himself stated on the floor of the Senate, "It is my hope that in the event the leagues are merged, New Orleans might be able to obtain a franchise." And Boggs wrote one constituent "This is, of course, a subject in which I have long been interested, and I'm sure I don't have to tell you how pleased I am that a professional team for New Orleans may at last become a reality." The deal reaped almost immediate political dividends for Boggs. Within a week of the announcement that New Orleans had been awarded the franchise, the congressman won reelection with 69 percent of the vote.[27]

On October 25, Pete Rozelle and members of the NFL's joint committee on expansion arrived in New Orleans to meet with three prospective owners: Louis Roussel, Jack Sanders, and John Mecom Jr. (who was eventually awarded ownership). The committee also met with representatives of Tulane University. Although Cincinnati and Seattle were ostensibly in the running and no official announcement had been made, New Orleans seemed a sure-shot to most Louisiana observers. "All of this . . . is just like a lot of window dressing as far as we're concerned," wrote *Times-Picayune* sports columnist Bob Roesler. "The decision has been made and our town is in like old Flynn." Governor McKeithen took a more cautious, but no less certain, approach: "Of course, I have no assurance that this is so, but I just think we have it [the expansion franchise]. If there were any doubts, they disappeared after what Senator Long and Congressman Boggs did in Washington last week."[28] Mayor Schiro wrote to Commissioner Rozelle, "It is a pleasure for me to join Pro Football fans throughout the Nation in expressing satisfaction at the House action which grants antitrust immunity to the National and American Football Leagues . . . . Naturally, we in New Orleans are proud of the fine job done by Hale Boggs and Russell Long, and we are hopeful that the sixteenth franchise will find its home in this City."[29]

On Tuesday, November 1—All Saints Day, appropriately enough—Pete Rozelle announced that NFL owners had unanimously chosen New Orleans for an expansion franchise. No owner for the franchise was announced, and the commissioner stressed the importance of building a new stadium for the team. Rozelle set up a temporary headquarters at the Royal Orleans hotel, where he oversaw more interviews of prospective team owners.[30]

Deeper causes were at work in the awarding of the new franchise than the politically expedient bargain Long and Rozelle struck. The NFL, by granting New Orleans a team, reflected a post-World War II trend among all professional sports leagues. At a time when sports became more and more significant in the lives of everyday Americans, the traditional regional stronghold of professional sports, the so-called Rustbelt of the industrial Northeast and Midwest, was being challenged and in some cases supplanted by the population-booming Sunbelt of the South and West as a potential source of fans—and of profits. Professional baseball had led the way in seeking out new markets when the Giants and Dodgers moved to California in 1958. The NFL, whose team owners tended to view their franchises as rare commodities that only increased in value due to scarcity, only reluctantly followed baseball's lead, although they had allowed the Rams to move from Cleveland to Los Angeles and had absorbed the San Francisco 49ers from the All-America Football Conference in 1950.[31]

This reluctance on the part of the NFL owners opened the door for the success of the AFL in the early 1960s. The older league—or at least factions within it—refused to recognize the post-World War II population and business resettlement and failed to take advantage of expansion opportunities, sometimes due to the veto of only one team owner. In fact, the impetus to create the new rival league came from just such reluctance. In the late 1950s, business and civic leaders in Dallas, Houston, and Minneapolis-St. Paul, clamored for expansion franchises. Tiring of delays, the groups, along with representatives from other western and southern cities, agreed to form the American Football League. The threat of aggressive AFL expansion, coupled with the salary wars, pressured the NFL into a new round of expansion in the mid-1960s. The New Orleans franchise would be the second new team in this movement, coming a year after the creation of the Atlanta Falcons.[32]

On the opposite side of the coin were the citizens and leaders of the cities themselves. For urban areas of the South and West, such as Miami, Atlanta, Houston, Denver, San Diego, Seattle, professional sports franchises further reflected their arrival on the scene as centers of population and business growth. Professional sports also brought media recognition; a football team or baseball team became a badge of honor, a status symbol, for cities. Professional sports, in other words, made a city "big league."[33]

In the eyes of most observers, the arrival of professional sports in New Orleans marked a new stage in the city's history: the Crescent City had finally become "big league." Attempts at defining just what "big league" meant proved illusory at best and nonexistent at worst. What were the conditions for being a big-league city? What was the impact of having that descriptive term added to a city's public image?

For cities as a whole, a professional sports franchise brought a number of positives that one might term "big league." Of course, proponents always pointed to the potential financial benefits of adding a sports team to a city's entertainment scene, but these financial benefits, which often went unrealized, do not completely explain the appeal of professional sports. Bringing an NFL team to New Orleans allowed the city to measure itself against other US cities; without a team, measurement—good or bad—would be impossible. Just as important, a sports team created free publicity for a city, as Bob Roesler noted in the *Times-Picayune*: "The sports pages, and the front pages [,] of the nation's press, have New Orleans qualified as a major league city." Finally, receiving a sports franchise boosted the morale of the city as a whole. "A city without the stimulation and excitement of good sports," Roesler noted, "is a city without a spirit, a city that ultimately would grow gray and lifeless."[34]

New Orleans Mayor Victor Schiro remarked during a 1966 speech that the city's residents had always been football fans. New Orleanians had supported Tulane's teams until, in his words, "Tulane de-emphasized football." Since then, Crescent City citizens had begun trekking "every Saturday to Baton Rouge, filling the 68,000 seat Tiger Stadium, selling out virtually every home game . . . . They love [football] so much they don't mind driving miles and miles on crowded highways to and from the game to pull their team through." And with the advent of televised professional games, the city had become "National Football League conscious." Schiro concluded that if New Orleanians "had the opportunity to see top football, professional football, right at home, they would keep any stadium packed."[35]

For sports fans and residents of New Orleans and other expansion cities, a professional franchise had more immediate and personal effects. For some city-dwellers, a professional team was a basic necessity of life. Not only did the new team place their city on a level with other cities, but it also brought the residents themselves up to the level of the residents of other "big league" cities. Sports became a defining characteristic in a time when distinctiveness, even in such a distinctive city as New Orleans, gradually faded, thanks in large part to a media of mass culture that homogenized national and regional tastes and to suburbanization that fractured local communities. As Kenneth Jackson noted in 1987, "Citizen identification with the city is now less than it was a century or more ago," when nineteenth-century cities and their populations "possessed a significant sense of local pride and spirit as a result of their struggles with other cities for canals, railroads, factories, and state institutions."[36] By the mid-twentieth century, this competition for infrastructure and institutional improvements had largely been replaced by a competition for sports franchises, and local pride and spirit had begun to be based on such "big league" considerations. Although it might have been increasingly difficult to define exactly what a New Orleanian was by the mid-twentieth century—an influx of non-natives and American culture changed that definition—being a fan of the new football team certainly qualified a person as one. Additionally, for those city residents not terribly interested in sports, the new team did not endanger other forms of non-sports entertainment—theaters continued to show movies and plays, exhibits continued to arrive at museums and galleries, musicians continued to play concert halls and clubs. But for those who did care, even if only on occasion, a sports franchise became, in the words of authors James Quirk and Rodney Fort, a "common identification symbol, something that brings the citizens of the city together." This sense of togetherness characterized a "big league" city.[37]

New Orleans, however, differed in one key circumstance from most of the other US cities clamoring for "big league" status: its past. Compared to the other expansion cities of the South, and even the West, New Orleans had been a city of consequence, in terms of population and economics, for most of its history. Therefore, the city did not really fit into the category of a "new growth" area. Just as important, though, New Orleans had a distinguished history as a center of professional sports.

Writing in 1968, a year after the Saints' first season, Crozat Duplantier addressed this topic. As early as 1837, he noted, New Orleans established itself as a center of sport—at first, horse racing. Following the Civil War and into the early twentieth century, the city's sports emphasis shifted to professional boxing. As enthusiasm for boxing declined in New Orleans, the city's image as a "big-league" sports center waned, leading to "years of frustration when New Orleans watched its spectator sports decline while other cities moved ahead into the big-league picture." Duplantier added, "its citizens developed a complex that their city was a 'two-bit town.'" Not until the creation of the New Orleans Open, a Professional Golf Association tour stop, in 1957, did major professional sports once again make inroads into the Crescent City. The success of the golf tournament prompted calls for other professional sports possibilities, particularly professional football, which culminated in the awarding of the NFL franchise in 1966 and hopes for a major league baseball team, as well. "New Orleans," Duplantier concluded, "on the eve of its 250th birthday, was big league again."[38]

After the granting of an NFL expansion franchise, New Orleans needed to add one final piece to its "big league" puzzle: a new stadium. Only eight days after the franchise announcement, Louisianans voted on Amendment 10, which allowed for the construction of a 60,000-seat covered stadium in Orleans or Jefferson Parish, to be financed by a four-and-a-half percent hotel tax in the two parishes. In addition to serving as a home to the new professional football team, the stadium would, according to proponents, attract other major sporting events, including high school football, baseball, basketball, tennis, polo, soccer, harness racing, professional and amateur boxing, track and field events, gymnastics—even the Spanish Riding School of Vienna and bullfighting.[39]

Although receiving the NFL franchise had been recognition of New Orleans as a "big league" city, many observers viewed Amendment 10 as the chance to secure, once and for all, the city's right to that description. Months before the vote, Dave Dixon had written to Governor McKeithen that in order to win support for a new stadium, citizens of the city and the state "don't need to like football, or baseball, or any other sport . . . [they] need only to like money, because it will mean money in the pockets of every man, woman, and child. . . ." He added that, in order to win votes for the stadium, it might be useful to compare New Orleans to rival cities: "In New Orleans this may be more than normally effective, because there is a deep resentment here that Houston, Atlanta, Dallas, and Miami have moved past us during recent years."[40] To Mayor Schiro, Dixon noted that "Long after people will ever care over who appoints the registrar of voters, they will remember you and your role in passing our Superdome legislation. This stadium will be built during your administration, and it will be a monument such as few American mayors have ever possessed."[41]

Sports columnist Bob Roesler wrote, "Every city in the nation, cities that have written us off ten years ago, envious cities, are watching us. With the vote coming on the heels of the franchise announcement, we will have a double-barrel load of great national publicity when the dome amendment is passed." Conversely, failure to pass the amendment would have only been detrimental, as *Times-Picayune* writer Ed Staton noted: "If Amendment No. 10 falls on its face, then New Orleans and Louisiana have fallen on their faces, locally and nationally. We'll look like a 10-horse town with a one-horse perspective."[42]

Louisiana politicians also emphasized the importance of a domed stadium in securing New Orleans' big-league status. Senator Allen Ellender said that the football team and stadium would "put our largest city and our state in the big leagues where they belong." Russell Long noted that "if we want to compete with the kind of leadership that exists in Houston, Dallas, Atlanta, and Miami, we must be prepared to go first class. That is what Amendment No. 10 proposes." Governor McKeithen added, "the domed stadium can do nothing but help the state."[43]

Louisiana voters approved Amendment 10 on November 8, 1966, but Governor McKeithen's prediction of it doing nothing but helping the state proved false. Indeed, it is ironical that so many observers hailed the expansion franchise and the stadium as proof of New Orleans' status as "big league," for both the team and the stadium turned out to be utter embarrassments. The New Orleans Saints became a virtual laughingstock, perhaps the worst franchise in professional sports. They certainly did provide New Orleanians with a common identifying symbol, as had been predicted, but the "Aints," as they were dubbed in the late 1970s and early 1980s, came to symbolize eternal losers. It seemed as if the "city that care forgot" had a team that care forgot, as well.[44]

The controversy surrounding the Superdome, as the home of the Saints came to be called, overshadowed even the frightfully poor play of the team itself. The last jewel in New Orleans' "big league" crown, the Superdome did not open until 1975. Its construction displaced hundreds of families and dozens of businesses. At its completion, what was originally planned as a $35 million, 55,000-seat stadium, had been bloated to 97,000 seats at a cost of $163 million. Adding to the problems of cost overruns, "Except for the New Orleans Saints and the original New Orleans Jazz, who came and went, the major league professional teams that were going to flock to the city never materialized," noted *New Orleans Magazine* in an August 2000 article. "When the Dome opened, New Orleans had one major-league professional team, the Saints; a quarter century later that is still all it has."[45] Eventually, the city did profit from the domed stadium. It attracted papal visits, concerts, exhibits, Mardi Gras balls, and political and other conventions. The Superdome hosted Super Bowls and Sugar Bowls, the Bayou Classic and high school football tournaments. New office buildings and hotels line Poydras Street, which borders one side of the dome.

In 1966, however, New Orleanians could not have known what the future held. Instead, they focused on the present. Their city, which had once ranked among the biggest of the big leagues, had returned to its status as a professional sports market. Thanks to the efforts of Senator Russell Long and Representative Hale Boggs, the National and American Football Leagues had been granted an antitrust exemption and New Orleans had been granted an expansion franchise. Capping the return, Louisiana voters had approved Amendment 10, which provided for the creation of a new stadium in New Orleans. The embarrassments would come soon enough—when the Saints took the field and when the Superdome costs piled up—and although the successes would take longer, they would come as well. For this brief period, however, New Orleans took its place in the spotlight as a "big league" city once again.

CHAPTER EIGHT

Professional Sports, Hurricane Katrina, and the Economic Redevelopment of New Orleans

Revisited[1]

ROBERT A. BAADE, VICTOR A. MATHESON, AND CALLAN HENDERSHOTT

Hurricane Katrina devastated New Orleans physically and economically after making landfall on August 29, 2005. Full recovery, which generally follows natural catastrophes in the United States given the inflow of funds for reconstruction, seemed less certain in the Crescent City. Citizens and businesses that left New Orleans following the storm exhibited a reluctance to return, and in many ways, the city has yet to fully recover from the devastation of the event even over a decade later. The city's professional sports teams were among those enterprises that departed New Orleans in the wake of Hurricane Katrina. The National Football League (NFL) Saints played home games in three different cities (San Antonio, Baton Rouge, and New York City) during 2005. The National Basketball Association (NBA) Hornets took up residence in Oklahoma City for 35 of their 41 home games during the 2005–2006 season, returning to Louisiana (although playing in Baton Rouge and not New Orleans) for a largely symbolic six games. The Arena Football League's VooDoo abandoned their entire 2006 schedule. The University of New Orleans and Tulane, both National Collegiate Athletic Association (NCAA) Division 1 schools,

A desperate, waterlogged citizen makes his way to shelter in the Superdome during the aftermath of Hurricane Katrina. Photo courtesy of *New Orleans Times-Picayune* and Barcroft Media.

either cancelled entire seasons for individual sports or played "barnstorming" seasons with no home games.

When we first conducted this analysis, we focused on two questions: what was and is the future of professional and spectator sports in New Orleans, and what roles did sports play and continue to play in the economic redevelopment of the city? The purpose of this paper is to analyze the extent to which the city of New Orleans directed its redevelopment dollars toward its sports infrastructure and to ask whether New Orleans benefited economically from its role as host to major professional sports teams and a disproportionate number of mega-sports events given its size and demographics. Did commercial sports enable a rebuilding of New Orleans's storm-ravaged infrastructure or did it force civic trade-offs made even more painful by the storm?

Independent scholarship in general has not supported the thesis that professional sports induce significant increases in economic activity for host cities. New Orleans, however, may be different. The city is smaller and less affluent than other host cities in general, and it may be that the frequency with which large sports events are hosted by New Orleans makes the area an exception to the experience of most cities with regard to sports and economic development.

The gravity of the city's economic situation in the wake of Katrina necessitates an individual and more complete appraisal as the strategies for economic redevelopment are evaluated thirteen years after the storm. Answers to the questions raised in this introduction require a review of, among other things, New Orleans's place in the national professional sports landscape, the extent of the damage Katrina wrought, the amount of redevelopment money the city must commit, and the evidence with regard to the impact sports has on host city economies with special attention to the circumstances that surrounded New Orleans in its rebuilding period.

While New Orleans hosts major league franchises in both the NFL and NBA, with a pre-hurricane metropolitan area population of less than 1.6 million residents, the city was already a small market for any of the major sports leagues in the United States. As shown in Table 1, in 2004 New Orleans was the 37st largest metropolitan area in the United States by population and was the 35th largest city out of the 39 hosting a team from one of the five large professional sports leagues in country.

The situation became markedly worse in the following decade. Katrina caused a significant dislocation of the city's residents, resulting in the New Orleans metropolitan area suffering the largest percentage drop in population among large American cities between 2004 and 2016. As seen in Table 1, by 2016 New Orleans had dropped to the 41st largest metropolitan area in the US and was the 36th largest city out of 40 "Major League" cities. Furthermore, four metro areas in the country without any major sports franchises, Austin, Virginia Beach/Norfolk, Greensboro, and Louisville, are all larger than New Orleans. Another sixteen larger cities are without an NBA team, including several with strong ambitions to attract a franchise such as Kansas City and St. Louis. Fifteen cities without an NFL franchise have larger population bases than New Orleans, including St. Louis and San Diego, both of which recently lost franchises to Los Angeles, and football hungry San Antonio, which played host to the New Orleans Saints for three of their "home" games during the 2005 season. Not only is New Orleans small, but it is also relatively poor, ranking 35th in per capita personal income among the cities listed in Table 2 and 32nd out of the 40 cities with major professional sports franchises. To be fair, however, the city is relatively richer now than in 2004 when it ranked 47th out of the 48 largest US cities in per capita income. Many of the city's poorest residents who were displaced by Katrina did not return.

Table 1: Summary Statistics for US Metropolitan Areas (2004)

Metropolitan Area	Population	Rank	Per Capita Income	Rank	NFL	NBA	NHL	MLB	MLS	Total
New York-Newark	22,662,795	1	44,959	2	2	2	3	2	1	10
Los Angeles-Riverside	17,284,575	2	35,305	18	0	2	2	2	2	8
Chicago	9,629,435	3	38,389	11	1	1	1	2	1	6
Washington-Baltimore	8,470,401	4	44,836	3	2	1	1	2	1	7
Boston-Providence	7,760,397	5	42,457	4	1	1	1	1	1	5
San Jose-SF-Oakland	7,753,167	6	48,091	1	2	1	1	2	0	6
Philadelphia	6,852,767	7	39,365	9	1	1	1	1	0	4
Dallas-Fort Worth	6,074,414	8	33,923	23	1	1	1	1	1	5
Miami-Fort Lauderdale	5,868,202	9	37,808	12	1	1	1	1	0	4
Detroit-Warren	5,480,176	10	35,374	17	1	1	1	1	0	4
Houston	5,321,109	11	35,124	19	1	1	0	1	1	4
Atlanta	5,220,858	12	35,714	15	1	1	1	1	0	4
Seattle-Tacoma	3,935,449	13	41,338	6	1	1	0	1	0	3
Phoenix	3,637,332	14	32,220	39	1	1	1	1	0	4
Cleveland-Akron	3,564,308	15	33,087	32	1	1	0	1	0	3
Minneapolis-St. Paul	3,490,160	16	40,374	7	1	1	1	1	0	4
San Diego	2,930,007	17	40,314	8	1	0	0	1	0	2
St. Louis	2,822,926	18	35,701	16	1	0	1	1	0	3
Denver	2,799,868	19	39,012	10	1	1	1	1	1	5
Pittsburgh	2,699,639	20	33,533	27	1	0	1	1	0	3
Portland, OR	2,685,494	21	33,045	33	0	1	0	0	0	1
Tampa-St. Petersburg	2,587,771	22	33,034	34	1	0	1	1	0	3
Orlando	2,488,765	23	29,743	45	0	1	0	0	0	1
Sacramento	2,255,401	24	35,912	14	0	1	0	0	0	1

Another strike against New Orleans is its business climate, as corporations play a major role in keeping a team financially competitive. It is one thing to provide highly profitable luxury seating; it is another to fill those seats. The city is home to just two Fortune 500 companies: CenturyLink, ranked 168 in 2018, and Entergy, ranked 241th, and there is, therefore, not the market for loges and club seats that can be found in the other NBA and NFL cities with which New Orleans competes. One writer somewhat whimsically stated the NFL financial equation in the following way:

Metropolitan Area	Population	Rank	Per Capita Income	Rank	NFL	NBA	NHL	MLB	MLS	Total
Kansas City	2,213,656	25	32,380	37	1	0	0	1	1	3
Columbus	2,170,450	26	32,413	36	0	0	1	0	1	2
Indianapolis	2,123,265	27	33,639	26	1	1	0	0	0	2
Cincinnati	2,101,112	28	34,970	21	1	0	0	1	0	2
Charlotte	2,035,782	29	33,119	31	1	1	0	0	0	2
Salt Lake City-Provo	1,981,051	30	27,901	48	0	1	0	0	1	2
Milwaukee	1,979,716	31	35,921	13	0	1	0	1	0	2
Las Vegas	1,880,581	32	33,688	25	0	0	0	0	0	0
San Antonio	1,857,602	33	29,683	46	0	1	0	0	0	1
Virginia Beach-Norfolk	1,736,907	34	33,862	24	0	0	0	0	0	0
Raleigh-Durham	1,606,502	35	34,991	20	0	0	1	0	0	1
Nashville	1,587,444	36	34,399	22	1	0	1	0	0	2
New Orleans	**1,578,179**	**37**	**29,043**	**47**	**1**	**1**	**0**	**0**	**0**	**2**
Greensboro-Winston-Salem	1,472,314	38	30,731	43	0	0	0	0	0	0
Hartford	1,451,200	39	41,348	5	0	0	0	0	0	0
Austin	1,410,058	40	33,347	28	0	0	0	0	0	0
Louisville	1,371,885	41	32,121	40	0	0	0	0	0	0
Grand Rapids	1,355,200	42	30,489	44	0	0	0	0	0	0
Jacksonville	1,341,793	43	33,268	30	1	0	0	0	0	1
Birmingham	1,289,938	44	32,297	38	0	0	0	0	0	0
Memphis	1,287,853	45	32,933	35	0	1	0	0	0	1
Greenville, SC	1,262,050	46	27,394	49	0	0	0	0	0	0
Buffalo	1,238,934	47	31,002	42	1	0	1	0	0	2
Oklahoma City	1,212,596	48	31,067	41	0	0	0	0	0	0
Green Bay	294,570	NA	33,329	29	1	0	0	0	0	1

Instead of fans, the NFL seeks corporations . . . While the NBA and Major League Baseball have guaranteed contracts for their players, the NFL with its exorbitant TV rights deals and corporate backing has practically given their owners guaranteed dollars . . .

The way business is done now is the owner convinces his buddies who own the largest businesses in their respective cities to buy majority [*sic*] of the season tickets and luxury boxes. The result: a term exclusive to the NFL, the

Table 2: Summary Statistics for US Metropolitan Areas (2018)

Metropolitan Area	Population	Rank	Change	Per Capita Income	Rank	NFL	NBA	NHL	MLB	MLS	Total
New York-Newark	23,689,255	1	-	65,960	2	2	2	3	2	2	11
Los Angeles-Riverside	18,688,022	2	-	52,166	13	2	2	2	2	2	10
Chicago	9,882,634	3	-	55,005	11	1	1	1	2	1	6
Washington-Baltimore	9,665,892	4	-	62,317	4	2	1	1	2	1	7
San Jose-SF-Oakland	8,751,807	5	+1	76,988	1	2	1	1	2	1	7
Boston-Providence	8,176,376	6	-1	62,790	3	1	1	1	1	1	5
Dallas-Fort Worth	7,673,305	7	+1	50,344	18	1	1	1	1	1	5
Philadelphia	7,179,357	8	-1	56,314	8	1	1	1	1	1	5
Houston	6,972,374	9	+2	51,442	15	1	1	0	1	1	4
Miami-Fort Lauderdale	6,723,472	10	-1	52,206	12	1	1	1	1	0	4
Atlanta	6,451,262	11	+1	46,204	31	1	1	0	1	1	4
Detroit-Warren	5,318,653	12	-2	47,758	26	1	1	1	1	0	4
Seattle-Tacoma	4,684,516	13	-	61,104	5	1	0	0	1	1	3
Phoenix	4,661,537	14	-	42,218	45	1	1	1	1	0	4
Minneapolis-St. Paul	3,894,820	15	+1	55,486	9	1	1	1	1	1	5
Cleveland-Akron	3,483,311	16	-1	46,444	29	1	1	0	1	0	3
Denver	3,470,235	17	+2	56,319	7	1	1	1	1	1	5
San Diego	3,317,749	18	-1	55,168	10	0	0	0	1	0	1
Orlando	3,202,927	19	+4	39,929	48	0	1	0	0	1	2
Portland, OR	3,160,488	20	+1	47,845	25	0	1	0	0	1	2
Tampa-St. Petersburg	3,032,171	21	+1	43,807	41	1	0	1	1	0	3
St. Louis	2,911,769	22	-4	48,950	21	0	0	1	1	0	2
Pittsburgh	2,635,228	23	-3	49,633	19	1	0	1	1	0	3
Charlotte	2,632,249	24	+5	45,980	32	1	1	0	0	0	2

> guaranteed sellout. Saints owner Tom Benson can't do that in New Orleans because there are no major corporations other than Entergy to back him.[2]

The competition to host a professional sports team is often as fierce as the competition among athletes on game day, and the lack of population base and both personal and corporate wealth places New Orleans at a considerable disadvantage in supporting and, therefore, retaining either the Saints or

Metropolitan Area	Population	Rank	Change	Per Capita Income	Rank	NFL	NBA	NHL	MLB	MLS	Total
Sacramento	2,567,451	25	-1	50,829	17	0	1	0	0	0	1
Salt Lake City-Provo	2,514,748	26	+4	42,886	44	0	1	0	0	1	2
Kansas City	2,446,396	27	-2	46,911	27	1	0	0	1	1	3
Columbus	2,443,402	28	-2	45,904	34	0	0	1	0	1	2
San Antonio	2,429,609	29	+4	44,284	38	0	1	0	0	0	1
Las Vegas	2,404,336	30	+2	41,120	46	0	0	1	0	0	1
Indianapolis	2,386,199	31	-4	47,956	23	1	1	0	0	0	2
Cincinnati	2,224,231	32	-4	48,429	22	1	0	0	1	0	2
Raleigh-Durham	2,156,253	33	+2	47,885	24	0	0	1	0	0	1
Austin	2,056,405	34	+6	51,566	14	0	0	0	0	0	0
Milwaukee	2,043,274	35	-4	49,548	20	0	1	0	1	0	2
Nashville	1,987,778	36	-	51,270	16	1	0	1	0	0	2
Virginia Beach-Norfolk	1,830,629	37	-3	46,693	28	0	0	0	0	0	0
Greensboro-Winston-Salem	1,650,019	38	-	40,112	47	0	0	0	0	0	0
Jacksonville	1,603,497	39	+4	44,325	37	1	0	0	0	0	1
Louisville	1,510,945	40	+1	44,525	36	0	0	0	0	0	0
New Orleans	**1,501,213**	**41**	**-4**	**45,245**	**35**	**1**	**1**	**0**	**0**	**0**	**2**
Hartford	1,476,637	42	-3	58,346	6	0	0	0	0	0	0
Oklahoma City	1,445,501	43	+5	44,172	39	0	1	0	0	0	1
Grand Rapids	1,443,508	44	-2	43,570	42	0	0	0	0	0	0
Greenville, SC	1,442,117	45	+1	38,977	49	0	0	0	0	0	0
Memphis	1,369,038	46	-1	43,175	43	0	1	0	0	0	1
Birmingham	1,361,299	47	-3	44,037	40	0	0	0	0	0	0
Buffalo	1,210,481	48	-1	45,933	33	1	0	1	0	0	2
Green Bay	318,236	NA	NA	46,362	30	1	0	0	0	0	1

the Hornets. Prior to Hurricane Katrina, in fact, New Orleans appeared to be on the verge of losing its NFL franchise. Tom Benson, the owner of the Saints at the time, had reportedly rejected the state's final offer to keep the Saints in New Orleans in late April of 2005. Benson died in March 2018 at which time his wife took over control of the team.[3] The state's offer included not only public financing of over 75 percent of a proposed $174 million Superdome renovation, but also direct cash payments to the Saints totaling $64 million through

2008 and $9.5 million per year after the completion of the renovations to the Superdome in 2008.[4] The state's offer to the Saints, including the annual cash subsidy, would have placed the team in the top half of the financial standings in the NFL.

The fact that Benson would reject such an offer, which included a direct cash subsidy to the team, speaks volumes about the financial realities of the NFL and the inordinate transfer of business risk from teams to their host cities. While the state struggled to meet its contractual cash payments to the team in the wake of reduced tax revenues following the terrorist attacks of September 11, 2001, the only significant financial risk facing Tom Benson was the $81 million he would have been required to pay (representing the subsidies that the Saints have received since 2001) if he broke his Superdome contract, which he could have done following the 2006 season.[5] That risk pales in comparison to the $1 billion written offer Benson claims to have received for the team in 2005, a 1,400 percent increase over the $70 million price Benson paid for the Saints in 1985.[6] The lucrative offer Benson received for the team reflects at least in part the money-making potential of NFL teams, which is explained in large part by the subsidies cities extend to attract a supply of teams that is limited by the NFL and its owners. The value of the Saints has only risen since 2005. Forbes estimates that the franchise was valued at $2 billion in 2017.[7]

While recognizing New Orleans's shortcomings as it relates to its ability to host professional sports, on the other side of the coin, the city caters to the tourist trade to an extent that distinguishes itself from almost every other American city. The infrastructure that New Orleans has created arguably provides a comparative advantage in hosting events to include commercial sports over most cities in the United States. The city's performance in attracting outside events supports the idea that it has exercised its comparative advantage. Even though New Orleans is a relatively small city, it ranked fifth in the United States in the number of conventions hosted.[8] Prior to the storm New Orleans annually attracted more than 10 million visitors who spent in excess of $5 billion per year according to the New Orleans Metropolitan and Tourism Bureau.

The information recorded in Tables 3 and 4 in a general sense indicates the extent to which New Orleans is geared to tourism. The fraction of the New Orleans economy both before and after Katrina that was accounted for by the Department of Labor's "Leisure and Hospitality" metric, the North American Industrial Classification System (NAICS 7) in 2004 indicated that New Orleans had a significantly larger tourist component than did the United

States overall and most other southern cities in the United States. that hosted NBA or NFL teams. It is noteworthy that New Orleans tourist sector as measured by employees and payroll in NAICS 7 is roughly 25 percent larger than that of Miami, Florida, which is among the most tourist-friendly cities in the country, and trails only Orlando, home of Disneyworld.[9]

Commercial sport, of course, is one important aspect of the tourist/leisure industry, and it could have played a role in the economic revitalization of New Orleans. Since opening in 1975, the Superdome has hosted numerous sporting events of national significance including the NFL's Super Bowl in 1978, 1981, 1986, 1990, 1997, 2002, and 2013 and the National Intercollegiate Athletic Association Men's Basketball Final Four in 1982, 1987, 1993, and 2003.[10] Furthermore, the Superdome annually hosts the Sugar Bowl, one of college football's top post-season matches and a game which has determined college football's national champion nine times since 1975. Post-Katrina, New Orleans has continued to host numerous mega-events such as the 2013 Super Bowl, the 2012 NCAA Men's Basketball Final Four, and the 2007 and 2012 College Football National Championship game.

Replacing the infrastructure for professional sports and mega-sports events can be justified if the benefits provided by the facilities exceed the costs incurred in the reconstruction. Both costs and benefits have to be measured over time since the facilities provided a stream of benefits as well as generating costs associated with operations and maintenance (O&M). Comprehensive economic analysis would include not only the explicit benefits but also the implicit benefits and costs, which are difficult not only to measure but in many cases hard to identify.

Data do exist for New Orleans for the number of establishments, annual payroll, and number of employees for a variety of entertainment related industries defined according to the NAICS and these data are recorded in Table 5.

All data point to the fact that the economic activity accounted for through the "Arts, Entertainment, and Recreation" industry (NAICS 71) for New Orleans is absolutely small, but large when compared to the United States overall.[11] Census data, thus, supports the idea that New Orleans is a tourist-based economy that exhibits an arts-entertainment-recreation industry that is larger than that characterizing the United States as a whole.

The contribution of "Spectator Sports" (NAICS 7112), however, is less than 1 percent by any of the measures identified in Table 3. Despite the high salaries paid professional athletes, the spectator sports industry typically accounts

Table 3: Aggregate Measures of the Fraction of the Economic Activity for Selected Cities and the United States Represented by "Leisure and Hospitality" (NAICS 7) for 2004

Geographic Area/Statistic	NAICS 7 Employees as a % of Total Area Employees	NAICS 7 Annual Payroll as a % of Total Area Payroll	NAICS 7 Establishments as a % of Total Area Establishments
Atlanta	9.67	3.93	7.70
Charlotte	9.34	3.99	7.82
Greenville	9.94	3.62	8.83
Houston	9.14	3.36	7.72
Memphis	11.22	5.58	7.66
Miami	10.75	5.51	7.22
New Orleans	**13.93**	**7.22**	**9.74**
Orlando	19.39	11.93	8.19
Tampa	9.42	4.62	7.78
United States	9.64	4.07	8.10
Atlanta	9.67	3.93	7.70

Source: https://www.bls.gov/cew/
MSA, quarterly census of employment

Table 4: Aggregate Measures of the Fraction of the Economic Activity for Selected Cities and the United States Represented by "Leisure and Hospitality" (NAICS 7) for 2017

Geographic Area/Statistic	NAICS 7 Employees as a % of Total Area Employees	NAICS 7 Annual Payroll as a % of Total Area Payroll	NAICS 7 Establishments as a % of Total Area Establishments
Atlanta	11.18	4.11	8.86
Charlotte	11.72	4.91	9.26
Greenville	11.15	4.14	10.37
Houston	10.85	3.78	8.88
Memphis	11.14	4.87	10.31
Miami	12.70	6.80	7.54
New Orleans	**16.30**	**8.51**	**11.38**
Orlando	21.36	12.52	9.36
Tampa	12.03	5.63	8.64
United States	11.05	4.62	8.51
Atlanta	11.18	4.11	8.86

Source: https://www.bls.gov/cew/
MSA, quarterly census of employment

Table 5: Aggregate Measures of the Fraction of New Orleans Economic Activity in Total Represented by Spectator Sports for 2004 and 2017

	2004			
Ratio/NAICS number	NAICS 71	NAICS 711	NAICS 7112	NAICS 72
Industry Employees/ New Orleans Total	2.33% (1.43%)	0.43% (.29%)	0.13% (.10%)	11.60% (10.52%)
Annual Industry Payroll/ New Orleans Total	2.20% (1.01%)	1.00% (.47%)	0.83% (.22%)	5.03% (5.54%)
Industry Establishments/ New Orleans Total	1.42% (1.38%)	0.51% (.50%)	0.11% (.07%)	8.32% (8.33%)
	2017			
Ratio/NAICS number	NAICS 71	NAICS 711	NAICS 7112	NAICS 72
Industry Employees/ New Orleans Total	2.31% (1.59%)	0.76% (.34%)	N/A (.10%)	13.99% (9.45%)
Annual Industry Payroll/ New Orleans Total	2.36% (1.09%)	1.62% (.55%)	N/A (.27%)	6.15% (3.54%)
Industry Establishments/ New Orleans Total	1.75% (1.43%)	0.71% (.55%)	0.10% (.06%)	9.64% (7.08%)

NAICS 71: Arts, entertainment, and recreation
NAICS 711: Performing arts and spectator sports
NAICS 7112: Spectator sports
NAICS 72: Accommodation and food services
US percentages given in parentheses. (US)
Source: https://www.bls.gov/cew/

for less than 1 percent of a city's payroll, and, by that measure, the industry is not economically vital to cities in the United States in general to include New Orleans.[12]

Numerous studies of both professional sports franchises and stadiums as well as of mega-events, furthermore, lend support to the notion that sports have little impact on local economies. Analyses of the Super Bowl, NCAA Final Four, and mega-events in general, for example, have all concluded that these big sporting events have no statistically significant impact on any number of economic variables such as employment, per capita income, metropolitan area-wide gross domestic product, or taxable sales.[13] Coates and Depken (2006) indicated ambivalence about the economic contribution of sports mega-events concluding, "The upshot is, therefore, that these mega-events are not necessarily the economic windfall that their proponents portray them to be."[14] Stadiums and professional franchises similarly show little in the way of economic benefits for host cities.[15]

Given the economically tenuous state of professional sports in New Orleans prior to Hurricane Katrina, it is difficult to imagine that a disaster of its magnitude would improve prospects for the industry in the city. The next section of the paper summarizes the extent of the damage with a particular emphasis on the demographic changes that may be sufficiently long-lived to have adversely influenced the prospects for supporting professional sports in New Orleans in the long term.

Hurricane Katrina, which swept into New Orleans and the Gulf Coast on August 29, 2005, caused far and away the largest damages in real dollar terms of any hurricane in US history, with uninsured losses topping $100 billion and insured losses estimated at $34.4 billion.[16] Its final death toll of over 1,400 also places it among the worst natural disasters ever suffered by the United States. New Orleans was particularly hard hit by the storm, as flood waters remained for weeks after Katrina while levies were repaired, and rebuilding the city was an epic undertaking unmatched in scope and expense in recent US history.

The cost of reconstructing New Orleans itself has been placed at more than $100 billion. Approximately 80 percent of New Orleans's 188,000 occupied housing units were severely damaged by the storm. Furthermore, more than half of the city's 100,000 owner-occupied homes were built before 1950, and their repair and replacement will require expensive modifications to meet modern building codes designed to prevent future hurricane damage.[17]

The damage to middle class neighborhoods has substantial implications for the redevelopment effort both as it relates to production and consumption. Without a middle class, New Orleans will not have the workers it needs to run the economy that existed prior to Katrina, and the spending necessary to restore the economy to pre-hurricane levels will be deficient. Katrina devastated the housing stock, schools, and other infrastructure vital to normal life for all socio-economic classes.

The extent of the damage to the social infrastructure must also be carefully assessed since the return of middle class workers and consumers is essential to the revitalization of the New Orleans economy. Even before Katrina, by nearly every measure of economic development, New Orleans lagged behind other large American cities. Labor force participation rates and employment to population ratios in New Orleans averaged 5 to 10 percent below national levels for most demographic groups. Hurricane damaged areas in Louisiana had poverty rates above the national average (21.4% vs. 12.4%), and New Orleans residents were less likely (55% vs. 66%) to live in owner-occupied housing than residents of other large cities. Finally, the educational attainment of younger adults (age 18 to 34) for storm-damaged areas was generally below that for the rest of the nation. For example, 22.9 percent of young adults in hurricane damaged areas had not completed a high school degree compared with 20.6 percent nationwide, while only 22.5 percent had completed a college degree compared with 29.3 percent nationwide.[18]

These figures had several implications for the likelihood that displaced people would return. First, Katrina hit the economically disadvantaged hardest. Statistics indicate that other places in the nation to which they have relocated improved their opportunities for employment. Second, significant portions of the middle class were displaced in the storm-ravaged area; 47.4 percent of those displaced had education equivalent to some college or above.[19] Third, 45 percent of those displaced did not live in homes that they owned indicating that a significant portion of the people displaced by Hurricane Katrina had weak financial ties to the communities they abandoned. A significant permanent displacement of the population affected by the storm undermined or may have substantially altered the socio-demographic character of neighborhoods most adversely affected by the storm. It should also be noted that virtually entire neighborhoods and parishes were wiped out by the storm, and devastation of that magnitude may well negate any pull that community loyalty and ties may exert in bringing people back. It has been estimated, for example, that Orleans Parish and St. Bernard Parish lost 65.9 and 89.8 percent of their populations over the period October 2005 to January 2006.[20] Even if people were inclined to return, much of the infrastructure necessary to rebuild and sustain people had been eliminated. Government programs, furthermore, were unable to fully compensate for lost private infrastructure.

The New Orleans economy served the nation as a tourist center and transportation hub for water transport in particular, as previously noted, and therefore, any economic redevelopment effort should focus on those industries, an opinion endorsed by members of an *ad hoc* committee of urban experts assembled under the auspices of the Urban Land Institute. The information in Table 6, to be specific, indicates that in July 2005, 32.9 percent of the labor force in New Orleans was employed in the "Trade and Transportation" and "Leisure and Hospitality" sectors. The numbers recorded in Table 6 indicate several things worthy of note as it relates to characterizing the New Orleans

Table 6: Comparing the Pre- and Post-Katrina Economies for the New Orleans MSA

Statistic/Date	July 2005	July 2006	July 2017
MSA Population	1,313,787	1,024,678[a]	1,275,762
Unemployment Rate	[Louisiana = 5.6%] New Orleans = 6.1% (United States = 5.0%)	[Louisiana = 4.2%] New Orleans = 4.9% (United States = 4.7%)	[Louisiana = 6.1%] New Orleans = 5.5% (United States = 4.3%)
Labor Force Size	645,907	507,621 (Down 21.4% from July 2005)	601,519 (Down 6.9% from July 2005)
Population Employed in the Transportation and Trade Sector	122,300	105,200 (Down 14.0% from July 2005)	112,800 (Down 7.8% from July 2005)
Population Employed in the Hospitality and Leisure Sector	86,200	60,600 (Down 29.7% from July 2005)	88,700 (Down 2.9% from July 2005)
Public Transportation: % of the System Operational	100%	17%	100%
Number of Workers Employed by Government	103,100 or 16.0% of the labor force for government at all levels; 15,700 for the federal government or 2.4%	73,600 or 14.5% of the labor force for government at all levels; 12,400 for the federal government or 2.4%	69,800 or 11.6% of the labor force for government at all levels; 12,700 for the federal government or 2.1%
Number of Open Hotels	142	116 (Down 18% from July 2005)	n.a.
Open Retail Food Establishments	100%	44%	100%
Number of Passengers Arriving at the New Orleans Airport	438,578	282,137 (Down 35.7% from July 2005)	525,822 (Up 19.9% from July 2005)

Source: Greater New Orleans Community Data Center, *The Katrina Index*, February 15, 2007, www.gnocdc.org. Accessed on March 3, 2007.

[a] January 2006 statistic. Note the metropolitan population for New Orleans fell by 29.2 percent from July 2005 to January 2006.

economy pre- and post-Katrina. First, the transportation/trade and leisure/hospitality industries, the cornerstones of the New Orleans economy, did recover to some extent. Employment in the transportation and trade sector remain below their pre-Katrina levels, but the numbers employed in the leisure and hospitality sector have fully recovered and now exceed their pre-Katrina levels by a modest amount.

Hurricane Katrina led to a significant temporary contraction of the leisure industry. In the immediate aftermath of the storm there were fewer people flying into New Orleans in comparison to pre-Katrina levels, and a smaller number of establishments to accommodate them. Nearly one year after Katrina, the number of retail food establishments was 44 percent of the level prior to the storm, and the number of hotels open remained below the pre-Katrina level.

Even now over a decade after the storm New Orleans has not fully returned to the population and economic activity levels that existed prior to the storm, although tourism appears to be a fairly bright spot overall. There is compelling scholarship by Davis and Weinstein to suggest that population and economic activity across cities and regions within a country are not random occurrences, but rather reflect "locational fundamentals," e.g., location on a coast or significant river (physical geography), and economies of scale emanating from "economic clustering." The Davis and Weinstein study is based on 8,000 years of data on Japanese regions, and Japan's population is far more homogenous than that characterizing the United States. The population of New Orleans is particularly diverse.[21]

Other scholarship supports the importance of locational fundamentals in explaining developments relating to population movements following catastrophic events. Evidence following the Chicago Fire of 1871, indicates that the city's recovery from that event depended on location fundamentals specific to neighborhoods.[22] More recently, economic recovery from the 1992 Rodney King riots in Los Angeles was notably slow as compared to Miami's experience following the devastation of Hurricane Andrew in the same year.[23] Taken together, these findings suggest that heterogeneity as it relates in part to ethnicity, shared values and culture, income and wealth, and education can retard redevelopment and efforts to resettle. Many New Orleans neighborhoods where redevelopment has been slow to occur exhibit marked variation in these characteristics and relatively low rates of home ownership as previously mentioned.

So, what role did spectator sports play in the economy of New Orleans as it attempted to recover from Hurricane Katrina's devastation? First, it is important to note that the Superdome itself, which served an ill-fated role as a center for 30,000 refugees who were unable to escape the city prior to the storm, suffered extensive damage due to Katrina as did other sports facilities throughout the city. In the immediate aftermath of the storm, immediate decisions needed to be made as to the extent of repairs that the city would undertake. Following any emergency repairs, additional consideration would be given towards long-term upgrades to the facility. Finally, the city needed to decide the extent to which it would make direct subsidies available to the city's professional sports teams in order to have them return to and remain in the city.

The extent of the devastation caused by Katrina coupled with the demographic character of New Orleans prior to the storm led to the prospect that residents of the city would resettle elsewhere in the country. The likelihood that New Orleans would return to its pre-Katrina state, in turn, clearly had a bearing on the probability that professional sports teams would be able to remain in the city for the long-term. If the chances increased that pro-sport teams would eventually leave due to a lack of fan support, that had implications for the efficacy of substantial public investments to replace or repair the professional sports infrastructure.

Following Katrina, plans for completely replacing the Superdome were scuttled, and instead, the city embarked on a multi-stage and multi-hundred million-dollar repair and renovation of the Superdome. The first stage involved repair of the direct wind and water damage caused to the facility by the hurricane as well as the deterioration of the stadium caused by its use an emergency shelter. These repairs cost roughly $200 million and were finished in time for the Saints to open their season back in New Orleans on September 25, 2006, just over a year after Katrina. An extensive set of renovations was then undertaken including new or refurbished seats, new club facilities and luxury suites, expanded bathrooms, new scoreboards and video systems, and a doubling of the locker room space. This phase was completed for the opening of the 2011 NFL season. The total cost of these two phases of construction cost a reported $336 million, of which $156 million was paid for by the Federal Emergency Management Agency (FEMA).[24] While the NFL as a league pledged $20 million towards these repairs, Saints owner Tom Benson, the primary tenant of the facility, paid nothing towards its reconstruction. Louisiana had only a $500 million insurance policy on state buildings along with $100 million in flood insurance, and the Superdome was just one of the many public buildings including schools damaged by the storm, so some have questioned the priority placed on this facility.[25]

Paradoxically, the extent of the devastation and the significant pressure exerted on the public sector to demonstrate its resolve and ability to help the city recover enhanced the prospects that those edifices most representative of the city to the outside world would be restored. Delaney and Eckstein identified the strength of "local growth coalitions" as vital to understanding public choices regarding the construction of sports infrastructure.[26] The public choice theory detailed by Delaney and Eckstein helps explain decision making in New Orleans with regard to the rapid reconstruction of the Superdome, and the successful floating of the $294-million bond issue that financed the repair. Not only was there a strong local growth coalition following Katrina, but that local effort was bolstered by a strong national sentiment for helping New Orleans get back on its feet. Ironically, the ineptitude that government displayed arguably at all levels immediately following the storm increased the pressure on government to correct the negative perceptions about its performance. Louisiana Governor Kathleen Babineaux Blanco in announcing the bond sale remarked that, "Rebuilding and reopening the Superdome were critical steps in Louisiana's recovery from hurricanes Katrina and Rita and this bond sale made them possible."[27] The Superdome as a symbol of the city's ability to survive and its struggle to recover achieved particular significance as Katrina's impact played out.

The demand for the Saints, the primary tenant of the Superdome, had been given a boost by the increase in the political demand for the Superdome. The political resistance for public subsidies to keep the Saints from marching elsewhere eased, and the successful sale of the bonds to repair and renovate the Superdome corroborates that assertion. The NFL, furthermore, had to temper Tom Benson's desire to move the franchise to keep the League's image from being tarnished further by widely criticized franchise moves from Los Angeles to St. Louis and Oakland and from Cleveland to Baltimore. Indeed, many observers believe that the Saints would certainly have ended up in the greener fields of Los Angeles within a few years after 2005 had Hurricane Katrina not occurred. The "good-cop" role played by the NFL in keeping the Saints in New Orleans may well have facilitated financial transfers to Tom Benson from a grateful city. All in all, in a peculiar way, financial transfers to Tom Benson had been made easier as a consequence of the storm.

Once again, the efficacy of those transfers can be questioned. Given the very small percentage of economic activity in New Orleans accounted for by the sports industry, it may have not been prudent to devote a disproportionate share of scarce redevelopment funds to that sector. An even stronger argument can be made against refurbishing the Superdome to accommodate the financial needs of the NFL Saints since their owner had consistently sought economic concessions from a city and state that were financially stressed even prior to Katrina. In 2001, Saints' owner Tom Benson signed an agreement that required the city to pay him $186 million over the next 10 years in exchange for the "privilege" of having the team play in the Superdome. A fifteen-year extension to this agreement signed in 2011 guaranteed the Saints' owner an additional $392 million in revenues through taxpayer subsidies through 2025.[28]

The economic incentive for the Saints owner to keep the team in New Orleans was compromised by Katrina. As the small economy of New Orleans lacked the financial wherewithal to support professional sports in the same manner as other cities, especially following Katrina, the Saints increasingly turned to public subsidies to generate revenues for its billionaire owner. Furthermore, unlike the efforts made by large oil companies and small business alike to repair the capital-intensive oil refineries as well as small restaurants and shops in and around the city, there existed little motivation for the Saints to recoup their small investment in infrastructure. This points to a larger problem with the financial structure of the professional sports industry throughout the United States. Namely, the existence of substantial subsidies for infrastructure undermines a team's commitment to its host city. Absent any meaningful risk to their own capital, what incentive does a team have to stay in a city that experiences a catastrophe on the scale of Hurricane Katrina if the team has little in the way of permanent infrastructure invested in its host city? There is little question that in the vast majority of cases the financial risk accompanying hosting professional sports in the United States is disproportionately borne by the host community. Katrina provided striking testimony to the reality of how subsidies for sports infrastructure have contributed to that financial vulnerability.

Consumer spending on spectator sports by local residents probably also serves to slow down the recovery of the local economy after a natural disaster. The money spent on attending a sports event by residents of the home-team community necessarily precludes them from spending that money on other locally owned and operated entertainment. Furthermore, local expenditures on professional sports may actually reduce total spending in the economy as opposed to simply reallocating money among competing ends. Professional sports, which use national resource markets as opposed to locally owned and operated resources for alternative entertainment or recreational activities, may foster a net outflow of money. Most of the money spent on a night at a professional sports event goes to the athletes and owners of the team who may not live in the community in which they play. Siegfried and Zimbalist note that while 93 percent of average employees live in the area where they work, only 29 percent of NBA players do the same (and the figures are likely to be similar in the NFL and other major leagues).[29] Given the generally poor condition of the city following Katrina, it is even less likely that millionaire athletes, and those with the financial wherewithal to live elsewhere, chose to reside in the Big Easy in the immediate aftermath of the hurricane. Certainly, owner Tom Benson, who had business interests in San Antonio among other cities, showed little interest in spending money in the city.

Furthermore, the devastation of the middle and lower classes in New Orleans eliminated not just the customers, but also the labor upon which professional sports relies. Each large event at the Superdome requires approximately 2,500 part-time workers. Unfortunately, the lack of housing in New Orleans meant that no such pool of potential part-time workers was readily available in the city. Indeed, a good fraction of the workers at the facility will very likely have to come from outside the city. The leakage of money from New Orleans through athletes repatriating their incomes to their primary residences were further enhanced by ordinary workers doing the same thing in some appreciable amount because of a lack of housing in many New Orleans neighborhoods. Post-Katrina, it was even less likely that income generated through commercial sports activities remained in the city.

The prospect of hosting mega-events was perhaps a more important incentive in repairing the city's sports infrastructure. As noted previously, the city was a frequent destination for major sporting events such as the Super Bowl or college bowl games. Mega-events have the economic advantage over hosting professional franchises in that much of the spending comes from outside the region. Most spectators at regular season home games are local residents and their spending at an event does not represent new spending in the region but rather simply reallocates where economic activity occurs in the metropolitan area. A football team's gain may represent a loss for a local restaurant or music club where the local resident would have spent their entertainment dollars in the absence of a professional sports franchise. On the other hand, attendees at a mega-event are typically from out of town, so their spending represents in inflow of money to the region. Furthermore, mega-events can serve to advertise the city to national or international markets, and especially in the wake of Hurricane Katrina, might serve as an indicator that the city is open for business.

Although the direct economic impact of the return of professional sports to New Orleans was likely small, a strong case can be made for sports having an important psychological impact. While much of New Orleans's Lower 9th Ward remained a tangle of rubble and destroyed houses more than one year after Katrina, the Superdome reopened for the 2006 NFL season. The restoration of the Superdome and the return of the Saints had clear symbolic significance. In fact, the Saints' return to New Orleans on September 25, 2006, received significant national attention. The game was nationally televised on Monday Night Football and featured musical performances by U2 and Green Day before the game. The team scored their first points in their home city with a dramatic blocked punt in the first quarter. That play is immortalized in a large statue outside the stadium erected in 2012 and named "Rebirth." The statue is said to be "symbolic of New Orleans'[s] resilience in the face of disaster."[30]

Those residents who returned to the city embraced the team by purchasing a record number of season tickets for the 2006 season. In fact, in their return to the Superdome following Katrina, season ticket holders purchased every available regular season ticket for the first time in the history of the franchise.[31] The fact that the Saints played for the National Football Conference title in January of 2007, the best performance in the history of the team to that point, further cemented the team in the hearts of the city's residents. And in the decade that followed, the fan base remained solid, selling out every home game, and the waitlist for season tickets grew to 60,000. Their success at the box office was helped in large part by the success of team. In the 39 years prior to Katrina, the Saints had a 0.386-win percentage and had won only one playoff game in their history. In the twelve seasons since returning to New Orleans, a period coinciding with the acquisition of future Hall of Fame quarterback Drew Brees, the team has amassed a 0.583-win percentage and six playoff wins, including their only Super Bowl Championship in 2010.

The fans' response, however, failed to impress the Saints owner who noted that, "You haven't seen the total commitment yet. No National Football League team can live on tickets alone . . . . The next big step is that the business community needs to step up."[32] Limited by the small number of large corporations in the city and the redevelopment priorities faced by the city's small businesses, 40% of the Superdome's luxury suites remained unsold as of May 2006. As luxury suites are not part of the league's revenue sharing deal, they provide significant profits to a team's owner. The fact that Tom Benson was unsatisfied with the millions spent on the first wave of stadium repairs and improvements entirely paid for by others and with record season ticket purchases by local residents boded ill for the Saints' long-term future in New Orleans. Indeed, as noted previously, it took another nearly $400 million in tax subsidies and another round of taxpayer financed improvements to the Superdome to convince Benson to commit the team to New Orleans through 2025.[33]

It remains to be seen whether the team will be able to maintain its extraordinary level of fan interest in such a small market if the team's fortunes on the field wane. And as noted by Benson, relatively high revenues are the key to keeping teams, but that requires more than ticket sales. Even with strong attendance and generous revenue sharing from the league, the team only ranks in the middle of NFL franchises in terms of annual revenue and is near the bottom in franchise valuation.[34]

While the majority of the media attention focused on the return of the Saints to the city, New Orleans's other franchises experienced changes in the wake of Katrina. The NBA's New Orleans Hornets, renamed the Pelicans in honor of Louisiana's state bird in 2013, were relatively new to the city when Katrina hit, having arrived in only 2002 after relocating from Charlotte. Prior to the arrival of the Hornets, New Orleans had been without an NBA team since 1979 when the New Orleans Jazz moved to Utah after suffering financial difficulties in Louisiana. Prior to Katrina, the Hornets, like the Jazz before them struggled financially. They were dead last in attendance in the league during the 2004–05 season.

While not as badly damaged as the Superdome, the New Orleans Arena, built in 1999 and currently named the Smoothie King Center, was also unusable in the wake of Hurricane Katrina, necessitating a change in venue for the Hornets. An attempt to move the team to Baton Rouge was scuttled because the sports arenas in Baton Rouge were commandeered for coordinating relief efforts for New Orleans. Instead, the team was officially renamed the Oklahoma City/New Orleans Hornets for 2005–06 and 2006–07 NBA seasons, and they played 35 of 41 home games in Oklahoma during each of those seasons. Only six games were played in Louisiana in the first season, with the team splitting time between Baton Rouge and New Orleans. On March 8, 2006, the Hornets became the first professional team to play in New Orleans following the disaster. Six games were played in New Orleans in the 2006–07 season.

Given the substantial increase in attendance that the team experienced in Oklahoma City, it was somewhat surprising that the NBA and the Hornets' owner George Shinn committed to keep the team in New Orleans. In retrospect, it appears that the decision to the return the franchise to New Orleans was based more on Shinn's troubled personal history than any sound financial decision-making. By December 2010, without the means to cover the continuing losses of the team and unable to find another buyer, Shinn sold the franchise to the league.[35] Tom Benson, owner of the Saints, later purchased the team. The team has languished in the bottom quarter of the league in attendance since their return to the city.

Minor league franchises experienced the same sort of temporary boost in attendance due to civic pride as witnessed by the Saints. The New Orleans VooDoo, an Arena Football team owned by Benson, suspended play for the 2006 season due to the damage to the New Orleans Arena. When the team returned in 2007, it led the league in attendance and posted one of the highest average attendance marks in the history of the league. However, the financial success was short-lived. After the 2008 season, Benson announced that the VooDoo were ceasing operations, and the entire league declared bankruptcy within a year.

The New Orleans Zephyrs (now known as the New Orleans Baby Cakes), the city's AAA Minor League Baseball team, suffered only moderate damage to its playing facilities and was able to open its 2006 season at home. Taxpayer funded repairs cost $21 million, and the team supplemented this figure by another $5 million to add new amenities including 16 luxury suites, a swimming pool, and two hot tubs. The stadium also hosted the Tulane University baseball team in 2006 and 2007 as the university's athletic facilities suffered more extensive damage. Like many of the other local sports franchises, the team did experience a bump in attendance in its first year back with a roughly 10% increase in fans during the 2006 season over the previous season (which had ended just a few days before Katrina made landfall). Over the course of the next decade, attendance remained relatively stable for the team at roughly the same level the franchise had experienced prior to Katrina, but one-third below the peak the team reached immediately after opening their new ballpark in 1997.

Professional sports teams were not the only organizations to engage in sports-related investment following Hurricane Katrina. Tulane University, for example, engaged in a significant reconstruction program for its athletic complexes as part of its $250 million campus-wide rehabilitation effort following the hurricane.[36] Tulane, unlike the Saints, has a huge financial commitment in its campus, and it is motivated to recoup its past investment. Division 1 intercollegiate sports serve as a recruitment tool for both athletes and prospective students as the school attempts to rebuild its student body.

Apart from permanent sports franchises, mega-events also contributed to the redevelopment of the city. The country's major sports leagues were eager to appear as helpful contributors to the reconstruction of New Orleans, and the city received favorable treatment in the awarding of major events to the city. The NBA played the 2008 All-Star Game in the city. The College Football National Championship games were played at the Superdome in 2007 and 2012 and will return in 2020. The NCAA Men's Basketball Final Four was played in the city in 2012 and will return in 2022, and the Women's Final Four was played at the New Orleans Arena in 2013. The nation's biggest sporting event, the Super Bowl, took place in New Orleans in 2013 although the event was marred by a 34-minute power outage during the middle of the game. Of course, this type of incident demonstrates the importance of properly maintaining general infrastructure, investments that can often take a back seat to spending on sports infrastructure and the subsidies to the owners of sports franchises in order to convince them to keep their teams in an otherwise unattractive city, economically.

Hurricane Katrina induced a massive outflow of residents and businesses from the city of New Orleans. The city's two major professional sports teams, the NFL Saints and NBA Hornets, were among the businesses that had to leave due to the extensive damage to their infrastructure. The capital costs and other financial commitments necessary to encourage the return of the Saints and the Hornets for the long term were substantial. The images of the NFL and NBA would have been damaged if the Saints and Hornets had not at least made cameo appearances, but in the longer term, the teams and their leagues demand greater revenue streams than can be generated in their current facilities. The fact that New Orleans and the State of Louisiana were already directly subsidizing the teams indicates that pre-Katrina the teams were not generating revenues in their venues that allowed them to be financially competitive in their leagues. This paper has concluded that it may have been financially ill-advised in the post-Katrina world to direct substantial funds at refurbishing and upgrading the Superdome and New Orleans Arena or to continue to directly subsidize the franchises specifically to make the teams financially competitive.

Capital expenditures on the Superdome supplant capital expenditures on housing, schooling, and other middle-class amenities that will bring the middle class back, and the reconstruction of the Superdome in the short run should have been undertaken only after spending on housing and other infrastructure repairs. Furthermore, restoration efforts for the Superdome and New Orleans Arena should not necessarily be directed towards amenities that provide the highest revenues for sports franchises, but instead provide a multipurpose facility for the general tourist trade. Providing physical accommodation for professional sports teams did not advance the economics interests of New Orleans in the short term. Having done so exacerbated the economic problems that existed in the aftermath of the storm.

One odd consequence of Katrina is that it may well have made it virtually impossible for the Saints to leave New Orleans in the short term, while at the same time requiring substantial public investment to provide accommodations in order to keep the team in the long-run. The opportunity costs for the funds necessary to rebuild the sports infrastructure have never been higher, but the political demand for demonstrable recovery from Katrina to include the highly symbolic reconstruction of sports facilities had sharply shifted the demand for their restoration to the right. The fact that a year after the storm, a bond issue for $294 million to refurbish the Superdome was sold with relatively little resistance provided striking testimony to this assertion. Tom Benson and the Saints have benefited from financial transfers from the City of New Orleans and the NFL. These transfers very likely would have been strongly contested and may not have occurred at all in the absence of the storm.

Cities in general should be mindful of the fact that subsidies for professional sports teams eliminate the financial incentives teams would have to remain in the community following a natural or manmade disaster. Businesses that have risked their own capital and built infrastructure have a financial stake in their host community, but the Saints and Hornets, as well as most professional sports teams in the United States, have few such ties to their local communities. Paradoxically, cities have contributed in a very substantial way to the incentive for teams to abandon a city in the face of a disaster on the scale of Katrina. The owner of the New Orleans Saints was making his way out of New Orleans before Katrina, and the storm probably has increased his perception of risk and diminished his long-term financial prospects in New Orleans to a point that it is not in his financial interest to stay there without the significant public subsidies that the city has provided.

New Orleans will be rebuilt at the grassroots home by home and business by business. Locational fundamentals may well lead to the restoration of New Orleans long term. The rate at which the city was resettled and restored affected the ability of the NFL Saints and NBA Hornets to generate revenues that encouraged them to remain in the community. The Saints and the Hornets have invested little in infrastructure, and are motivated in large part by the size of future revenue streams in New Orleans relative to other cities that would like to host them. The City of New Orleans, on the other hand, has invested substantially in infrastructure for the teams, and, as a first step found it necessary to invest further in that infrastructure necessary to encourage the teams to stay. That stay would have been short-lived in the absence of the return of the middle class so necessary to support the team and give the city any chance to recoup its infrastructure investment. To achieve this end, the order of capital expenditures in New Orleans should have been levees, housing, middle class amenities, infrastructure for nonresident businesses, and lastly those industries that cater to the entertainment needs of the middle class.

The role of sports in the economic recovery of the city is dubious aside from serving as a symbol that the city remains vital. The repair of the Superdome and the New Orleans Arena was an expensive tease in that regard. The investment in sports infrastructure did little to provide what was needed for the community to recover from the storm. Sports and the hosting of mega-events may actually undermine longer-term recovery through deflecting capital spending from where it is needed most and crowding out those workers and residents who are involved in the essential rebuilding process. Sport may have provided a pleasant recreational amenity to returning residents, but it is reasonable to ask whether the economic interests of the sport elites, out of financial and economic development necessity, should have taken a seat on the bench in the interest of the greater good.

III

Race and Respectability

CHAPTER NINE

The Sugar Bowl

Manhood, Race, and Southern Womanhood in New Orleans, 1935–1965

STEPHEN H. NORWOOD

During the Great Depression of the 1930s, southern business, civic, and university leaders determined to use college football to transform northerners' image of the South from an economically stagnant, impoverished "hookworm belt" into a modern, dynamic society in order to attract outside corporate investment capital and tourism. By establishing New Year's Day bowl games scheduled a few weeks after the college football season ended, which the North was not able to host for climatic reasons, the southern business elite hoped to forge strong intersectional bonds that could erase the longstanding stigma of southern economic inferiority and insularity and Civil War defeat. When the Sugar Bowl began in New Orleans on January 1, 1935, the only major existing postseason college football contest was the Rose Bowl in Pasadena, California, which was first played in 1902 and then every year after 1916. Optimally, Dixie's bowl games would pit a southern host team against a Northern opponent. The southern elite believed that inviting northern college teams and accompanying journalists and radio broadcasters to their section of the country would promote a better understanding among northerners of Dixie's racial segregation system.

By 1941, there was a general consensus among the nation's major sportswriters that the Sugar Bowl ranked behind only the Rose Bowl as a postseason football game; some believed that it had surpassed the Rose Bowl. The other two major bowl games were Miami's Orange Bowl, which began at the same time as the Sugar Bowl, and the Cotton Bowl, first played in Dallas in 1937. The 1941 Sugar Bowl matched the nation's only two undefeated and untied college

The festivities of the 1942 Sugar Bowl between the Fordham University Rams and the University of Missouri Tigers. Photo courtesy of The Historic New Orleans Collection, Williams Research Center, New Orleans, Louisiana.

teams, Boston College and the University of Tennessee, providing what football experts considered the best contest of any of the postseason games, including the Rose Bowl. Grantland Rice, the nation's most well-known sportswriter at the time, found it significant that neither of these teams had waited to hear from the Rose Bowl before accepting the Sugar Bowl's invitation.[1] The Sugar Bowl was the only postseason contest scheduled as the culmination of a week-long sports extravaganza, a "Carnival of Sports" that included yachting races, basketball games, tennis and boxing matches, golf contests, and track and field competition. This "gave New Orleans the appearance of an Olympic city" in the days before the Sugar Bowl, except for the absence of African American athletes during the event's first decades.[2] Only the Rose Bowl had a greater seating capacity than Tulane Stadium, where the Sugar Bowl was played. Many college football powers considered the Sugar Bowl the most attractive post-season contest to which they could be invited because of New Orleans' exotic image and superior reputation as a tourist destination, with many opportunities for revelry. New Orleans's appeal to northern schools declined dramatically during the 1950s, as teams became increasingly uncomfortable over segregationist practices that required them to leave their African American players at home for the Sugar Bowl or bench them.

C. Vann Woodward noted that when the South first started to industrialize in the 1880s, backed by Northern, British, and French investment capital, its staging of massive industrial expositions that celebrated manufacturing and technological progress was accompanied by a "cult of archaism," a romanticizing of an agrarian Old South and its Lost Cause. This reflected the mixed feelings many southerners harbored about modernization and the loss of a distinctive regional identity.[3] The Sugar Bowl and other Southern bowl games similarly combined aggressive promotion of the New South's industrial and commercial opportunities with nostalgia for a mythic antebellum past. The Sugar Bowl, more than the other southern bowl games, surrounded itself with parties and pageants honoring an idealized antebellum southern womanhood, in which Louisiana women appeared in the elaborate dress of the plantation mistress. By contrast, the Orange Bowl, staged in Miami, a city that (like Dallas) lacked New Orleans's lineage and roots in the antebellum past, more often presented women as modern bathing beauties to advertise its beaches.

By the 1930s, the South, having emerged as one of the nation's leading college football regions, was at the forefront in offering scholarships to prospects. This was in part because the South's relative poverty and economic underdevelopment made it difficult for college football players to obtain jobs or bank loans.[4] Southern athletes' semi-professionalism and proficiency in a sport closely associated with modern industrial and bureaucratic values: time-discipline, tightly coordinating the work of several persons within a group, specialization of roles, and precise statistical measurement, made the southern athlete appear as modern as his northern counterpart, or more so.

In late 1927, New Orleans *Item* sports editor Fred Digby conceived the idea of New Orleans hosting a postseason football classic, and a year later secured the backing of the city's Association of Commerce sports committee. Initially Digby encountered resistance from persons of influence who believed a bowl game in New Orleans would fail to attract a significant attendance unless a Louisiana or Texas team participated. Although Digby and New Orleans mayor A.J. O'Keefe argued that a postseason bowl game in New Orleans would enhance the South's image, the Southern Conference rejected their request to sponsor the project, preferring to keep its members free to accept Rose Bowl invitations. During the next several years, however, prominent business and civic leaders became convinced that a postseason football game featuring major college teams, particularly a North-South contest, would provide a needed economic stimulus for New Orleans. Sponsors of the classic organized in March 1934 as the Mid-Winter Sports Association, and decided on the game's name by polling city residents.[5]

The Sugar Bowl started on "a shoestring," but within a few years was firmly established, receiving extensive press coverage across the nation. By the late 1930s, hordes of tourists were pouring into New Orleans during the week before the game, filling up the hotels and restaurants and making major purchases in local stores. New Orleans *Times-Picayune* sports editor Bill Keefe reported two weeks before the 1941 Sugar Bowl that the Mid-Winter Sports Association was receiving checks for seats from people in "nearly every city in the nation and some from foreign countries."[6] The passage of bond issues allowed Tulane Stadium to expand its seating capacity twice between 1935 and 1940, to 70,000, with parking space for 20,000 automobiles. Jerry Nason of the Boston *Globe* described it as "massive, double-decked, and a spectator's paradise," with seats close to the field "even behind the goal posts." There were numerous ramps throughout the stadium to the upper levels, so visitors were required to do very little stair climbing.[7] Wirt Gammon of the Chattanooga *Times,* covering the 1941 Sugar Bowl, celebrated Tulane Stadium as "majestic." From the "high press box" he was enthralled with the view of New Orleans's skyline, which "streaks along the horizon," a symbol of dynamic urban growth. It was like being at the top of a New York skyscraper: "the field appear[s] small and the players midgets."[8]

The first Sugar Bowl game featured the desired North-South matchup, which packed more emotional intensity than the Rose Bowl's East-West or East-Midwest competition. The Mid-Winter Sports Association signed up two imposing teams, Philadelphia's Temple University Owls (7–0–2), coached by the legendary Pop Warner, representing the North, and New Orleans's Tulane University Green Wave (9–1), as the southern host team. Warner had coached Jim Thorpe at Carlisle Indian School from 1907 to 1912. He later recalled that Temple's fans "were wildly enthusiastic" that their school had been selected to play in the first Sugar Bowl, an indication that the new post-season contest had already developed significant prestige. Several hundred Temple fans came to New Orleans for the game by train; the school band made the two-day trip from Philadelphia by bus. The game was played before a sellout crowd at Tulane Stadium, whose capacity at the time was about 24,000 (compared to the Rose Bowl's 85,000).[9] The New Orleans *Item* invoked Civil War imagery in describing Tulane's victory, seizing the opportunity to praise the South's martial spirit: "The band played Dixie! And the flaming courage of Chancellorsville, the daring of Jeb Stuart's raiders, and the gallant defense of the Seven Days around Richmond were reenacted yesterday as Tulane defeated Temple, 20–14, in the North-South football game that inaugurated the Sugar Bowl series."[10]

The inaugural Sugar Bowl included pageantry similar to that accompanying dedication ceremonies for monuments to the Lost Cause that the United Daughters of the Confederacy erected in the late nineteenth and early twentieth centuries, highlighting southern feminine purity, innocence and delicacy.[11] At halftime an enormous sugar bowl was placed on the fifty-yard line. Inside were standing "two little girls dressed in the colors of the two [competing] colleges." They were greeted at midfield by "Father New Orleans, dressed in the costume of the Cavalier," projecting to Yankee visitors an image of southern aristocracy and cultivation.[12] Little girls were the most vulnerable females. The halftime event was designed to draw a sharp distinction between the sexes, and to emphasize the South's determination to provide the "weaker sex" with male protection. The football player could be seen as a stand-in for the vanished Confederate soldier.

The seventh Sugar Bowl on New Year's Day, 1941, between the Boston College Eagles and the Tennessee Volunteers, was considered by its boosters and the local and national media as the most successful to date, revealing the advantages New Orleans enjoyed over other cities in staging postseason contests. Some northern commentators found the game deeply upsetting, however, because Boston College, a Jesuit institution, agreed to the Mid-Winter Sports Association's demand that the Eagles' lone African American player, first-string running back Lightnin' Lou Montgomery, not play to comply with New Orleans custom. Boston College had benched Montgomery the previous year when it played Clemson in the Cotton Bowl in Dallas and withheld him from 1939 home games at Fenway Park in Boston at the insistence of its Southern opponents, Auburn and Florida. Curtis Sanford, president of the Cotton Bowl Athletic Association, had announced two weeks before the 1940 Cotton Bowl that Montgomery would not be allowed to play in the New Year's contest "in view of the general attitude toward Negroes in Texas." He could travel to Texas with the team, but not play. Montgomery therefore declined to go.[13] On the day of the Cotton Bowl, Montgomery telegraphed his teammates that he had driven to Philadelphia so that he could get better radio reception of the game. He told them he would be with them "in spirit while listening to the game from Philadelphia."[14]

The African American press expressed disgust that Boston College had readily capitulated to southern demands to discard Montgomery. The Baltimore *Afro-American* condemned the school's administration for "repeating the jellyfish act for the third time" for the Cotton Bowl. The New York *Amsterdam News* denounced Boston College as "spineless." Chicago *Defender* sports editor Fay Young considered it ominous that Boston College had allowed "the old Confederacy to dictate" to it and denied Montgomery the right to play "within the shadows of the Robert Gould Shaw monument . . . and near . . . the spot where Crispus Attucks fell." African American journalist Mabe Kountze, "speaking for the Negro National Newspaper All-American Association and other sports editors of more than 100 weeklies of the Associated Negro Press," published a letter to the editor in the Boston *Globe* expressing outrage with "the utter indifference" of many of Boston's civic leaders toward Boston College's treatment of Montgomery. The *Afro-American* derided Northern white colleges' excuse that they "make their schedules decades ahead of time." When Boston College opened its 1940 season in New Orleans against Tulane, it acceded to Tulane's demand that Montgomery not play. The *Afro-American* pointed out that Boston College had only recently placed Tulane on its schedule, at a time when Montgomery was enrolled there.[15]

A few sportswriters in the mainstream press similarly accused northern colleges of complicity in the South's segregation system for benching their African American players when they played southern schools. Jesse Abramson of the New York *Herald Tribune* in 1938, for example, condemned New York University and the University of Michigan for holding their African American players out of games against southern universities. Abramson demanded that the northern schools cancel any game in which an African American was not permitted to play.[16]

Southern sportswriters like Fred Digby, by contrast, considered Boston College's enthusiasm for scheduling games with southern opponents an important step forward in promoting "a better understanding" in the North of Dixie's "traditions and institutions." He quoted from an editorial by sportswriter Bill Cunningham in the conservative Boston *Post* that praised the 1941 Sugar Bowl as an important "milepost in the era of good feeling" between the sections that had developed because the Boston College administration had sought out southern competition. Cunningham described Boston College's 1941 football schedule as "so Southern in complexion that Boston College can almost be cast as a member of that faraway conference." He reported approvingly that a Bostonian who had attended the Eagles' game with Tulane in September had told him: "You know, I've had the South all wrong."[17]

The 1941 Sugar Bowl between Boston College and Tennessee was a "matchmaker's paradise," with the two top scoring teams in the nation, one northern and one southern. *Washington Post* sportswriter Shirley Povich stated that the Rose Bowl, "once reserved for the Brahmins of college football," would "be playing No. 2 fiddle to the Sugar Bowl." Boston College had attracted the attention of Sugar Bowl officials with a convincing 27–7 victory in New Orleans over a highly regarded and heavily favored Tulane team, played "in the worst Louisiana humidity imaginable." Boston College again agreed that Lou Montgomery would not play. Further intensifying southern institutions' objection to African American players' participation in football games was the fear of their coming into contact with white women at the social festivities accompanying the games. Tulane University arranged a postgame football dance for the players after its game with Boston College. The Eagles handily beat another southern team, Auburn, later in the season, 33–7, earning southern sportswriters' respect. Atlanta *Constitution* sports editor Jack Troy noted that Auburn rarely lost a game by more than one touchdown. He remarked that Boston College's "mastodonic men" had "ripped the Auburn line to shreds."[18]

The 1941 Sugar Bowl also had great appeal because of the teams' contrasting style of play. Slightly favored Tennessee was, according to the Boston *Globe*'s Jerry Nason, "what the Southern scribes call a bang-bang team," with a punishing ground game and "smashing" blocking and tackling. It was the first team ever to play in three bowl games, having beaten Oklahoma in the 1939 Orange Bowl and losing to Southern Cal in the 1940 Rose Bowl. Boston College was credited with a more versatile offense that included a dangerous passing game centered on tailback Chuckin' Charlie O'Rourke. Grantland Rice, who had succeeded Walter Camp in selecting All-American teams and had been covering college football for decades, stated that he considered Boston College "one of the greatest teams ever developed in the East." Eight of its players were chosen in that year's National Football League draft, along with four of Tennessee's.[19]

Boston College's Frank Leahy and Tennessee's Major Bob Neyland were both considered top-flight head coaches. Leahy had been a regular tackle at Notre Dame under the legendary Knute Rockne, and then, as line coach at Fordham, had charge of the famed Seven Blocks of Granite.[20] Neyland's record at Tennessee before the 1941 Sugar Bowl was an incredible 119 wins, 13 losses, and 8 ties. His coaching reflected the influence of New South values in southern college football. The Nashville *Banner* reported that Neyland emphasized "precision and timing." He inculcated a strong work ethic in his players. They "rehearsed and rehearsed" his plays until they could perform them "with split second accuracy."[21]

Coach Frank Leahy decided to leave for the South two weeks before the Sugar Bowl, ascribing the previous year's Cotton Bowl loss to insufficient training. He had concluded that teams remaining in the North too long before a bowl game were at a disadvantage because snow and ice cut down their practice time. A noisy and highly enthusiastic crowd of 5,000 people assembled at Boston's South Station to see the Eagles off, a clear indication that the Sugar Bowl had become a subject of major interest in New England. Boston mayor Maurice Tobin "had to battle his way through the mob to board the train and wish the players good luck." Massachusetts governor Leverett Saltonstall wired Coach Leahy his best wishes for victory.[22]

The Boston College Eagles' lengthy chartered railroad trip from Boston to their training camp in the tiny Gulf town of Bay St. Louis, Mississippi, fifty-two miles from New Orleans, provided many opportunities for forging and celebrating bonds of friendship between the North and the South. St. Stanislaus Academy, a Catholic school in Bay St. Louis, provided the training facilities. The Boston *Herald* reported that the Eagles' "most successful stop" on their way to Mississippi was at Spartanburg, South Carolina, where they "bumped into fifty Converse College girls who were leaving for their Christmas vacation." The *Herald* remarked that the train "almost didn't leave, so interested were the athletes" in the young South Carolina women. The Boston College newspaper noted that when their school's football team had traveled through the Palmetto state earlier in the season on its way to play Tulane in New Orleans, its train had been pursued by a fleet of cars carrying the Clemson football team, who yelled out "good-luck cheers" to the "happily surprised" Eagles.[23]

The train trip from Boston at the same time exposed Boston College players and students traveling to the Sugar Bowl to the grinding rural poverty below the Mason-Dixon Line, an image of the South that New Orleans boosters hoped the Sugar Bowl could help erase in Northern minds. The Boston College student newspaper, *The Heights,* reported that the first contingent of the school's students riding buses to New Orleans were shocked while stopping in Bristol, Virginia, to see the condition of hillbillies who came into town from their shacks on Saturday night. At the depot, the team encountered "an old man and his two grandchildren" who were entirely illiterate, "had never heard of Boston, or Massachusetts, [and] did not know what a college was." The trio "had walked ten miles," as they did every Saturday night, into Bristol "just to sit in the depot, say nothing, and watch the crowds go by." On the bleak Alabama prairie, the Bostonians saw similar "tumble-down" shacks, and occasionally a town, with "red-dirt roads, some blocked with knee-deep mud." The Boston *Herald* reported that the train carrying the Boston College football players to Mississippi had slowed down at Readville, North Carolina, to allow them to "get a good look" at a wrecked train, which had spilled a massive amount of coal along the tracks. The *Herald* stated that "pickanninies by the score" were busying themselves "collecting the coal in big burlap sacks." This meant that hundreds of southern families, who ordinarily would go through the winter shivering in their domiciles, would have some coal for heating.[24]

The Boston College Eagles received "a grand welcome" from city and state officials and members of the Sugar Bowl executive committee when they arrived in Bay St. Louis. Mississippi Lieutenant Governor Dennis Murphree and the city commissioner presided at "a gala reception breakfast" for them. Every store window was "plastered" with signs reading "Welcome, Boston" and displaying Boston College's maroon and gold colors. Every passing automobile that encountered an Eagle on the street offered him a ride.[25] In yet another gesture of sectional reconciliation, Murphree reminded the Eagles that they were not the first residents of their state to visit Bay St. Louis; many Massachusetts men in blue uniforms had been through the town "from 1861 to 1865." The lieutenant governor also mentioned that a great Bostonian, former world heavyweight boxing champion John L. Sullivan, had been jailed in or near Bay St. Louis for participating in an illegal prizefight during the 1880s. Murphree then told the Boston College players "to go out and fight Tennessee tooth and nail." He assured them: "If there is any talk of punishment, I'll just pardon you."[26]

Joseph David, vice-president of the Mid-Winter Sports Association and head of the Sugar Bowl ticket committee, invited the Boston College football team to a Christmas party at his "palatial residence," and arranged for them to meet an equal number of the "fairest" young women from local colleges. New Orleans' mayor Robert Maestri's personal chef was in charge of the "feast."[27]

Lou Montgomery came to Bay St. Louis from New Orleans to watch the Eagles' practice but was not invited to the Christmas party and was confined to attending exclusively African American events. He did not stay with the team but was housed in New Orleans and at the all-African American St. Augustine's Seminary, a quarter of a mile from where the Eagles trained. The New Orleans African American community enthusiastically welcomed Montgomery, who was "hard pressed to stay up with the social functions" it staged for him. Shortly before the Sugar Bowl, Montgomery starred in New Orleans' third annual Chocolate Bowl, a game between two African American professional football teams played at Xavier University, a black New Orleans school. The Boston *Globe* reported that Montgomery's drawing power was responsible for the capacity 4,000-person crowd that packed tiny Xavier Stadium. Montgomery led his team of New Orleans black all-stars to a 12–6 come-from-behind victory over the Baton Rouge Patriots. Park officials called the crowd the largest ever assembled for an African American football game in New Orleans history. Montgomery threw a thirty-yard touchdown pass and ran seventy-yards to the Baton Rouge one-yard line. He burst into the end zone on the next play to account for both of his team's scores.[28]

Boston College's lopsided victories over Tulane and Auburn had convinced most southern sportswriters and football fans that the Eagles were a worthy opponent for Tennessee. Several of the South's leading sportswriters had been in attendance at Tulane Stadium and Fenway Park for both games. Atlanta *Constitution* sports editor Jack Troy was impressed with the Eagles' balanced offense and "elephantine" linemen. Boston College tailback Charlie O'Rourke, the team's "sparkplug," was a genuine triple threat: one of the nation's best passers and an excellent runner and kicker.[29]

Boston College enjoyed much more support in the Crescent City than other northern teams that played there because it was a Jesuit institution and New Orleans' population was heavily Catholic. Ten of the Eagles' starters, however, were from Massachusetts or Rhode Island, where the Catholic population was more ethnically diverse than in Louisiana.[30] The presence of Polish-Americans and those of other Eastern European ethnic backgrounds on the Eagles' roster caused many southerners, including the sportswriters, to perceive Boston College's team as strikingly different. The Nashville *Banner,* praising Boston College's Henry Toczylowski as one of the nation's premier blocking backs, referred to him as the "quarterback on this team of unpronounceable names." *Banner* sports editor Fred Russell stated that the person with the most difficult task at the Sugar Bowl would be the radio announcer, whom he joked "broke the fan belt on an adenoid" rehearsing how to say the Eagles' names on the air.[31]

Birmingham *News* sportswriter Zipp Newman predicted that southerners outside Louisiana would view the Sugar Bowl as the occasion for Tennessee to avenge Boston College's defeats of the southern schools, Tulane and Auburn. The honor of southern football was at stake. Newman emphasized that the Sugar Bowl "definitely puts the Southeastern Conference on the spot."[32]

The New Orleans press, aware of the large influx of northern corporate executives into New Orleans for the Sugar Bowl, used the game as an opportunity to run features about the city's business opportunities and tourist attractions. The *Sunday Item-Tribune,* for example, published a thirty-page rotogravure Mid-Winter section to publicize "the beauties, attractions and advantages of our region to people in other parts of the Americas." It was modeled on the Los Angeles *Times*'s Mid-Winter issue, which had contributed enormously "to the advertisement and up-building of Southern California."[33]

Sugar Bowl promoters alleviated any anxiety they experienced about highlighting their city's dynamic industrial and commercial development and fraternizing with thousands of northern guests by simultaneously immersing themselves in the Lost Cause mystique. They sponsored as a Sugar Bowl attraction a gala "Beauregard Ball" at the Municipal Auditorium to raise funds to restore the home of Confederate general Pierre G.T. Beauregard, a Louisianan. It was billed as "a real Carnival ball with a Confederate theme." The ball followed tableaux and exhibition dances "commemorative of the Old South." Attendees wore elaborate antebellum costumes. The wife of Louisiana's governor occupied a special box, along with two women who were descendants of General Beauregard. Two Confederate veterans who resided at the Soldiers' Home were brought to the ball.[34] The gala premiere of the movie *Gone With the Wind* a year before in Atlanta had similarly combined aged Confederate veterans, waitresses in antebellum hoopskirts, and leaders of Atlanta society with celebrities from Hollywood's technologically advanced film industry and northern journalists and guests.[35]

As the Sugar Bowl game approached, it was evident that it had become a major focus of national, and even some international interest. The New Orleans *Item* reported on December 29 that the Sugar Bowl was filling up New Orleans "with folks from Keokuk to Johannesburg, South Africa, and from San Francisco to Costa Rica." The thousands of people converging on the city for the Sugar Bowl constituted the largest number to visit New Orleans for any occasion in the city's history.[36] Nashville *Tennessean* sports editor Raymond Johnson commented that New Orleans on the eve of the Sugar Bowl resembled

Louisville just before the Kentucky Derby or Indianapolis "the morning of the 500-mile auto race." "Boisterous crowds" packed hotel lobbies sporting Boston College's maroon and gold colors and the orange and white of Tennessee. Life-sized portraits of players on both teams were displayed in shop windows. Even "shops devoted exclusively to women's wear" were "dressed up with pictures, pennants, and signs having to do with the game." The *New York Times* reported the erection of enormous electric signs, "Times Square fashion," to welcome those attending the Sugar Bowl."[37]

The president of the Mid-Winter Sports Association declared that the Sugar Bowl surpassed any other advertising medium in drawing out-of-town visitors to New Orleans. It provided thousands of outsiders the opportunity "to see the vast resources of the great state of Louisiana." New Orleans hotels were totally booked, and tourist cabins were taxed to capacity. The New Orleans Association of Commerce and the Hotel Association placed more than 4,000 Sugar Bowl visitors unable to find lodging in private homes. Those fortunate enough to find hotel rooms had to fight their way through the lobbies to reach the sidewalk. Restaurants and bars were jammed. Downtown auto traffic slowed to a crawl.[38]

The 1941 Sugar Bowl, attracting enormous national attention by matching the only undefeated and untied college teams, forged bonds among sportswriters from all sections of the United States. The New Orleans *Item* reported that the Tulane Stadium press box, the nation's largest with a capacity of 261, "for the first time was loaded to the gills." Seated there "were big names from all sections of the United States." Among them were Stan Woodward, sports editor of the New York *Herald Tribune* and president of the New York Football Writers' Association; Arthur Daley of the *New York Times;* Arch Ward of the Chicago *Tribune,* founder of the annual College All-Star Game; and Frank O'Gara of the Philadelphia *Inquirer.* New Orleans newspapers published Boston sportswriters' columns about the game, and Boston newspapers ran those of southern sportswriters. The Sugar Bowl committee feted 100 of the visiting sportswriters at a New Year's Eve party at the famous New Orleans French restaurant Antoine's, where they were served café brulot, oysters à la Rockefeller, and poulet chanteclair.[39] Crews from all five of the nation's major newsreel companies were in New Orleans to film the game: MGM, Paramount, Fox Movietone, Universal, and Pathe, assuring coast-to-coast coverage of the Sugar Bowl in movie theaters.[40]

Fans poured into the Sugar Bowl from all parts of the United States on sixteen special trains, as well as on regular trains, in automobiles, and even on airplanes, including Boston mayor Maurice Tobin, Tennessee's governor Prentice Cooper, US Senator Kenneth McKellar, and Memphis political machine boss Edward Crump. Birmingham, Alabama was the first out-of- state city to put on special trains for the Sugar Bowl.[41] Knoxville, Tennessee, home of the Volunteers, made sure that residents unable to travel to New Orleans could hear the game on the radio by making January 1, 1941 what the Knoxville *News-Sentinel* called "the most widely observed New Year's Day probably in the city's history." City, county, and federal offices, railroad shops, most retail stores, beauty parlors, the city library, and military draft and recruiting offices shut down, and no mail was delivered. Only the textile mills, most of them with defense orders, and some other large factories were operating.[42]

The 1941 Sugar Bowl game, ending in a 19–13 Boston College victory, was considered the most thrilling yet played, and set a new attendance record of 73,181, despite the fact that for only the second time since 1935 the host team was not a Louisiana school, either Tulane or Louisiana State (LSU). Stan Woodward in the New York *Herald Tribune* called it one of the greatest games in football history, a "rock and sock" contest that left those in the stands and the press box "goggle-eyed." The Boston *Herald* reported that "the tackling and blocking were so fierce that even veteran observers of college football said they had never seen anything to equal it outside of professional competition." The Boston *Globe* dwelled on the battering meted out to players on both teams. The Eagles' Henry Woronicz had taken an elbow to the cheek, which was badly puffed out. He growled that he had "paid back the score." The game had at times devolved into a boxing match. Boston College end Gene Goodreault's mouth was so swollen he could barely speak. He stated that Tennessee blocking back Ike Peel "almost took my head off. He came up with those hands so fast I didn't have a chance to duck." The Volunteers "put in a sorry appearance" the next day at breakfast, looking like "they'd been tagged with everything but the goalposts." The New York *Herald Tribune* reported that Boston College had been the crowd favorite, even though it faced a southern opponent.[43] The Eagles' Catholicism was obviously an important factor, along with their being the underdog.

Boston College's upset victory was particularly dramatic because the Eagles overcame a 13–7 halftime deficit and broke a 13–13 deadlock with only two minutes and forty seconds left in the game. Tailback Charley O'Rourke moved the Eagles eighty yards down the field, passing to receivers Ed Zabilski and Monk Maznicki "with the unerring marksmanship of a Kentucky mountaineer," in

Arthur Daley's words. With the ball on the Tennessee twenty-four-yard line, the 158-pound O'Rourke faked a pass from the T-formation, ran one way, and then cut back in another direction, as the Eagles' blockers "chopp[ed] down everyone in sight." Like a "whirling dervish," O'Rourke faked out the two remaining Volunteers between him and the goal line, leaving the first "flat on his face" and handing the second a similar "New Year's Day gift."[44]

Southern sportswriters praised the Eagles' grit and determination in coming from behind and defeating an outstanding Tennessee team. The nation's press and the Sugar Bowl's promoters claimed that the strong performances of both teams and the participants' intensity showed that both sides had covered themselves with glory, as in the Civil War. The postgame celebrations also underscored the theme of intersectional unity and romance. While the Volunteers departed for home quickly, the Eagles found "a plentiful supply of gorgeous southern belles on hand" to help them forget the austerity of their football training. A supper dance was given for the Boston College players, and "many a sweet smile rewarded the 19–13 conquerors of Tennessee."[45]

The largest crowd ever to assemble at Boston's South Station, estimated between 60,000 and 100,000 people, provided a "monster reception" for the returning Eagles in "swirling" snow when they returned to the Hub on January 4. The Associated Press's Frank Carey guessed that the cheers that greeted Charlie O'Rourke when he stepped off the train equaled anything General Andrew Jackson might have received following his victory over the British in 1814 in the only comparable battle ever waged in New Orleans.[46]

On January 9, 1941, the Boston College Eagles were the guests of honor at the first Boston Chamber of Commerce dinner ever held for a football team, attended by more than 1,000 people. It featured speeches by Governor Leverett Saltonstall, Mayor Tobin, Boston College president the Rev. William J. Murphy, Eagles quarterback Henry Toczylowski, and New Orleans Association of Commerce president John Dane. Boston College's participation in the Sugar Bowl had clearly contributed to forging stronger North-South bonds. In his address, John Dane not only used the Sugar Bowl to extol the New South, boasting of how New Orleans benefited from having a "huge" modern stadium, but even recommended to Boston's civic leaders that they consider building a bigger one for their city, like Tulane Stadium.[47]

In 1956, Lou Montgomery told reporters that he resented that Boston College had required him to sit out games against southern schools, including home games in Boston, as well as the 1941 Sugar Bowl and 1940 Cotton

Bowl. Responding to Montgomery, John P. Curley, Boston College graduate manager who had charge of travel arrangements for the football team, declared that "Jim Crow seemed to be the accepted thing" at the time. Curley confirmed that Boston College had not disputed the southern colleges' demands to bench Montgomery. The Rev. Fr. Maurice Dulles, Boston College faculty moderator, added that "it might have been physically unsafe for Lou to play in the Sugar Bowl."[48]

After 1942, in which another Jesuit school, New York City's Fordham University, defeated the University of Missouri 2 to 0, there were no more Sugar Bowls matching northern and southern teams until the mid-1950s, unless St. Mary's of California, which played Oklahoma A & M in 1946, or West Virginia, Georgia Tech's opponent in 1954, can be considered northern. This absence of northern teams was likely due to World War II travel restrictions and to postwar complications involving race. By the late 1940s, northern colleges, whose teams contained many war veterans, were less willing to placate southern schools by benching their African American players in football games.[49]

The next Sugar Bowl in which segregation became a factor was the 1955 game between the US Naval Academy (Navy) and the University of Mississippi (Ole Miss). The former, although located in Annapolis, Maryland and notorious for its past racist practices, was considered "northern." The New Orleans *Item* ran a cartoon showing a uniformed sailor offering a bouquet of flowers to a smiling, attractive blonde woman labeled "Sugar" Bowl, as an older, mustachioed and goateed man identified as "Ole Miss" rushed up waving a cane, yelling angrily, "Clear Out Ya' Yankee Gob!" The US Navy, as Cold War tensions with the Soviet Union intensified, saw an opportunity in the Sugar Bowl to promote enlistments and showcase its modern fleet and advanced weaponry in the Gulf of Mexico near New Orleans. It plastered New Orleans with recruiting posters. Navy had only appeared in a bowl game once before, in Pasadena in 1924.[50]

The Sugar Bowl was the only 1955 bowl game matching two teams that the wire services ranked in the top ten, with Navy fifth and Ole Miss's Rebels sixth. It was an ideal matchup, with Mississippi (9–1) considered the nation's best defensive team, having allowed only forty-seven points in ten games, and Navy (7–2) ranked fourth in total offense, with 393.8 yards a game. For the first time since 1941, the Sugar Bowl pitted the Eastern against the Southeastern champion, and again clearly overshadowed the Rose Bowl.[51]

Indicative of the importance the US Navy placed on the Sugar Bowl game as an opportunity to display its power and readiness, many of its top brass were conspicuously in attendance. The Navy's delegation, headed by US Secretary of the Navy Charles S. Thomas, included ten admirals and the Naval Academy superintendent. In the obligatory reference to the Civil War that accompanied North-South Sugar Bowl contests, the New Orleans *Item* described the Navy's "invasion" of the Queen City of the Bayous as ranking in scale only behind that led by Union Navy Admiral David Glasgow Farragut's in 1862. The *Item* reported that the largest US Navy warship capable of navigating the Mississippi River, the aircraft carrier *Monterey,* was steaming to New Orleans from Pensacola for the game. An enormous Navy blimp brought from South Carolina hovered over New Orleans for the Sugar Bowl. The chancellor of the University of Mississippi joked that he hoped the Sugar Bowl was not causing the Navy to leave the nation's Atlantic and Pacific coasts undefended.[52]

Navy's presence in the Sugar Bowl made the audience truly international for the first time in the history of any bowl game. US Navy vessels in ports all over the world staged an "open house" for people to come on board and listen to the Sugar Bowl game over the radio or to watch it on television. Army's policy was not to participate in bowl games. Within the United States, the Sugar Bowl was televised coast-to-coast.[53]

The 1955 Sugar Bowl was marked by the first challenge to its segregated seating policies to have any effect. The US Navy, under strong pressure from civil rights organizations, insisted on its personnel being seated together, without regard to race. The Navy, which had proportionately more southerners in its officer corps than the other armed services, was long considered the most racist branch of the US armed forces. African Americans in the Navy had been largely confined to jobs as mess-men and to other menial work. The US Navy high command argued that it was unfeasible to mix white and black seamen together, given the tight quarters on ships. Navy had no African Americans on its football team. In April 1941, Harvard University had acceded to the Naval Academy's demand not to play the African American member of its lacrosse team, Lucius Alexis, Jr., in a game in Annapolis. Boston sportswriter Dave Egan, among others, had forcefully condemned the Navy's "brass hats" and Harvard for preventing Alexis from playing.[54]

The National Association for the Advancement of Colored People (NAACP) protested to the US Navy several weeks before the 1955 Sugar Bowl against the stipulation printed on nearly all the tickets that they were to be used by "Caucasians only." The Navy then secured permission to seat persons in the 13,000-seat section it had been allocated on the east side of Tulane Stadium without regard to race. As a result, eleven African American recruits among the 196 the Navy inducted in the week prior to the Sugar Bowl sat with the white enlistees. A few African American Navy personnel already in the service also sat in this section. The Sugar Bowl segregated the remainder of seats in Tulane Stadium, whose capacity had been expanded to 85,000. African Americans not associated with the Navy purchased only 550 tickets of the 700 Jim Crow seats set aside for African Americans, located in what was called "the Eagle's Nest" in the uppermost part of the north end zone. A coach at Dillard University, an African American school, declared that the Sugar Bowl's segregationist policy had destroyed any interest in the game among New Orleans blacks. He told the *Atlanta Daily World* that he had tried to give away Sugar Bowl tickets to local African Americans but found no takers.[55]

The crowning of a Sugar Bowl Queen for the first time in the game's existence was undoubtedly motivated by increasing white anxiety in Louisiana over civil rights pressure to erode the barrier between the races. Segregationists argued that racial integration would lead to miscegenation, and thus threatened the purity and innocence of the southern white female, for whom the white-gowned, gloved Sugar Bowl Queen provided a model. The first Sugar Bowl Queen was a student from Thibodaux, Louisiana, attending St. Mary's Dominican College.[56]

To solidify North-South bonds in a time of stress, and to publicize the bowl games nationally, Jimmy Patton from Ole Miss's football team, along with a player from Arkansas's Cotton Bowl team and one from Duke's Orange Bowl team, joined their respective Bowl Queens in New York in an appearance on television's *Two for the Money* quiz show. The Bowl Queens assisted the football players in answering the quiz questions, and then accompanied them to the Copacabana night club and to see the Manhattan sights.[57]

Navy "torpedoed" Ole Miss in the 1955 Sugar Bowl by a score of 21–0 before a record crowd of 82,100, while delivering a small blow against racial segregation. The Middies "blocked and blockaded the Rebels just as effectively as did Admiral David Glasgow Farragut's flotilla" in capturing New Orleans during the Civil War. They "shredded" Ole Miss's line despite giving away eighteen pounds-a-man. As with Boston College in 1941, northern inventiveness helped make the difference for Navy against the more stolid southerners. Navy used "fourteen variations" on defense, and "against these bewildering and tricky techniques the Mississippi attack was stagnant."[58]

During the mid-1950s, Louisiana segregationists waged a determined, often violent campaign to maintain the Jim Crow system, as African American grassroots civil rights activists, the *Louisiana Weekly,* including sports editor

Jim Hall, and the NAACP pressed their efforts to desegregate public facilities in New Orleans, including those related to sports. These protests caused some concern among Sugar Bowl committee members and southern football coaches, because they feared northern schools might no longer be willing to bench their African American players, who were becoming more numerous in the postwar period. Northern schools might also balk at playing in a stadium in which segregated seating was required in all sections, as the Naval Academy had. Because New Orleans boxing promoters were reluctant to stage interracial bouts because of stiff local opposition, they were having difficulty attracting national television coverage for their fights.[59] This was particularly disturbing to the promoters because boxing matches were being heavily televised by the mid-1950s.

In 1955, African Americans launched a boycott of the New Orleans AA minor league baseball team, the Pelicans, when they released their five black players after spring training, leaving the club all-white, and continued to maintain segregated seating. The boycott also protested the absence of any African American players in the eight-club Southern Association, with which the Pelicans were affiliated. The Pelicans were a vulnerable target because minor league attendance was declining as a result of competition from television, which provided people everywhere in the country access to major league games. Partly as a result of the boycott, Pelicans' home attendance dropped significantly.[60]

The national media gave unprecedented attention to the race issue in covering the 1956 Sugar Bowl after the University of Pittsburgh (Pitt), a team with one African American player, substitute fullback Bobby Grier, accepted an invitation to play Georgia Tech. As had been the case the previous year, the stadium required African American spectators to sit in the "Negro section." Tickets for Pitt's 10,200 seats, however, like those allotted to Navy the year before, were not restricted by race, and many African Americans purchased them.[61] This twenty-first Sugar Bowl precipitated some conflict between members of the southern business elite intent on promoting New Orleans as part of a dynamic New South and Louisianans committed to fighting desegregation efforts encouraged by the Supreme Court's 1954 *Brown v. Board of Education* decision. Many New Orleans business leaders were willing to accept Pitt as Georgia Tech's Sugar Bowl opponent, even with Grier playing, in order to showcase to corporations outside the region the investment opportunities their city offered. The *Dixie Roto Magazine,* a weekly published jointly by the New

Orleans *Times-Picayune* and the New Orleans *States,* boasted that the Sugar Bowl game would be played in what had become "the largest double-decked steel stadium in the world."[62] Militant segregationists considered sports an opening wedge in the civil rights movement's campaign to topple Jim Crow in schools and other public facilities. The 1956 Sugar Bowl took place at the time segregationist mobs violently resisted Autherine Lucy's attempt to desegregate the University of Alabama and less than a month after the Montgomery bus boycott began.

The availability of seats in Pitt's section to anyone regardless of race made the Sugar Bowl for the first time popular among African Americans. Navy's desegregated section the previous year was open only to naval officers and servicemen, the navy's new recruits, and Naval Academy midshipmen. The *Atlanta Daily World* reported that "throngs of Negroes who heretofore had only passing interest in the Sugar Bowl carried new money through the turnstiles" in order to sit in an unsegregated section. The 1956 Sugar Bowl was the first to permit African American journalists entry to the stadium press box.[63]

For several years the African American press had condemned the national news media for televising what they increasingly nicknamed the "Segregation Bowl." In 1952, *Atlanta Daily World* sports columnist Marion Jackson denounced ABC television for broadcasting nationally the "For 'Caucasians Only' Sugar Bowl game . . . featuring Georgia Tech and Mississippi, [from] two . . . of the most prejudiced states in the union." Jackson pointed out that African Americans had played in the other three major bowl games, including the two in southern states with legalized segregation. Racially mixed college teams had even participated in a regular season game at Miami's Orange Bowl in 1950 between the University of Miami and the University of Iowa, which had five African American players.[64]

In 1956, New Orleans remained a heavily segregated city. Buses and streetcars were segregated until 1958. Louisiana's Catholic Church kept its parochial schools totally segregated until 1962, providing, in the words of civil rights historian Adam Fairclough, "an example of procrastination and delay" in a state whose southern half was largely Catholic. Louisiana's public schools began desegregation only in 1960. The undergraduate school of Jesuit Loyola University of New Orleans did not admit any African American students until 1962. The only blacks admitted to "white" New Orleans hotels were African leaders like Emperor Haile Selassie of Ethiopia and President William Tubman of Liberia and their entourages, and some foreigners attending international conventions. When Loyola built a new gymnasium during the winter of 1954–55, it announced that seating would not be segregated. By May 1955, however, pressure from whites had forced the university to restore segregated seating "for non-university functions." New Orleans public libraries had desegregated in 1954, and the city hired two African American policemen in 1950.[65]

The Sugar Bowl again celebrated white female purity by incorporating beauty queens into its televised pregame ceremonies. Significantly, the 1956 Sugar Bowl Queen was the daughter of US Representative F. Edward Hébert (D-La.), a militant segregationist who represented a New Orleans district. New Orleans Mid-Winter Sports Association chair Bernie Greenwood crowned nineteen-year-old Dawn Hébert, a sophomore at Tulane's Newcomb College, Sugar Bowl Queen at the center of the field, flanked by her maids of honor and their escorts. As a Cherry Blossom Princess in Washington DC in 1952, "Queen Dawn" had posed before a large Confederate battle flag.[66]

After Georgia Tech's president Blake Van Leer and head football coach Bobby Dodd signed a contract to play Pitt, Georgia Governor Marvin Griffin demanded that Tech's board of regents meet in special session to prohibit the state's universities and colleges from participating in games with desegregated teams or before non-segregated spectators. Dave Rice, one of the few Georgia Tech regents willing to speak to the press, expressed concern that reneging on the Sugar Bowl commitment would adversely affect the ability of Georgia Tech and the University of Georgia to recruit out-of-state athletes, thus harming their prospects of fielding winning teams. The segregationist Augusta (Ga.) *Chronicle* published an editorial similarly warning that Griffin's stand would damage the Georgia Tech and Georgia football programs, which had "brought fame, glory, and prestige" to the Peach State. The *Chronicle* maintained that were Georgia Tech to break its contract with the Sugar Bowl, it would spell "the end of the line for the [Georgia Tech] Yellow Jackets as a national football power, with no more intersectional and bowl games." Associating university prestige with college football prowess, the *Chronicle* claimed that this would cause "irreparable damage" to Georgia's institutions of higher learning. The Georgia Tech and Georgia football teams had appeared in fourteen bowl games during the previous fifteen years.[67]

Upon learning of Griffin's effort to prevent their school's participation in the Sugar Bowl, Georgia Tech students spontaneously protested on campus by burning him in effigy, and then marched to the state capitol and to the governor's mansion before dispersing. While rejecting Griffin's call for Georgia

Tech not to play in the Sugar Bowl, the school's board of regents reaffirmed the policy of most southern colleges and universities to play teams with African Americans only in states without legal segregation. Blacks were prohibited from playing in Georgia Tech home games, and stadium seating would remain segregated. Dave Rice's resolution criticizing Governor Griffin's attempt to overturn Georgia Tech's acceptance of its Sugar Bowl invitation died when it failed to obtain a second from any regent. The regents voted thirteen to one to demand an investigation of the students' "riotous" conduct, which they said they would not tolerate.[68]

Public opinion in Georgia remained divided over Georgia Tech's willingness to play a desegregated team in the Sugar Bowl, even a team with just one black player. *Sports Illustrated* magazine, published in New York City, stated that there were enough "sensible" Georgians to fill a twenty-car train from Atlanta to the Sugar Bowl in New Orleans. A considerable number were also traveling there from Georgia by automobile, bus, and airplane. But Georgia's major politicians followed the governor's lead and boycotted the game, and many Georgians expressed support for Griffin's stand.[69]

Pitt provided a little more support for Bobby Grier than Boston College had for Lou Montgomery, but still made a significant concession to New Orleans' Jim Crow system. The Pitt football team, the Panthers, stayed at Tulane University, a private school, in order to accommodate Grier, who was barred from the city's "white" hotels by New Orleans housing law. Georgia Tech's team was lodged at the upscale St. Charles Hotel. Grier was, however, kept out of the dinner-dance held there for both teams. Instead he attended a "function" at African American Dillard University.[70]

The Rose Bowl provided a stark contrast to New Orleans' segregationist practices. In the reviewing stand for Pasadena's Tournament of Roses parade, which preceded the Michigan State-UCLA game, were Chief Justice Earl Warren, who had presided over the *Brown v. Board of Education* school desegregation decision, and Michigan governor G. Mennen Williams, who had in 1950 refused to sign extradition papers for convicted Scottsboro Boy Heywood Patterson, who two years before had escaped from a prison work gang in Alabama and fled to Detroit.[71] Both Chief Justice Warren and Governor Williams were reviled in the South.

The 1956 Sugar Bowl game went down to the wire, with the clock running out on the Panthers, trailing 7–0 and only four-and-a-half yards from the Yellow Jackets' goal line. An earlier seventy-nine yard Pittsburgh drive died on the Georgia Tech one yard line. New Orleans *Times-Picayune* sports editor Bill Keefe considered the game "maybe the hardest fought of all the great Sugar Bowl" contests. Just as both the Blue and the Gray covered themselves with glory in Civil War combat, the "desperate and dynamic effort" of the "Pennsylvania invaders" at the end "was so magnificent that even the most ardent Tech rooters hailed the explosive, eleventh hour attack." When the final gun sounded, "a great rebel yell" rose from the Georgia Tech bench and stands.[72]

Grier played well substituting for Pittsburgh's injured starting fullback, gaining fifty-one yards on six carries to finish as the game's leading rusher, but he remained a focus of controversy. On defense Grier was called for pass interference in the end zone, which placed the ball on Pitt's one-yard line and led to the Yellow Jackets' touchdown two plays later. Grier denied that he had committed pass interference; the Georgia Tech receiver claimed that he had. Pitt head coach Johnny Michelosen said the play could have been called either way; Georgia Tech head coach Bobby Dodd could not see the play from where he was standing. The Pittsburgh *Courier,* a leading African American newspaper, insisted that Grier had been victimized by racist southern officials. It also claimed that late in the first half, when Pitt moved within Georgia Tech's ten-yard line, its signal callers declined to give Grier the ball. The *Courier* emphasized that "four of the six officials were from Dixie," including the back judge who called pass interference on Grier. It claimed, moreover, that the intended receiver could not have caught the pass "on a five-foot stepladder," so interference never should have been called.[73]

Intensifying segregationist militancy in Louisiana resulted in the state legislature passing, "with only token opposition," a bill shortly after the Pittsburgh—Georgia Tech game prohibiting the races from mixing in sports events, either on the field or in the stands. Louisiana governor Earl Long signed the bill into law. Long claimed that eighty percent of the "messages" he received about the bill favored it. The Mid-Winter Sports Association had initially expressed no opposition to the bill but reversed itself as many Northern schools signaled they would not participate in the Sugar Bowl if it passed.[74]

In July 1956, Bill Keefe, sports editor of the New Orleans *Times-Picayune* and one of the South's most well-known and influential sportswriters, acknowledged that Louisiana's law against race mixing in sports would adversely affect the Sugar Bowl's ability to set up the best possible match of teams, but he nonetheless aggressively defended racial segregation. Keefe's views were common among white southern sportswriters. What was important to Keefe was that "the stand of the people of Louisiana was forcefully presented by the legislators, who voted 100 percent for the new law . . . public sentiment was overwhelmingly in favor of segregation in sports." Keefe proceeded to denounce Jackie Robinson for publishing an article "in which he abused the South for its fight for segregation." Robinson had written that he would not be satisfied until "hotels in the South accepted Negroes just as they admitted whites." Keefe argued that this would drive away the hotels' white clientele and jeopardize the hotel owners' investments. "Perhaps Southern hotel owners will get together and decide to bankrupt themselves so Robinson will be satisfied," Keefe sneered.[75]

The Sugar Bowl immediately suffered a drastic loss of prestige as a result of Louisiana's legislation barring race mixing in sports. Northern schools did withdraw from participation for the next eight years, until the legislation was overturned. Baylor, situated in Waco, Texas, played Tennessee in the 1957 Sugar Bowl, and for the next seven years only teams from the segregated Southeastern Conference, to which LSU belonged, were represented. Shirley Povich of the Washington *Post,* a strong civil rights advocate, wrote in January 1957 that the Louisiana legislature had reduced the Sugar Bowl from "a major football game that could challenge the Rose Bowl, to second-rate status." He noted that "the Sugar Bowl is now scrounging for attractive competition." The Pittsburgh *Courier* in November 1962 stated that the Sugar Bowl, "once ranked No. 2 in the national bowl picture behind the Rose Bowl . . . has consistently lost ground to the Cotton and Orange Bowl games solely because of its racial policy." In December 1964, the *Courier* commented that the Sugar Bowl had "moved into virtual oblivion as it invited only Southern teams." For eight years, the Sugar Bowl had featured "mediocre teams" and "suffered malnutrition at the gate."[76] Northern colleges also now refused to schedule games against LSU and Tulane in Louisiana, and the Chicago Cubs moved their spring training camp from Lafayette, Louisiana to Mesa, Arizona.[77]

Only in 1965, after the Congress had passed the Civil Rights Act, did the Sugar Bowl desegregate, inviting Syracuse University (7–3), whose team included eight African Americans, to play LSU (7–2–1). Five of Syracuse's African American players were starters. The Pittsburgh *Courier* reported that African Americans were now "buying tickets by the scores." Syracuse trained for the Sugar Bowl at the Naval Air Station in Pensacola, Florida, and flew to New Orleans on December 30. The game pitted Syracuse's highly touted ground game, spearheaded by All-American halfback Floyd Little and fullback Jim Nance, both African Americans, against LSU's stingy defense.[78]

LSU overcame a 10–2 halftime deficit to win 13–10, before what the Associated Press called a "disappointing" turnout of about 65,000 spectators, well below the stadium's 81,585 capacity. The previous two Sugar Bowl games, between Alabama and Mississippi the previous year, and Mississippi and Arkansas in 1963, each drew more than 80,000 spectators. The low 1965 turnout probably resulted from southern white resistance to watching a northern team with several African American players, and from the failure to impose a local television blackout. "Scattered pickets" outside Tulane Stadium carried signs reading "Integration has ruined the Sugar Bowl."[79]

The Sugar Bowl in the three decades after its founding in 1935 served an important function in promoting New Orleans as a glittering, economically dynamic New South metropolis, and attracting northern investment capital. It quickly established itself as the second most important bowl game in the United States, and sometimes, as in 1941, it overshadowed the Rose Bowl. The Sugar Bowl usually attracted tens of thousands of tourists to the Crescent City during the last week of December and the first week of January, many of them from the North and some even from abroad. The Mid-Winter Sports Association, the New Orleans businessmen's group that had charge of the Sugar Bowl, made a concerted effort during the game's early years to attract a northern team to play a southern host team, exploiting the most potent sectional rivalry in American history and in American sports. It used these North-South games both to promote sectional reconciliation and to celebrate a mythic antebellum plantation culture overshadowed by New South economic development. The Sugar Bowl possessed an element of mystery in almost always matching teams that had never faced each other before, like baseball's World Series before the onset of interleague play.

To impress northern investors arriving in New Orleans for the Sugar Bowl, the New Orleans press published features highlighting the city's business growth. In early January 1965, for example, the *Times-Picayune* boasted of the "eye-catching" thirty-three story Trade Mart Tower, built by the Dock Board of New Orleans at a cost of $11 million and scheduled for completion in October. The main hall would seat 17,000 people. The *Times-Picayune* noted that the Trade Mart Tower's status as the city's tallest building would be short-lived. Piles were "already being banged into the ground . . . for the forty-five story Plaza Tower" office and apartment building. A developer had also just announced plans to build a seventy-two story, $25 million convention hotel, the

Place Vendome. The *Times-Picayune* added that New Orleans had completed several new wharves and wharf extensions for its "bustling port, ranked No. 2 in the nation for total tonnage." It reported that new chemical, cement, and soft drink plants had also been recently built.[80]

Only two schools with an African American player went to the Sugar Bowl during its first thirty years, both northern institutions, and both made significant concessions to New Orleans' Jim Crow system. When Boston College participated in the 1941 Sugar Bowl, its administration and athletic officials readily agreed to the Mid-Winter Sports Association demand to bench their African American player, Lou Montgomery. Boston College also placated its southern opponents by keeping Montgomery out of games in Boston. Although Pittsburgh's lone African American, Bobby Grier, was permitted to play in the 1956 Sugar Bowl, and the team was housed together at Tulane University, Grier was excluded from a dinner-dance for the teams to avoid violating the taboo on black men mingling socially with white women. National network television did not hesitate as late as the first half of the 1960s to broadcast segregated Sugar Bowl games.

The Sugar Bowl was notable for the kind of pageantry that accompanied it, incorporating chaste beauty queens into pregame and halftime festivities. It gave greater emphasis than other southern bowl games to celebrating the Confederacy and the antebellum southern woman. Sugar Bowl queens and members of their courts were usually gloved and attired in flowing gowns that reached to their heels, never in swimsuits like Miami's Orange Bowl queens or the contestants at Galveston's International Pageant of Pulchritude during the 1920s and 1930s. The Sugar Bowl, the only postseason game played in the Deep South, embraced a highly traditional image of womanhood that changed very little over the decades. The halftime show at the 1972 Sugar Bowl featured a parade of floats, each of which carried a beauty queen from a southern state. The *New York Times* published a photograph of Miss Tennessee with a beatific smile, upswept hair, and long, shoulder-length strands, standing on a float wearing a full-length ruffled cloak covering an elaborate gown.[81]

The determination by Louisiana's legislature and white population to maintain racial segregation, which became even more intense in the mid-1950s, contributed to the Sugar Bowl's significant loss of status in the next decade. Despite challenges from the African American press and civil rights activists inside and outside Louisiana, and some white northern journalists, who repeatedly condemned the Sugar Bowl's segregationist practices, it proved impervious to change until after the passage of the Civil Rights Act of 1964. Although purporting to promote improved intersectional relations and southern economic advance, the Sugar Bowl helped solidify an image of New Orleans outside the South as stagnant and insular.

CHAPTER TEN

"No Room for Such a Club in Our Organization"

The Southern Association of the Amateur Athletic Union's Long Fight for White Supremacy in New Orleans and the South

MARK DYRESON

In 1935, the Southern Association of the Amateur Athletic Union (SAAAU) held its annual meeting at the swanky headquarters of the New Orleans Athletic Club, a French Quarter institution located on Rampart Street that counted on its membership rolls the leading movers and shakers in the city. Born in 1893, the SAAAU made its headquarters in New Orleans. Clubs from the South's largest metropolis had long dominated the Southern Association and they gave it a peculiarly New Orleans flavor—though the SAAAU originally spanned Florida, Tennessee, Alabama, Mississippi, and Texas, as well as the rest of Louisiana.[1] A reflection of the unique and heterodox oligarchy that governed the Crescent City, the SAAAU's governing councils drew leadership mainly from among the elites in the Catholic and Jewish communities who ruled New Orleans.[2] In contrast to much of the rest of the American South, urban or rural, where Protestant majorities with ethnic roots in the British Isles dominated the upper echelons of society and anti-Semitic and anti-Catholic attitudes were not uncommon; a coalition of Catholics—mainly Italian and Irish—and Jews played key roles in governing New Orleans.[3]

The SAAAU's leaders reflected that social demography, a fact that put the major controversy that confronted delegates at this 1935 gathering into a different relief than might otherwise be expected in the American South. At that moment, a titanic internal struggle raged in the many branches that formed the national

The track at Southwestern Louisiana Institute prepared for the Southern Amateur Athletic Union track and field meet in May 1926. Edwin Lewis Stephens, "Track Ready for Southern Amateur Athletic Union Meet," May 1926, Southwestern Louisiana Institute Photograph Album No. 1, 1922–1927, p.#225 photo #896. University Archives and Acadiana Manuscripts Collection, Edith Garland Dupré Library, University of Louisiana at Lafayette, Lafayette, LA.

Amateur Athletic Union (AAU) over whether or not American athletes should boycott the 1936 Berlin Olympics. The International Olympic Committee (IOC) originally awarded those games in 1929 to the Weimar Republic. By the early 1930s, the republic had collapsed and the National Socialists (Nazis) led by Adolf Hitler came to power. Global concerns over the rise of Hitler's regime and Nazi racial and religious discrimination—particularly against Jews but also against Catholics and Protestants—had created an international furor over whether the world should gather in Berlin for an Olympian celebration. In the United States many Jewish and Catholic groups, as well as some Protestant organizations, favored a boycott. Jeremiah T. Mahoney, an Irish Catholic scion from New York and the newly elected president of the AAU, led the boycott effort. The opposition gathered around the man whom Mahoney had just replaced as the AAU's chief executive, Avery Brundage. The formidable Brundage also served as the president of the American Olympic Committee (AOC). An anti-boycott firebrand who argued that the Olympics must continue regardless of any discomfort or discontent the world felt for the emerging Nazi regime, Brundage sought to make his case amongst the AAU branches that he had recently ruled. In every one of the AAU's multiple national branches, Mahoney's troops fought Brundage's cabal over the proposed Berlin boycott.[4]

In the boardrooms of the New Orleans Athletic Club, the boycott question dominated the SAAAU's 1935 agenda. The president of the SAAAU, Joseph Dresner, had been a founding member of the Young Men's Hebrew Association of New Orleans and a former basketball and baseball star in the city.[5] Dresner began the Southern Association's annual convention by inviting Rabbi Louis Binstock to give a talk on "Amateur Sport and Its Values," in which the rabbi outlined German persecution of Jews, Catholics, and even Protestants. Next, Dresner introduced a letter from the Southern Young Judea Association pleading with the SAAAU to support the boycott. Other delegates joined in the boycott calls, decrying Nazi Germany's treatment of Catholics, Jews, and Protestants. All of the speakers concurred that a withdrawal by the United States from the Berlin games would send a powerful message to the world. The SAAAU leadership created a committee to draft a resolution on the matter—a statement they planned to read at the upcoming AAU national convention in New York City in December of 1935. The committee quickly composed a declaration that condemned Nazi religious and racial policies and demanded that the American team refuse Berlin's Olympic invitation. The manifesto passed without a single dissenting vote or abstention. The SAAAU proclaimed: "by unanimous approval and consent of all members present, [we] have instructed our representatives, without qualification, to vote for the withdrawal of the American team from the Olympic Games to held at Berlin in 1936."[6]

The SAAAU's unwavering and undivided support for upholding the fundamental equality of all of the world's athletes against Nazi discrimination seemed to mark them as enlightened defenders of human rights. Led by cosmopolitan New Orleanians, an organization with members from throughout the Deep South—from Shreveport to Jackson to Birmingham—rejected religious and ethnic discrimination. The SAAAU's bold stance against anti-Semitism, as well as against other forms of anti-religious and anti-ethnic discrimination, came just two decades after the infamous lynching of Leo Frank, a prominent member of Atlanta's Jewish community whose murder helped spark a revival of the Ku Klux Klan that started in Georgia and spread through the nation. In a region in which anti-Semitism and anti-Catholicism thrived, as the strident pronouncements of the resurgent Ku Klux Klan and the less strident but no less discriminatory practices of white, Protestant southern elites betrayed, a civil rights cause seemed to have won an unexpected victory.[7]

At the 1935 national convention of the AAU, the Southern Association's Lawrence di Benedetto forcefully made his branch's case to his assembled comrades from across the United States. Di Benedetto, who immigrated as child to New Orleans from Italy, was a fixture in the Crescent City's Catholic hierarchy. A founding member of the SAAAU, he had served from 1906 as the powerful secretary-treasurer of the organization. Well connected in city government, he ran New Orleans's municipal parks and playgrounds and helped to found and lead both the Public School Athletic League and the Catholic School Athletic League. He also worked as a sports reporter for the *New Orleans Times Picayune*.[8] In New York at the AAU national meeting, Di Benedetto declared that it would be a "betrayal of honor and sportsmanship by any Catholic, Protestant, or Jew who loves his God" to support United States participation in the 1936 Olympics. The veteran SAAAU leader's words thrilled Mahoney's pro-boycott faction. However, Brundage and the pro-participation faction outmaneuvered their pro-boycott colleagues in a series of parliamentary skirmishes. By a razor-thin margin the AAU's members rebuffed a motion to prohibit American athletes from taking part in the 1936 Olympics. Mahoney, disheartened after failing in his boycott crusade, refused to stand for re-election as AAU president. Brundage once again assumed that mantle, adding the AAU post to his presidency of the AOC and all but guaranteeing US athletes would enter the "Nazi Olympics"—as the American press increasingly called the 1936 games.[9]

Though boycott advocates continued to fight rearguard actions against the decision, the AAU's convention decision had effectively ended the war. The SAAAU and its allies had lost their fight to protest Nazi discrimination by keeping the American team away from Germany.[10] Meanwhile, at nearly the same moment as Di Benedetto and the SAAAU vigorously defended the civil rights of Jewish, Catholic, and Protestant athletes to compete in Berlin, they were also promoting a new track meet slated for the end of December of 1935 in an effort to bring a world-class field of Olympians and Olympic hopefuls to New Orleans. The Midwinter Sports Association, which Di Benedetto and other SAAAU members dominated, had decided to add a track meet to Sugar Bowl festivities that drew national attention to the city for the annual gridiron clash of leading college football teams that debuted earlier that year in January 1935. Di Benedetto, who created and led the new Sugar Bowl track meet, promised that "every competitor in this midwinter sports carnival is a potential Olympic candidate."[11] The new track meet in fact drew a stellar field of athletes from around the United States, including several who would medal in the 1936 Berlin Olympics. Di Benedetto's brainstorm also garnered national attention for New Orleans.[12]

Unnoticed—or at least unmentioned—in the mainstream white press was the fact that while Protestants, Catholics, and Jews were welcome to run, jump, and throw in the Sugar Bowl showcase, African Americans were excluded. The omission of African-American stars from the New Orleans invitational—including the three fastest men in the world in the 100-meter dash in 1935—American sprinters Ralph Metcalfe, Eulace Peacock, and Jesse Owens—did not escape the attention of the black press—particularly since just a few weeks earlier Di Benedetto and the SAAAU had mounted such a strident opposition to Nazi racial ideology and proclaimed such a stirring defense of religious and racial fair play at the AAU convention. The Goodfellows Club of Chicago penned an open letter to Di Benedetto and the SAAAU that the *Chicago Defender* published. "Your organization has gone on record as opposing American participation in the Olympic Games of 1936 because of alleged racial discrimination in Germany," the missive began. "It is such a wonderful sentiment we wonder why you do not apply it to your New Orleans Track and Field Meet," the Goodfellows inquired of their New Orleans brethren. The letter then quoted the entire SAAAU declaration of support for the boycott of the Nazi Olympics. "By the same high moral sentiments the Negroes of America might ask the athletes invited to your New Orleans track and field meet to withdraw because of discrimination against the three fastest humans in the world today—Owens, Metcalfe and Peacock," the Goodfellows observed.[13]

Sports columnists in two other leading African-American newspapers, the *Philadelphia Tribune* and the *New York Amsterdam News,* also highlighted the hypocrisy of the SAAAU in drawing a color line in New Orleans while advocating against discrimination in Berlin. The New York and Philadelphia opinion-makers expanded their criticism to the national AAU, condemning the leadership for permitting the SAAAU to segregate at the very same time that the organization castigated the Germans for their brand of segregation. The journalists lamented that track and field, which they characterized as the sport where African Americans had the greatest freedom to compete, still permitted the drawing of color lines, if not on Olympic teams or in AAU national championships, at least in the large swath of the American South where the SAAAU ruled. They demanded the national AAU take action to end discrimination in the Southern Association.[14]

Neither the SAAAU nor the AAU responded publicly to arguments raised by the black press. A year later, however, the SAAAU provided a clear retort through its executive actions. In 1936, the SAAAU reconvened in New Orleans for its annual meeting, hosted this time by the Young Men's Hebrew Association in their splendid Athenaeum at the corner of Clio Street and St. Charles Avenue.[15] Once again, a civil rights issue appeared on the agenda. In this case, however, the issue generated no debate whatsoever. Once again, the delegates fully supported the decision they made with nary a dissenting voice. This case involved an application from the Elverillo Athletic Club of New Orleans, located at 1934 St. Louis Street, for membership in the SAAAU. This bastion of amateur athletes, as the application revealed and the New Orleans delegates well knew, was a "colored" club. Secretary-treasurer Di Benedetto, who had eloquently defended the principle that no individual should suffer discrimination at the hands of the Nazis just months earlier at the national AAU convention in New York City, captured the spirit of the quick dismissal of the Elverillo Athletic Club's petition. Di Benedetto wrote in the official report of the meeting that it "was the sense of the meeting that there is no room for such a club in our organization."[16]

The Southern Association of the AAU, which sometimes fought vigorously for the rights of minority athletes—especially Catholics and Jews from New Orleans—to compete on level playing fields throughout the Deep South, had in 1936 "no room" for African Americans in "our organization." Had the other subdivisions of the AAU been as vigorous as the southern branch in championing segregation, the 1936 US Olympic team would have looked very different without Jesse Owens and the other "black auxiliaries" who challenged Nazi and other white supremacist ideologies on the American squad.[17] Indeed, from its foundation in 1893 the SAAAU staunchly supported white supremacy and the necessity of segregation. On the question of the necessity of keeping people of African descent separate and unequal, the SAAAU shared the sentiments of Adolf Hitler and the Nazis—a stance at odds with their egalitarian sentiments on other forms of ethnic and religious discrimination at the Olympics. In fact, the SAAAU was not merely a silent partner in segregation and racism but a leader in New Orleans and southern efforts to draw color lines. The SAAAU consistently excluded African Americans from their organization, sought to draw color lines in AAU events that frequently put them at odds with the national AAU, and launched a series of pro-segregation boycotts against AAU events that included black competitors.

In American track and field from the 1890s through the 1960s, the SAAAU, led by a heterogeneous cabal of New Orleans elites from the Crescent City's Irish, Italian, and Jewish communities, policed the color line between white and black with an unrivalled ferocity, as the SAAAU was a constituent group of a national organization that demonstrated relatively progressive credentials on race relations. The national AAU permitted black membership, although not always encouraging or enabling it, from its 1888 founding. Especially in track and field, however, the AAU resisted drawing color lines more energetically than any other national sporting organization in the United States. Black track and field athletes competed in AAU national championships in segregated cities straddling the Mason-Dixon Line at Washington, DC in 1890, at St. Louis in 1904, 1917, and 1963, at Baltimore in 1914, and at College Park, Maryland, in 1954. They even defended the right of black athletes to compete in the Deep South, at Jamestown in 1907, at Dallas in 1936 and 1937, and at San Antonio in 1946.[18]

In this particular arena New Orleans, in spite of its reputation as a city with greater tolerance of racial mixing that the rest of the American South, served as a fortress of segregationist fervor and white privilege. The SAAAU built the foundation of their Jim Crow citadel in track and field from the moment they set foot on the national stage, when they began in the early twentieth century to send teams to national meets and became the first city in the South to host an AAU national championship. The SAAAU won the right to host the 1910 national track and field championships at the AAU's November 1909 convention. Residents cheered the news that the city had garnered such a prestigious meet, an event that the *Times Picayune* labeled "one of the biggest affairs of its kind in the world and second only to the Olympian games in importance."[19] With the city's political establishment, including Mayor Martin Behrman, a major figure in the Jewish community, behind the effort, New Orleans boosters quickly raised the $3000 subsidy that the AAU demanded for hosting rights. They also drummed up more funds to build a state-of-the-art track at Tulane University. Harry Fitzpatrick, the president of the SAAAU, promised that the event would put New Orleans on the national map. "I bear you the assurance of the national championship committee that in making this departure from their custom of ignoring the South when championship favors are distributed, the gentlemen composing the committee will bend every energy to make this meet a success which will place it on a plane with the most notable competitions ever held under A.A.U. auspices," Fitzpatrick cheered. Fitzpatrick also promised his fellow New Orleanians that they would see the world's best athletes compete in the Crescent City. The AAU, Fitzpatrick bragged, "have promised an entry of at least fifteen teams from all sections of the United States, whose personnel will be as high as that of those attending the Olympic games in London last year."[20]

In order to guarantee Olympic-caliber competition, Fitzpatrick would potentially have to allow African-American athletes to compete in the New Orleans national championship. Indeed, John B. Taylor, the reigning AAU national champion in the quarter-mile was also the nation's first African-American gold medalist when he sprinted the 400-meter leg with the victorious US medley relay team in 1908 at the London Olympics. The early accounts of New Orleans as the host had not raised the issue of color lines and black athletes, but Harry Fitzpatrick made his position clear a few months before the October 14 opening day of the championships were scheduled. Fitzpatrick not only served as the chief executive of the Southern AAU but was also an accomplished all-around athlete. In August of 1910, Fitzpatrick took the train to Chicago to compete in the AAU All-Around championships—that era's version of the decathlon. When he discovered that Charles White, an African-American intercollegiate star from the University of Pennsylvania had entered the competition, Fitzpatrick balked.[21]

Fitzpatrick wired his dissatisfaction with the integrated field to the sports editor of the *Times Picayune*. "Nothing doing with me in national all-around tomorrow," Fitzpatrick moped. "Negro entries from University of Pennsylvania," he complained.[22] The New Orleans daily supported Fitzpatrick's stance on the color line, while admitting that a "dusky lad," John B. Taylor, "was one of the top-notchers" at the recent Olympics.[23] In spite of the prominence of a few African Americans in the highest echelons of American track and field, the *Times Picayune* sports editor then threw down the racial gauntlet to the national AAU. "The surest way to ruin the good results of the A.A.U.'s work in the South would be to allow the smart Mr. James E. Sullivan, secretary-treasurer of the A.A.U., to use some of the funds sent him by New Orleans in paying the expenses of a big team of Eastern athletes that contained a negro or two," warned the *Times Picayune* correspondent. The sports editor pegged Fitzpatrick's stunt in Chicago for precisely was it was, a shot across the bow of the national AAU's tradition of allowing racial mixing in tracking and field meets. "It is felt that Harry W. Fitzpatrick's withdrawal will wake up the big guns of the organization in time," asserted the *Times Picayune* editor, "and that the national field and track meet of the A.A.U., here, . . . will be held without any unpleasant and unnecessary arguments about the 'color line.'"[24]

Arguments about the "color line" would have been unavoidable had John Taylor, who for a time competed for the nation's leading track club in that era—the Greater New York Irish American Athletic Club (IAAC)—tried to enter the championships. Many of the Southern Association's leaders, including the bombastic Fitzpatrick, came from New Orleans's Catholic community and were especially eager to see the IAAC bring its world-class squad to the Crescent City.[25] The IAAC's athletic prowess had transformed it into a national symbol of Irish Catholic pride. In contrast to the elitist New York Athletic Club (NYAC), the IAAC fielded a heterogeneous team that included not only Irish competitors but also immigrant athletes from many backgrounds, including Jewish stars as well as stellar black athletes such as Taylor. Tragically, Taylor had contracted what the press identified as "typhoid-pneumonia" on his way back from London's 1908 Olympics, and he died in December of that year.[26] Thousands crowded his funeral service in Philadelphia, including many of the leading stars of the IAAC who were Taylor's former Olympic as well as club teammates.[27]

Taylor's death and the absence of any other African-American athletes on the national scene at that particular moment represented a stroke of luck for New Orleans' athletic bigots. New York City's new black athletic organizations—the Salem-Crescent, St. Christopher's and Alpha Physical Culture clubs—did not seek to enter the 1910 meet. Had the New Orleans event been just the next year, new African-American stars from Massachusetts such as Howard Drew of Springfield and Irving Tecumseh Howe of Boston would have burst onto the scene and created a "color line crisis." In 1910, however, the AAU's national leaders could ignore the issue since no black athletes entered the meet, permitting the Southern Association and Fitzpatrick to stage a "lily white" meet. Fitzpatrick himself competed in the meet, earning a third-place medal in the "junior" shot put—junior being the AAU designation for a competition open only to those who had not won a major national title. Lest his accomplishment seem too incredible, only three shot putters entered.[28]

Absent the fight over the "color line," the national leaders exulted in expanding the AAU's reach into the Deep South. AAU chieftain James Edward Sullivan blustered that New Orleans had drawn the largest crowd ever to attend a national track and field championship and praised the Southern Association for pulling the event off "without a hitch." Sullivan even provided a historical perspective on where the Crescent City ranked as a host: "'I have seen them all since 1888, and New Orleans surpasses everything.'"[29] "Without a hitch" meant, among other things, without any African Americans challenging segregation. Indeed, the only appearance of black citizens in the *New Orleans Times Picayune*'s extensive coverage of the meet was the mention that while the AAU's national stars and administrators quaffed post-contest cocktails at an exclusive club, a "'classy' negro band" played popular tunes for the partygoers. That seems a not insignificant oversight by white interpreters given that New Orleans in 1910 ranked as the fifteenth largest city in the nation with a population of about 340,000, a little more of quarter of whom were categorized as black—almost all of whom, save for the 'classy' band, were apparently invisible.[30] The one place that African Americans appeared in the SAAAU's official production of the meet was as cartoon caricatures adorning several pages of the program that the editors of the compilation added as "comic" levity to spruce up the otherwise tedious recitation of entry lists and statistics that they offered to spectators.[31]

Harry Fitzpatrick, flush with success at hosting an all-white national track and field championship in New Orleans, did not give up on his quest to segregate AAU competitions beyond the Southern Association's borders. Fitzpatrick, once again re-elected to the presidency of the Southern Association, decided to return to Chicago for the 1911 AAU all-around championships. Arriving from New Orleans in Chicago, he once again discovered an African American entered in the national field. Fitzpatrick then once again demanded that the AAU bar African-American competitors, threatening that he would once again withdraw if they were not removed. He once again wrote the sports editor of the *New Orleans Times Picayune.* This time, Fitzpatrick enclosed a clipping from the *Chicago Examiner,* that, he insisted, "reveals the motif [*sic*] of the officials in permitting the negro Holmes to enter after date advertised for closing." The clipping touted F.A. Holmes, "colored star" of Chicago's Gaelic Athletic Association, as the favorite to win the national all-around crown. "It is patent they desire the championship at any price, and figure this Ethiopian will materially improve their prospects," Fitzpatrick fumed. "It seems to be a matter for much jubilation whenever a wearer of the bar sinister enters any contest in this section, as evidenced by the press notices Holmes has received, which same exceed those bestowed upon all the other candidates for honors in the national all-around," Fitzpatrick ranted.[32]

This time both the white press and the black press in Chicago covered Fitzpatrick's racial tantrum. Walter Eckersall,[33] reporting for the white *Chicago Tribune,* interviewed the man to whom Fitzpatrick addressed his formal complaint, Everett Brown, the president of the National AAU and a native Chicagoan. "I believe in giving everybody a chance, regardless of color, race, religion, and as long as Holmes is an American citizen I cannot see any reason why he should not be allowed to pit his skill on the athletic field against other men," Brown proclaimed. Brown did admit that a technical matter had briefly clouded Holmes's application for the meet. "Holmes telephoned Martin Delaney on the night the entries closed that he had mailed his blank, but did not reach the club in time for us to send it to New York with the other entries for approval," the AAU president admitted. "In my mind, there is no question as to the validity of the entry, and I shall do my best to allow him to compete," Brown argued. He noted that when Delany received Holmes's application "it had the proper postmark, which showed us he had lived up to the requirements, and I cannot see any reason why he should not be a contestant."[34]

Writing for the *Defender,* Chicago's leading black daily, correspondent Julius Avendorph used precisely the same quotation from President Brown of the AAU in decrying Fitzpatrick's challenge to Holmes. Avendorph pegged Holmes as the favorite to win the meet, noting that the versatile "colored star athlete" of Chicago's Gaelic Athletic Association had just a few days earlier triumphed in the Central Association of the AAU's all-around final. In his story, Avendorph took an editorial step beyond Eckersall and the *Tribune* and saluted Brown for rising to the defense of Holmes's right to compete. "This and this kind of grit alone, in the breast of the white man, is the only thing that is going to help the black boy," Avendorph contended. "The *Defender* congratulates Mr. Brown," Avendorph concluded.[35]

Fitzpatrick's antics caught the attention of the national black press, as well. The *Crisis,* the journal founded in 1910 as the publishing arm of the crusading NAACP, itself founded the year prior in 1909, scoffed that a "Southern athlete, Harry Fitzpatrick of New Orleans, traveled all the way to Chicago to take part in the contest of the Amateur Athletic Union, but when he found a colored man, F.T. [F.A.] Holmes, was to compete he withdrew his name." Joining in the *Defender*'s praise for the national AAU's president, the *Crisis* cheered that "Mr. Everett C. Brown, president of the union, made no move to prevent Mr. Fitzpatrick's withdrawal, remarking that he could see no reason why a colored athlete should not be treated exactly like a white athlete."[36]

Fitzpatrick followed through on his one-man boycott, once again sitting out the national all-around contests. Holmes finished a respectable seventh in the meet, failing to live up to pre-competition predictions of some members of the press. Fred Thomson of Los Angeles, the defending champion, won his second consecutive all-around crown in Chicago. Another athlete from Los Angeles, J.W. Donahue, took second prize. The same Avery Brundage who would later play a pivotal role in administering amateur athletics in both the United States and internationally as the leader of the AAU and the IOC,[37] finished fourth in the 1911 meet. James Sullivan, the AAU's leader, once again served as the head referee for the contest, continuing his string of work in that position that stretched back to 1887 when he refereed the very first all-around meet in American history, as well as underscoring the national AAU's commitment to racial inclusion.[38]

Fitzpatrick's back-to-back boycotts against black athletes picked up traction nowhere but in his hometown. In the wake of his Southern comrade's withdrawal, the sports editor of the *Times Picayune* opined that "Chicago has shown entire unworthiness to be allowed to conduct a national meet of the A.A.U., and that New Orleans may have the privilege of pulling off the all-around championship of the A.A.U. next year." The New Orleans daily endorsed the idea of an all-white national championship in the South and dismissed Holmes's performance in the 1911 nationals as inconsequential. "As was published Sunday morning in papers throughout the country, Fred Thompson repeated his 1910 success by once more winning the national all-round," the *Times Picayune* averred. "Several Chicago athletes, . . . [who were] white men, did far better than the smoke [Holmes] who entered."[39]

New Orleans would not get the AAU all-around meet in 1912. Instead, it went to Celtic Park in Long Island, the home ground of the Irish American Athletic Club. Fresh off his grand performance in the 1912 Stockholm Olympics where he vanquished the world in both all-around events—the decathlon and pentathlon—Jim Thorpe, the great Native American athlete from Carlisle Indian School, dominated the American field. The *New York Times* headline blared "Indian Thorpe is Best Athlete," a common refrain in 1912, as the press marveled at Thorpe's record-setting performance in piling up more points than had ever been scored in an AAU championship.[40]

Harry Fitzpatrick was not at Celtic Park to challenge the Sac and Fox tribesman Thorpe, nor was Fitzpatrick a member of the 1912 American Olympic decathlon team that included both Thorpe and Avery Brundage.[41]

Still, Fitzpatrick patiently bided his time and nurtured his network of AAU connections. In spite of his history of confrontations with national officers over color lines, the national organization granted his wish for the SAAAU to host a national all-around championship contest.[42] On September 19, 1914, the Southern Association of the Amateur Athletic Union staged the national competition at Alabama's Birmingham Athletic Club. The *Birmingham Ledger* provided additional sponsorship. Only five athletes, all of them white, showed up for the national championship. Harry Fitzpatrick, representing the Young Men's Gymnastic Club of New Orleans (the precursor of the New Orleans Athletic Club) finished a distant fifth with just 3460 points, more than 2500 points behind the victor. Nathan Tycer of St. Paul's Athletic Club of Covington, Louisiana, finished fourth. Patrick O'Connor of New York City's Pastime Athletic Club, a well-known all-around athlete on the national circuit and the reigning Eastern champion, was third while local favorite Gilbert Ritchie of the Birmingham Athletic Club, the reigning southern champion, garnered a surprising second place. The national championship honors fell to an athlete who had sought the crown for many years and placed among the top three or four on numerous occasions in the past. In the crowning achievement of his athletic career, with a respectable score of 6999 points, the Chicago Athletic Association's Avery Brundage finally won his long-sought national championship.[43]

Brundage would become in the 1920s the president of both the AAU and the American Olympic Committee. In 1936, he would become a member of the International Olympic Committee. From 1952 to 1972, he would serve a tumultuous two decades as the most important president in the IOC's history. In each of those capacities, Brundage would become embroiled in series of racial and political controversies.[44] As a member of the inner circle of the AAU beginning in 1919, Brundage would regularly encounter Harry Fitzpatrick and deal with his quest to exclude black athletes from AAU national championships. During this period, the Southern Association sent athletes to compete in national meets in which black competitors were also welcomed. On some occasions, the white southerners even competed directly against black contestants, though Fitzpatrick counseled withdrawal to his charges facing African-American rivals. Fitzpatrick frequently accompanied the southern team to nationals, sometimes even competing in walking races when black competitors were not entered.[45]

In 1919, in spite of Fitzpatrick's consistent challenges of AAU racial policy at the national level, Brundage and his fellow delegates awarded New Orleans the 1920 AAU national convention. The meeting took place without any public ripples regarding race, though Fitzpatrick launched a failed candidacy for the AAU presidency.[46] In 1925, Brundage won a vice-presidential slot in the AAU while he and the other delegates rejected Fitzpatrick's request to bring the national track championships back to New Orleans. The AAU instead granted the meet to Philadelphia, also the site for the 1926 sesquicentennial celebration of American independence.[47] Undaunted, Fitzpatrick set his sights on a 1927 bid for New Orleans—a bid that the Crescent City would win.[48] Early press coverage of New Orleans winning the meet made no mention of racial policies or color lines.[49] Later stories in the press reported that New Orleans athletic leaders had agreed to abide by the AAU's national policy and permit blacks to compete.[50] One cannot imagine Fitzpatrick ever making such a concession—and the venerable defender of racial segregation initially spearheaded New Orleans' bid. In September 1926, a few months before New Orleans officials would travel to Baltimore and make a formal and successful pitch for the championships, Fitzpatrick committed suicide. Reportedly despondent over health issues, he blew his brains out with a pistol.[51]

Fitzpatrick's demise seemed to clear the main hurdle facing New Orleans—the refusal to permit blacks to compete in a Crescent City championship. Satisfied that New Orleans would acquiesce to AAU tradition, national leaders gave the event to the city. The business community set about to raise the necessary funds to guarantee the meet, grown to $15,000 from the $3000 required in 1910, and began construction on a new facility at Loyola University, an institution next door to 1910 host Tulane. Arthur O'Keefe, a friend of the deceased Fitzpatrick, a prominent member of the city's Irish-Catholic elite, and the mayor of New Orleans, was elected in the wake of Fitzpatrick's suicide as the president of the Southern AAU. O'Keefe began public negotiations with the AAU to change the dates of the meet from the Fourth of July weekend—when Crescent City residents generally fled the swelter to Gulf Coast beaches—to a later date in July.[52]

In New York, the black press and a few athletic leaders questioned the wisdom of selecting New Orleans and warned that any effort to draw a color line would be met with a united boycott of both black and white competitors.[53] A columnist in the *New York Amsterdam News* observed, "Down there in that benighted part of the United States known as the 'dear Old Southland', 'Dixie,' etc., Negro athletes have been barred from open competition with the young cracker boys." However, the columnist assured readers that New Orleans would not attempt to draw a color line at the AAU meet since white athletic leaders in New York had promised a boycott in response. "We . . . have it that the officials down in the old Creole city have decided not to buck the union and will not start any trouble when the colored athletes start to pull down the points," the *Amsterdam News* correspondent promised.[54]

Behind the scenes, Mayor O'Keefe and Southern AAU officials were not only lobbying for a calendar change but "bucking the union" for an exemption from any racial "square deal" that would include black athletes. By April of 1927, the secret negotiations became public. In what the *Times Picayune* labelled an "ultimatum," AAU president Frederick W. Rubien informed Mayor O'Keefe that New Orleans was forbidden from barring black athletes from the championships.[55] In a public statement reported nationwide by the Associated Press and other media outlets, Rubien declared that the "Amateur Athletic Union, being a national and patriotic body, has no right to bar any man from its game because of race or creed." The AAU leader regretted that New Orleans had taken a hard line on the color line. "I had hoped that such a stand never would be taken in America," he lamented. "Negroes in the past have competed for the United States in the Olympic games abroad and have won high honors there," Rubien reminded the nation. "What a strange situation to refuse them the right to compete in the national games of their own country," he concluded.[56]

The entry request of DeHart Hubbard, the reigning AAU and Olympic champion in the long jump, had precipitated the crisis. The *Times Picayune*'s sports editor blamed Hubbard, who apparently from a white southern vantage did not have the good grace that John Taylor had demonstrated decades earlier, to perish from a dread disease acquired on a return trip with a gold medal from Europe thus sparing New Orleans from the prospect black participation. "Everything was all set for the meet, until an entry came from DeHart Hubbard, a dark-complected young man whose athletics might be up to the standard but whose color and social standing would not permit Southern athletes measuring strides with him," the New Orleans editor contended, blaming Hubbard for the Crescent's City's misery.[57]

Responses from outside the South to the sports editor's accusations and to New Orleans's decision were swift and emphatic. Both the black and white press championed Hubbard's right to defend his crown and lionized Rubien and the AAU's leadership for holding firm against Southern designs to draw race lines.[58] The "big guns" of national sports journalism, Paul Gallico of the *New York Daily News,* John Kieran of the *New York Times,* and Charles E. Parker of the *New York World,* filleted the Crescent City's turnabout.[59] The black press in the North condemned New Orleans's actions in a torrent of editorials. An impassioned piece in the *Pittsburgh Courier* typified the response. "In the midst of the talk about the New South, little incidents arise to demonstrate the fact that much of spirit of the old South still remains below the celebrated line of Messers. Mason and Dixon," the editorial began. After several scornful paragraphs, the editorial concluded: "It may be perfectly all right to cut off one's nose to spite one's face, but the loss hardly adds to one's attractiveness. Some day even New Orleans will learn that."[60]

The decision by New Orleans powerbrokers to punt the national championships out of the South rather than to permit African Americans to compete drew fire from within the Crescent City. In contrast to the *Times Picayune*'s support of the city's segregationist intransigence, the *Louisiana Weekly,* a New Orleans-based black newspaper, cheered the AAU's decision. "If these young men were good enough to help the United States win the Olympics, they and other colored young men should certainly be good enough to compete in a national event of this great country of which they are citizens."[61] The *Weekly* also added a distinctively local set of perspectives to the controversy: "The hue and cry about mixing with the Negro on the field of honor is ridiculous," the editors contended. "In fact they show no fear of not only sleeping in the same house or room with, but even seem perfectly willing to share their beds with black folk," the *Weekly*'s editors observed, juxtaposing New Orleans's well-known reputation for a certain libertine tolerance in personal relations with the hypocrisy that drawing color lines in a famously "mixed" city produced. Public mixing, the editors noted, was quite a different matter. "In the final analysis, we must conclude that it is 'Fear' alone that keeps up this 'traditional' idea. Fear of what, then, do you ask? It is the fear of being beaten in fair play, by their black neighbor."[62]

The AAU relocated the 1927 national championships to Lincoln, Nebraska.[63] At the University of Nebraska's Memorial Stadium on Fourth of July weekend, DeHart Hubbard defended his long jump title with a national record leap. Other African-American athletes competed in Nebraska as well, earning high places.[64] Ironically, the Southern Association of the AAU sent two white long jumpers to Lincoln to compete against Hubbard.[65] Reporter Milton Bledsoe of the *Pittsburgh Courier,* in Lincoln to cover the meet, declared, "[p]ersonally the correspondent felt like extending a vote of thanks" to the AAU's national leadership "for their holding the 1927 meet in a place where color was no barrier to participation." Bledsoe contended that the accomplishments of Hubbard and other athletes of color in Lincoln highlighted why white southerners were committed to excluding blacks. "Judging from the performance of our boys it is little wonder New Orleans wanted to bar them from the meet if it had been held there," he concluded.[66]

Bledsoe and his fellow commentators in the black press hoped that the AAU's decision to defend African-American participation in track and field and strip the segregated SAAAU and New Orleans of the prize would mark a turning point in the long struggle to desegregate the sport—and the nation. In some ways, it did. In practical terms, the AAU's decision to keep the national championship racially inclusive had a tremendous impact at the national level and even in the American South. The SAAAU's affirmative defense of segregation began to erode its power from within.

Just a few years after the New Orleans debacle, AAU leaders in Texas broke away from the Southern Association and created a new branch of the organization, the Southwestern AAU, with membership open to all races. In breaching the solid southern ranks of the AAU, Texas boosters sought to bring high-profile national track meets for the emerging metropolis of Dallas. They made bids for the 1936 Olympic trials and for an AAU championship meet, promising that unlike their brethren in New Orleans, the people of Dallas would welcome black competitors. The endeavors of the new Southwestern AAU should not be misunderstood as an early step toward dismantling segregation in a major southern city with a large black population. The Southwestern AAU endorsed interracial competition to sell Dallas to the rest of the nation as a modern and progressive metropolis but had no plans to support dismantling Jim Crow beyond the walls of stadiums. Still, this shift in strategy, in an era when Jackie Robinson was still a schoolboy in California, is significant. Amateur athletic officials in Texas went from demanding that the national AAU forge "gentlemen's agreements" with Southern sites that prevented black athletes from competing in their region to acquiescing to inter-racial competition in Texas track meets. Dallas boosters could not convince the AAU to give the city a national championship or an Olympic trial, but they did manage to get the AAU's sanction for the first two major sporting events in the ex-Confederate South since the 1907 AAU meet in Norfolk that featured "mixed" competition—the 1936 Texas "Centennial Olympics" and the 1937 Pan American Olympics. When a year after the end of the Second World War the AAU finally relented nearly two decades after the New Orleans fiasco and once again granted the national track and field finals to a southern city, San Antonio (a part of the Southwest AAU's region) garnered the 1946 championships.[67]

In other ways, stripping New Orleans of a national championship had little immediate impact on the SAAAU and New Orleans. As the Southern Association's territory shrank with the secession of Texas, the organization remained committed to racial segregation. The national AAU did not pressure their southern wing to admit blacks into the SAAAU. In November of 1927, when Lawrence di Benedetto returned from the national AAU convention in Cincinnati, he told the *Times Picayune:* "Nothing was said . . . about the 1927 national championships which we were forced to give up because of the negro question and I felt that since the national officers very diplomatically kept the discussion out of the convention that I should not bring it up."[68]

In contrast to Fitzpatrick's earlier fiery assaults on African-American inclusion, Di Benedetto sought to avoid public conflict about race questions while quietly supporting racial segregation in his city and region. For instance, in 1932, Di Benedetto privately assured an inquirer that while the national AAU permitted interracial contests the southern branch did not, but he refused to debate the issue in public when his message was leaked to the press.[69] Di Benedetto also refused to enter the public fray that erupted in battle over boycotting the 1936 Olympics, leaving unanswered the charges of blatant hypocrisy in the SAAAU's vociferous condemnation of German discrimination against Jewish athletes while his organization barred blacks from membership. Nor did Di Benedetto lash out against the African-American press when it criticized his new creation, the Sugar Bowl track invitational, for its lily-white invitation list. Di Benedetto worked quietly behind the scenes to keep the walls of segregation intact in the South while acquiescing to the AAU's national policy of guaranteeing the participation of all races in national track meets. Mastering that divide let him accomplish something Fitzgerald failed to achieve. Di Benedetto became a major player in national sporting circles, serving as AAU president from 1939 to 1943 and playing key roles in the administration of track and field for both the AAU and the US Olympic Committee. In national affairs, he did not push to limit the growing African-American participation in the Olympics and US track meets outside of his region—diverging from the ardent advocacy for promoting segregation that Fitzpatrick had practiced. In New Orleans, he kept his Sugar Bowl track meet, which quickly became one of the most prestigious events in American athletics, and his SAAAU empire for whites only.[70]

In 1958, Di Benedetto passed away at 75 years of age, with Jim Crow still mostly intact in amateur sport in New Orleans.[71] Two years before he died, Di Benedetto, who had been one of the founders of the Sugar Bowl, witnessed the emergence of a huge crack in segregated sport in his hometown when Bobby Grier of the University of Pittsburgh became the first African American to play in the New Year's Day gridiron extravaganza. Louisiana's legislature quickly spackled the crack by introducing a law prohibiting both interracial sporting contests and integrated seating at sporting events. Local civil rights groups sprang into action and launched boycotts against white teams and events. They drove the city's white baseball team, the New Orleans Pelicans of the segregated Southern Association, to financial ruin and relocation. They pushed the struggle against Jim Crow into the daily life of the city. The local civil rights coalition also launched lawsuits. Federal courts struck down the laws, but state officials tried to maintain the racial barriers.[72]

In the midst of these battles, Di Benedetto's cronies at the SAAAU raised funds and pushed the national AAU to create a Lawrence di Benedetto Memorial Award, a yearly prize inaugurated in 1959 to honor the best performance in track and field by a male athlete from any nation in the world. The second and third Di Benedetto awards, given for performances in 1960 and 1961 and inscribed on a huge silver cup displayed in the swanky headquarters of Di Benedetto's beloved New Orleans Athletic Club, went to Ralph Boston. Boston was an African-American long jumper who set world records in both of those years and also won the gold medal at the 1960 Rome Olympics in his event. Boston, who was born in the heart of the SAAAU's territory in Laurel, Mississippi, and competed for a historically black college, Tennessee State University, had his name ensconced on a trophy in a city where he was not allowed to compete in 1960 or 1961 against white competitors.[73]

Two years later, New Orleans athletic leaders received news that their national showcase, the Sugar Bowl track meet, would face a major challenge. The Orange Bowl in Miami, Florida, had added a track meet to the festivities surrounding its New Year's Day college football spectacle. The Orange Bowl's boosters announced their track gala would be open to black as well as white athletes. "This could mean that the Sugar Bowl will have a rough time getting the top talent," worried *Times Picayune* sports columnist N. Charles Wicker.[74] In 1964 the newly minted Civil Rights Act empowered the Supreme Court to strike down of all Louisiana's Jim Crow statutes. Faced with the new legal realities, and perhaps more importantly, the prospect of losing power, prestige, and revenue to southern rivals like the Orange Bowl and Cotton Bowl that encouraged interracial competition, the SAAAU and the Midwinter Sports Association that ran the Sugar Bowl festivities dropped their color lines in sporting venues. On December 29, 1964, four African Americans received invitations to the Sugar Bowl track classic. Richard Stebbins of Grambling University won the 100-meter dash while Theron Lewis, a New Orleans native and Southern University star, set a meet record in the 400-meters and walked away with the award the for top performer in the meet. Lewis could not stay to collect his award as he was already on a plane, bound for the Orange Bowl track meet held the next day.[75]

Three days later, Syracuse University's football team played eight African Americans, including stellar running backs Floyd Little and Jim Nance, in the Sugar Bowl. Though Syracuse lost, 13–10, to an all-white Louisiana State University squad, the racial dynamics of American sport were clearly changing. Commenting on both the desegregated track meet and the desegregated football game and all the hoopla that surrounded them, Jim Hall, correspondent for New Orleans' African-American newspaper, the *Louisiana Weekly,* heralded the dawn of a new era: "Judging from what was passed on to us, the Mid-Winter Sports Association, scored a direct hit, in making the switch. Both the Syracuse players and the trackmen, were high in their praises for the Sugar Bowl Committee. From the playing field, to the sets in the stands, and up in the Stadium press box, and over at the Jung Hotel, for the Sugar Bowl's Award Dinner, it was sweet as Sugar with the unwanted guy—Jim Crow—missing."[76]

A year later, in 1966, the records of the SAAAU reveal the first inclusion of African-American athletes in a Southern Association track meet. In a package dated October 27, 1966, John O. Brown, the track coach at historically black Dillard University, enclosed official registration cards for three athletes—Michael Bucksell, Charles John Nizalak, and Raymond Nathaniel Horne.[77] Though a search of the *Times Picayune* reveals no mention of the meet, the Southern Association of the AAU seemed to have finally dropped their long championing of Jim Crow on the tracks and in the fields of New Orleans.

In 1967, the AAU returned to New Orleans, nearly a half-century after its leaders pulled the 1927 national championship track meet from the city after local officials refused to permit black athletes to compete. Hundreds of delegates, including Rafer Johnson, a prominent African-American athlete who won gold in the decathlon at the 1960 Rome Olympics, gathered in the Roosevelt

Hotel. Press coverage of the meeting did not mention any local racial incidents or protests as the Crescent City welcomed the AAU. The delegates discussed a variety of issues, including United State versus USSR track meets and schedules for future championships. They selected a slate of finalists for the James E. Sullivan Award—given to the nation's top amateur athlete—that included seven women among the fourteen-person list. The major racial controversy swirling around the convention was not the SAAAU's historic embrace of segregation but the news that Black Power activist Harry Edwards and his Olympic Project for Human Rights (OPHR) had threatened that if the AAU and other sporting organizations did not submit to a catalog of OPHR demands then African-American athletes would boycott the US Olympic team for the 1968 Mexico City games[78] The *Chicago Defender* noted that the "convention follows closely behind reports that some Negroes will boycott the United States Olympic team at Mexico City next year to dramatize their demands for better racial relations."[79] Edwards's list included barring the apartheid regimes of South Africa and Rhodesia from the Olympic movement, restoring Muhammad Ali's world heavyweight boxing title, hiring more black assistant coaches on the US Olympic team, and a boycott of the New York Athletic Club, a leading organization in American track and field, for refusing to admit black or Jewish members. Edwards and OPHR also demanded the resignation of Avery Brundage as president of the International Olympic Committee, charging the IOC potentate with decades of consistently denying the rights of racial and religious minorities.[80]

Brundage vociferously denounced the charges that he harbored any racial or religious bias. He did admit that, as Edwards charged, he owned the Montecito Country Club in Santa Barbara, California. However, he claimed that he played absolutely no role in managing the club and had no idea that it barred blacks and Jews from membership. In demonstrating his commitment to racial justice, Brundage harkened back to the 1920s when he led the AAU. He claimed that he had "once removed the American track and field championships from New Orleans because the organizers refused to allow Negroes to compete." After invoking his commitment to racial justice by resurrecting the AAU's old battle with New Orleans in 1927, Brundage proclaimed, "I have opposed racial and religious discrimination all my life."[81]

In harkening back to the historic confrontation over color lines between the AAU and the city of New Orleans to bolster his credentials as a crusader for civil rights, Brundage highlighted both the centrality and complexity of the Crescent

City's role in American racial struggles. The city's leaders had once upon a time condemned Brundage and his allies for failing to adequately defend the civil rights of American athletes against Nazi racial policies. A coalition of Catholic and Jewish leaders from New Orleans vigorously opposed Brundage's claim that participating in the 1936 Olympics did not offer aid and comfort to Nazi segregationists and white supremacists. At the same time, those same eloquent champions in the fight against religious and ethnic discrimination encouraged by the Third Reich worked tirelessly to keep African Americans out of their own white sporting institutions. Sometimes they were outspoken apostles of white supremacy, boycotting events where they faced black challengers. Sometimes they were discreet defenders of the segregated status quo, a regiment in the army of bureaucrats who maintained the machinery of Jim Crow.

In the 1960s, as the world around them changed and they found it impossible to keep even a modicum of power and prestige as long as they kept color lines intact in their beloved Sugar Bowl track carnival and in their Southern Association meets, they acquiesced to the surges of social transformation. Of course, the floodtide of the 1960s did not instantaneously vanquish all of the residues of segregation in the Crescent City and in the Southern Association. The New Orleans Athletic Club, the elite institution that once counted the likes of Fitzpatrick and Di Benedetto on its membership rolls, did not permit black members until 1986. Still, that was three years before the venerable New York Athletic Club—an institution that counted on its rosters many of the AAU's national leaders who had stood firm against the efforts by New Orleans and the SAAAU to draw color lines in national meets—finally in 1989 added the first African-American member to its roster.[82]

CHAPTER ELEVEN

Called Off, On Account of Darkness

The AAU, the AFL, and Civic Development in Jim Crow New Orleans

GREGORY L. RICHARD AND THOMAS AIELLO

In 1927, the Amateur Athletic Union (AAU) canceled its scheduled national track and field championship in New Orleans because city officials refused to allow black athletes to participate. In that incident, the city's white population was in agreement with its government, as civic officials willingly took a hit to the city's economy and reputation in order to uphold the racial line. Thirty-eight years later, the American Football League's All-Star Game was scheduled to be played in New Orleans, but the virulent and overt racism of whites in the city led black athletes to threaten a boycott unless the game was moved. Just as they had in the 1920s, civic leaders had sought the AFL All-Star Game in a specific, targeted effort to boost the city's reputation and economy. This time, civic leaders agreed that racial inclusion should not be a hindrance to progress, but the city's white population went the other way. A vocal segment of New Orleanians were not yet ready for that kind of change and precipitated the boycott with their overt racism. The fiasco was not a federal court seeking to impose integration on a population, and that group fighting back with the aid of its city government. Instead, it was a city government itself seeking that imposition, leaving the citizens themselves to take matters into their own hands.

Examining these two incidents together demonstrates two different paces of racial change, one for officials seeking notoriety and economic growth, one for white citizens who had been taught their entire lives to uphold the racial line because the racial line put a premium on whiteness. Most studies of southern regimes during Jim Crow interpret a symbiotic relationship between white

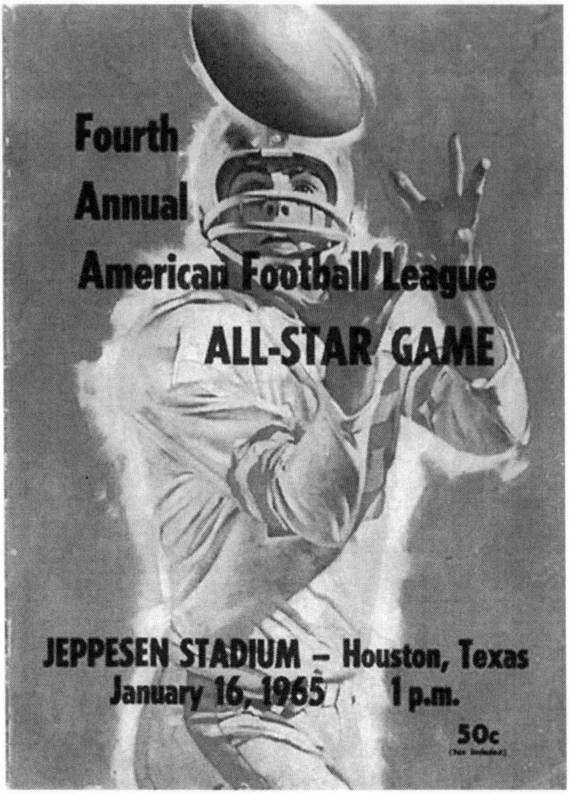

After the players threatened to boycott the AFL All-Star Game, the league moved the contest to Houston's Jeppesen Stadium. This is the cover of the program for the game after its move to Texas. It unsurprisingly featured a white player catching a pass. Program cover in the public domain.

leaders and the white governed, with politicians playing to their most virulently racist base to gain political advancement and maintain power. Dan Carter's famous *Politics of Rage,* for example, describes the life of George Wallace, who combined a working-class white populism with an overt, pragmatic, segregationist racism that kept him beloved by those who could vote without incident.[1] New Orleans's two sports segregation fiascos demonstrate a different dynamic, one where city officials ready to move away from segregationist politics for the sake of postwar Sunbelt civic improvement could not escape the monster they had created over previous Jim Crow decades.

The national AAU track and field championship was one of the largest, most prestigious sporting events in the country in the first three decades of the twentieth century. As Mark Dyreson explains in his broader study of the Southern Association of the Amateur Athletic Union in Chapter 10, New Orleans had managed to host the event once before, in 1910, a lily-white affair that went off without real controversy. In 1926, with an expanded media presence driving an increased interest in sports and a local desire to showcase New Orleans as a pre-Sunbelt example of southern civic development, the city made a bid to host the 1927 championship, winning the honor in November. The games had not been lily white for a number of years, but leaders assumed that the presence of the games in the Deep South would act as its own warning to keep black athletes from the competition. Those assumptions would be wrong, and the games would be defined by racial controversy.[2]

Hopes, however, remained high in the early months of 1927. The national AAU indoor championships were held in early March in Madison Square Garden, a city and venue that hosted everything of consequence. That was the company that New Orleans wanted to keep. Knowing that Louisiana would be hosting the larger outdoor championships in July, New Orleans newspapers covered the event assiduously, both as a preview of the kinds of athletes that the city would see in the summer and a preview of the features of hosting a good tournament. The city was so invested in the tournament that the mayor, Arthur J. O'Keefe, also served as President of the Southern Association of the AAU and chairman of the executive committee of the national AAU track and field championships.[3]

In early March, the city petitioned the national AAU to change the scheduled dates of the tournament from July 1, 2, and 4 to July 8, 9, and 11. The Fourth of July was on a Monday in 1927 and officials were worried that the city would largely clear out for trips to the coast over the holiday weekend. The event was a national showcase for New Orleans, a showcase that would become far less effective with sparse crowds in the grandstands.[4]

It was a busy Spring for the Southern Association of the AAU and its secretary Lawrence di Benedetto, with New Orleans hosting both the regional gymnastics and wrestling championship in May, the men's track and field regionals in Houston, the girls' track and field regionals at Loyola in early June, and continued work taking place to prepare for the men's track and field nationals.[5]

The city had more than forty AAU clubs, all of whom were joining forces to work for a strong showing at the crowning achievement of the city's events, the national track and field championships. Organizing committees planned a campaign to raise $15,000 for the tournament, led by the mayor who spanned both civic and athletic worlds. When officials from the national organization arrived in late February to inspect the facilities at Loyola University, where the contest would be held, they were incredibly pleased. "You have a wonderful track," said Tom Thorpe of the AAU's New York office, "and I look for many records to be broken." With O'Keefe's responsibilities extending to the entire city government of New Orleans, Di Benedetto was the day-to-day point man preparing for nationals. He assured everyone that preparations were progressing smoothly and that "world's record-holders and national champions" would be participating, the "cream of the nation's athletes."[6]

In early April, the committee in charge of the meet, led in name by O'Keefe, held a working luncheon at the Elks' Club to discuss preparations, with another scheduled for the April 17 and general meeting scheduled for April 20 in the council chamber of City Hall. To interest people in the event, the New Orleans *Times-Picayune* began running profiles of athletes expected to attend, athletes like Charlie Paddock, former USC standout, world champion, and Olympic gold medalist sprinter. It was working. Even though the fundraising campaign was not scheduled to start officially until April 25, it had already earned almost $2,000 by April 10. The luncheon meeting on April 17 reported positive results and optimism about the progress of the fundraiser and preparations for the tournament.[7] And then everything collapsed.

The beginning of the end came after William DeHart Hubbard, Olympic gold medalist and University of Michigan standout submitted his entry form, and Frederick W. Rubien, president of the Metropolitan Association of the AAU, told southern officials that black athletes had to be allowed to compete.[8]

DeHart Hubbard was a superstar, the first black man to win an Olympic gold medal in an individual event when he won the long jump competition in the 1942 Paris Games. He was the world record holder in the event, a three-time NCAA national champion and seven-time Big Ten champion. Though he was one of the best athletes in the country, however, and though no legitimate contest of track and field superiority could be judged without his presence, he was black. City officials responded by conferring with representatives of the AAU, an easy process considering that Mayor O'Keefe was president of the group's Southern Association. Initially, city leaders considered asking Hubbard not to participate, but other applicants were planning to attend, as well, all hoping to compete in the Deep South for the first time. Syracuse's Cecil Cook, champion of the quarter mile, Olympic gold medalist Ned Gourdin, St. Bonaventure high jumper Charles Major, Morgan State's Charles Drew, national junior hurdle champion, and Wesley Foster, national junior sprint champion, all planned to participate. Thus the city and tournament organizers decided that the national event and the economic boon that accompanied it were not worth the racial trouble, cancelling the event and leaving AAU officials to scramble for a new location.[9]

The meet was "called off, on account of darkness," in the words of *Times-Picayune* columnist William McG. Keefe. Hubbard, he admitted, might have had worthy athletic prowess, but his "color and social standing would not permit Southern athletes measuring strides with him." The cancellation was, thus, in the mind of Keefe, all Hubbard's fault. "The apparent determination of Northern institutions to force negroes into amateur competition with white youths of the South is one of the biggest obstacles in the way of intersectional games," he wrote, citing an earlier incident when Tulane's football team travelled to Northwestern and refused to play until its black player was benched. "The negro has no place in competition with whites in Dixie," he concluded. "Southern negroes, who are sensible, realize that; they get along much better and are happier."[10]

Keefe's article was blasted by the *Chicago Defender*'s Frank A. Young, who took apart the racist column bit by bit. "He forgets that every year southern high schools enter northern interscholastic games where our boys walk off with many of the first places," wrote Young, "and we dare say if the gods of fate haven't washed away all their coin, many southern institutions will send men to the Penn relays, where loads of our boys will not only be seen warming up, but will be out there after first places." Young praised the national AAU for not compromising on race, the group "being well acquainted with the fact that the southern white man fears real competition."[11]

Charles E. Parker of the *New York World* joined his counterparts in the black press in praising Rubien's stand for racial fairness and assured his readers that "if messages received yesterday at the local headquarters of the Amateur Athletic Union are indicative, every section of the land except the far South heartily approves of the action of the AAU in refusing the request of New Orleans authorities to bar Negro athletes."[12]

"The sunny south is a very romantic land, with colonels and golf links and all that," wrote Paul Gallico in the New York *Daily News*, "its hospitality is famous and its sportsmanship is not so hot. It is a much more youthful section of the country though not from the point of view of physical age. Spiritually it falls short of the adult class in many cases." Racial trouble was the given reason for the withdrawal, wrote Gallico, but "it is the holler that the superior white gentleman can be counted on to raise whenever he is on the point of not giving his colored brother a square deal." For Gallico, "the unforgivable breach of sportsmanship is not the barring of the colored athlete from New Orleans," as cities had the right to make such decisions, but instead it was to bid for the AAU championships, "the greatest title meet the country has to offer, and then propose to bar from competition some of the most brilliant and loyal athletes in the country."[13]

There was relatively long history of the kind of southern athletic intransigence displayed by New Orleans officials. In 1907, Penn runner John B. Taylor was threatened with lynching if he competed at the AAU meet at Jamestown, Virginia. He did, however, and broke a national record in the process. In 1910, white southerners again protested the participation of black athletes in AAU meets and again were thwarted. They tried again and failed to bar black competitors in 1914 when the championships were held in Baltimore. New Orleans, however, was not on the South's periphery, not in the upper South. It was the first Deep South location to host such an event, and it was not ready for black participation.[14]

"I had hoped that such a stand would never be taken in America," said Fred Rubien. "Colored men in the past have competed for the United States in the Olympic games abroad and have won high honors there. What a strange situation to refuse them the right to compete in the national games of their own country."[15]

The *Daily News* explained to its readers that "the city of New Orleans would have the world believe that the colored man of New Orleans is only waiting for DeHart Hubbard to make a winning jump in the gulf city to pick up his machete and automatic and go fantee." The newspaper was certain that the city "has not yet attained its mental majority."[16] The *Boston Globe* lamented that "because of Southern feeling against negro athletes," the city and "the South loses the most popular and interesting general sports event held in America."[17]

Bids to host the short-notice meet came from Boston, Baltimore, Chicago, New York, and other locations. After a vote by telegraph in early May, however, the event was finally awarded to Lincoln, Nebraska and the facilities at the University of Nebraska. The only representatives not to vote for Lincoln's bid were those from the Southern Association, who stubbornly lodged a protest vote for New Orleans.[18]

Meanwhile, white amateur athletes from New Orleans began making their way to Houston for the Southern Association meet, held at the stadium of Rice University. Lawrence di Benedetto (who would rise to the national organization's presidency in 1939 and carry the AAU into the war years) arranged for Texas governor Dan Moody to serve as an honorary referee. New Orleans mayor O'Keefe would be there as well, in his capacity as president of the Southern Association.[19]

Only one New Orleans athlete, however, won his event in Houston and qualified for the nationals in Lincoln. Lloyd Bourgeois was an employee of the Southern Pacific Railroad and was part of the company's AAU team. A husband and father of two, Bourgeois was an unlikely champion who had not gone to college, though he trained at Tulane Stadium and at a local track near his Algiers home. He went to Houston and dominated his chosen event, the triple-jump. His dedication to the craft would lead the following year to Bourgeois becoming the city's first representative in the Olympic Games in Amsterdam. In 1927, however, the nationals at Lincoln would be the most prestigious tournament in which he participated. Just as in Amsterdam in 1928, he would be the only New Orleanian there.[20]

In the run-up to the event, Roland Locke, world-record holder in the 220-yard dash and University of Nebraska standout known as the Nebraska Flyer, told an interviewer that he planned on skipping the national tournament in New Orleans, much to the dismay of many who hoped to see him race USC's Charley Borah, another star collegiate sprinter. The hopes of those awarding the games to Lincoln was that the move would convince the school's star runners to participate in the event. It would.[21]

The Lincoln championships were an unqualified success, for the city, the university, and the successful athletes at the competition. The governor of Nebraska joined roughly twelve thousand others to see the games at Lincoln. Hometown University of Nebraska star Fait Elkins won the all-around competition. Known as "Chief," Elkins was an Indian often lauded as "another Jim Thorpe."[22] New Orleans probably would have accepted Elkins, the legacy of Thorpe and the particular contours of southern racial lines, which emphasized blackness as the cardinal form of inferior difference, facilitating that willingness to stomach the presence of an Indian athlete, but it is still significant that a non-white star dominated the contest that otherwise would have taken place in New Orleans.

New Jersey's Johnny Gibson, a white hurdler, broke the world record for the 440-yard hurdles, another laurel not going to New Orleans. In the final of the 440-yard relay, held in two heats on the closing day of the Lincoln meet, four of the teams broke the world record in less than five minutes. Meanwhile, DeHart Hubbard, whose application began the process of venue change, won the broad jump at 25 feet 8¾ inches, breaking the AAU record while nursing a sprained tendon.[23]

In 1967, two years after the city's second racial media fiasco, sociologist Harry Edwards began organizing a black boycott of the 1968 Olympics. Among the goals of the effort was to have Avery Brundage removed as president of the International Olympic Committee. Brundage had a long history of racism and anti-Semitism, but in answering new charges brought by the Edwards boycott, Brundage cited in particular his time with the national AAU in 1927, claiming that he removed the national track and field championships from New Orleans because the city "would not accept negro entries." Like so many of Brundage's other racial statements, that, too, was intentionally misleading. While Brundage was AAU vice president in 1927 and would become president in 1928, the national AAU president was Murray Hulbert and the point-person for the track and field nationals was Metropolitan Association president Fred Rubien.[24]

More importantly, Brundage's prevarications masked the larger truth: that it was New Orleans officials themselves who made the decision not to keep the games if the games were going to include black athletes. There was no space between city government and Southern Association leadership. Mayor O'Keefe was president of the Southern Association. Responses from that organization were also official responses from the city. The decision to forfeit the games was, despite the rhetoric of Brundage and the newspapers that celebrated the city's demise, solely the result of the racial intransigence of New Orleans civic leadership. That would not be the case a generation later.

The United States Supreme Court spoke for the judiciary in *Brown v. Board of Education* in 1954, proclaiming that separate could never be equal, thus deeming public schools segregated by race unconstitutional. Then the legislature passed and the president signed the Civil Rights Act of 1964, which officially outlawed segregation in those areas where it still existed. With the death of Jim Crow came the birth of new political and social norms. Hundreds of stories exist where these changing generational patterns in wake of *Brown* produced a struggle between the races. One of those struggles involved the American Football League's scheduling of its yearly 1965 All-Star game in New Orleans. The city once again had a legitimate chance to promote improved race relations and its own civic standing when two professional squads, with almost half of both rosters filled with African American players, met on the gridiron, an event that New Orleans hoped would serve as a showcase that would ultimately lead to a permanent professional football franchise of its own. If New Orleans impressed the AFL, the league might consider locating a team, along with all the grandeur and money that came with it, in the Deep South. Nevertheless, the city's history, and the 1927 AAU track meet in particular, demonstrated that age-old norms, stubbornness, and an inability to accept and promote change often overcame progressive ideals and new and lucrative business and entertainment ventures. While accounts of the infamous AFL All-Star game and the city's pursuit of a professional team have been told ably but separately by others, the two events were fundamentally linked, as professional sports in the 1960s provided much the same cache and civic validation that the AAU national championships provided in the 1920s.

Unlike the older, more recognizable National Football League, the American Football League actively scouted and drafted African-American athletes from its inception. Although the Los Angeles Rams of the NFL signed Kenny Washington and Woody Strode to its roster in 1946, the move did not lead to immediate and widespread integration. While it took the NFL seventeen years to complete its task of integrating black players into its league, the new AFL accomplished the feat during its first season in 1960, when seven of its eight teams had at least one black player. By the start of the 1962 campaign, forty-seven African Americans were on the eight rosters. The league's practice of incorporating black players, however, could not completely overcome generations of bigotry. Stacking occurred regularly, as black athletes did not fill the positions that some coaches thought required more decision-making ability and responsibility than other roster spots. In 1960, for example, only five-and-a-half percent of linebackers and guards were black; none played regularly at center, kicker, punter, or quarterback. Coaches and personnel responsible for filling AFL squads "established an unwritten policy that created a positional system of racial quotas and set-asides." Even with the still discriminatory system, however, the American Football League created opportunities that the NFL closed. As historian Charles K. Ross notes, "black players brought a new style of play to the football field, one born of pride in their accomplishments, an increased assertiveness because they were no longer tokens, and a rise in levels of self-esteem brought about by the black social revolution."[25]

New Orleans had hoped that the promise of positive treatment of African-American players would create a welcome environment for professional football. The city experienced what officials considered something of a renaissance in race relations just a few weeks before the AFL All-Star game when the 1965 Sugar Bowl between Syracuse and Louisiana State University became the first integrated football game of national importance in the state since the legal end of segregation. Jim Hall of the *Louisiana Weekly,* New Orleans's African-American newspaper, praised the event, writing that the year's classic "will be sweeter because some brown coloring has been added to the mixture in the bowl. The flavor will make the pigskin dish more tasty to all." It was a milestone, however, long in coming.[26]

Unlike the Rose Bowl, which from its first contest in 1916 never discriminated against African-American athletes, the Sugar Bowl did not allow black players to participate in its New Year's' classic until 1965. The brainchild of the Mid-Winter Sports Association, the first Sugar Bowl took place on January 1, 1935, with a ban on black players on the field and a segregation of fans in the stands. Coupled with the already prevalent de facto residential segregation in the Big Easy, such race-fueled practices created a Sophie's choice for northern colleges and universities. Southern schools forced visiting squads from the north to bench their African-American players or leave them home. Demonstrating the power of southern collegiate football at the time, many southern schools even demanded black players not play in contests that took place during away games at the northern school's stadium. Segregationist policies in the South, however, did not only affect student athletes. By the late 1940s, a ticket to the Sugar Bowl contained a disclaimer: "This ticket is issued for a person of the Caucasian race." And while most northern teams did not have black players on their squads, African American students increasingly became involved in the ancillary factions of football, such as cheerleading and the marching band.[27]

The Mid-Winter Sports Association found it increasingly difficult to attract exciting match-ups to its New Year spectacle. Southern legislators continued to make the task more arduous after the Supreme Court's decision in *Brown.* The case, which famously desegregated the nation's public schools, ran counter to the prevailing notions of the White South and its ideal of a pre-Civil War paternalistic society. Sugar Bowl officials, realizing the need to keep their January tilt prevalent, loosened the racial restrictions on the bowl game by inviting an integrated University of Pittsburgh team to play Georgia Tech in the January 1, 1956 contest. The Pitt squad had one African-American footballer, Bobby Grier, who was "sufficient to alarm rabid segregationists in both Georgia and Louisiana." Georgia Tech's athletic department accepted the bid, but it knew passing the decision by boosters and the governor would be necessary. After receiving numerous complaints from donors and fans of Yellow Jackets' football, Georgia Governor Marvin Griffin reversed his original support for the squad playing in the game. He also urged the board of regents to rescind the invitation. "The South stands at Armageddon," he said. "The battle is joined. We cannot make the slightest concession to the enemy in this dark and lamentable hour of struggle. There is no more difference in compromising the integrity of race on the playing field than in doing so in the classroom. One break in the dike and the relentless seas will rush in and destroy us." Even if officials wanted to desegregate their bowl games for the sake of competition and money, clearly state actors had other things in mind.[28]

For many southern collegiate campuses, the most progressive voices came from students themselves, and Georgia Tech's students went out of their way to express disapproval of the governor's decision to keep the team out of the game. Students burned images of Griffin in effigy while organizing a group of nearly two thousand students into a march to the Georgia state capitol and the governor's mansion. Eventually, the university system board of regents reversed its decision and agreed to allow the team to compete in New Orleans for the bowl game. They did, however, note that officials would uphold the traditions of the sovereign state of Georgia at future home football contests. The "Georgia Tech Riot" did nothing to make New Orleans more appealing to professional sports leagues, especially football leagues. For a city that was hoping to present itself as a beacon of post-war diversity and progressivism, the idea of integrated sporting events taking place in The Big Easy seemed like a pipe dream. The Louisiana legislature of the 1950s did all it could to prevent desegregated contests in all sports. The Sugar Bowl's unwillingness to allow African-American players to compete hurt other sports as well. The annual collegiate basketball tournament that accompanied the football contest, for example, remained an all-white regional affair between southern teams. Northern schools also began canceling regularly scheduled matchups with Deep South schools in basketball as well as football.[29]

Eventually, in one of many showdowns between the federal government and the South, the United States Supreme Court would deal yet another death blow to Jim Crow. In 1958, United States federal courts invalidated the Louisiana law segregating athletic competition, and the United States Supreme Court upheld the decision in May 1959. The lower court case, *Dorsey v. State Athletic Commission,* began as a suit from an African-American prizefighter.[30] The court ultimately declared that the *Brown* ruling applied to athletic contests. The Louisiana State Athletic Commission's act of preventing an African-American boxer from competing violated the Constitution. The Commission's argument that the state had the right to prevent black prizefighters from competing within its borders as a constitutional use of the state's police power fell on deaf ears to the three federal judges, led by Judge Minor Wisdom. The Constitution did limit that police power, Wisdom argued, if a state took away a constitutionally protected right. The judiciary continued the work of desegregating sports by ridding the South of the last vestige of segregated athletics, segregated fan seating, in January 1964.[31]

Many in New Orleans hoped that the first desegregated Sugar Bowl would represent a bright future for race relations and a welcome stage for big-time professional football. The introduction of integrated games would only make the city's image as a potential home for a national football franchise, either from the NFL or the AFL, that much more attractive. Officials in New Orleans, especially Dave Dixon of New Orleans Professional Football, Inc., figured their best option for bringing professional football to the city was the younger AFL. Dixon hoped to use the upcoming All-Star game as New Orleans's best chance at attracting an expansion franchise to the Crescent City. Sporting his best pair of glasses with rose-colored lenses, he claimed that New Orleans set itself apart in the area of progressive race relations: "New Orleans is a different kind of a city," he claimed, ignoring the AAU debacle of 1927. "New Orleans was a better city about race than any other Southern city because of a long tradition of people living right on top of each other. I lived in a pretty nice home, and we were never more than two or three blocks from black families. We had no problems in New Orleans at all."[32]

That was, of course, a lie, but one in service to civic development, even though that development seemed far-fetched in the racial climate of the city a decade after *Brown.* In interviews with reporters during the week of the 1965 Sugar Bowl, Dixon expressed little faith in the NFL giving New Orleans a club. "All we ever get from Pete Rozelle and the NFL is politeness," said Dixon, not wanting to offend a league that could still have New Orleans in its sights. "He acts as interested in New Orleans as an Eskimo visiting here in the middle of the summer. Joe Foss [commissioner of the AFL]," however, "looks more kindly towards New Orleans." Dixon hoped to fill Tulane Stadium, which seated 80,000 fans, for the AFL All-Star Game. Realistically, he figured about 45,000 fans would attend the event, which would still double the average annual attendance at previous years' matches. The largest crowd of the past three AFL All-Star games, for instance, numbered 25,500 at an event in San Diego. Dixon also hoped a great All-Star game would add to the two successful AFL exhibitions already on the city's resume. Compared to Houston's regular-season attendance figures, New Orleans totaled around 21,000 paying attendees. Dixon and other optimists thought little stood in New Orleans's way of impressing Joe Foss and other AFL officials when they considered expansion.[33]

The game was to take place on January 16, 1965. The players slated to participate in the contest only increased the interest of Louisianans, both black and white. Three players hailed from Grambling State University. Ernie Ladd of the San Diego Chargers, Buck Buchanan of the Kansas City Chiefs, and Willie Brown of the Denver Broncos would be on the field playing for the West squad. The league named Ladd and Brown unanimous All-Pro selections. Kansas City selected Buchanan with its first pick in the 1962 draft. Other local stars included LSU legend and Heisman Trophy winner Billy Cannon. Drafted by the Houston Oilers in 1960, he now played for the Oakland Raiders. Johnny Robinson of LSU would also be on the field. Anticipation and excitement kept building for New Orleans and its officials hoping to bring professional football to the city on a more permanent basis.[34]

The emotional high of all involved in the concerted effort to bring pro football to Louisiana, however, died quickly. Black players on both the East and the West squads complained of widespread discrimination and poor treatment from New Orleans citizens and business owners. According to some, that mistreatment began at the airport. Ernie Warlick told of African-American players having to wait almost an hour to hail a cab from the Moisant International Airport to their hotels. "It seemed that if Negro players were with several white players they were serviced by the cab drivers," he said. "But the ones who were not with white teammates were refused service."[35] While Warlick never experienced trouble at the airport, transportation from the hotel presented another set of obstacles. "Several cab drivers outside the Fontainbleau refused to take me," said Warlick. Halfback Clem Daniels of the Oakland Raiders stated that he was part of a group that had to wait about twenty minutes for a cab outside of the hotel. "There were five or six cabs lined up outside the hotel but the divers began getting out of their cabs and walking away rather than service us," stated Daniels. He continued, "Finally, we stood in the middle of the street and a cab stopped rather than run us down." Dick Westmoreland, a defensive back for the San Diego Chargers and West squad alternate, said that one cab driver stopped and "told us he couldn't take us because he'd be arrested if the police saw him carrying Negro passengers. He suggested that we call a Negro cab." While black players had to physically hail cabs in unheard of ways, taxi drivers were not the only New Orleanians giving the players grief.[36]

Westmoreland also spoke of owners and personnel preventing them from entering certain clubs and bars in the French Quarter. "We weren't looking for trouble. We were just sightseeing. Doors were shut in our faces as we attempted to enter several establishments and some people hurled insults at us," he said. "We could plainly see that we were not wanted and felt it best to return to the hotel but being unfamiliar with the city we didn't know the way." Warlick told reporters that the treatment took the players by complete surprise. "We were led to believe that we could relax and enjoy ourselves in New Orleans just like other citizens. Maybe if we had been alerted to the fact that we wouldn't have the run of the town, we could have avoided this unpleasant situation." The African American players eventually met with each other at the Roosevelt Hotel to discuss matters.[37]

White player Ron Mix, concerned about the black players' feelings and their solutions to the problems faced on the streets of New Orleans, decided to walk over to the Sunday, January 10 meeting at the Roosevelt as well. Mix "felt something was wrong about what the Negro ballplayers were doing. Not wrong to protest, but wrong in method. An action such as this must lead to a favorable result. What would be accomplished by their actions? Nothing that I could see." While discussing methods with the players, Ernie Warlick interrupted and brought up previous poor treatment black players received in Atlanta. "A definite action must be taken," he said. Art Powell agreed. "Look, we know we aren't going to change these people. But neither are they going to change us. We must act as our conscience dictates," he told the room. "I suppose it would be better to stay here and by doing so, imply that we accept such treatment for ourselves and our people? Do you want us to condone that?" he asked. The players became even more candid in speaking to Mix. Abner Hayes told a story of asking a taxi to take him to a nightclub; the cab driver instead drove him to one that Hayes claimed "is a hangout for perverts." He wasn't the only one. "Ernie Ladd, Dick Westmoreland and a couple of others had been turned away from one Bourbon Street club by a man who indicated he had a gun." Mix sympathized with the players even if he did not agree with their methods of protest. In the end, however, he made it known that he would stand next to his fellow players and not participate in the All-Star game if they chose to sit out.[38]

Later at that meeting, the African American players announced that they would present a united front and boycott the game as scheduled in New Orleans. Most of the players arranged to leave the city as soon as possible. Ernie Warlick served as the spokesperson for the group and made an official statement on its behalf. He stated that being a part of such a progressive sports league regarding African American participation meant that the black players should not play in New Orleans that Saturday. The players felt they could not perform one hundred percent in the contest. "With the exception of the hotels where the squads were quartered," Warlick said, "recreational facilities and transportation were not available to the Negro players and service was refused." Commissioner Joe Foss, called that night by the protesting group, assured them that the league would stand behind whatever decision they made. The commissioner officially announced the decision the next morning.[39]

The AFL, siding with its disgruntled players, moved the game to the 37,000 seat Jeppesen Stadium in Houston, Texas. Foss, on the phone all night before making the decision, agreed that the players had adequate reason to walk out. African Americans across the city and state agreed with the decision, as well. Jim Hall of the *Louisiana Weekly* wrote that New Orleans probably lost pro football altogether due to the treatment of the players. "This shocking blow, knocked New Orleans down the ladder in its bid to reach the top," wrote Hall. "The years of work to push the city into 'Big Time' sports went down the drain Sunday, when the racial discrimination snake in the French Quarter and the local cabs sank its ugly fangs in the Negro players here for the game." There would be no way to stop the racial downpour, as Hall called it, "and because of the 'hate' shower, which has been continuous in certain quarters, New Orleans chances of being a sports center, have been drowned."[40]

Ernest N. Morial, the New Orleans NAACP president, also agreed with the players' decision. He met with the black players during their afternoon meeting in response to an invitation from the protesting players. Morial told players that he would support whatever they decided to do, but that they should consider giving the city twenty-four hours to determine if officials could do something to keep the game in New Orleans. The affected parties attempted to make contact with New Orleans Mayor Victor H. Schiro, but he could not meet with them that night due to illness. Morial told them that the NAACP would continue to push for changes in the city, regardless of the decision they made. The city's black leadership presented a solid front in support of their fellow African Americans' actions and their attempts to enlighten the community to their plight.[41]

The white leadership of New Orleans and Louisiana, meanwhile, solidly opposed the actions of the black players. Mayor Schiro, for example, began his official statement by saying that "if these men would play football only in cities where everybody loved them, they would all be out of a job today. Their reaction would only aggravate the very condition they are seeking, in time, to eliminate. We are a very cosmopolitan and tolerant city, but we are also a Southern city, and there are times when personal reaction is unpredictable." The mayor used the recent Sugar Bowl as an indication that integrated sports do have a place in New Orleans, even though Syracuse had only eight African American players and LSU had none. Schiro continued by stating that the players who walked out "should have rolled with the punch. Almost all of them are educated, college men, who must be aware that you cannot change human nature overnight." He criticized them as doing "themselves and their race a disservice by precipitous action. Not to mention the irreparable harm they inflicted on the future of professional football in New Orleans." Schiro, unlike O'Keefe a generation prior, had no position of authority in athletics decisions and, barred from helping choose the city's fate, instead lashed out at the players, only adding further fuel to the racial fire. Importantly, however, Schiro was not doing so in aid of a desire to keep the game and the players in New Orleans. He was clumsy and frustrated in his handling of the debacle, but he was not taking a roundly white supremacist stand.[42]

Chairman E.M. Rowley of the Citizens' Special Committee expressed a similar regret, though better expressed, especially since, in his opinion, New Orleans was making great strides in race relations since the passage of the Civil Rights Act. Nicholas Tedesco, director of the City Cab Bureau, injected a little realism into the city's response. While stating that those cabs with Negro permits could carry whites and white-permit cabs could now carry African Americans, individual drivers did not have to cater to them. Section 12–91 of the city code still gave individual permit holders the right to carry only those passengers that their permit designated. The discussion of these city leaders merely reinforced the uncertainty of race relations following the Civil Rights Act and the problems the city would face in the future.[43]

A *Times-Picayune* sports editorial stated that the players should have fulfilled their obligations to their employers and to the city. The writer mentioned an issue he had with getting a cab in New York City to the Aqueduct racetrack to cover the Belmont Stakes, wherein the driver refused him service not because of his race but because of the location of the track. The writer went on to praise Dave Dixon for the work he did in procuring the contest for the city and told citizens of New Orleans to keep their heads held high, for a chance for the Crescent City to get a professional franchise still remained. Governor John McKeithen, speaking at a Chamber of Commerce luncheon in New Orleans, stated that he was proud of Louisiana and its racial progress. The players acted unreasonably, in his opinion, because they did not tell the mayor or himself that they were leaving. McKeithen declared that the "black players should have given the city a chance. There are some clubs on Bourbon Street that won't even let our D.A. in."[44]

It was a good line, and very likely true. But blame for the game's absence belonged solely on white New Orleans. The boycott of New Orleans by black AFL players represented a milestone for civil rights in sports. While other African-American athletes had protested against discrimination before, this hugely powerful move forced the league to move its All-Star game due to player concerns. The players' efforts also hammered the last nail into the coffin of American Football League action in New Orleans.[45]

Ultimately, professional football would march into New Orleans, but it would not be a team from the American Football League. Louisiana utilized its political muscle in wrangling a professional football franchise for the Big Easy via the National Football League. Dave Dixon's dreams finally materialized due to the political clout of the state's representatives in the United States Congress. NFL owners did not mind early on keeping their numbers small, as a lucrative profit-sharing agreement kept their pockets full. But the league's practice of absorbing smaller leagues before they became competitive enough to take away from the NFL's spotlight eventually led league officials to the AFL. Owners knew, however, that they would not be able to get a merger as large as the NFL-AFL past federal trade regulators unless they had an antitrust exemption. Major League Baseball had such an exemption, but earlier efforts at the NFL gaining something similar fell short.[46] The league would finally get that congressional exemption through the efforts of Louisiana's Senator Russell Long and Congressman Hale Boggs. As a reward for their efforts, the newly-created NFL, which had absorbed its AFL rival and now had two conference components, the National Football Conference and the American Football Conference, awarded a franchise to New Orleans.[47]

It was a post-*Brown* story that began with hope—hope from the Mid-Winter Sports Association that its Sugar Bowl could become the draw of the nation's eye, pitting two of the best collegiate football squads in competition, and hope from Dave Dixon and others that New Orleans could become the beacon of success for southern Jim Crow cities to emerge from the ashes and become the phoenix of progressive race relations. But the city did nothing to create a welcome environment for professional sports in Louisiana. The actions and reactions of both African Americans and whites involved in the AFL's boycott of New Orleans demonstrated how far the Crescent City still had to go in achieving improved race relations after the passage of the Civil Rights Act. Officials in New Orleans hoped the game would serve as a stage for the city to show off progressive race relations to the nation and those in control of the AFL, but for a segment of the city's population the continued mistreatment of blacks and the maintenance of segregation outweighed the importance of the city gaining a professional football franchise.

Despite Schiro's clumsy, vindictive response to the boycott, the incident demonstrated a situation where a southern metropolitan government attempting to establish itself as a Sunbelt power was ahead of its population on race relations. These politicians were not playing to the racist whims of their citizens like white populist leaders in statehouses across the region. Instead, they were attempting to remedy the problems that occurred at events like the 1927 AAU national track and field championships. While civic leaders had made the changes to remedy the city's early failings, a segment of their citizens had yet to come around. That the pace of change between governments and governed would not be uniform is not a radical notion, of course, but the history of post-*Brown* southern populism demonstrates that usually the politicians followed the racial whims of a given constituency to curry favor and maintain power. The progression of New Orleans from 1927 to 1965, however, told a different story, one where the city government, in an effort at civic development, had learned from past mistakes and sought to put racial differences behind it while a vocal part of its citizenry stayed behind. The differentiation would not produce electoral consequences for Schiro because the city was still able to secure the Saints two years later, but it was differentiation nonetheless.

Such is not to say that all white citizens of New Orleans were atavistic racists. Demonstrating the lack of monolithic uniformity in the city's racial thinking, two years after the AFL All-Star Game debacle, in 1967, the fully-integrated Saints played their inaugural season in the city. Two years after the AAU track and field debacle, in 1929, New Orleans industrialist and Assistant Secretary of the Navy Ernest Lee Jahncke became a United States representative on the International Olympic Committee, a tenure that would end in 1936 when Jahncke refused to support the location of the summer Olympics in Hitler's Berlin. Jahncke became the only man in the twentieth century to be "fired" from the IOC after his moral stand against the Nazis. Jahncke was very much part of the New Orleans elite that produced O'Keefe and the other civic leaders who turned against an integrated AAU meet, but racial thinking was never uniform in New Orleans.[48]

That reality makes understanding the pace of racial awakening between government and governed all the more significant. Civic leaders had no moral epiphany by the time of the AFL All-Star Game. There was instead an economic epiphany, one that average white citizens could not see as being in their interest. A team of their own like the Saints, however, was a legitimate carrot, not just for civic boosterism, but for disaffected white citizens who could fold the new team into their own self-identity. The pace of such racial awakenings, then, was never about moral reckonings. It was instead about proximity to tangible economic benefits, a proximity that would always redound to civic leaders and thus skew the pace of racial change in the city.

CHAPTER TWELVE

'In Spite of Ourselves' They Were the Pride of New Orleans

The Role of Race, Gender, and the Media in the Demise of the Crescent City's Women's Professional Basketball Franchise, 1979–1981

STACY LYNN TANNER

An important accomplishment of the American women's rights movement was the passage and implementation of Title IX, and an important accomplishment of the civil rights movement was the passage of Title VI.[1] The timing of the passage and execution of these laws facilitated the establishment of racially integrated women's professional sports leagues across the nation. However, a backlash against the civil rights and women's rights movements led to the abrupt fall of these leagues.

New Orleans was always a prime candidate for inclusion in those leagues. In many ways New Orleans served as an economic, political, and a social exception to the South and the nation as a whole. Certainly, New Orleanians thought of themselves and their city as exceptional. The fight to regulate women's bodies and vice along with the historically racial and ethnic diversity of the city are but a few things that help explain the residents' historically unique experience.[2] Much has been written about the cultural history of New Orleans, yet Dale A. Somers' *The Rise of Sports in New Orleans, 1850–1900* is the only significant work that comprehensively deals with sports in New Orleans. And his work contains few references to the discourse on physical education and sports programs for women in the city. Historian Joan Paul has supplemented his work by describing

A game program from the New Orleans Pride's inaugural season. Program cover in the public domain.

early women's physical educator Clara Gregory Baer and her expansion of the women's version of basketball at the city's Newcomb College. [3]

Certainly from Baer's time until the last part of the twentieth century (and arguably into the twenty-first) the more aggressive the model of the sport, the less ideal the model was considered for women. Basketball was considered one of the more aggressive and less feminine sports, especially after changes to the women's game that happened in the 1970s. At the beginning of the decade, the women's game changed to a five-on-five full-court game from a more static half-court game, but also to what some would consider street ball, a game that many African American women already knew how to play, particularly by the end of the decade, when entrepreneur Bill Byrne organized the Women's Professional Basketball League (WBL).[4] The experience of many black women players would offer them the opportunity to thrive in the new league, provided that the league itself could thrive.

Throughout the 1970s women's basketball saw tremendous growth. In 1976, women's basketball became an official Olympic sport. In the 1970s NCAA officials looked to takeover women's sports championships, then held by the Association of Intercollegiate Athletics for Women (AIAW). In the context of this increased interest in women's sports and a new interest in the potential financial benefit of women's sport, Byrne hashed out and executed a plan to create the first women's professional basketball league in the summer of 1977. In October of 1977 the league was born when Bryne, David Almstead, and Carew Smith incorporated in Ohio. The initial bylaws required eight teams for play to begin but offered room to grow with a plan for twelve. This group's optimism was infectious enough in the right circles because within about eight months the league had the necessary number of investors. And in December of 1978 those eight teams, the Chicago Hustle, Dayton (previously DC) Rockettes, Houston Angels, Iowa Cornets, Milwaukee Does, Minnesota Fillies, New Jersey Gems, and the New York Stars, began the league's inaugural season.[5] With the anticipated slow start, but hopeful growth of the WBL, expansion investors emerged in the second year. Those investors included Dr. John W. and Claudette Simpson who, with their stockbroker, Steve Brown, worked out a deal to fund the New Orleans franchise.[6]

The WBL became possible and built strength from the sweat of evolving women's high school and college programs. By the late 1970s the impact of Title IX began to be felt at the college level. In 1975, an important women's basketball program was evolving at Louisiana Tech under the leadership of Sonja Hogg. She remembered how then-university president F. Jay Taylor told her, "I do not want you to be an appendage of the men's program." Mickie Demoss, former point guard and current associate head coach for the team, described Hogg: "She was very much a Southern Lady. She carried that over to the basketball court. Of course, she wanted to win, but we had to win the right way and we had to conduct ourselves in the right way." [7] Hogg and her program would in many ways define post-Title IX women's basketball. Louisiana Tech quickly earned three titles, the first of which was the inaugural NCAA women's basketball title in 1982. Clearly there was pressure at all levels to emphasize the differences between the men's and women's game, and one of the reasons for Hogg's success at Tech was her feminine branding of women's basketball, so clearly recollected by players such as DeMoss thirty-four years later. This legacy loomed in New Orleans when the city got a franchise in the WBL, the New Orleans Pride.

The challenge that the team's management, its coach, and the city's media continuously discussed was how to sell the game, the team, and the idea of women's sports more generally to New Orleanians. For the most part, those involved relied on the same model upon which Hogg relied at Tech, a model thought most culturally acceptable, emphasizing white hegemonic femininity and leaving, with few exceptions, the players of color out of bounds.[8] The management's attempt at branding the team and the "new" women's game frequently meant emphasizing gender difference and collapsing black women's identity within the media, habitually ignoring the race of the woman player. For promoters, this meant abandoning a key segment of the city's population who might otherwise have been very interested in supporting a women's basketball team that embraced the talents of each of its players, one that was truly different than the men's game and the teams of the NBA.[9] While the game changed, it also stayed much the same for the white and black women of the New Orleans Pride.

Many forces contributed to the demise of the Crescent City's first women's professional basketball team. On a local level, the media's treatment of race had a detrimental impact on the public perception of the team. The media and the management of the team took several approaches to avoid illustrating race. Through my study of the products of the local media, several things became abundantly clear. First, the media coverage of the sporting performances of people of color on the New Orleans Pride team was frequently missing. Second, when coverage was present, it was commonly limited to a statistic or to one sentence. The statistic and/or sentence was nearly always an addendum to a stat or comment regarding a player of a different race. Third, when the infrequent opportunity presented itself, black players spoke for themselves. Fourth, the team and its players of color were taken seriously and often fiercely defended by Champ Clark in his column, "The Sports Parade," within the city's major African American newspaper, the *Louisiana Weekly.* The irreverence shown by the staff writers of the *States Item* and the near silence from those at the *Times Picayune,* however, meant that any late support for the team was truly fallacious fanfare. Of the television coverage available, one program has survived, WVUE-TV's *Project 8* feature, "Pride of New Orleans," which aired in October 1979. Even when race was visible, as it was on this television program, the themes and discussions within the program reflected a similar disregard for race found in the pages of the *States Item* and the *Times Picayune.*

Opportunities for the New Orleans Pride to win games often materialized as a result of the talent and experience of black players. Those players included Queen Brumfield, Coretta Bloom, Wanda Ard, Beverly Crusoe, Betty Booker, and, especially, Augusta Forest and Bertha Hardy. The quality and quantity of the media coverage of the players was never apparently nor necessarily fair and balanced in either of the city's mainstream dailies.

Early on, much of the media attention directed at Queen Brumfield seemed appropriate. After all, she was the team's inaugural number one draft pick. In a *Times-Picayune* feature article by Lily Jackson, Queen Brumfield was interviewed regarding being the Pride's number one draft pick of 1979. Brumfield explained her position about women's basketball. "The game is played exactly like the men's, but the women's game is generally more intense . . . . [The women's game] is played with more heart." Jackson explained of Brumfield, "She graciously acknowledges the ability and agility of the men in the sport but feels that women are equally adept in professional basketball, where the men and women will continue to play in separate courts."[10] With special emphasis on the separate but equal frame for sport, Jackson subordinated and, if not for the photos, eliminated Brumfield's identity as a black player.[11]

It was also commonplace to subordinate race and sometimes even erase race from the WBL court within the coverage of players and games within the *States Item,* led by Ron Brocato, the paper's beat reporter for the Pride's games. He pithily reported the accomplishments of the team's star player, Augusta Forest, but his decorative language typically tarnished otherwise positive reports. For example, Brocato titled one article, "Pride's Forest a One Girl Gang." While the article seems to acknowledge Forest's exceptional performance, he calls her a girl and a gang. At best, it reads as a back-handed compliment. At worst, it is a racist comment meant to single her out. Somewhere in the middle was a reporter trying to garner the attention of his readership. Either way, the article did not focus on Forest's play. Instead, it discussed a number of players, including new addition Bertha Hardy, from the perspective of the coach, Butch van Breda Kolff. [12]

Brocato's brief reporting of the performance of black players was frequently an addendum to reports of the performance of other players on the team. On the surface this seems fair, particularly for a team whose coach stressed the importance of team-oriented play and combinations. In a discussion of this team-oriented play and in an effort at balanced coverage, Brocato wrote that no player ranked among the league leaders in scoring, listing those who came closest. Forest was closest, then Smallwood, Hardy, and Blalock. He also referenced Wanda Ard and Cindy Williams in the same breath, but in very different ways. He called them both "floor burners" but described Cindy Williams as "a petite blonde who married her high school math teacher" and Wanda Ard as having a "five-year-old daughter."[13] The likely intent was to feminize both Williams as a wife and Ard as a mother, but without a mention of a marriage for Ard, Brocato's audience is left to assume a lot about her personal life. One need not count the words on the page to notice the disparity in the number of interviews and quotes from white and black players within Brocato's reports. The white player interviews far outnumbered those of the black players, and it is clear that his coverage was not equitable. It seems that Brocato's brevity assuaged those associated with his newspaper who had interest in balanced coverage.

In *Mad Seasons: The Story of the First Women's Professional Basketball League,* Karra Porter acknowledges the "racial disparities [that were] being debated in all the professional sports leagues."[14] For the WBL and the New Orleans Pride, there was less a debate than a consistent disavowal of racial disparity from major media outlet coverage of the league and the team. In an interview by Porter, Bill Byrne, a founder of the WBL, purportedly said, "In women's basketball the black and white thing is just so easy for me, because in sports you don't look at that."

Clearly Ray Beard, who reported on the Pride for the *Times-Picayune,* got the memo. On the surface, Beard appeared to make a genuine attempt at balanced and accurate coverage of the Pride team. In an article meant to feature black Pride guard Wanda Ard, he offered questions and printed her answers. He ignored, however, the "black and white thing." He quickly collapsed her identity to that of a woman in order to align with the branding of the team and, clearly, the league. "Many college players—men or women—dream of playing professional sports when their collegiate career is over," Beard wrote, "and so far Ard has not been disappointed in the professional life."[15] Underneath this language was the intent to direct readers' attention toward her gender and likely less intentionally to divert it away from her race.

Bill Grady reported on the Pride in a feature article in the "Dixie Magazine" within the *Times Picayune* late in the team's first season. The article title, "Pride and Prejudice," suggested that the author might discuss issues related to race because the word prejudice was commonly used at this time to reference racism. Instead, his readers saw Sandra Smallwood, a white player, in action against a white opponent from the California Dream, and the words on the page did not refer to black players, but instead to sexist sports fans. Typical of articles related to the team, Grady's interview established the conversation about the fledgling team and league by comparing the women's game to the men's game and more generally women to men without regard to the pluralistic identities of the players. Steve Brown, then the Pride's general manager, said, "Our main problem is changing the minds of male sports enthusiasts." And Grady reiterated this idea. "The major obstacle is erasing from the minds of male-chauvinist sports fans their preconceived notions about women's basketball," he wrote, but without acknowledging the diversity of the team and the issues surrounding its integrated status.[16]

The absence of a conversation on race was typical of both the *Times-Picayune* and the *States Item*. Within her study of the WBL, Porter alleged again and again that team owners and coaches alike never took race into account when building their teams. Yet there were WBL staff members, Gail Marquis and Cardie Hicks, who admitted that there were inequities in the way that teams and players were promoted.[17] In New Orleans, such inequities seemed to spill over into the major media outlets.

Even after New Orleans became the team with the fewest black players (two) in the league during its final season after trading Betty Booker and Beverly Crusoe, reporters, players, and coaches vehemently denied claims of racial bias. And for all of the team's first and much of its second season, it remained unclear whether Butch van Breda Kolff and the management of the team made major personnel decisions together or if the coach called the plays and the management called the shots. The management in the 1980–1981 season was Mrs. Claudette Simpson, wife of majority owner Dr. John Simpson. Van Breda Kolff claimed that Mrs. Simpson called the shots, but later admitted that he approved of the Booker deal but wanted to keep Crusoe. Either way, Beverly Crusoe and Betty Booker were traded in January 1981, and the number of black players on the Pride roster dropped to two, top scorers Bertha Hardy and Augusta Forest.

Mike Strom of the *Times-Picayune* enumerated the disagreements between the Simpsons and van Breda Kolff, a list that grew longer than the team's losing streak late in the final 1980–1981 season. Strom made it clear that personnel decisions were at the heart of the disagreements between the Simpsons and van Breda Kolff that led to his late season suspension. He reported that Mrs. Simpson had the final say in regard to personnel decisions and quoting her as saying that while Butch, "approved all those trades," he also quoted Simpson as saying, "If I had fielded an all-black team out there, no one would have come out."[18] It was a comment that answered the question of racial bias and proved the racially motivated decisions made by Pride management. It may have taken almost two full seasons for the *Times-Picayune* to include such an overtly racist comment related the team, but another reporter from a different part of town recognized the problem all along.

While Ron Brocato demonstrated the desire of some New Orleanians to avoid discussion of race and Ray Beard sat on the fence, Champ Clark of the *Louisiana Weekly* was outspoken about the way the media treated the Pride and the team's black players. It is doubtful that anyone misunderstood Clark's opinions about the black women who played for the Pride. While Brocato, Beard, and others regularly disavowed race, it was ordinarily the focus of Champ Clark's coverage. This was both a strength and a weakness of his coverage. His emphasis on racial unity and his commitment to consistently cover the team was commendable and sent a cohesive message to his primarily black readership, but his focus on racial difference routinely displaced the sexist system of oppression that the black women players also faced.

Clark seemed to be the only person willing and able to stand up and speak out about racial issues. In November 1979, he used his column to call out racism in sport as he saw it. "In a moral sense, the malignancy (prejudice), which afflicts our American society is more vicious and disruptive than the cancer cells which heap destruction upon our physical well being," he wrote. "There is no question that the local sports media is infested with prejudice. Seldom, if ever, is there an objective reporting of the news."[19] In effect, Clark was proclaiming his personal commitment to objectively report the news, particularly when it came to the Pride.

The quantity of coverage found in any issue of the *Louisiana Weekly* and the frequency of publication could not compete with the local dailies, but the quality and consistency of Clark's articles could not possibly have gone unnoticed by his readership. If the Pride played, Champ was always there, always evaluating the team's performance. He said of van Breda Kolff's substitutions, "Augusta Forest tops the club in scoring, but she doesn't receive the playing time of Paula Dean. Neither does Coretta Bloom."[20] He also consistently connected such critiques to his promotion of the team.

He recurrently called on the black community to support the black players and the team. Clark nudged fans to attend the next home game, "On January 25 and down the stretch, the fans will be watching to see if the Pride are playing the best combinations. Sure I've heard it said: 'The coach plays his own combinations.' I've also heard it said, 'The cash customers are the ones, who control the destiny of the team.'"[21] He was clearly implying that if the attendance of black fans increased, it might exert pressure of the coach to be more strategic in his substitution of Forest and other talented black players. Clark was not reluctant to vocalize his assessment of the team, nor was he reticent to appraise the performance of other sports reporters.

Champ did not let the absence of reporters from other newspapers go unnoticed. He said, "Local promoters just do not exert the same enthusiasm in promoting black stars," he wrote. "If you do not believe that racism abounds in New Orleans then you do not believe that rice is grown in China."[22] In another column from the fall of 1980, he called on his community to support the team while calling on inattentive reporters from the "metro sheets" to pay closer attention to the team. He asked, "How many Orleanians can go out on the courts and recognize these players? Incidentally, I can because I attend all of the games. Do you? Let's get behind the Pride! They need our help." He also asked in November 1980, "I wonder what the Simpsons feel about the third-rate coverage the Pride are receiving?"[23] plainly pointing to the lack of support from the *Times-Picayune* and other daily newspapers. Such comments were not sporadic; they were part of his method.

When the team announced a possible move to Kenner in 1981, Clark spoke up about the economic impact the decision would have on the black community. He said that a move would "seriously impede patrons living in the CBD area getting out to Kenner. I could be wrong, but I just believe that New Orleans needs a franchise based within our own municipal limits." Black fans from the city likely wouldn't have the time or money to make it to games so far away from their homes, making it that much harder to attend games at a time when the Pride needed all the moral and financial support they could get. From Clark's perspective no one from the management or the media seemed to be concerned over whether the black community supported the team.[24]

Champ Clark's attention to covering the performances of white players was similar to those of Ray Beard and Ron Brocato in covering black players, in respect to his use of the addendum. In a report of a quarter-final game against the Minnesota Fillies, Clark rightly suggested that the Pride needed to have more height, more players capable of playing a physical game, and a better backcourt. He criticized van Breda Kolff's predictability to call plays for the white guards, Sandra Smallwood, Sybil Blalock, and Paula Dean. More physical players like Wanda Ard and sharper shooters like Coretta Bloom would have been a better fit.[25] Clark commonly juxtaposed a less than adequate performance of a white player with the strengths and reasons van Breda Kolff should have played a black player or left them in the game longer. Clark studied the team and its coach for an entire season (and likely studied van Breda Kolff longer, as he was the coach of the NBA's Jazz for a period). His coverage was neither inconsistent nor unobjective, but it did clearly place emphasis on the talents of black players and the coach's seemingly lackluster play calls. Clark used the addendum in the reporting of black players' performances, but the infrequency of his weekly newspaper in comparison with the "metro sheets" likely concealed the impact.

Clark's intentional use of the addendum is debatable, but its regularity is not. In an article in support of growing the fan base over the 1980–1981 season, Clark featured Augusta Forest's skills. He followed this with a brief description of what positions other primarily white players would play. "In the front line with Forest are Cindy Brogdon and Bertha Hardy. The starting guards are Beverly Crusoe and Sybil Blalock."[26] He also offered, "We wonder why Sybil Blalock gets so much press. The best guard combination for the Pride could be Bev Crusoe and Sharon Farrell."[27] In both of the examples, he clearly used the addendum in dropping the names of several of the players without including a balanced discussion of their performances.

Clark also consistently condemned what he rightly considered to be overt racism on the part of the Pride organization. One of Clark's most vehemently anti-racist rants came on the heels of the Booker-Crusoe trade in January 1981. He jibed, "All that is needed now is to trade off Hardy and Forest. The Pride are going to continue to win, but they will continue their course of financial fiascoes as long as personality, not talent, is the guideline." And far more seriously he countered, "Why cannot coaches and athletic directors be colorblind?"[28] He likely never expected a response, but his rhetoric was clear; he was certainly frustrated by the Pride's inability to recognize and correct their weakness if for no other reason than the sake of the game.

Consistently throughout the franchise's existence, Champ criticized van Breda Kolff's lineup and bench. He snapped, "From my opinion, and this is purely my opinion, some of the players like Tesa Duckworth and Coretta Bloom have the potential, but they are not getting the playing time needed. We, also, wonder why Queen Ann Brumfield and Augusta Forest are seldom in the lineup together," he asked. We're not saying van Breda Kolff is not doing a good coaching job—we're simply saying that the Pride needs more rebounding strength, they need more height and proficiency inside."[29] Clark used the word "we" six times in the short article after explaining that the following response was his own opinion. Here he sent a cohesive message of the necessity for racial solidarity.

It is reasonable to conclude that Clark's readership expected that racial unity would be the fundamental message that would levitate from the pages of this African American newspaper.[30] In many ways, Clark was a standard bearer. His flag was no more prominent than in an article meant to glorify Bertha Hardy's accomplishments. Clark said,

> Whenever I think of Bertha Hardy, I think of the infantry. The soldiers in the trenches rarely get the credit of other branches. Likewise, Hardy, who is a complete player, seldom gets the gobs of publicity that the high scorers get such as Cindy Brogdon. But, if you compare Cindy and Bertha on their defensive genius, it isn't close.[31]

Here, Clark clearly grounded the players' differences in race. And this kind of comparison left black women players, in this case Bertha Hardy, genderless. They were genderless because everyone knew Hardy was a basketball player; that women were not infantry soldiers. Through the common omission of pronouns and his infantry soldier analogy, Clark stripped Hardy of her gendered identity and fortified her identity as a black person.

Coverage of the sporting performances of people of color on the New Orleans Pride, however, was frequently missing or scant in both mainstream print and televised media programs. Save for the enthusiastic WVUE-TV *Project 8* feature of the team that aired prior to the Pride's first season, television coverage of the team more generally is commonly missing from the catalogs within the archives of local media stations. Interestingly, the surviving program's narrative focused on the long-term approach of the management, the coach, and the owners of the team. Although the players were not the focus of the program, it provided opportunities for them to speak for themselves. This meant that there were moments when black players also spoke for themselves, thus providing an important glimpse into the minds and experiences of some of the women players of color. This single known remaining television program, while purposefully encouraging in tone, fell short of the long-term goal of increasing support for the team. The producers' careful deference to white men and the director's focus on whiteness meant that once again media coverage of the team did not represent all or even most of the city's population and potential fan base. Hence, contrary to the creator's intent, the *Project 8* feature, much like the city's print sources, contributed to the dissolution, not the growth, of the New Orleans Pride.

The establishing scene framed the feature around whiteness and about white men's ideas. The program opened with a close-up of a white woman's fast, low dribble of basketball followed by her completion of a layup. The audience never sees the woman's face and is left with the image of a white woman as player. The director then cuts to a medium close-up of a fifty-something white man wearing a baseball cap with the American flag on it. The program's writer, narrator, and producer, Patricia Gormin, asks in a voice over, "What do you think of the idea of a women's professional basketball team?" To which he responds flatly, "Well I think the men didn't make it. Maybe the girls will." The producers then cut to a ten-second clip of the women practicing a jump ball as if to emphasize that the fate of the team is still up in the air. There were at least two important ideas stressed in this establishing scene, which are reinforced throughout the program: whiteness defines the woman basketball player and the male voice of approval is a clear priority.

Director Robert Weaver appended the establishing scene to one with another brief interview with a white man, the apparent owner of a deli or a short order restaurant. In a medium shot with Gormin's back to the camera, in order to emphasize and capture the cook/owner's reaction, she asks, "Do you think most of the guys who come in here will go see it [the women's game]?" To which he says, "I think they will. I think they'll support them more than they do the Saints." The reporter countered, "Why is that?" The local man says, "Nawlins ain't got nuttin'. Maybe the ladies'll help it out." To which she rejoined, "You think the team will be taken seriously?" He says, "Yes. M'ame" As the camera zooms in for a close up, the reporter is no longer in the frame. She asks, "Would you take your wife to see it?" His response included a sly smile. "I'm not married, but I would take somebody else's wife to see 'em." It was evidence of the underlying sexism within society and its impact on the growth of women's sports. Here, the filmmakers send a complex message, because while the owner says others will go see the Pride, he never commits to attending a game, never commits his own time or money in support of the team. At the same time, he subtly includes his opinion about the position of women. He makes it clear that he had more interest in other people's wives than the women's game.

A scene with a white woman and her baby completes the sequence that establishes the dominance of whiteness and white men within the program. When asked the same question regarding whether the women's team will be taken seriously, the mother said that the Pride would not be taken seriously at first. "It might take some effective PR, but I think that eventually it will be a good entertainment for the whole family," she said, "especially if they have male cheerleaders." This scene solidifies the subordination women to men, black women to white women, and, less legibly, heterosexuality to homosexuality. Up to this point in the film, the only people who speak are white, the only women who speak are white, and the only woman interviewed is a mother, further framing women's sports under the veil of white hegemonic femininity.[32]

The creators of the program committed an inordinate amount of camera time to the management, coach, and owners of the team in what appeared to be a half-hearted effort to convince the viewership of the team's potential. After the introductory sequence, Gormin sits down with Steve Brown, the team's general manager and "biggest booster." Brown is exuberant in his descriptions of what he believes the league can achieve and bases his conclusions on the growth of other women's sports such as tennis. He likely carefully chose this example given the growth of the sport nationally, which stemmed at least partially from the attention that erupted from the 'Battle of the Sexes' contest between Bobby Riggs and Billie Jean King in 1973.[33] Brown sought to link the potential of the franchise's success to King's success in defeating Riggs and her subsequent battle for equal pay for women tennis players and other athletes.

Brown embeds these comparisons within his enthusiasm for the community that he is trying to build through constructing this WBL organization. For example, he unequivocally proclaims that the best coach for this city is Butch van Breda Kolff because "he is loved by the people of this city and he is a great coach." Van Breda Kolff has spent the last several years in New Orleans, first coaching the NBA's Jazz (1974–1977), then the University of New Orleans (1977–1979).[34] Brown works to tie the community's affinity for the fiery coach to the hypothetical affinity that the community might acquire for the team.

He also underscores the differences between the Pride and the community's other sports programs. He says that the team came to New Orleans to build the "number one women's basketball franchise in the United States" and that the community should come out and "root for their team and have their team win for a change." Brown works to convince the viewership that the difference between this team and the others is not just about sex or gender or race, which was not discussed at all, but about winning, community, and local money. He spent no time defining the "community" outside of the white male sporting institutions. After the Brown interview, it becomes clear that the primary focus of the program would remain on the men off the court, given the emphasis placed on discussing van Breda Kolff and the investment team.

The program returns from a commercial break to a long shot of Coach van Breda Kolff and Gormin, her back once again to the camera, sitting on the stoop outside the Tulane gymnasium where the team practiced. She asks, "What did you expect from the players when you first took this job?" Van Breda Kolff responds, "intelligence," and laughs, suggesting that this would be a welcomed difference after coaching men. He claimed that he had no real expectations because he did not have experience with women's basketball, but he

> "thought they ought to be able to play pattern basketball fairly well because they can't do some of the wild physical things that the men can do. And men who are very good physically don't like to play the sort of patterned game, the finesse game. So I thought that the girls would probably be a heck of a lot better. People who like the, whatever you want to call it, nuances of basketball will appreciate watching girls play."

Women's basketball is also good, explains van Breda Kolff unconvincingly, but it is different. He could simply have focused on similarities between the men's and women's games in order to relate to much of the community's knowledge of professional basketball. In a valiant and surely genuine comment, even the Pride's coach focuses only on gender difference. He later comments that the "girls" are tougher that he thought. He suggests progress for women as a whole when he adds, "Years ago, when a girl gets a little a hangnail, she sniffs and she cries. These girls are getting banged around. Not a peep, not a whimper out of any of them. I'm really proud of them that way." In this exchange, as in the previous, the focus is on gender difference not racial difference. As with the Brown and van Breda Kolff interviews, there is no discussion of race present in interviews with the team's investors.

Dr. and Mrs. John D. Simpson were the majority investors in the team. In an interview with them in their "peaceful Covington home," Gormin presses for an answer as to why they would invest in this "women's team when the league is *so* new." John Simpson fielded most of the questions, and he responded that, "Well one of the reasons is because the *league* is *so* new . . . [it is] something that has probably considerable potential." Without confidence in this last statement, his reply is far from persuasive. His reticent tone resonates throughout the interview and contrasts with that of Brown's earlier optimism. It is clear that they care about women, the team, and their investment, but neither John nor Claudette Simpson exude the confidence or enthusiasm that Brown had in the previous interview. Part of this has to do with the leading questions Gormin uses in the interview and part is a result of the gendered divide within the replies.

Gormin asks whether Claudette Simpson had any influence in the decision to invest in the team, and Simpson offers that she was "for it," supporting her statement by counting her children. "We have six girls," she said. "That's the thing that played a pretty big part in it. Of course we also have one son. I don't want to leave him out." Underlying her statement is a fallacious idea that permeates societal ideas about gender in sport: if women gain opportunities in sport, then men lose opportunities (and if black players gain opportunities, then white players lose opportunities).[35] Gormin passes on the opportunity to develop Mrs. Simpson's response and proceeds without transition.

Instead of developing the concern for the future of women and women in sport, Gormin moves on to discussing the men involved with the team and directs these questions to Dr. Simpson. She asked, "How did you come to pick Butch as your coach?" to which he answered, "Who else could we select with Butch in this area? We are just real lucky that he's in the New Orleans area." Gormin follows up with, "Will you take part in any active parts in the team management or any other activity?" Dr. Simpson states, as a matter of fact, "Only in maybe a business sense. We don't intend to do any coaching or player selection at all." Yet, in the Pride's second season, Mrs. Simpson would manage the team and provide the public with a new face of the organization.[36] Claudette Simpson's words may have been few in the Gormin interview, but her many actions would be felt in the coming year, proving her understated influence in the decision to invest in the franchise.

Gormin consistently framed the program around ideas of whiteness and deference to gender roles, even within interviews with the team members. The interviews with the players demonstrated that the women's game in New Orleans was defined by the white players, though, when the infrequent opportunity presented itself, black women players spoke for themselves about their experiences. A discussion about race was once again all but absent from Gormin's player interviews—women were far more likely to conform to patriarchal ideas of womanhood and sport than they were to displace them.

From the establishing scene with the white woman's low dribble, to the first player interview featuring Paula Dean, to the first player addressed within the broader team interview, Karen Logan, it is clear that Gormin defined this sport and this team by its white players. When there were frames that included white and black players, many began with a close up of a white player and upon zoom out a player of color was included in the frame. Until the team interview, there were no close-up shots of a black player or players. There were a few long shots of black players, but they were never the only ones in the shot. It reinforced the whiteness that pervaded the television program, the team, and the league.[37]

There were a number of other Pride players of color who were talented athletes, few of whom were featured in the program. *Project 8* aired in October 1979 just before the WBL season began, yet there was no mention of the team's first draft pick. It is likely that the feature was filmed months before its air date, but Queen Brumfield, the first player drafted to the New Orleans Pride, was picked in the first round of the draft in June 1979.[38] Instead of Brumfield, Gormin chose Paula Dean, a southern white player, to feature first.

Gormin's interview with Dean focused on gender difference while completely excluding race. She asked Dean a number of leading questions, such as, "Will you be satisfied with the salary that you can earn as a member of this team, say eight, nine and ten thousand dollars whereas men starting out get so much more?" and "Is it a rough life? Are you sure this is what you want to do?" She subtly reinforced the fallacious ideas about white women's sporting bodies and reproductive capacities with the question, "How many years can a woman do this?"[39] Gormin's pointed questions focused on gender differences and reinforced that, at least within this media coverage, the women's game in New Orleans would be defined by conceptions of white femininity.

Gormin included one sequence in the program wherein she interviewed the team. The team members were sitting in the living room at their boarding house, some on the floor, some on the stairs. They fill the room. Not surprisingly—and not close in ratio to the races of the players—white voices dominate the narrative and the frame. Gormin asked the team generally, "Do you think you will run into any kind of particular prejudice because you are women?" Wanda Ard replied to Gormin's question and provided examples to support her responses. The director, however, had hard time anticipating that a black woman (Ard) would respond. He took a moment to zoom in on the respondent. However, he never zoomed in as close to Ard or other black players as he did to the white players. Ard and two other players including the white player, Sybil Blalock (and probably Augusta Forest) remained in the visual frame. Ard responded to the question quickly, "Yes we have. Like we were on the trolley the other day [and] a couple of guys saw us. And we was all together as a team and they said, you know, 'You all play basketball?' They looked at me and said, 'You too short.' (Smiling) I said, 'Well it's all in the game. Shortness can make it just like quickness and height and all that.'" She was the most vocal black woman player interviewed and demonstrated that when the opportunity presented itself, black women players spoke for themselves about their experiences with the team and the sport.

Despite these brief moments, a discussion that acknowledged race was very nearly completely absent the program. Gormin asks the team, "Why would you want to play basketball professionally, especially in a new league, a new team?" Wanda Ard also answers this question, "Well I've been playing basketball really all my life and it's an experience for myself because I never did anything really on my own, going out and seeking a goal. I said if anyone can go out and play women's professional basketball, I feel that I can do it, you know." Gormin tries to offset her response by asking, "Is it hard work?" Ard swiftly returns, "No. I've been playing rough basketball all my life. In other words, outdoor basketball they would say. So it is competition, but it is not rough. I feel a person should be able to take the licks and give the roughness, if they're able to be playing in the league. That's the way I feel." When she adds, "That's the way I feel," she subtly suggests that her ideas on this subject may not be the answer Gormin was looking for. During this scene, the camera zooms to a close-up of Ard, marking the single moment within the feature when a black woman filled the frame. Ard shared her experience with basketball, likely emphasizing that she had a different and now more pertinent experience with the sport than white women players. This, combined with the close-up of Ard, also marked the singular moment when racial difference is referenced within the program, a moment not intentionally initiated by the filmmakers, but by a confident, black player.

It was nearly always a white woman player who responded to the interviewer's prompts related to gender differences. In a question that seems particularly irrelevant given the topic of the feature, Gormin asked, "What would you all be doing if you weren't playing basketball?" A white player, Kathy Swilley, replied, "Going back to school, physical therapy school." After this, Gormin stumbles through another leading question, "Is that what most everybody is interested in, either teaching or coach or some other things connected with sports?" It becomes clear through the player responses that the women already understood that they needed long-term career plans (for life after basketball). A sea of voices mostly affirmed the response embedded in her question.

Those affirming voices did not include Karen Logan's. She symbolized gender difference in sport because she convinced the leadership of the WBL to adopt a smaller basketball purportedly more suitable for the women's game.[40] Logan remarked, "Usually everybody that's an athlete is, interested in sports, but I think if you make a career out of it. If you do it for fun and make a career out of it too then it gets old . . . . I think that's one of the things that's real important for women to realize is that just because you are an athlete doesn't mean you can't do other things too." Gormin cuts her off to counter, "But isn't it all consuming? . . . . There is nothing else. You just always have to be in training?" At this point, the director zooms in on Logan's face as she explains this seemingly foreign idea (at least to Gormin) that women athletes can think and are not one-dimensional. She says, "Well yeah, but you work out two or three hours a day, and there is a lot of the rest of the day that you can think of, at least try to get active in other things . . . . If you don't, I think in the end, I think you'd go crazy." When Gormin asks why she would go crazy if she only played sports, Logan said, "Because it's too limited to be nothing but an athlete. It's also socially, it limits you as far as the people and how they view [you] as, well you're just a basketball player. You know, I think it's not good for women."[41] These words end the sequence of the team interview and do not mark a significant shift in the picture of women in sport as historically impermanent.

On one hand, Logan complicates her attachment to gender difference in sport when she adds that the sports world is socially isolating for women. Still, through her previous comments about her plans after basketball (while vague, and her vision for the future of women athletes ill-defined), she essentially asserts that some women are still not comfortable with being defined as an athlete because an athlete is still defined by Gormin and others through the masculine. The feminine athlete, according to Logan, was, at best, a temporary definition. A woman, then, would need to become accomplished outside of sport. She could be an athlete for a while and still be a woman, if she later became other things that were likely to be more socially acceptable. Clearly, the final moments of Gormin's team interview sequence reinforces the idea that women (and especially white women) were far more likely to conform to patriarchal ideas of womanhood and sport than they were to displace them.

Throughout the program, Gormin's marked physical detachment from the interviewees and ignorance of the topic intimates that she is in uncharted territory, one that she seems uncomfortable occupying. As program producer, she consistently pays special attention to men and to whiteness. In fact, the deference she shows in *Project 8* shifted the focus of the program from the team to the actions that white men took off court. Most of the scenes were established to focus on the opinions and ideas of the general manager, the coach, and the investment team. Her leading questions with both the white men and the players typically called into question the potential success of women's sports in general and the Pride in particular.

Overall, it becomes clear that the manner with which Gormin posed leading questions in interviews suggested that she thought that the players' fate was prescribed by their gender but influenced by the opinions and actions of white men. It was not prescribed by the race of the players, because race was completely ignored by all those interviewed except for Wanda Ard. While black women were likely to speak for themselves when the opportunity presented itself, their important ideas about the direction of the sport were diluted by the number of white voices present. When white women players spoke for themselves, they were more unlikely to displace conceptions of gendered sport. While *Project 8* was meant to encourage support for the new local professional sports team, it seemed instead to predicate its failure by not fostering community around *all* the team members.

Clearly, television and newspaper reporters struggled to find a medium in coverage of the Pride players. The racism and sexism that permeated the league and sports was not eliminated by the reporters' silence. The readership of the *Times-Picayune* and the *States Item* and the viewership of the WVUE-TV *Project 8* feature took white racial unity as a given and centered the conversation and branding of the team on gender, effectively leaving the players race-less. If the players were race-less, then the reporters and papers could not be perceived as racist.

In "Sportswomen in Black and White: Sports History from an Afro-American Perspective," Linda D. Williams asserts that during the twentieth century, white presses and media primarily concerned themselves with the quantity of stories related to black athletes and only much later to the quality of that coverage.[42] It is clear that the major white presses in New Orleans were no exception to this rule. At best, black players were a postscript in sport media conversation, an addendum quota to fill that proved the self-defined equity of the city's largest media outlets.

Williams also notes, "The inattention to and disregard of the black female athlete by white culture has resulted in a distorted picture, which suggests that the black sportswoman's experience in sport paralleled that of her white sisters."[43] The black woman athlete's experience is collapsed under the category of woman, and woman was historically defined through cultural productions as white. In the vast majority of the surviving media coverage related to the Pride, the black and white women athlete's experiences were defined through her gender and not race. This quite likely meant that the reporters and promoters for the team missed out on addressing segments of the New Orleans population who may have otherwise identified with and supported those players by attending games.

Patricia Hill Collins discussed race and identity in her work, *Black Sexual Politics,* asserting that the antiracist African American political message prioritized racial solidarity above all other methods of self-identity and organization because it was thought to weaken racist movements.[44] In other words, prioritizing any other part of a black person's identity was thought to undermine the strength of the anti-racist movement and black communities. With a surplus of external pressures meant to divide the black community's strength, there was a silencing of forms of organizing in relation to other subjectivities from within the community and movement.

The sports reporting within the *Louisiana Weekly* commonly focused on race, resulting in the subordination and near erasure of gender. This weakened the ability of the organization and the media to garner the fan support necessary to keep the team afloat. One force among many that likely kept many black people from attending games was Clark's focus on the racist nature of the ball club. Both racism and sexism require "visible communities," Collins claims, and communicate a binary that subordinates white women and black women.[45]

With no clear critique of the dual (and multiple) systems of oppression present in the media, the league, and the Pride organization, the media missed its shot. Clearly race and gender (and likely class and sexuality) played roles in the perception of the team and therefore very likely impacted ticket sales. When the management and the media singled out one system of oppression, they missed others; race and gender were divisive and contributed to the dissolution of the New Orleans Pride.

Late in the first season, Ron Brocato foretold the demise of the organization and concurrently acknowledged and disavowed racism and sexism as factors in a string of complex explanations as to why the community failed to support the Pride. Ticket sales plummeted over the course of the next year in New Orleans and elsewhere, resulting in the quiet dissolution of the team and league in 1981. Brocato lamented what became a futile attempt to foster support for the team, "For months many of us have all but ignored their existence for several reasons. But, those reasons no longer exist because the local entry in the Women's Pro Basketball Association has given the city a team to be proud of; one to take to heart in spite of ourselves."[46]

CHAPTER THIRTEEN

When the Saints Went Marching In

Social Identity in the World Champion New Orleans Saints Football Team and Its Impact on Their Host City[1]

ELIZABETH BOOKSH BURNS

One of the more succinct descriptions of social identity theory (SIT) has been provided by Hogg, Terry, and White.[2] They describe SIT as a social psychology theory that focuses on intergroup relations, group processes, and the social self. According to SIT, people classify themselves into social categories such as nationality, political affiliation, or sports team. These categories provide a definition of who the person is in terms of the defining characteristics of the category. People's actions, feelings, and emotions are prescribed by the stereotypical attributes of a particular group of which they are members, otherwise known as the in-group. Similarly, stereotypes are applied to members of the out-group as well. There is a strong tendency for individuals to adopt behaviors and beliefs that favor the in-group over the out-group, thereby increasing positive perception of the self.

Hargie, Dickson, Mallett, and Stringer pointed out that the tendency to favor the in-group over the out-group accentuates the differences between groups as well as the similarities within groups.[3] Groups or social categories appear difficult or impossible to change. At times, a perceived inferior position of the in-group can lead to negative social identity that can trigger an attempt to move status position. These researchers have identified three factors that affect the preference for identity management: perceptions of stability of the group, legitimacy of the status inferiority, and the permeability of the boundaries between groups. Based on these factors, people are more or less willing

Drew Brees and Sean Payton celebrate the New Orleans Saints' 2010 victory in Super Bowl XLIV. Photo courtesy of *New Orleans Times-Picayune* and Barcroft Media.

to engage in individual or collective modes to change their present situation. Unstable and illegitimate status relations cause members to think that there should be an alternative to their present situation while permeability between in-group and out-group raises the possibility of individual mobility between groups. Mummendey, Kessler, Klink, and Mielke listed six identity management strategies individuals and groups use to handle negative social identity.[4] The first two are individual methods, individual mobility and recategorization, whereby an individual will choose to switch to a higher status group or choose to consider his own group of a higher status. The next two are collective methods, social competition and realistic competition, whereby the in-group as a whole will attempt to reverse their status or to compete for resources that will allow the in-group to gain higher status. The last two are creative methods, preference for temporal comparison and reevaluation of the material dimension, whereby groups will choose another comparison point (instead of a higher status out-group) that gives them a higher status or devalue the comparison with the out-group as unimportant to increase their positive social identity.[5]

The process of categorization simplifies the social environment and relationships between individuals. This theory can be helpful in creating a better understanding of "the communicative processes upon which judgments about group membership are made, relationships sustained, or outgroup attitudes ameliorated."[6]

Substantial research has been conducted on the issue of professional sports teams and the real economic impact made on their host cities. Over the last two decades, numerous studies have shown that investment in sports facilities and teams are not correlated with regional economic development.[7] Baade argued that professional sports teams do not increase income or create enough jobs to justify cities' staggering financial support.[8] The primary beneficiaries of these investments are the owners and players, not the tax-paying public. Baade and Dye found no evidence that a sports stadium or franchise increases the level of real income in a sample of nine cities studied between 1965 and 1983.[9] Coates and Humphreys found, after studying 37 standard metropolitan statistical areas in the United States between 1969 and 1994, that the existence of professional sports franchises in some cities actually reduces the level of per capita personal income with no effect on growth per capita income.[10] Previous research by Baade and Dye, Baim, and Euchner reported that professional sports have an insignificant impact on metropolitan economies.[11]

Several researchers have pointed out that, while it has been proven that sports-led development strategies are ineffective engines of economic growth, the presence of professional sports in a city can increase the overall well-being of the city's residents.[12] Rosentraub's study of the $450 million sports-led development project in downtown Cleveland confirms that the city will likely not experience substantial changes in development patterns or a great many new jobs.[13] However, he argues that Cleveland is now a more exciting place with a greater sense of civic pride and that the city is creating an increasing impression among young people that Cleveland is the center of the region, causing them to return to the previously deserted downtown for recreation. The citizens of Cleveland and Cuyahoga County should determine if these intangible benefits, not the supposed economic benefits, are worth the price tag.

Rosentraub posed the question, "What is the cost to cities without major league sports franchises?" He questioned if the city without a team becomes a second, third, or fourth-tier community and claimed, "Any community or city in our society that is striving to become a major center must also establish and maintain its sports identity."[14] He used the example of employers, looking for a high quality of life for their employees, who might not choose a city that lacks cultural amenities like theaters, museums, and professionals sporting events. He argued that sports are an important part of the marketing image of a city with "free" publicity broadcast on a regular basis to hundreds of thousands, maybe millions, depending on the event.

Regardless of the macro-view, individual sports fans can be affected strongly by their sports teams. One study demonstrated that individuals with a strong identification with their local team report healthier mood profiles than those with low identification.[15] Individuals can be affected positively and negatively by this connection. Hirt, Zillman, Erickson, and Kennedy found that sports fans' judgments of their personal capabilities are influenced by the performance of the team with which they identify; high-identifying fans who witnessed a victory report higher personal competencies on mental, social, and motor skill tasks than highly identified fans who witness a defeat.[16] Highly identified individuals also report a decrease in self-esteem following their team's defeat.[17] Another study found that citizens of Germany report higher levels of life satisfaction after a national soccer team victory than prior to the game.[18]

Judge and Watanabe argued that positive mood in one context (i.e., life satisfaction) can spill over to other contexts such as work environment.[19] This spillover effect can account for the strong positive correlations between life satisfaction and job satisfaction.[20] This can be translated to sports fans of successful teams whose joy may spillover to positively influence job satisfaction and, subsequently, their performance at work.[21] Isen found that positive mood, similar to the mood experienced by fans of successful sport teams, can positively impact the economy through increased consumption and spending.[22]

Austrian and Rosentraub noted other intangible benefits. They pointed out that "sports teams provide a common denominator among people of different age, race, and income."[23] Platow et al. concluded that charitable contributions increase following a sports team's successes.[24] Sports also help in the healing process following a tragedy. Brown discussed the role Major League Baseball and National Football League (NFL) games played in the nationwide healing process after the September 11 terrorist attacks. Instead of merely escaping reality, Brown claims sport can address the nation's pain and invite spectators to deal with their feelings from a number of perspectives. He quotes *USA Today* writer Erik Brady, reflecting on September 11 a year after the attacks,

"Ballparks became home to sacramental ceremony. It seemed natural to salute and sing and cry and then settle in for a game that meant exactly nothing and everything all at once."[25]

In 2005, the *Wall Street Journal* summed up the Saints' history with this statement: "The Saints have been perennial losers, winning just 40 percent of their games in 38 seasons. For years they were dubbed the 'Aints.' But their fans have stood by them."[26] Four years later, the 2009 Saints team would win the ultimate championship in American football, the Super Bowl, and finally bring legitimacy to the fans who had stood by them for 43 seasons.

The team was born on November 1, 1966—All Saints Day—and named for the spiritual jazz song "When the Saints Go Marching In."[27] From that day, the identities of the largely Catholic city and its football team were permanently intertwined.[28] Even though the Saints had only nine winning seasons in their history, the team is "unconditionally loved in its native city."[29] In 1980, the Saints hit rock bottom, winning only one game. Throughout the early 1980s, the fans still supported the team, although they wore bags over their heads to express their shame in the team's poor performance at the prompting of the iconic sportscaster Buddy "Buddy D" Diliberto.[30] In 1985, current owner Tom Benson purchased the Saints.[31] The mid-1980s to early 1990s took a turn for the better with five winning seasons, the first in Saints history.[32] Returning to mediocrity in 1993, the Saints did not see another winning season until 2000, when they won their first playoff game. The franchise "took 21 years to celebrate its first winning season, 35 years to win its first playoff game, 42 years to have a chance to play for a world championship."[33]

New Orleans is a small, relatively poor city by professional sports standards. It is the 36th largest city out of the 40 cities hosting a team from one of the five large professional sports leagues and holds the same rank when measuring per capita personal income. Lacking in large corporations, New Orleans finds it more difficult to fill the luxury suites and to achieve the "guaranteed sellout" like other NFL cities.[34]

While New Orleans may seem to be an unlikely choice for a professional sports team, "the city caters to the tourist trade to an extent that distinguishes itself from almost every other American city." Its tourist-based economy relies on an arts-entertainment-recreation industry that is much more prevalent than most other United States cities.[35] With the addition of the Superdome in 1975, a monumental structure that could fit the Houston Astrodome comfortably inside, New Orleans could market itself to a growing demand for convention space and sporting events. The Superdome "would host concerts and conventions and impact the landscape and economics of New Orleans like no other institution."[36]

New Orleans has used its infrastructure, including the Superdome and an extensive convention center, to its advantage, ranking 4th in the United States in number of conventions hosted. Prior to 2005, the city attracted more than 10 million visitors who spent in excess of $5 billion per year. For this reason, Baade and Matheson suggest that New Orleans may be different than other cities in regard to the lack of economic activity for host cities of professional sports teams. The city is smaller and less affluent than other host cities in general, and it may be that the frequency with which large sports events are hosted by New Orleans makes the area an exception to the experience of most cities with regard to sports and economic development.[37]

On August 29, 2005, Hurricane Katrina made an indelible mark on New Orleans and its iconic structure, the Superdome. The largest natural disaster in United States history flooded almost 80 percent of New Orleans and caused the deaths of nearly 2,000 people in the Louisiana and Mississippi Gulf Coast region. The Superdome stood as a visual symbol, broadcast around the world, of the city's suffering and the government's incompetence.[38] The home field of the Saints served as the center for 30,000 refugees who could not escape the city; catering freezers in the basement were used as a morgue for the dead. Flood waters remained in the below-sea-level city for weeks as levees and pumps were repaired, causing even more extensive damage to residential and business communities. Approximately 80 percent of New Orleans's 188,000 occupied housing units were severely damaged. The cost of reconstructing New Orleans was estimated at more than $100 billion.[39]

Even before Katrina, New Orleans lagged behind in nearly every measure of economic development. By January 2006, New Orleans had lost 29.2 percent of its residents as compared with July 2005. The workforce size had decreased by 30.9 percent by July 2006. The displaced residents were largely middle-class or economically disadvantaged. Entire neighborhoods were destroyed, and 45 percent of those displaced did not live in homes they owned, leaving many residents with weakened ties to the community and less incentive to return. Those missing citizens were needed to support the tourism industry so vital to the economic stability of New Orleans.[40]

In New York City after the September 11 terrorist attacks, the city had the home baseball and football teams to help rally the city's spirits; but New

Orleans's sports teams did not have a city to rally or even a stadium to play in. Before the hurricane in early 2005, Tom Benson, the Saints owner, made it known that he was interested in moving the Saints to another city. With the severe damage inflicted on the Superdome in Katrina, the Saints were forced to play "home" games in San Antonio, Baton Rouge, and even New Jersey. It was estimated that the renovations to the Superdome, and the adjacent arena that housed the National Basketball Association's Hornets, would cost $400 million; according to their contract, the Saints could opt out of their contract with the Superdome in January 2006.[41]

It seemed that New Orleans was about to lose the Saints for good; the city was downtrodden and the Saints were a vagabond team without a home. A *Times-Picayune* editorial stated, "Before Katrina, Saints fans wanted their team to stay. Now they need it to stay."[42] Then in early 2006, Tom Benson hired Mickey Loomis as general manager; Loomis, in turn, hired Sean Payton as coach. Payton signed 27 new players, including Drew Brees, an injured quarterback from the San Diego Chargers who hoped to fully recover by the start of training camp.[43]

After a $200 million renovation, the Superdome reopened for the team's first home game since Hurricane Katrina on September 25, 2006, with a Monday Night Football national broadcast.[44] Set before a national stage, the country saw New Orleans rising from the ashes. "Then New Orleans celebrated its NFL franchise like never before, as the team galvanized the community like never before, giving the downtrodden a pleasant distraction from their worries about reparations, FEMA money and the absence of electricity."[45]

The city identified with their new team, particularly with Brees. He was unwanted by his former team or any other team in the NFL. The Miami Dolphins were interested at one time but thought he had only a 25 percent chance of regaining full use of his injured shoulder.[46] When Payton first drove Brees through New Orleans, he gave him the pitch: you can be part of the rebuilding. "When I visited New Orleans, I saw it all, the good and the bad," Brees said in a 2010 interview. "I just thought, this is a chance to be part of something incredible—the rebuilding of an American city. I felt like it was a calling. Like I was destined to be here."[47] Brees's dedication to the city through his words and his charitable actions, not to mention his on-field performance, garnered the city's support and appreciation. "Ninety percent of people who come up to me on the street don't say, 'Great game,'" Brees said in 2006, when he first arrived in New Orleans. "They say, 'Thank you for being part of the city.'"[48]

The team went from a 3-win season in 2005 to a 10-win season in 2006. This was their first winning season since 2002, finishing with the second playoff win in team history. A record number of season tickets were sold in 2006, although only 40 percent of the luxury suites were sold by May 2006. By the 2007 season, the Superdome sold out of all 137 suites and 68,000 season seats with a waiting list of more than 30,000. The stadium has sold out of season tickets every year since.[49]

The newly formed team under Sean Payton hit its stride in 2009. The Saints won a franchise-record 13 games and 2 playoff games including the National Football Conference (NFC) Championship on January 24, 2010, giving the team its first chance to play for the ultimate prize, a Super Bowl Championship. After the NFC win, the city burst into a fury of joy and excitement at a level never reached in this party-loving city. Without violence or riots, the city celebrated a victory all its own, and grown men had trouble keeping their emotions in check. "The truth is, if Katrina never had happened, a river of tears still would flow through the Superdome on Sunday," according to the *Times-Picayune.* It was "the ultimate Saints experience . . . a championship in our house, shared by 70,000 cheering, singing, dancing, hugging, high-fiving, crunking and, yes, crying Saints fans. Along with a few million more watching on television."[50]

While the city celebrated another victory, the "Who Dat Nation" joined in vicariously through their television sets.[51] Bobby Hebert, Saints sportscaster, coined the phrase in the 2006 season based on the popular chant associated with the team, "Who dat! Who dat! Who dat say dey gonna beat dem Saints!"[52] With displaced New Orleanians cheering on from around the country and new fans joining by the thousands interested by the team's and the city's compelling stories, the Who Dat Nation had grown to epic proportions by the time the Saints hoisted the Lombardi Trophy.

The Saints defeated the Indianapolis Colts two weeks later on February 7 in the most widely watched Super Bowl, and the most widely watched scheduled program, in United States television history, attracting more the 106.5 million viewers. The 51.7 million households watching the 2010 Super Bowl topped the previous record holder, the 1983 finale of the CBS sitcom "M*A*S*H."[53]

Throughout the 2009 season, the country saw New Orleans again in a new light. Instead of death, destruction, and ineptitude, they saw life, energy, and excellence executed at the highest level. The television cameras swarmed New Orleans; some say it was difficult to tell the Super Bowl was actually in Miami with all the coverage of the Saints' hometown.[54]

State economic officials hoped to parlay the Saints' Super Bowl debut into a powerful start to a long-term rebranding of Louisiana's image. They saw it as their chance to show that the state is strong and rebuilding. "Unlike the Saints, we're not necessarily at Super Bowl level, but we're clearly headed in the right direction," said Stephen Moret, secretary of economic development for Louisiana. Austin Marks, chief of staff of Greater New Orleans Inc., used the Saints' dream season as a recruiting tool, bringing site selection professionals to town for meetings and visits to the Superdome, courtesy of Saints executives.[55]

By the end of the season, owner Tom Benson had secured a lease extension to keep the team playing in the Superdome through the 2025 season and convinced fellow NFL owners to vote New Orleans as the Super Bowl host city for a record-tying 10th time in 2013. By this time, nearly every national-profile sports event hosted in New Orleans before Katrina, including college football's Sugar Bowl, college basketball's championship tournament, and the Professional Golf Association's Zurich Classic, had returned or made plans to return to the city.[56]

The history of the relationship between the Saints football franchise and its host city leads to the following research question:

> **Research Question 1:** What is the association between the positive self-image of Saints fans and the success of the Saints football team?

National, regional, and local newspapers and sports magazines were reviewed from August 2009 to February 2010 using the search terms *Saints* and *Super Bowl.* The publications selected for review were *Sports Illustrated,* the *Washington Post,* and the *New York Post* on the national level; the *Baton Rouge Advocate* and the *Mobile Register* on the regional level; and the *Times-Picayune* on the local level. In total, 1,885 articles were reviewed to discover the reported association between the positive self-image of New Orleans citizens, as well as of Saints fans in general, to the success of the Saints football team. Articles were classified as showing a positive association, a negative association, positive and negative association, or no association at all. Articles with no association contained no information about the effect of the football team on its fans. Post hoc content analysis was undertaken of 1,885 articles by two coders. The intercoder reliability was .99.[57]

Of the 1,885 articles reviewed, 46 (2.44%) were in *Sports Illustrated,* 126 (6.68%) were in the *Washington Post,* 217 (11.51%) were in the *New York Post,* 283 (15.01%) were in the *Baton Rouge Advocate,* 335 (17.77%) were in the *Mobile*

Register, and 878 (46.58%) were in the *Times-Picayune.* In *Sports Illustrated,* 8 (17.39%) articles were coded to the positive self-image of Saints fans and 38 (82.61%) were not relevant. In the *Washington Post,* 16 (12.70%) articles were coded to the positive self- image of Saints fans and 110 (87.30%) were not relevant. In the *New York Post,* 20 (9.22%) were coded to the positive self-image of Saints fans and 197 (90.78%) were not relevant. In the *Baton Rouge Advocate,* 33 (11.66%) articles were correlated to the positive self-image of Saints fans, 1 (0.35%) was coded to the negative self-image of Saints fans, 1 (0.35%) was coded to positive and negative self-image of Saints fans, and 248 (87.63%) were not relevant. In the *Mobile Register,* 34 (10.15%) articles were coded to the positive self-image of Saints fans and 301 (89.85%) were not relevant. In the *Times-Picayune,* 94 (10.71%) articles were coded to the positive self- image of Saints fans, 1 (0.11%) was coded to positive and negative self-image of Saints fans, and 783 (89.18%) were not relevant.

The articles reviewed showed that the Saints and their fans have had a long-standing relationship that has been through many more downs than ups. As Lagasse wrote in *Sports Illustrated,* "There's something about the Saints and their relationship with the city that is indescribable. Wins and losses aren't just felt on the field and by the 53 guys on the roster but by everybody in town. I've been all over the country, and there is a correlation between the success of the Saints and the success of the city unlike any other I've seen."[58]

Mickey Loomis, General Manager of the New Orleans Saints, also noted the strong connection in an article in the *Washington Post:* "There's always been a unique relationship between the fans of the New Orleans Saints and their team. . . . There's a connection between the team and the city that's unusual."[59] Toni Trapani, a Saints season-ticket holder and lifelong New Orleans resident, attempted to explain why the citizens of New Orleans were so connected to the team. He said, "The team gets into your blood at a young age the same way the city does. This isn't a transient town like Dallas or Houston or Atlanta. Everyone who lives here chooses to live here. It's not like your company sent you here. You're here because you want to be here."[60]

Many residents of the Gulf Coast region were severely impacted by Hurricane Katrina in 2005. Numerous articles included references to the rise of the city paralleling the rise of the Saints. LeCharles Bentley, drafted by New Orleans in 2002, described the complementary resurgence of the city and the team in a *Times-Picayune* article:

> What no camera was able to capture or mouths able to articulate was the emotional and mental devastation that laid in the wake of Katrina . . . The irony is the city and the people were made whole in the same building that ended up being a tomb for so many. Fans cheered the Saints to their first Super Bowl berth at the Superdome—a place that is synonymous with one of the darkest periods in natural disaster history . . . the Saints and the city of New Orleans have shown that perseverance and faith eventually will yield sweet rewards.[61]

The successful 2009 season was reported to have a unifying effect on the city and the region. The *Mobile Register* wrote, "The Saints brought us together, my family, my community, my coast, my state, my brothers and sisters in Louisiana, and yes, gathering from the record-breaking television ratings for the game, my nation. For one great shining moment, we were all Saints fans."[62]

A *Times-Picayune* article discussed the concept of the Who Dat Nation, described as "a post-Katrina phenomenon that has tied together Orleanians, suburbanites and displaced former residents of all ethnicities, ages and socio-economic classes based on their love of the Saints."[63]

The players recognize the strong ties their team has to the city, and to its recovery from Katrina. Quarterback Drew Bees was quoted in a *Washington Post* article as saying,

> It's surreal . . . Coming here four years ago, post-Katrina . . . It's unbelievable, it's unbelievable. You can draw so many parallels between our team and our city. In reality we've had to lean on each other in order to survive. The city is on its way to recovery. We've used the strength and resilience of our fans to go out and play with confidence on Sundays. It's been one step at a time, and we've had to play through plenty of adversity. Just like this town has.[64]

After the devastation caused by Hurricane Katrina, the city and the team were ready for a change in status from losers to winners. The *Washington Post* wrote, "Had a town ever craved a victory more than New Orleans? All across the city, people who had lost everything needed so desperately to win something. Even the cops on street corners chanted, 'WHO DAT?'"[65] After the Super Bowl win, a *Sports Illustrated* article said,

> The triumph capped a lovefest between the city and the team that began in 2006 with the hiring of coach Sean Payton and the signing of quarterback-community institution Drew Brees just months after Hurricane Katrina had devastated New Orleans and left tenuous the Saints' future in the town. "This is for everybody in the city who had homes that used to be wet," Payton said after the game. "This is for New Orleans."[66]

The change in the Saints' self-identification from losers to winners allowed the fans as a group to change categories themselves, an example of one of the six identity management strategies for groups with a negative social identity described by Mummendey et al.[67] The Saints and their fans are typical of *realistic competition,* whereby the in-group as a whole attempt to compete for resources that will allow the in-group to gain higher status. This change in status is evident in several articles in the *Times-Picayune.* One article stated, "For so many years, we followed what had been our lovable losers. But Sunday's victory against the Indianapolis Colts seemed to change the local perspective in an instant. There seemed to be a greater sense of civic pride on Monday morning. People hugged, they kissed, they danced, they cried."[68]

Dr. Adrianne Brennan, an assistant professor of clinical psychiatry at LSU Health Sciences Center, was quoted in the *Times-Picayune* as saying, "New Orleanians have this new identity now," she said. "We're not the underdogs. We're on top."[69]

Most of the articles that mentioned the effect of the Saints on the city of New Orleans and on Saints fans were positive in nature. Saints fans' sense of identity is in some ways prescribed by their sports team. Linebacker Jonathan Vilma said, "The New Orleans Saints are Super Bowl champions and the city of New Orleans is Super Bowl champions."[70] The *Mobile Register* article went on to say, "You hear that kind of sentiment and it's hard for civic pride to not burst through, impossible for provincialism to not intensify even more than it already has." The *Baton Rouge Advocate* recorded Saints receiver Robert Meachem as saying, "A few weeks ago, a fan walked up to me and just started crying and said, 'Thank you for what you did for our city.' That makes you know that you are not bigger or better than anyone else, but you are doing something that's good for our city."[71]

The *Washington Post* reported that NFL Commissioner Roger Goodell said, "When you think about the relationship between the Saints and the Gulf Coast and the Saints and New Orleans, it was more than just a football game and more than just a football team . . . The hopes and dreams and struggles of the people in that region were reflected in that team."[72]

One article also mentioned the positive effect a winning team can have on the work environment. The *Baton Rouge Advocate* reported, "The New Orleans Saints' Super Bowl win may have long-lasting, positive effects on the region's Hurricane Katrina-damaged psyche, rebuilding residents' self-confidence and self-esteem, and making them more productive at work, according to at least one expert."[73] The article went on to quote Seymour Adler, senior vice president in the Human Capital Practice at Aon Consulting, "Winning the game makes people feel good about being in New Orleans and around the city . . . . Boosting self-confidence, security and self-esteem have been scientifically proven to increase productivity." Jean Kelley, president and founder of Jean Kelly Leadership Consulting in Tulsa, said winning can also lower productivity temporarily because of the adrenaline rush as well as heavy drinking and eating. While consultants Challenger, Gray, and Christmas estimated the Super Bowl would cost employers as much as $900 million on the following Monday, Paul Damiano, president of Good Works Consulting in Summerfield, North Carolina, said there are too many variables and measurement errors to get a reliable numerical answer. Although there may be short-term decreases in productivity, the article said Damiano predicted "a corresponding gain in non-traditional measures such as better communication and employee relations and even higher short-term motivation."[74]

Only two articles mentioned a negative effect of the Saints' presence in the state. One appeared in the *Baton Rouge Advocate* and concerned the high price state taxpayers had to pay to keep the Saints profitable over the years. The article questions if the Saints, even after such a successful year, are worth the high price tag. Mark Ballard wrote,

> Since 1985, Louisiana taxpayers have given the Benson family of San Antonio, Texas, almost a half-billion dollars in subsidies and cash—without ever getting any ownership interest that would be recognized by a court. In essence, a succession of Louisiana governors used the state's treasury to reward managers who apparently could not succeed in the National Football League, a business that has grown to astounding heights of profitability.[75]

The other appeared in the *Times-Picayune* and was a mix of positive and negative references. The article questioned the long-term effect the team's success could have on the city. Rice University professor and former New Orleans resident Douglas Brinkley was quoted as saying, "Saints mania is very exciting, but sports can be an opiate for the masses . . . . You can't build a sustainable urban community on football wins." The article goes on to comment, "No one thinks that, but the Saints do inspire those of us who've chosen to stay and rebuild."[76]

Besides these two articles concerning economic factors, the articles reviewed in this study contain only positive subject matter in reference to the city's and fans' connection with the Saints football team. The intangible benefits commonly referenced are the unity among fans in the "Who Dat Nation" and the ecstatic joy experienced by the citizens of New Orleans and the Gulf Coast region, examples of accentuating similarities within the in-group, as well as the corresponding good feelings about the city and the region and the positive impression it may create in the rest of the viewing public around the country, and the world, as a result of the positive media coverage of the 2009 season, both examples of positive self-perception of the in-group.

Baade and Matheson argued that New Orleans would have a difficult time retaining their professional sports teams over the long run.[77] They predict that any efforts to rebuild sports facilities would hinder development. It is questionable whether the extensive investment New Orleans made in its sports team was worth it when so many other essential services and publicly funded projects are still struggling. Baade and Matheson allow that hosting professional sports and mega-events has symbolic significance, but they argue it is an amenity the city simply cannot afford.

Supporters of investment in the sports infrastructure say, "There's a preservationist case to be made, in which sports in New Orleans muscle their way alongside cuisine and music—all worth saving because they make life worth living, especially when people the world over want to sample that very culture."[78]

It remains to be seen if the investment New Orleans has made in the Saints, their winning season, and the ensuing publicity will make a long-lasting effect on the community. In the short term, it seems to have created a positive effect for the citizens of the city and the surrounding region who identify as fans of the team.

Research has shown that professional sports teams can provide intangible benefits for their host cities, while the economic benefits have been shown to be inconsequential. In the case of New Orleans and its Super Bowl–winning NFL team, the Saints, more research needs to be conducted to determine what benefits may be experienced by the city. A few suggested areas of future research include level of identification Saints fans have with their team as compared with other teams' fans, tourism levels before and after 2009, changes in media coverage post-Katrina compared with post-Super Bowl win, changes in economic climate, and measurements of life satisfaction, job satisfaction, and/or work performance post-Super Bowl win. Ultimately, the goal of such research should be to obtain a better understanding on the relationship of sports to a variety of intangible benefits to a community.

Notes

Introduction

1. New Orleans *Times-Picayune*, 9 January 1925; Jeff Davis, *Papa Bear: The Life and Legacy of George Halas* (New York: McGraw-Hill, 2005), 80–81; and Gregory Richard, email correspondence in possession of the author.

2. Michael S. Martin, "New Orleans Becomes a Big-League City: The NFL-AFL Merger and the Creation of the New Orleans Saints," in *Horsehide, Pigskin, Oval Tracks, and Apple Pie*, ed. James A. Vlasich (Jefferson, NC: McFarland & Co., 2006), 123–125, 128–129.

3. Martin, "New Orleans Becomes a Big-League City," 128–129; and *Louisiana Weekly*, 16 July 1966, 2–9, 1 October 1966, 2–6, 5 November 1966, 1, 10, 25 July 1970, 2–6.

4. Though their stories are readily available. For the story of Algiers bullfighting, German gymnastics, and the Jesuit-St. Aug basketball game, see the podcast "Tripod: New Orleans at 300," by Laine Kaplan-Levenson, presented by 89.9 WWNO, New Orleans Public Radio. For the Negro Leagues in New Orleans, see Thomas Aiello, *The Kings of Casino Park: Race and Race Baseball in the Lost Season of 1932* (Tuscaloosa: University of Alabama Press, 2011), or the pioneering work of Ryan Whirty, most of which is presented on his blog "The Negro Leagues Up Close," https://homeplatedontmove.wordpress.com/. For the Bayou Classic, see Thomas Aiello, *Bayou Classic: The Grambling-Southern Football Rivalry* (Baton Rouge: Louisiana State University Press, 2010).

5. Peter Finney, *The Best of Peter Finney, Legendary New Orleans Sportswriter* (Baton Rouge: Louisiana State University Press, 2016), 5.

Chapter 1

1. Originally published in *Louisiana History* 8 (Summer 1967): 219–238.

2. Quoted in Harry T. Paxton (ed.), *Sport USA: The Best from the* Saturday Evening Post (New York: Thomas Nelson and Sons, 1961), 3. For accounts of the rise of sports, see John A. Krout, *Annals of American Sport* (New Haven: Yale University Press, 1929); and Foster Rhea Dulles, *America Learns to Play: A History of Popular Recreation, 1607–1940* (Gloucester, MA: D. Appleton-Century Co., 1959). [Note format has been changed from the original for contemporary consistency. –*Editor*]

3. Frederic Logan Paxson, "The Rise of Sport," *Mississippi Valley Historical Review* 4 (September 1917): 145.

4. Quoted in Paxton (ed.), *Sport USA*, 4.

5. John Higham, "The Reorientation of American Culture in the 1890's," in John Weiss (ed.), *The Origins of Modern Consciousness* (Detroit: Wayne State University Press, 1965), 27.

6. "The World Awheel," *Munsey's Magazine* 15 (May 1896): 131.

7. For a history of the development of the bicycle, see Arthur J. Palmer, *Riding High: The Story of the Bicycle* (New York: Dutton, 1956).

8. Luther H. Porter, *Wheels and Wheeling: An Indispensable Handbook for Cyclists* (Boston: Wheelman Company, 1892), vii. For accounts of cycling in America, see Palmer, *Riding High;* and Norman L. Dunham, "The Bicycle Era in American History," (Ph.D. diss., Harvard University, 1956).

9. Cited in "Velocipede Notes," *Scientific American* 20 (27 February 1869): 131.

10. New Orleans *Daily Picayune,* 20, 29 March, 4, 13 July 1869. All newspaper citations, unless otherwise noted, are from New Orleans newspapers.

11. *Picayune,* 25 June 1871.

12. *Picayune,* 16 May 1880.

13. *Picayune,* 11 January 1892; *Bicycling World* (Boston), 4 (2 December 1881): 42.

14. *L.A.W.* [League of American Wheelmen] *Bulletin* (Boston) 3 (27 August 1886): 204.

15. *L.A.W.,* 5 (22 July 1887): 41.

16. *Picayune,* 20 September 1884.

17. *Picayune,* 20 February 1882; *Bicycling World* 4 (10 March 1882): 209; and Palmer, *Riding High,* 182.

18. *Picayune,* 12, 14, 15 February, 9 March 1885.

19. Quoted in Dunham, "Bicycle Era," 203; and *Bicycling World,* 8 (7 March 1884): 223.

20. Karl Kron, [Lyman H. Bagg], *Ten Thousand Miles on a Bicycle* (New York: s.p., 1887), 654, 670; and *Bicycle South* 3 (May 1886), passim.

21. *Picayune,* 4 May 1885.

22. *Picayune,* 27 August 1886.

23. *L.A.W. Bulletin* 5 (30 September 1887): 205.

24. *L.A.W.,* 5 (22 July 1887): 39; and *Bicycling World* 24 (19 February 1892): 468.

25. *Picayune,* 16 August 1892.

26. *Picayune,* 12 June, 29 November 1893.

27. *Picayune,* 29 November 1893, 21 February 1894.

28. Robert P. Scott, "Cycling Art, Energy, and Locomotion: A Series of Remarks on the Development of Bicycles, Tricycles, and Man-Motor Carriages" (Philadelphia: J.B. Lippincott, 1889), 96, quoted in Dunham, "Bicycle Era," 403.

29. *Picayune,* 21 June 1891, 23 April 1895.

30. *Picayune,* 15 June 1890, 7, 9 January, 26 April, 22 June 1891.

31. *Picayune,* 22 June 1891.

32. *Bicycling World* 18 (29 March 1889): 388; and *Picayune,* 3 August 1891.

33. *L.A.W. Bulletin* 3 (27 August 1886): 204.

34. *Bicycling World* 18 (2 November 1888): 8.

35. *Picayune,* 2 June, 16, 23 August 1891.

36. Dunham, "Bicycle Era," 241–74.

37. *L.A.W. Bulletin* 5 (2 September 1887): 133; and *Picayune,* 16 June 1890.

38. *L.A.W. Bulletin* 5 (2 September 1887): 133; and *Picayune,* 24 June 1896.

39. *Picayune,* 18 July 1891.

40. *Picayune,* 23 August 1891.

41. *Bicycling World* 18 (1 March 1889): 292; 19 (17 May 1889): 63; and *Picayune,* 4, 5 May, 25 December 1890.

42. *Bicycling World* 25 (28 October 1892): 119.

43. *Bicycling World* 25 (11 November 1892): 151.

44. *Picayune,* 29 March 1893.

45. *Picayune,* 24 October 1894, 10 April 1895.

46. *Picayune,* 13, 18 May, 2, 14 June, 7 July, 13 October 1895, 28 May, 1, 27 September, 1896.

47. *Picayune,* 18 October 1895.

48. *Southern Cyclist* 2 (12 February 1896): 2.

49. *Picayune,* 1 September 1896.

50. *Picayune,* 2, 14 June, 17, 18 October 1895.

51. *Picayune,* 18, 26 October, 14 December 1895, 14 June 1896.

52. *Picayune,* 22 July 1896.

53. *Picayune,* 25 October 1896, 18 May 1897, 13 February 1898.

54. *Picayune,* 23 January 1898.

55. Dunham, "Bicycle Era," 459–60.

56. *The* Picayune*'s Guide to New Orleans* (New Orleans: Picayune, 1897; 3rd. rev. ed.), 39; and *Picayune,* 19 October 1896.

57. *Picayune,* 31 August 1896.

58. Louisiana Road Club Broadsides, 1889–1898, Rosemonde E. and Emile Kuntz collection, LaRC/Manuscripts Collection 600, Howard-Tilton Memorial Library, Special Collections, Tulane University, passim.

59. *L.A.W. Bulletin* 5 (29 July 1887): 59; and *Bicycling World* 19 (17 May 1889): 63.

60. *Picayune,* 28 June 1896.

61. *Picayune,* 12, 14 August, 18 September 1896.

62. John R. Betts, "The Technological Revolution and the Rise of Sports," *Mississippi Valley Historical Review,* 40 (September 1953): 251.

63. *Picayune,* 4 August 1895.

64. *Southern Cyclist* 2 (12 February 1896): 2.

65. *Southern Cyclist* 3 (14 July 1896): 2; and "Official Programme of the Southern Athletic Club," Spring Games, at Athletic Park, Saturday, May 2nd, 1896, 3 P.M. (New Orleans: Southern Athletic Club, 1896).

66. "Official Programme of the Southern Athletic Club," Spring Games, Saturday, May 4th, 1895, 3 P.M. (New Orleans: Southern Athletic Club, 1895), 14; "Official Programme of the Southern Athletic Club," Spring Games, at Athletic Park, Saturday, May 2nd, 1896, 3 P.M. (New Orleans: Southern Athletic Club, 1896); and *Southern Cyclist* 2 (12 February 1896), 2–3.

67. *Bicycle South* 3 (May 1886): 13; and "Official Programme," 1896; "Official Programme," 1895, 6.

68. Mary Taylor Bissell, "Athletics for City Girls," *Popular Science Monthly* 46 (December 1894): 149.

69. *Bicycling World* 19 (5 July 1889): 269.

70. *Picayune,* 9 August 1891.

71. *Picayune,* 7 October 1895.

72. *Picayune,* 21 September 1895.

73. *Picayune,* 7 October 1895.

74. *Picayune,* 13 November 1891.

75. *Picayune,* 11 January 1892.

76. *Picayune,* 7 July 1895, 25 August 1896.

77. *Picayune,* 25 August 1896.

78. *Picayune,* 4 December 1896.

79. *Puck* 37 (7 August 1895): 391, quoted in Frank L. Mott, *A History of American Magazines, 1885–1905* (Cambridge: Harvard University Press, 1957), 359.

80. *Picayune,* 18 July 1891.

81. *Picayune,* 10 September 1894.
82. *Picayune,* 27 February 1897.

Chapter 2

1. "Great Four Mile Day," *New Orleans Picayune,* 9 April 1854, 1.

2. Eliza Ripley, *Social Life in Old New Orleans: Being Recollections of my Girlhood* (New York: D. Appleton and Co, 1912), 246.

3. Larkin, "'Larkin' at Home," *Spirit of the Times,* 31 March 1855, 79; and John Hervey, *Racing in America, 1665–1865,* vol. 2 (New York: Jockey Club, 1944), 302.

4. Toni Morrison, *Beloved* (1987; New York: Vintage, 2004), 43–4. My discussion of haunting owes much to Marisa Parham, "Event Horizons: Notes on Memory, Space and Haunting," (PhD diss., Columbia University, 2004).

5. Arvilla Taylor, "Horse Racing in the Lower Mississippi Valley Prior to 1860," (MA thesis, University of Texas, 1953), 31–2; Dale A. Somers, *The Rise of Sports in New Orleans 1850–1900* (Baton Rouge: Louisiana State University Press, 1972), 25; and Hervey, *Racing in America, 1665–1865,* vol. 2, 179.

6. Somers, *Rise of Sports in New Orleans,* 25–6.

7. Somers, *Rise of Sports in New Orleans,* 26; Hervey, *Horse Racing in America, 1665–1865,* vol. 2, 181–3; and Taylor, "Horse Racing in the Lower Mississippi Valley," 3–7, 71.

8. John Dizikes, *Sportsmen and Gamesmen* (Boston: Houghton Mifflin, 1981), 144–5.

9. Taylor, "Horse Racing in the Lower Mississippi Valley," 130–1; Somers, *Rise of Sports in New Orleans,* 27; and William H.P. Robertson, *The History of Thoroughbred Racing in America* (Englewood Cliffs, NJ: Prentice Hall, 1964), 71.

10. Larkin, "Racing Prospects in America," *Porter's Spirit of the Times,* 15 Nov 1856, 205.

11. Richard Campanella, "The St. Louis and the St. Charles: New Orleans' Legacy of Showcase Exchange Hotels," *Preservation in Print* (April 2015), 16–7; and "Very Famous Hotel in Ruins," *New York Times,* 30 April 1894, 1.

12. "The New Jockey Club at New Orleans," *Spirit of the Times,* 14 Jan 1848, 543; "On Dits in Sporting Circles," *Spirit of the Times,* 8 Jan 1859, 570; Taylor, "Horse Racing in the Lower Mississippi Valley," 5; and Martha Ann Peters, "The St. Charles Hotel: New Orleans Social Center, 1837–1860," *Louisiana History* 1 (Summer 1960): 199.

13. "On Dits in Sporting Circles," *Spirit of the Times,* 22 January 1842, 558.

14. "St. Charles Exchange Hotel, New Orleans," *Spirit of the Times,* 20 March 1841, 25.

15. "The New St. Charles Hotel," *New Orleans Picayune,* 9 January 1853, 1.

16. "Match Between Tom Parker and Picayune," *Spirit of the Times,* 24 September 1859, 386.

17. Walter Johnson, *Soul By Soul: Life Inside the Antebellum Slave Market* (Cambridge, MA: Harvard University Press, 1999), 78–116.

18. John S. Kendall, "Shadow over the City," *Louisiana Historical Quarterly* 22 (January 1939): 147; and Peters, "The St. Charles Hotel," 196–8.

19. "Imported Stock at the South," *Spirit of the Times,* 21 July 1838, 180.

20. Alexander MacKay-Smith, *The Race Horses of America 1832–1872* (Saratoga Springs, NY: National Museum of Racing, 1981), 211–4; Hervey, *Racing in America, 1665–1865,* vol. 2, 284–6; and Kent Hollingsworth, *The Great Ones* (Lexington: Blood Horse, 1970), 165–6, 169–71.

21. Equus, "The Turf and Turfmen," *Spirit of the Times,* 23 July 1853, 271.

22. "The Most Brilliant Sporting Event of the Age," *Spirit of the Times,* 12 February 1854, 19.

23. Hervey, Racing in America, 1665–1865, vol. 2, 286.

24. "New Orleans (La.) Spring Races," *Spirit of the Times,* 15 April 1854, 103.

25. "The Great Post Stake. Kentucky Victorious!," *Spirit of the Times,* 15 April 1854, 103.

26. "Great Four Mile Day," *New Orleans Picayune,* 9 April 1854, 1. For details of the contest see "Metairie Jockey Club Meeting," *Spirit of the Times,* 22 April 1854, 115; Larkin, "Lexington and Lecomte's Great Race," *Spirit of the Times,* 10 June 1854, 199; Hervey, *Racing in America, 1655–1865,* vol. 2, 288–90; and Hollingsworth, *The Great Ones,* 166–7.

27. "Sporting Challenges," *New Orleans Picayune,* 11 June 1854, 3; "The Turf," *New Orleans Picayune,* 21 June 1854, 1; "On Dits in Sporting Circles," *Spirit of the Times,* 14 August 1854, 318; and Hervey, *Racing in America, 1655–1865,* vol. 2, 291–4.

28. Larkin, "'Larkin' in New York!," *Spirit of the Times,* 10 February 1855, 614. Variant usages in original.

29. "Nine Cheers for Lexington!," *Spirit of the Times,* 7 April 1855, 90.

30. "The Great Four Mile Race," *Spirit of the Times,* 28 April 1855, 126.

31. Hollingsworth, *The Great Ones,* 167; and Hervey, *Racing in America, 1655–1865,* vol. 2, 297.

32. "Reminiscences of Seargent S. Prentiss of Mississippi," *Spirit of the Times,* 3 August 1850, 283; "New Orleans Jockey Club Races," *American Turf Register,* May 1843, 294; and "New Orleans Jockey Club Races," *Spirit of the Times,* 15 April 1843, 84. On the importance and meaning of the idea of progress to Whig ideology, see Daniel Walker Howe, *The Political Culture of the American Whigs* (Chicago: University of Chicago Press, 1979), 125, 131–3, 182–4.

33. "Great Four Mile Day," *New Orleans Picayune,* 9 April 1854, 1; and Observer, "The Racing at New Orleans," *Spirit of the Times,* 22 April 1854, 114.

34. For a more extensive discussion of the relationship of racing and Whig politics, see Katherine C. Mooney, *Race Horse Men: How Slavery and Freedom Were Made at the Racetrack* (Cambridge, MA: Harvard University Press, 2014), 79–88.

35. On Southern concerns over Cuba in the 1840s, see Matthew Karp, *This Vast Southern Empire: Slaveholders at the Helm of American Foreign Policy* (Cambridge, MA: Harvard University Press, 2016), 57–69.

36. "The Races at Havana," *Spirit of the Times,* 15 April 1843, 78. See also "An American Race Course in Havannas," *Spirit of the Times,* 8 January 1842, 534; "The Havana Races," *Spirit of the Times,* 6 May 1843, 114; Taylor "Horse Racing in the Lower Mississippi Valley," 117–8; and Hervey, *Racing in America, 1655–1865,* vol. 2, 207–8.

37. A Young Turfman, "Racing Prospects in Louisiana and Mississippi," *Spirit of the Times,* 8 November 1851, 450.

38. Americus, "Sale of Lecomte, Etc.," *Spirit of the Times,* 17 May 1856, 162.

39. Equus, "Letter from 'Equus'," *Spirit of the Times,* 10 June 1854, 200. The misspelling of abolitionist is in the original.

40. "Twenty-five Dollars Reward," *New Orleans Picayune,* 19 March 1854, 7; and "Twenty-five Dollars Reward," *New Orleans Picayune,* 31 July 1854, 3.

41. "Capt. Minor and His Stable," *Spirit of the Times,* 22 Jan 1848, 567. For a sample list of slaves that includes slave horsemen, see the slave lists, Box 1, Folder 3, Duncan Kenner Papers, Series 1, Louisiana and Lower Mississippi Valley Collections, Louisiana State University.

42. "The Turf and Turfmen," *Spirit of the Times,* 23 July 1853, 271.

43. W.J. Minor to T.J. Wells 5 Aug 1854, Box 1, Folder 3, William J. Minor Papers, Louisiana and Lower Mississippi Valley Collections, Louisiana State University.

44. Robertson, *History of Thoroughbred Racing in America,* 68–9; and Hervey, *Horse Racing in America,* 1655–1865, vol. 2, 281–2.

45. "The Late New Orleans Races," *Spirit of the Times* 10 Feb 1849, 606; and Untitled ms., Box 1, Folder 40, William J. Minor Horse Racing Collection, Beinecke Library, Yale University.

46. A Young Turfman, "Lexington and Lecomte Again," *Spirit of the Times,* 17 Nov 1855, 474; and "On Dits in Sporting Circles," *Spirit of the Times,* 14 January 1848.

47. "On Dits in Sporting Circles," *Spirit of the Times* 27 January 1855, 594.

48. "Third Day of the Metairie," *New York Tribune,* 10 April 1861, 3; and "The Great Day on the Metairie," *New York Tribune,* 18 April 1861, 7. The *Tribune*'s circulation was both national and immense, helping to boost Abe to fame across America.

49. "Metairie Jockey Club Spring Meeting," *Spirit of the Times,* 19 April 1851, 102; "Orleans Jockey Club Races," *Spirit of the Times,* 10 May 1851, 139; and "New Orleans Races," *Porter's Spirit of the Times,* 21 Jan 1860, 331. Abe was such a well-known figure that he was named even when he wasn't aboard a winner. See "New Orleans Jockey Club Races," *Porter's Spirit of the Times,* 16 April 1859, 108.

50. A Young Turfman, "Lexington's Great Time Match," *Spirit of the Times,* 24 March 1855, 67.

51. A Young Turfman, "Sporting Epistle from 'A Young Turfman,'" *Spirit of the Times,* 16 April 1853, 102.

52. "New Orleans Races," *Porter's Spirit of the Times,* 21 January 1860, 331; and "Metairie Jockey Club Races," *New Orleans Picayune,* 15 January 1854, 1.

53. "The New Orleans Races on the Old Metairie," *Porter's Spirit of the Times,* 21 January 1860, 328.

54. A Young Turfman, "Lexington and Lecomte: The Great Turf Events of the Past Season," *Spirit of the Times,* 8 Sept 1855, 355; and "New Orleans Spring Races," *Spirit of the Times,* 19 April 1856, 115.

55. "Metairie Jockey Club Races," *Spirit of the Times,* 28 July 1860, 607.

56. John Smith Kendall, *History of New Orleans,* vol. 2 (Chicago: Lewis, 1922), 690.

57. Hervey, *Horse Racing in America,* 1655–1865, vol. 2, 353; and Somers, *Rise of Sports in New Orleans,* 75.

58. "Metairie Jockey Club Races," *Spirit of the Times,* 13 April 1861, 153.

59. Louis Bringier to Stella Bringier 6 April 1861, Box 2, Folder 17, Louis Bringier and Family Papers, Louisiana and Lower Mississippi Valley Collections, Louisiana State University. The variant spelling of Lecomte's name is a fairly common one and in the original.

60. List of Horses Confiscated, Box 1, Folder 16, William J. Minor Horse Racing Collection, Beinecke Library, Yale University; "Sale of Thoroughbred Stock at New Orleans on Monday, January 23d, 1863," *Wilkes's Spirit of the Times,* 24 January 1863, 333; and "Thoroughbred Horses From the South," *Wilkes's Spirit of the Times,* 11 April 1863, 93.

61. J. Carlyle Sitterson, "The Transition from Slave to Free Economy on the William J. Minor Plantations," *Agricultural History* 17 (October 1943): 217; and John Blassingame, *Slave Testimony* (Baton Rouge: Louisiana State University Press, 1977), 392–3.

62. "The Turf in the South," *Turf, Field and Farm,* 4 November 1865, 232.

63. Rambler, "Observations by Rambler—No. 7," *New Orleans Times,* 15 October 1865, 8; "The Turf in New Orleans," *New Orleans Times,* 2 July 1866, 6; "Metairie Jockey Club," *New Orleans Times,* 15 November 1866, 2; and "The Louisiana Turf," *New Orleans Times,* 15 December 1866, 2.

64. "The Metairie Races," *New Orleans Times,* 20 December 1866, 8.

65. "The Turf in New Orleans," *New Orleans Times,* 2 July 1866, 6.

66. "The Turf As a Means of Restoring Cordial Relations," *Wilkes's Spirit of the Times,* 13 June 1868, 297.

67. "The Turf," *New Orleans Times,* 23 Dec 1866, 1; and "The Turf," *New Orleans Times,* 29 December 1866, 1.

68. Somers, *The Rise of Sports in New Orleans,* 92–109; Matthew S. Perreault, "Jockeying for Position: Horse Racing in New Orleans, 1865–1920," (MA thesis, Louisiana State University, 2016), 66–79; "Sporting," *New Orleans Times,* 8 November 1874, 1; "Sale of the Metairie Course," *Wilkes's Spirit of the Times,* 11 May 1872, 201; and Hervey, *Racing in America, 1655–1865,* vol. 2, 354–5.

69. Kendall, *History of New Orleans,* vol. 2, 691.

70. "Testimony of Duncan F. Kenner Before the Select Committee on the Privileges, Powers, and Duties of the House of Representatives in Counting the Votes for President and Vice-President of the U.S.," 44th Congress, Congressional Record, House Miscellaneous Documents, 44–42, 378–9.

71. Kenner testimony, 376–85. The Withers Stakes, a popular prep for the Wood Memorial and a stepping-stone to the Kentucky Derby, is named for Withers.

72. Dr. G.M.G. Stafford, *The Wells Family of Louisiana and Allied Families* (Alexandria, LA: Standard, 1942), 100.

73. *New Orleans Republican,* 4 April 1872, 1.

74. "Spring Races—First Day," *New Orleans Times,* 12 April 1866, 2.

75. "More Prejudice," *Semi-Weekly Louisianian,* 9 April 1871, 2; "Public Privileges," *Weekly Louisianian,* 2 May 1874, 2; Somers, *Rise of Sports in New Orleans,* 96–7; and Dale Somers, "Black and White in New Orleans: A Study in Urban Race Relations, 1865–1900," *Journal of Southern History* 40 (February 1974): 24–6.

76. "Racehorses for Mr. Leonard Jerome," *New York Sportsman,* 10 July 1880, 19; "The St. Louis Races," *Wilkes's Spirit of the Times,* 5 Nov 1864, 153; "The American Turf," *Wilkes's Spirit of the Times,* 17 June 1865, 252; and "The Paterson Races," *Wilkes's Spirit of the Times,* 18 June 1864, 244.

77. "The American Turf," *Wilkes's Spirit of the Times,* 16 June 1866, 243. The Kentucky Derby would not be run for the first time until 1875.

78. "Answers to Correspondents," *Spirit of the Times,* 15 September 1866, 37.

79. "St. Louis," *Spirit of the Times,* 25 June 1887, 729.

80. Broad Church, "New Orleans," *Spirit of the Times,* 16 March 1889, 289; "New Orleans," *Spirit of the Times,* 9 March 1892, 342; "Southern Racing" *Spirit of the Times and Sportsman,* 18 February 1893, 168; "Latonia," *Spirit of the Times and Sportsman,* 4 June 1892, 819; and "Kentucky in Front," *Spirit of the Times and Sportsman,* 30 November 1895, 646.

81. Vigilant, "The Metropolitan Meeting," *Spirit of the Times,* 15 October 1881, 303.

82. "New Orleans," *Spirit of the Times,* 8 May 1886, 456.

83. "New Orleans," *Spirit of the Times and Sportsman,* 22 Feb 1896, 156.

84. "Hicks, the Jockey," *Illustrated Sporting News,* 14 November 1903, 24; and "Suit Over Negro Jockey," *New York Times,* 11 November 1903, 5.

85. "J. Lee Equals World's Record at the Downs," *Louisville Herald,* 6 June 1907, 5; and Alfred S. Amer, "Souvenir of New Orleans, 'The Paris of America,'" 9th ed, 1924, Jack B. McGuire Louisiana History Collection, MSS 654, Folder 13, Historic New Orleans Collection, 14.

86. "Peeping Between the Ropes," *Louisville Times,* 8 June 1907, Sec 2, 7; "Wonderful Record Made by Jockey Lee," *Louisville Courier-Journal,* 6 June 1907, 8; and "Jockey J. Lee, the 'Black Demon' of the Turf,'" *Louisville Courier Journal,* 6 June 1907, 8.

87. "Restigouche Gains Fame," *Daily Racing Form,* 30 May 1908, 1; and "Jockeys Duel with Whips," *Daily Racing Form,* 30 December 1908, 3.

88. "Gossip of the Racetrack," *New York Sun,* 23 May 1908, 5.

89. "Black Star Shines," *Louisville Times,* 6 June 1907, 16.

90. Perreault, "Jockeying for Position," 47–50.

91. "Stake-winning Jockeys of This Year," *Daily Racing Form,* 30 Dec 1908, 3.

92. Ed McNamara, *Cajun Racing* (New York: DRF Press, 2008), 137–8; and Joe Drape, "It's a Long Uphill Ride to Racing's Big Leagues; But St. Julien, a Black Jockey, Is on His Way," *New York Times,* 21 July 1998.

93. Marcus Hersh, "Fair Grounds apprentice McMahon already riding like a pro," *Daily Racing Form,* 8 December 2011, http://www.drf.com/news/fair-grounds-apprentice-mcmahon-already-riding-pro, accessed 28 Jan 2017; and "Great Minds Outwits Shotgun Cowboy For the Victory in G3 Texas Mile," http://www.paulickreport.com/news/thoroughbred-racing/great-minds-outwits-shotgun-cowboy-victory-g3-texas-mile/, accessed 7 February 2017.

94. Mark Singelais, "Saratoga's 1st black jockey in decades tries to make name for himself," *Albany Times Union,* 12 Aug 2015, http://www.timesunion.com/tuplus-sports/article/New-York-racing-s-1st-black-jockey-in-decades-6438291.php, accessed 28 January 2017.

Chapter 3

1. Originally published in *The Ring* (November 2015): 54–61. *The Ring* is a magazine that does not utilize footnotes, and their absence here reflects the long-form journalistic style with which the article was originally intended.

Chapter 4

1. Ellen Gilchrist, "In the Land of Dreamy Dreams," in *In the Land of Dreamy Dreams: Short Fiction* (Fayetteville: University of Arkansas Press, 1981), 60–71.

2. Carolyn Kolb, "For the Love of Tennis," *New Orleans Magazine* 44 (December 2009): 54–55; New Orleans *Times-Picayune,* 25 February 1898, 14; and Elizabeth Wilson, *Love Game: A History of Tennis, from Victorian Pastime to Global Phenomenon* (Chicago: University of Chicago Press, 2014), 9–27.

3. See James G. Hollandsworth, *An Absolute Massacre: The New Orleans Race Riot of July 30, 1866* (Baton Rouge: Louisiana State University Press, 2004); Justin Nystrom, *New Orleans After the Civil War: Race, Politics, and a New Birth of Freedom* (Baltimore: Johns Hopkins University Press, 2010); and Khaled J. Bloom, *The Mississippi Valley's Great Yellow Fever Epidemic of 1878* (Baton Rouge: Louisiana State University Press, 1993).

4. Joy J. Jackson, *New Orleans in the Gilded Age: Politics and Urban Progress, 1880–1896* (Baton Rouge: Louisiana State University Press, 1969), 204–231. Quote from 231.

5. Eric Arnesen, *Waterfront Workers of New Orleans: Race, Class, and Politics,* 1863–1923 (New York: Oxford University Press, 1991), 74, 119–121, 160–1161, 204; and Roger W. Shugg, *Origins of Class Struggle in Louisiana: A Social History of White Farmers and Laborers during Slavery and After, 1840–1875* (Baton Rouge: Louisiana State University Press, 1939), 197–233, 274–314.

6. Kolb, "For the Love of Tennis," 54–55; "About Us," Westfeldt Brothers, Inc., Coffee Importers, http://www.westfeldtcoffee.com/about.html, accessed 13 January 2018; Andrew Morrison, *New Orleans and the New South* (New Orleans: Metropolitan Publishing Co., 1888),

10, 114; T.P. Thompson, "Early Financing in New Orleans, Being the Story of Canal Bank, 1831–1915," in *Publications of the Louisiana Historical Society,* vol. 7, 1913–1914 (New Orleans: Louisiana Historical Society, 1915), 57; *Biographical and Historical Memoirs of Louisiana,* vol. 2 (Chicago: Goodspeed Publishing Co., 1892), 441; and Missouri Pacific Railroad Co. v. International Marine Insurance Co., 84 Texas 149, in *The American and English Railroad Cases,* vol. 55, ed. William M. McKinney (Northport, Long Island: Edward Thompson Co., 1893), 549.

7. Kolb, "For the Love of Tennis," 54–55; Stephen Tignor, "The Survivor," *Tennis* 42 (September 2006): 86–89; and New Orleans *Times-Picayune,* 25 February 1898, 14. See also Ann Maden, "Popular Sports in New Orleans, 1890–1900" (MA thesis: Tulane University, 1956): 63–64, 80.

8. H.W. Slocum, "Lawn Tennis in the South," *Outing* 13 (March 1889): 496.

9. Larry R. Youngs, "The Sporting Set Winters in Florida: Fertile Ground for the Leisure Revolution, 1870–1930," *Florida Historical Quarterly* 84 (Summer 2005): 59. Pre-revolutionary Cuba was a similar kind of destination for Americans of wealth. A similar argument is made, for example, in Rosalie Schwartz, *Pleasure Island: Tourism and Temptation in Cuba* (Lincoln: University of Nebraska Press, 1997), and, to a lesser extent, in Louis A. Perez, *On Becoming Cuban: Identity, Nationality, and Culture* (Chapel Hill: University of North Carolina Press, 1999).

10. Steven A. Reiss, *City Games: The Evolution of American Urban Society and the Rise of Sports* (Urbana: University of Illinois Press, 1989), 53.

11. Alecia P. Long, *The Great Southern Babylon: Sex, Race, and Respectability in New Orleans, 1865–1920* (Baton Rouge: Louisiana State University Press, 2004), 66–69, 95–97. The case from which Long's analysis derives, and from which the quotes appear, is *Koehl, et al. v. Schoenhausen,* 47 La. An. 1316, 17 So. 809 (1895).

12. Elliott J. Gorn, *The Manly Art: Bare-Knuckle Prize Fighting in America* (Ithaca: Cornell University Press, 1986), 83.

13. Eric Danhoff, "The Struggle for Control of Amateur Track and Field in the United States," *Canadian Journal of History of Sport and physical Education* 6 (No. 1 1975): 43–85; and Richard Wettan and J.D. Willis, "Effect of New York Athletic Clubs on Amateur Athletic Governance, 1870–1915," *Research Quarterly. American Alliance for Health, Physical Education and Recreation* 47 (No. 3 1976): 499–505.

14. See Clifford Putney, *Muscular Christianity: Manhood and Sports in Protestant America, 1880–1920* (Cambridge: Harvard University Press, 2003).

15. *Harvard Crimson,* 5 April 1878, 2.

16. Wilson, *Love Game,* 19, 56–69, 74–79, 113–122. See also Marshall Jon Fisher, *A Terrible Splendor: Three Extraordinary Men, a World Poised for War, and the Greatest Tennis Match Ever Played* (New York: Broadway Books, 2010); Frank Deford, *Big Bill Tilden: The Triumphs and the Tragedy* (New York: Simon and Schuster, 1976); and Larry Engelmann, *The Goddess and the American Girl: The Story of Suzanne Lenglen and Helen Wills* (New York: Oxford University Press, 1988).

17. Benjamin G. Rader, *American Sports, from the Age of Folk Games to the Age of Televised Sports,* Fifth ed. (Upper Saddle River, NJ: Prentice Hall, 2004), 67.

18. New Orleans *Times-Picayune,* 26 July 1879, 4.

19. New Orleans *Times-Picayune,* 2 May 1880, 2, 7 September 1880, 4.

20. Jackson, *New Orleans in the Gilded Age,* 261–268. Quote from 261. The advertisements continued through much of the year. For an example, see New Orleans *Times-Picayune,* 28 March 1880, 8.

21. New Orleans *Times-Picayune*, 23 May 1897, 8, 24 June 1901, 8; and "Stenographic Report of the Discussion at the Meeting of the Louisiana Sugar Planters' Association," *Louisiana Planter and Sugar Manufacturer* 56 (17 June 1916): 394–395.

22. The SLTA's first championships, in the 1880s and 1890s, took place on the east coast, rotating between Wilmington, Washington, DC, and Baltimore. Slocum, "Lawn Tennis in the South," 496; and "Lawn Tennis," *Sporting Life* 11 (11 July 1888): 11.

23. *Atlanta Constitution*, 8 April 1902, 7, 15 February 1903, 2, 20 March 1904, B8, 26 May 1904, A3, 20 March 1908, 13, 8 April 1909, 11, 8 July 1909, 4, 28 April 1912, 16, 22 June 1913, 13, 24 March 1914, 9; *New York Tribune*, 10 March 1905, 6; *Christian Science Monitor*, 10 June 1912, 3, 22 June 1920, 10; New York *Herald Tribune*, 13 June 1947, 27; *Chicago Tribune*, 12 March 1905, A2; *New York Times*, 16 March 1901, 10, 15 March 1903, 10, 10 March 1905, 7, 11 March 1906, 11, 2 May 1920, 21; *Boston Globe*, 15 February 1903, 2; and *Los Angeles Times*, 5 June 1925, B1.

24. Reiss makes this case for both early northern, urban athletic clubs and northern, suburban country clubs. See Reiss, *City Games*, 57–59.

25. *Atlanta Constitution*, 28 May 1920, 9, 21 June 1920, 7, 22 June 1920, 11, 13 June 1947, 14, 7 June 1953, 4D, 12 June 1953, 30, 24 June 1956, 7D; *Atlanta Journal-Constitution*, 10 September 2005, A8; and *New York Times*, 10 June 1953, 40.

26. *Atlanta Constitution*, 7 May 1959, 48.; and *Atlanta Daily World*, 12 June 1953, 3.

27. Tignor, "The Survivor," 86–89.

28. Henry W. Slocum, Jr., "Lawn Tennis as a Game for Women," *Outing* 14 (July 1889): 289; and Somers, *The Rise of Sports in New Orleans*, 212.

29. The original 1902 City Park Tennis Club grew quickly in popularity, open to whomever wanted to play. Forty-five had joined within the first month of its existence. Two courts were reserved for the members. New Orleans *Picayune*, 9 June 1902, 3; and "City Park Tennis Club: A Brief History," http://cityparktennisclub.com/, accessed 13 January 2018.

30. New Orleans *Times-Picayune*, 23 September 1935, 12; and Sixteenth Census of the United States, 1940, Population Schedule, New Orleans City, Louisiana, Sheet No. 8A.

31. It is no coincidence that the city's *Picayune* newspaper's first mention of lawn tennis in 1879 was in a fashion column suggesting outfits for the outing. New Orleans *Picayune*, 13 July 1879, 11; and New Orleans *Times-Picayune*, 7 November 1937, 4–3.

32. New Orleans *Times-Picayune*, 7 November 1937, 4–3, 14 November 1937, 4–6.

33. New Orleans *Times-Picayune*, 20 February 1938, 4–6.

34. New Orleans *Times-Picayune*, 13 February 1938, 4–3, 10 March 1948, 18.

35. New Orleans *Times-Picayune*, 15 June 1923, 18, 22 May 1938, 4–2.

36. New Orleans *Times-Picayune*, 1 July 1901, 11, 9 December 1901, 7, 18 July 1937, 4–6, 10 September 1964, 2–14; *New York Herald Tribune*, 3 April 1930, 28; Jackson, *New Orleans in the Gilded Age*, 266; Dale Somers, *The Rise of Sports in New Orleans, 1850–1900* (Baton Rouge: Louisiana State University Press, 1972), 211; *Spirit of the South*, 2 February 1889, 1; and *New York Times*, 2 January 1967, 27. Further, when major national conferences like the American Legion's annual gathering in 1922 occurred in New Orleans, the NOLTC allowed the conventioneers to hold their tennis tournament on the property. *New York Tribune*, 10 September 1922, B10.

37. New Orleans *Times-Picayune*, 18 July 1937, 4–6.

38. See, for example, New Orleans *Times-Picayune*, 28 June 1934, 16, 22 May 1938, 49, 3 December 1944, 28, 30 October 1949, 88, 2 September 1956, 58.

39. Sundiata Djata, *Blacks at the Net: Black Achievement in the History of Tennis*, vol. 1 (Syracuse: Syracuse University Press, 2006), 2–4; Gerald F. Norman, "National American Tennis Association Championships," *Opportunity* 6 (October 1928): 306–307; and Bertram

Barker, "A Black Tennis Association: Active since 1916," in *American Tennis Association National Rankings, 1983–1984* (Philadelphia: American Tennis Association, 1984), 60.

40. John W. Blassingame, *Black New Orleans: 1860–1880* (Chicago: University of Chicago Press, 1973), 139–143.

41. *Weekly Louisianian*, 22 October 1881, 1.

42. *Weekly Pelican*, 25 December 1886, 3, 8 January 1887, 3.

43. Another such upper-middle class genteel tale used tennis as another respectability signpost in 1889. *Weekly Pelican*, 25 December 1886, 4, 15 January 1887, 4, 19 October 1889, 1.

44. *Weekly Pelican*, 8 January 1887, 1.

45. *Weekly Pelican*, 22 October 1887, 4.

46. *Weekly Pelican*, 26 October 1889, 3. There were other black weeklies in the city during this period, but what issues of those papers survive do not mention tennis. One of them, the Southern Republican, did, in 1900, demonstrate an interest in bicycling, but never expanded its coverage to any ball games. *Southern Republican*, 14 April 1900, 1, 3; *The Crusader*, 19 July 1890; *Black Republican*, 15 April 1865, 22 April 1865, 29 April 1865, 13 May 1865, 20 May 1865; and *Republican Courier*, 2 December 1899, 20 January 1900.

47. *Louisiana Weekly*, 9 January 1926, 7.

48. For further examples of some of these clubs, see the society page of the *Louisiana Weekly*. The listed entities, some of the most popular and continuous, appear in several of many mentions on 16 January 1926, 8; 9 October 1926, 5.

49. Such is not to say that black New Orleans did not participate in the athletic fads of the era. Bicycling was popular. One black student even planned a bicycling excursion from New Orleans to New York. *Louisiana Weekly*, 29 May 1926, 1.

50. *Louisiana Weekly*, 26 August 1929, 1.

51. *Louisiana Weekly*, 2 April 1927, 1, 14 April 1927, 1, 2, 23 April 1927, 2, 30 April 1927, 8, 28 May 1927, 8, 13 August 1927, 1, 27 August 1927, 1, 3 September 1927, 1.

52. *Louisiana Weekly*, 23 July 1927, 1, 8, 20 August 1927, 8, 16 June 1928, 8, 7 July 1928, 8; and William Ivy Hair, *Carnival of Fury: Robert Charles and the New Orleans Race Riot of 1900* (Baton Rouge: Louisiana State University Press, 1986), 177–178. For more on the influence of Thomy Lafon, see Frederick D. Smith, "Thomy Lafon," in *Encyclopedia of African American Business*, vol. 2, ed. Jessie Carney Smith (Westport, CT: Greenwood, 2006), 447–449.

53. The growth in availability of such courts benefited from a national boom in the production of places to play, particularly in urban areas. Between 1924 and 1931, the number of tennis courts in the United States increased by 81 percent. Reiss, *City Games*, 141–142; and *Louisiana Weekly*, 11 August 1828, 8. For more on Frances Joseph-Gaudet, see her autobiography, *He Leadeth Me* (New Orleans: Louisiana Printing Co., 1913).

54. *Louisiana Weekly*, 30 July 1927, 5.

55. *Louisiana Weekly*, 6 August 1927, 5, 20 August 1927, 5, 27 August 1927, 5, 10 September 1927, 5, 16 June 1928, 5; Vic Hobson, *Creating Jazz Counterpoint: New Orleans, Barbershop Harmony, and the Blues* (Jackson: University Press of Mississippi, 2014), 7–31; and Donald M. Marquis, *In Search of Buddy Bolden: First Man of Jazz* (Baton Rouge: Louisiana State University Press, 2005), 2, 109.

56. *Louisiana Weekly*, 13 August 1927, 5; and Sundiata A. Djata, *Blacks at the Net: Black Achievement in the History of Tennis*, vol. 1 (Syracuse: Syracuse University Press, 2006), 221.

57. *Louisiana Weekly*, 17 September 1927, 8.

58. *Louisiana Weekly*, 23 June 1928, 5, 14 July 1928, 8.

59. Burbridge would go on to become a sportswriter at the *Louisiana Weekly*, owned as it was by the Dejoie family. Fifteenth Census of the United States, 1930, Population Schedule,

New Orleans City, Louisiana, Sheet No. 3A, 11A; Sixteenth Census of the United States, 1940, Population Schedule, New Orleans City, Louisiana, Sheet No. 16B; and *Louisiana Weekly,* 16 July 1927, 5, 23 July 1927, 8.

60. Victor would not finish school, leaving after meeting and marrying her husband, Victor Hayes Labat, in 1931. *Soards' New Orleans City Directory, 1929* (New Orleans: Soards Directory Co., 1929), 1034; Fourteenth Census of the United States, 1920, Population Schedule, New Orleans City, Louisiana, Sheet No. 13A; Sixteenth Census of the United States, 1940, Population Schedule, New Orleans City, Louisiana, Sheet No. 7B; and *Louisiana Weekly,* 23 July 1927, 8, 3 September 1927, 8.

61. Fifteenth Census of the United States, 1930, Population Schedule, New Orleans City, Louisiana, Sheet No. 14B; 16B, 4A; and *Louisiana Weekly,* 23 July 1927, 1, 3 September 1927, 8, 7 July 1928, 8.

62. Lee Sartain, *Invisible Activists: Women of the Louisiana NAACP and the Struggle for Civil Rights, 1915–1945* (Baton Rouge: Louisiana State University Press, 2007), 85–88; and Harriet Elsa Weidman, "The Sylvania F. Williams Community Center (MA thesis: Tulane University, 1933), 2–10.

63. *Louisiana Weekly,* 30 June 1928, 8, 7 July 1928, 8, 21 July 1828, 8, 28 July 1928, 8, 11 August 1928, 8.

64. *Louisiana Weekly,* 18 August 1928, 8.

65. New Orleans *Times-Picayune,* 20 January 1974, 6–7.

66. Djata, *Blacks at the Net,* 2–4; and Barker, "A Black Tennis Association," 60.

67. New Orleans *Times-Picayune,* 13 August 1960, 22, 2 September 1960, 3–2, 20 January 1974, 6–7, 7 August 2012, B2.

68. Alan Wieder, "The New Orleans School Crisis of 1960: Causes and Consequences," *Phylon* 48 (2nd Qtr. 1987): 122–131; and Adam Fairclough, *Race & Democracy: The Civil Rights Struggle in Louisiana, 1915–1972* (Athens: University of Georgia Press, 1995), 234–264.

69. Wieder, "The New Orleans School Crisis of 1960," 122–131; Juliette Landphair, "Sewerage, Sidewalks, and Schools: The New Orleans Ninth Ward and Public School Desegregation," *Louisiana History* 40 (Winter 1999): 35–62; Diane T. Manning and Perry Rogers, "Desegregation of the New Orleans Parochial Schools," *Journal of Negro Education* 71 (Winter-Spring 2002): 31–42; and *Bush v. Orleans Parish School Board,* 138 F. Supp. 337 (1956).

70. Tim Lyman, "Jumping the Net," *Gambit,* 10 December 2002, n.p. (article available online at https://www.bestofneworleans.com/gambit/jumping-the-net/Content?oid=1240979, accessed 13 January 2018); and M.R. Werner, "Footloose: New Orleans—A Mixture Of the Old and the New and All That Dixie Jazz," *Sports Illustrated,* 21 March 1966, E1–E2.

71. Lee Stall, General Manager of the NOLTC, said that the club desegregated "sometime before 1987" but was unable to recall an exact date for the first black membership. Interview with Lee Stall, conducted by Kelley Clark, 15 February 2018; and *Atlanta Constitution,* 22 October 1968, 40. Boston's Longwood Cricket Club began playing tennis in 1878. Merion Cricket Club outside of Philadelphia, founded in 1873, began playing tennis in 1879. *Boston Globe,* 21 August 1977, K8.

72. New Orleans *Times-Picayune,* 3 December 1970, 1–22.

Chapter 5

1. Parts of this material were presented orally at conferences of the Popular Culture Association (1993), North American Society for Sport History (1994), and Louisiana Studies

(2015), and published in R.V. McGehee, "The New Orleans Athletic Club (Young Men's Gymnastic Club): A Crescent City Tradition," *Louisiana Association for Health, Physical Education, Recreation and Dance Journal* 65 (No. 1 2001): 3–8.

2. Dale Somers, *The Rise of Sports in New Orleans, 1850–1900* (Baton Rouge: LSU Press, 1972); Ann Maden, "Popular Sports in New Orleans, 1890–1900," (MA thesis: Tulane University, 1956); and Flora K. Scheib, *History of the Southern Yacht Club* (Gretna, LA: Pelican Pub. Co., 1986).

3. J. Calvin Williams, "YMCA New Orleans 1982: 130 Years of History on the Mississippi Crescent" (New Orleans: Metro YMCA, 1982). For more on Turnvereins, see Somers, *The Rise of Sports in New Orleans*, 69–71.

4. *The Punch*, 1972, 12. Other sources, such as Somers, *The Rise of Sports in New Orleans*, 240, give the initial club membership as thirteen.

5. *The Punch*, 1972, 12.

6. Somers, *The Rise of Sports in New Orleans*, 240. Somers cites an 1880 *Daily Picayune* entreaty to the YMGC to expand its gymnastics activities to track and field events, as in northern athletic associations, a direction finally taken by the club in 1886, when they staged a two-day meet that included track and field, boxing, wrestling, cycling, and gymnastics.

7. *The Punch*, 1972, 12–13. In *The Punch* of January, 1935, W.H. Heyl described his memories of the early installations and finances of the YMGC, including discrepancies with the account given in the 1972 anniversary issue. Heyl reported that in 1884 the stable owner demanded a rent increase from $40 to $50 per month and a five-year lease. The membership voted unanimously against accepting their landlord's demands, and they moved their belongings successively to two temporary locations before buying the high school for $6600. To cover the loan they needed, they issued certificates to members and moved into their new home in January of 1885. In 1888 the club organized itself into a stock corporation of 1500 shares at $50 each and began construction of a new gym and baths at a cost of $85,000. After purchase of the mansion on North Rampart for $18,000 and a little more for remodeling, "we celebrated the occasion by a grand musicale and dance. The singing and music were furnished by the artists of the French Opera Company. . . ." Heyl wrote that this opening event was so successful that membership soon rose to 1500 and that dues were raised from $6 to $15 per year. The street address of the mansion site was changed at some time from 44 to 224, and later to 222.

8. *The Punch*, 1972, 13. Beginning in 1911 swimming trunks were banned in the NOAC natatorium for purposes of hygiene. In 1930 the procedures for keeping the pool clean were described: every night the pool was drained and refilled from the club's salt water well. Swimmers took a hot soap bath before entering the pool, and being naked, no one could "enter the water with ring worms or other contagious disease but that he will be seen by someone." Also, "the possibilities of infected garments throwing off germs in the water is impossible" (*The Punch*, 1930). In an article in *The Punch* for September, 1935, W.H. Heyl described the circumstances of the drilling of the 1898 well and gave an analysis of its water compared to ocean water.

9. Baseball was a popular club activity, and in 1895 YMGC representatives joined others from the American AC, Southern AC, and Catholic Club to plan an amateur baseball league and schedule games for a tournament (*Daily Picayune*, 29 March 1895). A week later the paper called the new organization the "Southern Amateur Baseball League." In preparation for their first league game, the YMGC team traveled to Baton Rouge to play the Baton Rouge Baseball Club (*Daily Picayune*, 20 April 1895). Games were to be played at Sportsman's Park and on the Southern AC field. Competition among the city's athletic clubs seems to have been fierce, as

the *Daily Picayune* (12 April 1895) described "hard feelings" at the YMGC over the move of five of their best track and field athletes to the Catholic Club. The YMGC tried to block their deserters' representing the rival club in the 1895 Southern AAU spring meet.

10. Maden, "Popular Sports in New Orleans," 162; *The Punch,* 1972, 65. There was a "YMGC Park" on Tulane Avenue, between St. John and Carrollton Streets. This may have been the location of their cycling track. The *Daily Picayune* (17 March 1895, 8) reported YMGC members training at the YMGC athletic park, corner of Carrollton Ave. and Common St., for their annual spring games (track and field) that would be held at the fairgrounds on April 20. On March 24 the paper said that the YMGC park was also being used for training by the Jesuit College, American AC, and the YMCA. The Southern AC had its own training facility and also offered a spring track and field meet at the fairgrounds.

11. Somers, *The Rise of Sports in New Orleans,* 244. The *Daily Picayune* (31 January 1895, 8 and 1 February 1895, 8) reported that the Pelican Cyclers were also in the founding group in 1893, but by 1895 they had become the Crescent Wheelmen.

12. Program of the 1895 Spring Meet of the Southern Association of the AAU. No competitors were listed from the Pensacola AC. The events included 100- and 220-yd dashes; quarter mile, half mile, one mile, and five mile runs; 120- and 220-yd. hurdles; one-mile walk, running high jump; running and standing broad jumps; hop, step, and jump; pole vault; 16-lb hammer, 16-lb shot, and 56-lb weight throw; and quarter-, half-, one-, and two-mile bicycle races. There were between three and thirteen competitors in each event, the larger numbers all in the cycling races.

13. Maden, "Popular Sports in New Orleans," 182, gives the figure of 4500 for attendance at the "YMGC's spring games," which apparently were member-only meets.

14. Somers, *The Rise of Sports in New Orleans,* 244–245. Somers says that interest in track and field faded after this meet. The program of the AAU National Spring Championships, May 14, 1898 lists as officers of the Southern Association: the president from Birmingham AC, secretary from Southern AC, and vice-president J.J. Woulfe of the YMGC. The board of governors included three members each from Birmingham AC, Eagle Pass AC, Nashville AC, Southern AC, and the YMGC. An insert in the program shows an estimated attendance figure of 9,000 (6,000 civilians and 3,000 soldiers) and a tabulation of first, second, and third places (NYAC: 8 firsts, 3 thirds; Southern AC: 8 firsts, 7 seconds, 5 thirds; YMGC: 6 seconds, 4 thirds; and Birmingham AC: 1 first, 3 seconds, 1 third). The events were similar to those held in 1895. Only one cycling race (one mile) was held, and the five-mile run and hop, step and jump were eliminated. Discus and a one-mile relay race were added. Most events had only 3–4 competitors and the final activity, the mile relay, had only two entries (Southern AC won when Boston withdrew).

15. Somers, *The Rise of Sports in New Orleans,* 244; and Maden, "Popular Sports in New Orleans," 127.

16. Somers, *The Rise of Sports in New Orleans,* 174.

17. Maden, "Popular Sports in New Orleans," 56.

18. In 1893 T.L. Bayne, a Southern Athletic Club member and former star quarterback at Yale, sold Tulane students on the idea of forming a team. He coached them and organized a game between Tulane and the SAC for November 18. A week later Tulane played LSU (Tulane winning, 34–0) before a New Orleans crowd of 1500–2000 spectators, the Tulane squad being strengthened by several SAC players. LSU finally beat the SAC in 1896, the first time the club had lost to a college team [Peter Finney, *The Fighting Tigers II: LSU Football, 1893–1980* (Baton Rouge: LSU Press, 1980) 5, 7–8, 13–14]. Farther north, the Louisville

Athletic Club, established in 1888, was already playing football in 1890 and tied Sewanee College in 1892 [Brian S. Butler, "'Gain Ground and Glory:' Metropolitan Athletic Clubs and the Promotion of American football—the Case of the Louisville Athletic Club," *The International Journal of the History of Sport* 9 (No. 3 1992), 378–396].

19. Somers, *The Rise of Sports in New Orleans,* 154, 243; and Maden, "Popular Sports in New Orleans,"78–79.

20. *The Punch,* 1972, 13, says the YMGC bought the rowing club facility in 1900. An article in the *Times-Picayune* (4 September 1994) said the YMGC operated the rowing club from 1904–1913. Previously it had been the West End Rowing Club (since 1864) and after 1913 until a fire destroyed the clubhouse in 1929, it was the home of the Pontchartrain Rowing Club.

21. Maden, "Popular Sports in New Orleans," 78–79, 81, 137–143. In an article in *The Punch* for August, 1989, A.A. Crais, Jr., stated that during the 1890s the YMGC unsuccessfully tried to introduce soccer in New Orleans as well as sponsor women's basketball. Somers, *The Rise of Sports in New Orleans,* 244, states that both the YMGC and the Southern AC were involved in those unsuccessful endeavors.

22. *Daily Picayune,* 10 May 1900, 8, 17 May 1900, 8, 23 May 1900, 8. On the evening of May 23, the club was to hold a stag entertainment to raise funds for Prof. Schoenfeldt's travel to Paris. The program included "wrestling, sparring, broadsword contests and statue work by Prof. Schoenfeldt, one of the most perfectly formed men in the world. With the use of chalk and wigs, he will present a number of the famous Roman statues." In addition to the tableaux featuring Schoenfeldt alone and in groups, he was to do gymnastic and acrobatic work. Club members were to perform tumbling, and an eight-round glove contest would be fought "to a decision."

23. Maden, "Popular Sports in New Orleans," 183. In the late 1890s twenty New Orleans athletic clubs had a total of about 7,200 members. In 1897 there were 30 athletic clubs (the American AC had 1300, and the Southern AC, 1040 members), 30 rifle clubs, 25 bicycle clubs, 13 rowing clubs, and others for baseball, tennis and other sports. The Southern Yacht Club had 500 members. The *Daily Picayune* for 7 April 1895 said the American AC was celebrating its fifth anniversary, and the current membership was 750.

24. *The Punch,* 1972, 122.

25. Maden, "Popular Sports in New Orleans," 80.

26. *Times-Picayune,* 14 May 1995.

27. *The Punch,* April 1935, 7.

28. *The Punch,* November 1935, 10.

29. *The Punch,* December 1932, 9–10. The *Times-Picayune* (25 November 1993) reported the NOAC's annual 5-mile "Turkey Day Road Race" would be held that day, for the 86th time, starting on Orleans Avenue and ending on the track inside Tad Gormley Stadium. Proceeds were to go to the Spina Bifida Association.

30. *The Punch,* 1972, 71.

31. *Morning Advocate* (Baton Rouge), 26 June 1989.

32. The award was inaugurated by Jack Spellman, member of the Board of Directors and chairman of the NOAC Athletic Committee. After his death it was called the NOAC-Jack Spellman Outstanding Amateur Athlete Award. Female athletes received the award in 1952, 1957, 1967, and 1970 (*The Punch,* February 1971, 4–5). The winner received the Spellman Award each year at the club's "Banquet of Champions," an awards dinner, which included recognition of the club's best athlete and other outstanding club teams and athletes.

33. *The Punch,* March 1930, 8.

34. *The Punch,* February 1930, 5.

35. *The Punch,* September 1930, 9; November 1930, 15.

36. The website for the Louisiana Sports Hall of Fame describes how in 1914 Tad Gormley moved from Massachusetts, where he had trained two Boston Marathon winners (1903, 1906), to New Orleans to become track coach at Tulane and athletic director of the YMGC. Gormley later coached at LSU and Loyola. New Orleans' City Park Stadium, where the 1992 US Olympic track and field trials were held, was renamed Gormley Stadium in 1965. Promotional material (23 November 1989) from New Orleans' Spina Bifida Association announcing the NOAC's "82nd Annual Turkey Day Race" places Gormley in New Orleans at an earlier date, stating that the race was started in 1907 by Tad Gormley.

37. *The Punch,* 1972, 13. The NOAC sent athletes in boxing, wrestling, track, and gymnastics to the tryouts for the 1932 Olympics in Los Angeles. One of the gymnasts was a rope climber, the eight-meter rope climb being an official Olympic event at that time. This man had climbed within two seconds of the world record, but he was disqualified by the IOC because of a physical deformity (he only had one leg).

38. Somers, *The Rise of Sports in New Orleans,* 194. When the bowling alley was built in the 1890s, Thursday nights were set aside for ladies. The American AC may have had more extensive activities for women. The *Daily Picayune,* 2 February 1895, 8, mentions a "ladies class" in that club and the cancellation of their first performance due to bad weather, but it doesn't mention the nature of their "training." On February 7 (under the section heading "ATHLETIC") the young ladies' performance in the club's gym the previous evening is reported. It consisted of a marching drill with flags, and extensive comments described how pretty they were and how they were dressed. Also, one of the young ladies presented award buttons to the men who had recently won events in a club track and field meet.

39. *The Punch,* May 1933, 18.

40. *The Punch,* 1972, 89.

41. *The Punch,* March 1930, 16.

42. *The Punch,* 1933.

43. As early as 1925 the club was holding "bathing beauty" contests. *Times Picayune,* 12 July 1925. There were monthly bathing beauty contests in 1926, and the "final winner" of the contest that year was given a trip to Havana. *Times Picayune,* 3 June, 26 October 1926.

44. *The Punch,* 1972. Somers, *The Rise of Sports in New Orleans,* 282, cites an earlier song about the club, the "Progressive YMGC March."

45. Tennessee Williams frequented the club when he lived in New Orleans in the early 1940s. Williams loved to swim, and considering his sexual orientation, he must have found the nude swimming in the club's pool especially enjoyable. While at the club Williams observed with interest the behaviors of a masochistic young club member and a sadistic black masseur, and this theme became the basis for his 1948 short story, "Desire and the Black Masseur." Donald Spoto, *The Kindness of Strangers: The Life of Tennessee Williams* (Boston: Little, Brown, 1985), 90.

46. *The Punch,* 1972, 13.

47. *Times-Picayune,* 7 July 1984.

48. A *Courier* article (3 December 1975) reported NOAC president Dr. Robert Azar's editorial in a recent issue of *The Punch,* calling on the club to reverse its race discrimination policy. He wrote, "For more than a century the NOAC has been a center of civic and social, as well as athletic, activities. But . . . we are becoming morally moribund, social stagnant and

economically extinct." In response to his comments, Azar ("Mr. New Orleans" of 1952, former Golden Gloves boxer and black belt in karate) was attacked in letters, and he was opposed 8–1 by the members of the club's board of directors. Azar's proposal was voted down at the 14 January 1976 general membership meeting. With roughly 450 of the 1,759 members present, there were about 400 against (*Times-Picayune,* 16 January 1976). *Figaro* (21 January 1976) reported that two city council members and 34 priests had abstained from the vote. Azar was removed as president by the board at the end of January. This move may have been spurred largely by Azar's pre-vote threat that if the NOAC constitution were not changed to remove its exclusion of blacks, a new downtown athletic club would be established, formed by "the cream of our membership" (*States-Item,* 3 November 1975).

49. *Times-Picayune,* 7 July 1984; and *Morning Advocate,* 7 July 1984.

50. In a *Picayune* cartoon, a NOAC member is saying to his black masseur, "We've always been tolerant toward blacks. Right, Jefferson?" Undated clipping in NOAC club files.

51. *Times-Picayune,* 20 May 1976.

52. *Times-Picayune,* 7 August 1994. Lawyer, real estate investor, and long-time NOAC member and club president at the time women were admitted in 1989, More paid $400,000 for the club in 1991 and put $1.2 million into it over the next three years, hoping to be rewarded with its growth in value. Over that period it went from 400 to 1,650 members (including about 40% women and 20% black members in 1994) and annual revenue from $400,000 (in 1992) to $1 million. This article gave the club membership at the time of the 1972 centennial as 2,583 and attributed the decrease (to the low figure in 1991) as largely due to the deterioration of the club's facilities. One of the many improvements in the club's amenities was next-door parking for members, made possible by More's purchase of a parking building there.

53. Apparently the NOAC management seeks to preserve something of the historical social prestige of the club. Recent online promotional material states that its "clientele ranges from doctors and lawyers to poets, actors, musicians, and athletes. If you're lucky you may even bump into a celebrity or two while using the club." Actually, the social status of club members seems to have spanned a large range, from governors, judges, business owners, doctors, lawyers, and Central American and European consuls, to (at least as seen from occupations noted in membership applications) stevedores, clerks, and office boys.

54. Bucking its current trend and recalling the club's tradition of community outreach, in 2014 and 2015 the NOAC held a lecture series, open to the public, featuring speakers on New Orleans cultural topics from history to food to voodoo.

Chapter 6

1. Ron Smith, "Far More than Commercialism: Stadium Building from Harvard's Innovation to Stanford's 'Dirt Bowl,'" *International Journal of the History of Sport* 25 (August 2008): 1457.

2. "The Steel-concrete Work of the Harvard Stadium," *The American Architect and Building News* 85 (1904): 51–54.

3. Brian Ingrassia, *The Rise of the Gridiron University: Higher Education's Uneasy Alliance with Big-Time Football* (Lawrence: University of Kansas Press, 2012), 171.

4. Allen L. Sack, "The Commercialization and Rationalization of Intercollegiate Football: A Comparative Analysis of the Development of Football at Yale and Harvard in the Latter

Nineteenth Century (PhD diss., The Pennsylvania State University, 1974): 1–2. See also Andrew Doyle, "Turning the Tide: College Football and Southern Progressivism," *Southern Cultures* 3 (No. 3 1997): 28–51.

5. Raymond Schmidt, *Shaping College Football: The Transformation of an American Sport, 1919–1930* (Syracuse: Syracuse University Press, 2007), 5–6.

6. Ingrassia, *The Rise of the Gridiron University,* 9.

7. Ryan Whirty, "The History of Tulane Stadium(s)," *Gambit,* 26 June 2012, accessed August 15, 2016, http://www.bestofneworleans.com/gambit/the-history-of-tulane-stadiums/Content?oid=202894. See also Marty Mulé "Taking One Last Look Way Back to Tulane Stadium," *The Advocate,* n.d., accessed August 15, 2016, http://www.theneworleansadvocate.com/sports/10054807–171/taking-one-last-look-way.

8. Schmidt, *Shaping College Football,* 151.

9. Bayne Family Involvement in Tulane Football, n.d., folder 3, box 39, Denegre Family Papers, 1824–2000s, Tulane University Archives, New Orleans, LA. See also: "Football," *Times-Picayune,* 1 January 1890, 3; Marty Mulé, *Rolling Green: A Century of Tulane Football* (New Orleans, LA: Tulane University Athletic Department, 1993), 1; "Football: The Game at Sportsman's Park Yesterday, For the Benefit of the Ambulance Fund," *Times-Picayune,* 2 January 1890, 3; and Ned Hemard, "Football in New Orleans New Year's Day, 1890," *New Orleans Nostalgia* (2008), 1–2, accessed August 15, 2016, http://www.neworleansbar.org/uploads/files/FootballinNewOrleansArticle_001.pdf

10. *Southern Inter-collegiate Athletic Association* (Athens, GA: E.D. Stone Publisher, 1895), 1.

11. W. Curtis Miner, "Leveling the Playing Field: The Democratization of Amateur Sport in Pennsylvania" (PhD diss: University of Pittsburgh, 2006), 227.

12. *University Bulletin of the Tulane University of Louisiana: 1905* (New Orleans: Tulane University of Louisiana, April 1905), 6.

13. *Bulletin of the Tulane University of Louisiana: 1909–1910* (New Orleans: Tulane University of Louisiana, January 1909), 17, 22, 32, 143. See also Athletic Matters 1910–1912, folder 1, box 2, Edwin B. Craighead Papers 1904–1912, Tulane University Archives, New Orleans, LA. Professors Halsey, Anderson, Creighton, Smyth, Lemann, and Mr. Bruff made up the committee.

14. "Tulane Working for Increased Proficiency on Gridiron," *Times-Picayune,* 17 November 1909, 12. See also "All Ready to Rush Work of Constructing Stadium on Tulane University Property," *Times-Picayune,* 8 May 1910, 28, "Tulane's New Stadium," *Times-Picayune,* 20 August 1910, 10. Tulane engineering students helped build the facility. President Howard Taft spoke at the facility in 1909 when he visited New Orleans to promote various transportation improvement projects on the Mississippi River at the Lakes to the Gulf Waterways Convention.

15. W.W. Roberts, "American Universities: Tulane, New Orleans," *Journal of Education* 77 (1913): 236. The nine departments were: Arts and Sciences, Technology, Teachers, Young Women, Law, Medicine, Pharmacy, Dentistry, and Graduate. At this time, $20,000 was reserved for the improvement of Athletics.

16. E. Davis McCutcheon, Highlights of the Forty Years of Football at Tulane, folder 10, box 24, Charles DuFour Papers, 1803–1984, Tulane University Archives, New Orleans, LA. See also Athletic Matters 1912–1918, folder 1, box 2, Robert Sharp Papers 1912–1918, Tulane University Archives, New Orleans, LA; and "The Tulane Stadium," *The Tulane News Bulletin* 1.3 (1920): 37.

17. "Tulane Stadium Ordered Closed By City Officials," *Times-Picayune,* 29 February 1916, 7.

18. Athletic Matters 1912–1918, folder 1, box 2, Robert Sharp Papers 1912–1918, Tulane University Archives, New Orleans, LA.

19. "Historic Tulane Stadium Cannot be Used Any Longer," *Times-Picayune,* 27 February 1916, 38. When built, Tulane Stadium required hundreds of carts of dirt and cinders to level out the land above the swamp.

20. Letter from Tulane Athletic Association Board of Trustees to Clark D. Shaughnessy, 15 April 1915, Athletic Matters 1912–1918, folder 1, box 2, Robert Sharp Papers 1912–1918, Tulane University Archives, New Orleans, LA.

21. Athletic Matters 1912–1918, folder 1, box 2, Robert Sharp Papers 1912–1918, Tulane University Archives, New Orleans, LA. The university pursued donations of $5 to $10 from local citizens. See also "Cost of New Tulane Stadium Investigated by Committee," *Times-Picayune,* 5 March 1916, 29.

22. "Athletics at Tulane Now Reach a Critical Stage," *Times-Picayune,* 26 April 1916, 25.

23. "Cost of New Tulane Stadium Investigated by Committee," *Times-Picayune,* 5 March 1916, 29.

24. "Meeting Assures College of Fine Modern Stadium: Tulane Realization Day Plan Outlined at Enthusiastic Gathering," *Times-Picayune,* 18 March 1916, 1.

25. *Times-Picayune,* 18 March 1916, 1.

26. "Realization Day Nets $5000 For Tulane Stadium Chairman Jahncke Announces More Money Needed to Erect," *Times-Picayune,* 2 April 1916, 54, "Frank B. Williams' $10,000 Donation Assures Stadium Gift of Public Spirited Citizen Swells Tulane Fund," *Times-Picayune,* 7 December 1916, 1.

27. "Jahncke Directs Realization Day Campaign," *Times-Picayune,* 24 March 1916, 5. Newcomb College was the women's college of Tulane University. Approximately 1,500 students participated in Realization Day for $5 per day.

28. "The Tulane Stadium," 36.

29. "Frank B. Williams' $10,000 Donation Assures Stadium Gift of Public Spirited Citizen Swells Tulane Fund," *Times-Picayune,* 7 December 1916, 1. See also "Meeting Assures College of Fine Modern Stadium," 1.

30. "Tulane President Will Make Plea for New Stadium," *Times-Picayune,* 21 March 1916. See also "L.S.U. to Help Fund: Moving Pictures of Realization Day will be Shown in Baton Rouge," *Times-Picayune,* 25 April 1916, 4; and "Lionel F. Favret to Build Stadium before Next Fall: Stand is Promised for Next Season," *Times-Picayune,* 17 June 1917, 7.

31. "Frank B. Williams' $10,000 Donation," 1. See also "Lionel F. Favret to Build Stadium before Next Fall," 7; and Letter from Office of Registrar to Tampa Board of Trade, March 9, 1923, box 4, Albert B. Dinwiddie Papers, 1918–1935, Tulane University Archives, New Orleans, LA. The designer was Prof. Donald Derickson and contractor was O.M. Gwin Construction Company. Original estimates for the 1921 expansion were $8,934.

32. "Tulane to Build Stadium Big Enough to Seat Grid Crowds," *Times-Picayune,* 18 November 1925, 1.

33. Meeting with President Report, October 10, 1921, box 4, Albert B. Dinwiddie Papers, 1918–1935, Tulane University Archives, New Orleans, LA. See also "Tulane Stadium," *Times-Picayune,* 19 November 1925, 6.

34. "Tulane Stadium Fund," *Times-Picayune,* 7 December 1925, 7. See also "Tulane Stadium," *The Times-Picayune,* 2 December 1925, 10.

35. Athletic Sessions 1921–1922, box 5, Albert B. Dinwiddie Papers, 1918–1935, Tulane University Archives, New Orleans, LA. See also William M. Keefe, "Reverses of 1926 Don't

Daunt Wave in Schedule Plans," *Times-Picayune,* 27 October 1926, 11. The article highlights the stadium as useful to schedule high caliber opponents like Ga. Tech, Maryland, and others.

36. Summary Report of Committee on Ways and Means for Financing New Stadium. 1925. box 4, Albert B. Dinwiddie Papers, 1918–1935, Tulane University Archives, Tulane University, New Orleans, LA: 1, 3, 5–6.

37. Letter from Douglas Andrews to Albert B. Dinwiddie, May 25, 1925, box 5, Albert B. Dinwiddie Papers, 1918–1935, Tulane University Archives, Tulane University, New Orleans, LA.

38. Letters of Correspondence between John C. Futrall and Albert B. Dinwiddie, November 12 and 17, 1921, box 5, Albert B. Dinwiddie Papers, 1918–1935, Tulane University Archives, Tulane University, New Orleans, LA. See also "Citizens to Help Raise Tulane's Stadium Money," *Times-Picayune,* 22 November 1925, 3, "Interest in Tulane Team's Fortunes Increases while Stadium Nears Completion," *Times-Picayune,* 10 October 1926, 1. Tulane played a schedule that featured games against the Universities of Missouri, Mississippi, Mississippi State, Northwestern, Auburn, Louisiana Tech, and LSU.

39. Martin Behrman, "Mayor Behrman's Proclamation," *Times-Picayune,* 4 December 1925, 29.

40. "Interest in Tulane Team's Fortunes," 1.

41. "Football," *Times-Picayune,* 23 October 1926, 26.

42. "Institutions which are Cornerstones to Progress," *Times-Picayune,* 23 October 1926, p. 17.

43. Eric Seiferth, "Tulane Stadium: Fifty Years of Football in New Orleans," *Historic New Orleans Collection Quarterly* 27 (No. 3 2010): 6. See also "Tulane to Dedicate New Stadium," *Times-Picayune,* 23 October 1926, 1; and Bill to the Board of Administrators, Tulane Educational Fund (1927, January 27), Tulane University Archives, Tulane University, New Orleans, LA. Seats were industry standard 18–20 inches similar to the aforementioned Harvard Stadium. The cost of the scoreboard was $58,000, one of the most expensive of that era.

44. "Tulane to Dedicate New Stadium," 1.

45. Chad S. Seifried and Donna Pastore, "Analyzing the First Permanent Professional Baseball and Football Structures in the United States: How Expansion and Renovation Changed Them into Jewel Boxes," *Sport History Review* 40 (November 2009): 181.

46. "Tulane to Dedicate New Stadium," 1.

47. Letter from Frederick M. Mann to Albert B. Dinwiddie, June 18, 1925, box 5, Albert B. Dinwiddie Papers, 1918–1935, Tulane University Archives, New Orleans, LA.

48. "Ground is Cleared for Tulane Stadium," *The Times-Picayune,* 14 January 1926, 17.

49. "Interest in Tulane Team's Fortunes," 1.

50. RE Stadium Drive, (1928–1929), extract from *The Register,* Tulane University Archives, Tulane University, New Orleans, LA. See also College Stadium: Summary (1927, December 16), Tulane University Archives, Tulane University, New Orleans, LA.

51. Edward Branley, "NOLA History: Allstate Sugar Bowl," *Go NOLA,* 30 December 2013, accessed August 15, 2016, http://gonola.com/2013/12/30/nola-history-allstate-sugar-bowl.html.

52. Marty Mulé, *Sugar Bowl: The First Years* (Birmingham, AL: Oxmoor House, Inc., 1983), 6.

53. Associated Press, "What's in a bowl name? History and geography," *The New York Times,* 30 December 2007, accessed August 15, 2016. http://www.nytimes.com/2007/12/30/sports/ncaafootball/30sugar.html?_r=0.

54. "Tulane University will Spend $300,000 on its New Stadium," *The Times-Picayune,* 25 March 1928, 2. This specific dryer was noted as only being present in two other universities in the United States, "the Universities of Michigan and Minnesota."

55. Seifried and Pastore, "Analyzing the First Permanent," 189.

56. Mulé, *Sugar Bowl,* 3–4.

57. The Doll & Toy Fund provided nearly 4,000 children with 10,500 toys during 2015 and has been an annual activity for the *Times-Picayune* since 1895.

58. Chad Seifried and Matthew Katz, "The Creation of Domestic and International Bowl Games from 1942 to 1964: The United States and Football as Conjoined Twins," *Sport History Review* 42 (November 2011): 156.

59. Chad Seifried and Benji King. "The Postseason Payout History of the Division I Football Bowl Subdivision: Comparing Current Bowl Championship Series (BCS) and Non-BCS Institutions through the Lifespan of Defunct and Active Bowl Games," *Sport History Review* 43 (November 2012): 206–228.

60. Mulé, *Sugar Bowl,* 3–4. Tulane University won Southern Conference championships in 1929 through 1931 achieving a combined 28–2 record. The 1934 team was a co-champion of the Southeastern Conference finishing with a 10–1 record.

61. Mulé, *Sugar Bowl,* 8–9. See also New Orleans Mid-Winter Sports Association (Sugar Bowl), 1934–1984, box 12, Rufus C. Harris Papers, 1937–1960, Tulane University Archives, New Orleans, LA.

62. "Fans Invited to Select Name for Post-season Tilt," *Times-Picayune,* 8 July 1934, 8.

63. "New Year Tilt Called 'Sugar Bowl' Classic," *Times-Picayune,* 25 July 1934, 11.

64. Mulé, *Sugar Bowl,* 10–11; and New Orleans Mid-Winter Sports Association (Sugar Bowl), 1934–1984, box 12, Rufus C. Harris Papers, 1937–1960, Tulane University Archives, New Orleans, LA.

65. "Sugar Bowl Game Success Assured," *Times-Picayune,* 27 December 1934, 16.

66. "The Sugar Bowl Game," *Times-Picayune,* 31 December 1934, 8.

67. Mulé, *Sugar Bowl,* 10. See also New Orleans Mid-Winter Sports Association (Sugar Bowl), 1934–1984, box 12, Rufus C. Harris Papers, 1937–1960, Tulane University Archives, New Orleans, LA.

68. "Sugar Bowl Classic by the New Orleans Mid-Winter Sport Association," *Times-Picayune,* 1 January 1935, 16.

69. "Highlights of the Radio," *Times-Picayune,* 1 January 1935, 19.

70. Mark C. Bodanza, *1933: Football at the Depth of the Great Depression* (New York: iUniverse, Inc., 2010), 75. See also Kathleen O'Toole, "John L. Griffith and the Commercialization of College Sports on Radio in the 1930s," *Journal of Sport History* 40 (Summer 2013): 248–249.

71. O'Toole, "John L. Griffith," 242.

72. Christopher J. Walsh, *Where Football is King: The History of the SEC* (Lanham, MD: Taylor Trade Publishing, 2006), 13.

73. "Barney's Pass Wins as Owls Watch "Monk," *Times-Picayune,* 2 January 1935, 15.

74. William Keefe, "Viewing the News," *Times-Picayune,* 3 January 1935, 8.

75. "Expressing the Public Mind," *Times-Picayune,* 10 January 1937, 6.

76. "Stadium at Tulane to be Enlarged to Accommodate 55,000," *Times-Picayune,* 25 May 1937, 1.

77. "First Pile Driven for Extension for Tulane stadium," *Times-Picayune,* 31 July 1937, 3.

78. "No Plans for Expansion of Stadium Here," *Times-Picayune,* 6 January 1939, 14; "Three Stadium Enlargement Plans before Group Tonight," *Times-Picayune,* 27 January 1939, 14. See also New Orleans Mid-Winter Sports Association (Sugar Bowl), 1934–1984, box 12, Rufus C. Harris Papers, 1937–1960, Tulane University Archives, New Orleans, LA.

79. "Cleanup Squad Will Continue Stadium Drive," *Times-Picayune,* 25 March 1939, 1.

80. "Work to Start Thursday on Stadium Enlargement," *Times-Picayune,* 7 June 1939, 14.

81. Contracts 1939 and 1947 and Arrangements for Stadium Enlargement, box 10, Rufus C. Harris Papers, 1937–1960, Tulane University Archives, New Orleans, LA; and 1939–1958 Stadium Painting, Press Box, Drainage, Willow St. End, Maintenance Costs, box 10, Rufus C. Harris Papers, 1937–1960, Tulane University Archives, New Orleans, LA.

82. "Tulane Stadium Work Will Start Later This Week; Contract is Awarded for 30,000 Additional Seats in Sugar Bowl," *Times-Picayune,* 7 May 1939, 1.

83. Val Flanagan, "Sugar Bowl Sports Program Slated to Extend Over Six Days This Year," *Times-Picayune,* August 20, 1939, 6. See also New Orleans Mid-Winter Sports Association (Sugar Bowl), 1934–1984, box 12, Rufus C. Harris Papers, 1937–1960, Tulane University Archives, New Orleans, LA.

84. William Keefe, "Sure Enlarge it," *Times-Picayune,* 1 January 1941, 8.

85. Mulé, *Sugar Bowl,* 10.

86. Mulé, *Rolling Green,* 59.

87. Bodanza, 1933: *Football at the Depth of the Great Depression,* 75.

88. Bodanza, *1933: Football at the Depth of the Great Depression,* xxii. See also 1941–1942 Minutes of Faculty Committee on Athletics, box 10, Rufus C. Harris Papers, 1937–1960, Tulane University Archives, New Orleans, LA; and 1942–1943 Wartime Intercollegiate Athletics Policy Statement, box 10, Rufus C. Harris Papers, 1937–1960, Tulane University Archives, New Orleans, LA.

89. William Keefe, "Plan to Enlarge Stadium," *Times-Picayune,* 6 July 1947, 22. See also New Orleans Mid-Winter Sports Association (Sugar Bowl), 1934–1984, box 12, Rufus C. Harris Papers, 1937–1960, Tulane University Archives, New Orleans, LA.

90. "Sugar Bowl Enlargement Debenture Bond Issue Sale Opens," *Times-Picayune,* 13 July 1947, 25. See also Contracts 1939 and 1947 and Arrangements for Stadium Enlargement, box 10, Rufus C. Harris Papers, 1937–1960, Tulane University Archives, New Orleans, LA; and 1939–1958 Stadium Painting, Press Box, Drainage, Willow St. End, Maintenance Costs, box 10, Rufus C. Harris Papers, 1937–1960, Tulane University Archives, New Orleans, LA.

91. William Keefe, "World's Best Stadium," *Times-Picayune,* 30 May 1948, 25. See also "Tulane Stadium Work to Start," *Times-Picayune,* 29 February 1948, 8.

92. William Keefe, "The Perfect Stadium," *Times-Picayune,* 5 January 1949, 20.

93. Clarence L. Mohr and Joseph E. Gordon, *Tulane: The Emergence of a Modern University, 1945–1980* (Baton Rouge: Louisiana State University Press, 2001), 163–164. See also Rufus C. Harris, "Post-War Intercollegiate Athletics," *Southern Coach and Athlete* (April 1944), box 20, Rufus C. Harris Papers, Tulane University Archives, New Orleans, LA.

94. Mohr and Gordon, *Tulane,* 164–165.

95. Paul R. Lawrence, *Unsportsmanlike Conduct: The National Collegiate Athletic Association and the Business of College Football* (New York: Praeger, 1987), 41–42, 49.

96. Mohr and Gordon, *Tulane,* 165. See also Presentation by President Rufus C. Harris of Tulane University, "An Eight-Point Plan for the Restraint of Intercollegiate Athletics," to Presidents of the Southeastern Conference, December 1951, box 19, Rufus C. Harris Papers, Tulane University Archives, New Orleans, LA.

97. Chad Seifried and Patrick Tutka, "Southern Methodist University Football and the Stadia: Moving toward Modernization," *Sport History Review* 47 (November 2016): 180–181.

98. Mohr and Gordon, *Tulane,* 165–166. See also Letter from Rufus C. Harris to Joseph M. Jones, September 18, 1951, box 19, Rufus C. Harris Papers, Tulane University Archives, New

Orleans, LA; and Richard O. Baumbach, "Tulane's Athletic Policy," *Tulanian* 27 (February 1951): 16–17.

99. Mohr and Gordon, *Tulane,* 166. "Harris accordingly set targets of 90 football awards and an athletic salary budget of $50,000 for 1951–1952." See also Letter from Harris to Horace Renegar, February 7, 1951, box 19, Rufus C. Harris Papers, Tulane University Archives, New Orleans, LA.

100. Letter from Rufus C. Harris to Joseph Jones, September 18, 1951, box 19, Rufus C. Harris Papers, Tulane University Archives, New Orleans, LA.

101. Mohr and Gordon, *Tulane,* 167–168. See also Board of Administrators Minutes, June 19, 1952, item 31, Tulane University Archives, New Orleans, LA.

102. Mohr and Gordon, *Tulane,* 174. See also Richard O. Baumbach to Russel M. Geer, May 19, 1955, box 11, Rufus C. Harris Papers, Tulane University Archives, New Orleans, LA; and Russel M. Geer to Rufus C. Harris, September 28, 1955, box 19, Rufus C. Harris Papers, Tulane University Archives, New Orleans, LA.

103. Board of Administrators Minutes, December 10, 1958, Tulane University Archives, New Orleans, LA. See also Board of Administrators Minutes, October 12, 1955, May 9, 1956, Report of Meeting between Special Committee of Board of Administrators and a Committee of the University Faculty Senate on Athletic Advisory Committee, May 9, 1956, Tulane University Archives, New Orleans, LA.

104. Darwin Fenner, Statement to Board of Administrators, December 31, 1964, box 49, Herbert Eugene Longenecker Papers, Tulane University Archives, New Orleans, LA.

105. Walsh, *Where Football is King,* 17.

106. Mohr and Gordon, *Tulane,* 394.

107. Buddy DiLiberto, "Hey Atlanta . . . How Y'all," *Times-Picayune,* 10 August 1964, S2–11.

108. Buddy DiLiberto, "Pro Football and the SEC," *Times-Picayune,* 11 August 1964, S2–8.

109. Kelso Sturgeon, "Atlanta, NO to Combine Efforts," *Times-Picayune,* 15 August 1964, S2–5. See also "Three Cities in Battle for AFL Berth in 1963," *Lewiston Evening Journal,* 27 June 1962, 13; and 1966 Stadium and National Football League Franchise, Victor H. and Margaret G. Schiro Papers, 1904–1995, folder 56, box 12, Tulane University Archives, New Orleans, LA.

110. Peter Finney, "Franchise is Acquired," *Times-Picayune,* 1 November 1966, 1.

111. "Tulane, Saints Sign Contract," *Times-Picayune,* 29 August 1967, S2–5.

112. James Varney, "The Saints, the Early Years: The Times-Picayune Covers 175 Years of New Orleans History," *Times-Picayune,* 29 January 2012, accessed August 15, 2016, http://www.nola.com/175years/index.ssf/2012/01/the_saints_the_early_years_the.html.

113. Bob Roesler, "Welcome aboard NFL," *Times-Picayune,* 2 November 1966, S2–4. The eventual vote was 76% in favor of the Louisiana Sports & Entertainment District and subsequently the Domed Stadium project. See also Pamphlets: Louisiana Stadium and Exposition District (1967 Proposal), Victor H. and Margaret G. Schiro Papers, 1904–1995, folder 3, box 63, Tulane University Archives, New Orleans, LA.

114. "Night Football for Green Wave," *Times-Picayune,* 6 May 1956, S2–6. See also 1939–1958 Stadium Painting, Press Box, Drainage, Willow St. End, Maintenance Costs, box 10, Rufus C. Harris Papers, 1937–1960, Tulane University Archives, New Orleans, LA.

115. Bob Roesler, "Lights at Tulane," *Times-Picayune,* 31 January 1957, 38.

116. William Keefe, "Tulane Makes Night Stadium Debut against VPI Tonight," *Times Picayune,* 20 September 1957, 26.

117. William Keefe, "Engineering Baffler," *Times-Picayune,* 30 June 1957, S2–6.

118. Bob Roesler and Paul Atkinson, "Tulane's Stadium Ok'd for Pro Ball," *Times-Picayune,* 26 October 1966, 3. See also Chad S. Seifried and Donna Pastore, "This Stadium Looks and Tastes Just Like the Others: Cookie Cutter Era Facilities from 1953–1991," *Sport History Review* 40 (May 2009): 34–36; and "Updating and Reevaluation of Parking Demand for Domed Stadium," (Baton Rouge: Gulf South Research Institute, 1968), Jones Hall Southeast Architectural Archives, New Orleans, LA.

119. Michael Oriard, *King Football: Sport & Spectacle in the Golden Age of Radio & Newsreels, Movies & Magazines, the Weekly & the Daily Press,* (Chapel Hill: University of North Carolina Press, 2001), 99.

120. Howard Jacobs, "N.O. Chosen as Site of the Super Bowl," *Times-Picayune,* 23 March 1969, S3–8; and Bob Roesler, "Behind the Sports Scene," *Times-Picayune,* 19 March 1969, S3–1.

121. "Landrieu won't Approve Injurious Span for City," *Times-Picayune,* 18 March 1971, 1, 12.

122. Bob Roesler, "New Orleans Awarded 1972 Super Bowl Game," *Times-Picayune,* 24 March 1971, 1.

123. Bob Roesler, "Here to Stay," *Times-Picayune,* 28 May 1970, S5 1.

124. Seifried and Donna Pastore, "This Stadium Looks and Tastes Just Like the Others," 39.

125. Lynn Lashbrook, "The Facts about Fake Grass," *Journal of Health, Physical Education, Recreation* 42 (No. 9 1971): 28. Regional participants in the survey included Alabama, Ole Miss, Arkansas, Tennessee, Texas A&M, Texas Tech, Kansas, and Kansas State.

126. "Citywide Drive for Turf Hoped," *Times-Picayune,* 27 March 1971, 1–2; and Bob Roesler, "Super City USA," *Times-Picayune,* 11 April 1971, S6–2.

127. "Turf Telethon Sunday Night," *Times-Picayune,* 23 April 1971, 9. See also "Landrieu Ball Team Will Play," *Times-Picayune,* 8 August 1971, 18.

128. "First Steps Taken on Turf Installation," *Times-Picayune,* 14 April 1971, S3–1. See also "Super Bowl Turf Total is $96,000; Right on Schedule Officials Say," *Times Picayune,* 22 April 1971, S5–14.

129. "Drive for Turf Lacking $22,500," *Times-Picayune,* 27 April 1971, 11.

130. Ted Lewis and Marty Mulé, "Plunging from Peak Prestige," *Times-Picayune,* 24 October 2002, accessed August 15, 2016, http://www.tulanegreenwave.com/genrel/102702aac.html. See also Annual Report of the Budget Review Committee for the Year 1971–1972, separate typescript accompanying University Senate Minutes, May 1, 1972, and Budget Review Committee Report to University Senate, March 22, 1973, item 2-A, University Senate Minutes, April 2, 1973, box 73, Herbert Eugene Longenecker Papers, Tulane University Archives, New Orleans, LA, 9–11; and Wayne S. Woody to Harry B. Kelleher, May 2, 1973, box 75, Herbert Eugene Longenecker Papers, Tulane University Archives, New Orleans, LA.

131. Joe Belock, "Super Bowl IX: Steelers Launch Dynasty with Dominant Win over Vikings," *New York Daily News,* 26 December 2013, accessed August 15, 2016, http://www.nydailynews.com/sports/football/super-bowl-ix-curtains-vikings-steelers-launch-dynasty-article-1.1558548.

132. Gerald Eskenazi, "New Orleans, Hoping to Outdo Houston, Putting up Ultimate Stadium," *New York Times,* 26 March 1972, S6; and Steve Cady, "Food for Thought at Super Bowl: Just How Much Can 75,000 People Eat?" *New York Times,* 8 January 1978, S8. These luxury amenities were recognized as significant revenue contributors.

133. Joan Niesen, "Tulane Stadium Left Mark on New Orleans," *Fox Sports North,* 24 January 2013, accessed August 15, 2016, http://www.foxsports.com/north/story/tulane-stadium-leftmark-on-new-orleans-012413. The final game at Tulane Stadium occurred on

November 1, 1979, and featured De La Salle High School and Archbishop Rummel High School. On November 2, 1979, Tulane President Sheldon Hackney announced that the remaining areas of the stadium would be razed as previous metal sections were already removed, beginning in 1975.

134. Lloyd Brown, "Tulane Riding the Crest of a New Wave with Yulman Stadium," *Stadium Journey*, n.d., accessed August 15, 2016, http://www.stadiumjourney.com/stadiums/yulman-stadium-s2110/.

Chapter 7

1. Originally published in *Horsehide, Pigskin, Oval Tracks, and Apple Pie*, ed. James A. Vlasich (Jefferson, NC: McFarland, 2006), 119–131.

2. New Orleans *Times-Picayune*, 18 September 1967.

3. Charles W. Erdmann to Millard T. Lang, 10 June 1957, Morrison, De Lesseps S., Collection, 1946–1961, City Archives, New Orleans Public Library (hereinafter Morrison Collection), Subject File, Carton S57–36, "United States Football League-1957."

4. Dave Dixon to K. S. "Bud" Adams, Jr., 10 August 1959, Morrison Collection, Subject File, Carton S59–1, "American Football League-1959."

5. Dixon to Morrison, 10 August 1959, Morrison Collection, Subject File, Carton S59–1, "American Football League-1959."

6. Morrison to Dixon, 14 August 1959, Morrison Collection, Subject File, Carton S59–1, "American Football League-1959."

7. Morrison to D.C. Smith, 25 January 1961, Morrison Collection, Subject File, Carton S61–10, "Football-Professional-1961."

8. Dixon to Joseph V. Di Rosa, 26 October 1964, Di Rosa, Joseph V., Collection, 1962–66, 1970–1978, City Archives, New Orleans Public Library.

9. Dixon to Mayor Victor H. Schiro, 3 August 1964, Schiro, Victor Hugo, Collection, 1957–1970, City Archives, New Orleans Public Library (hereinafter Schiro Collection), Subject File, Carton S64–12, "Football Club, Inc.-1964."

10. Dixon to Schiro, Schiro Collection, Subject File, Carton S65–10, "Football Club, Inc.-1965."

11. Dixon to Schiro, Schiro Collection, Subject File, Carton S65–10, "Football Club, Inc.-1965."

12. Dixon to Schiro, Schiro Collection, Subject File, Carton S65–20, "N.O. FB Club Assn.-1965."

13. NFL Trip to Washington, memo, 13 May 1966, Schiro Collection, Subject File, S66–6, "Football Club, Inc.-1966."

14. New Orleans *Times-Picayune*, 25 October 1966.

15. James Quirk and Rodney D. Fort, *Pay Dirt: The Business of Professional Team Sports* (Princeton: Princeton University Press, 1992), 145, 359.

16. Quirk and Fort, *Pay Dirt*, 334–347, 359; and Steven Reiss, *City Games: The Evolution of American Urban Society and the Rise of Sports* (Urbana: University of Illinois Press, 1989), 238.

17. Randy Roberts and James S. Olson, *Winning is the Only Thing: Sports in America Since 1945* (Baltimore: The Johns Hopkins University Press, 1989), 139; and Benjamin G. Rader, *American Sports: From the Age of Folk Games to the Age of Spectators* (Englewood Cliffs, N.J.: Prentice-Hall, Inc., 1983), 256, 257.

18. Jerry Gorman and Kirk Calhoun, with Skip Rozin, *The Name of the Game: The Business of Sports* (New York: John Wiley & Sons, Inc., 1994), 170; Roberts and Olson, *Winning is the Only Thing*, 138; and Quirk and Fort, *Pay Dirt*, 349.

19. Quirk and Fort, *Pay Dirt*, 340.

20. *U.S. News and World Report*, 20 June 1966, 10; New Orleans *Times-Picayune*, 7 October 1966; and *Time*, 17 June 1966, 68.

21. New Orleans *Times-Picayune*, 9 October 1996, 14 October 1966, 19 October 1966; and *Los Angeles Times*, 25 January 1981.

22. *Congressional Record—Senate* (hereinafter *CR*), 30 June 1966, 14809, 14810; *Los Angeles Times*, 25 January 1981; and Robert Mann, *Legacy to Power: Senator Russell Long of Louisiana* (New York: Paragon House, 1992), 273.

23. *New York Times*, 15 October 1966.

24. *New York Times*, 21 October 1966.

25. *Congressional Record—House*, 20 October 1966, 28231.

26. *CR*, 14 October 1966, 26886; Los Angeles *Times*, 25 January 1981; and Rader, *American Sports*, 258.

27. *CR*, 14 October 1966, 26887; Hale Boggs to Dr. Walter J. Vinsant, 19 October 1966, Hale Boggs Papers, Legislation Series, Box 12, 1966–1967, "1966 Legislation, Ways and Means, October 1966"; and *Los Angeles Times*, 25 January 1981.

28. New Orleans *Times-Picayune*, 25 October 1966.

29. Schiro to Rozelle, 21 October 1966, Schiro Collection, Subject Files, Carton S66–8, "Football League-1966."

30. New Orleans *Times-Picayune*, 2 November 1966, 4 November 1966.

31. Gorman and Calhoun, *The Name of the Game*, 216.

32. Roberts and Olson, *Winning Is the Only Thing*, 140–141; Quirk and Fort, *Pay Dirt*, 350–351, 359; and Gorman and Calhoun, *The Name of the Game*, 221.

33. Roberts and Olson, *Winning Is the Only Thing*, 141; and Gorman and Calhoun, *The Name of the Game*, 45.

34. Gorman and Calhoun, *The Name of the Game*; Roberts and Olson, *Winning Is the Only Thing*, 49; and New Orleans *Times-Picayune*, 6 November 1966.

35. The Victor Hugo Schiro and Margaret (Sunny) Schiro Collection, Manuscripts Collection 1001, Box 6, "VHS Speeches, 1966, Football team and stadium," n.d., Manuscripts Department, Howard-Tilton Memorial Library, Tulane University, New Orleans, Louisiana.

36. Kenneth Jackson, *Crabgrass Frontier: The Suburbanization of the United States* (Oxford: Oxford University Press, 1985), 272.

37. Gorman and Calhoun, *The Name of the Game*, 215, 221; Roberts and Olson, *Winning Is the Only Thing*, 216; Leonard Koppett, *Sports Illusion, Sports Reality: A Reporter's View of Sports, Journalism, and Society* (Urbana: University of Illinois Press, 1994), 62; and Quirk and Fort, *Pay Dirt*, 176.

38. Crozat J. Duplantier, "A Sportsman's Town," in *The Past as Prelude: New Orleans, 1718–1968*, ed. Hodding Carter (New Orleans: Tulane University Press, 1968), 185–186, 189, 208, 209.

39. New Orleans *Times-Picayune*, 6 November 1966.

40. Dixon to McKeithen, 28 January 1966, Schiro Collection, Subject Files, Carton S66–8, "Football Club, Inc.-1966."

41. Dixon to Schiro, 6 July 1966, Schiro Collection, Subject Files, Carton S66–8, "Football Club, Inc.-1966."

42. New Orleans *Times-Picayune,* 4 November 1966.

43. *Times-Picayune,* 30 October 1966, 3 November 1966, 4 November 1966, 10 November 1966.

44. *Times-Picayune,* 10 November 1966.

45. Reiss, *City Games,* 242; and *Orleans Magazine* 34 (August 2000), 13.

Chapter 8

1. Significant portions of this paper originally appeared as Robert Baade and Victor Matheson, "Professional Sports, Hurricane Katrina, and the Economic Redevelopment of New Orleans," *Contemporary Economic Policy,* Vol. 25:4 (October 2007): 591–603. The paper has been updated to reflect the economic redevelopment of New Orleans and the role of sports in the city's recovery over the past decade.

2. Terrebonne *Parish Courier,* 15 May 2005, S2.

3. Nick Underhill, "Saints Owner Gayle Benson Says She Will 'own and operate this franchise until my death' in Letter to NFL Owners," *The New Orleans Advocate,* 12 April 2018, https://www.theadvocate.com/new_orleans/sports/saints/article_0296c2b4-3e9a-11e8-82c2-6f9a32789cba.html.

4. The Superdome, opened in 1975, is the home field for the NFL's New Orleans Saints and has also served as the home field for the Tulane University football team in the past. It is now known as the Mercedes-Benz Superdome.

5. Anne Rochelle Konigsmark, "Superdome Major Part of New Orleans Comeback," *USA Today,* 29 December 2005, 1C.

6. Charles Robinson, "Saints on the March?" *Yahoo! Sports,* 24 May 2005, article in possession of authors, no longer available online.

7. "Sport Money: 2017 NFL Valuations," *Forbes,* https://www.forbes.com/nfl-valuations/list/#tab:overall, accessed July 13, 2018.

8. "Rebuilding of New Orleans Incredibly Big, Far From Easy: Massive Job Will Take Billions Of Dollars And Tons Of National Resolve," *Nashville Tennessean,* 5 September 2005, 1.

9. Department of Labor, Bureau of Labor Statistics, North American Industrial Classification System 7, Leisure and Hospitality.

10. Larry Holder, "New Orleans Gets Another Super Bowl: What Happened The First Ten Times The City Hosted The Game," *Times Picayune,* 23 May 2018, https://www.nola.com/expo/erry-2018/05/ca85e887ec73/new_orleans_super_bowls_at_a_g.html.

11. Department of Labor, Bureau of Labor Statistics, North American Industrial Classification System 71, Arts, Entertainment, and Recreation.

12. Department of Labor, Bureau of Labor Statistics, North American Industrial Classification System 7112, Spectator Sports.

13. Robert Baade and Victor Matheson, "An Economic Slam Dunk or March Madness? Assessing the Economic Impact of the NCAA Basketball Tournament," in *Economics of College Sports,* J. Fizel and R. Fort, eds. (Westport, CT: Praeger Publishers, 2004), 111–133; Robert Baade and Victor Matheson, "Padding Required: Assessing the Economic Impact of the Super Bowl," *European Sports Management Quarterly* 6 (Issue 4 2006): 353–374; Robert Baade, Robert Baumann, and Victor Matheson, "Selling the Game: Measuring the Economic Impact of Professional Sports Through Taxable Sales," *Southern Economic Journal:* 74 (January 2008), 794–810; Dennis Coates and Brad Humphreys, "The Economic Impact

of Post-Season Play in Professional Sports," *Journal of Sports Economics* 3 (August 2002): 291–299; and Philip K. Porter, "Mega-Sports Events as Municipal Investments: A Critique of Impact Analysis," in *Sports Economics: Current Research,* ed. John Fizel, Elizabeth Gustafson, and Lawrence Hadley (Westport, CT: Praeger, 1999), 61–73.

14. Dennis Coates and Craig A. Depken, "Mega-Events: Is the Texas-Baylor Game to Waco what the Super Bowl is to Houston?" *International Association of Sports Economists Working Paper Series,* No. 06–06, 2006.

15. Robert A. Baade and Richard F. Dye, "The Impact of Stadiums and Professional Sports on Metropolitan Area Development," *Growth and Change* (Spring 1990): 1–14; Dennis Coates and Brad Humphreys, "The Economic Impact of Post-Season Play in Professional Sports," *Journal of Sports Economics* 3 (Issue 3 2002): 291–299; and Baade, Baumann, and Matheson, "Selling the Game," 794–810.

16. "Katrina cost: $100 billion," *Chicago Tribune,* 1 October 2005, 1; and Eileen Alt Powell, "Survey Foresees $34.4 B in Katrina Claims," *Associated Press,* 4 October 2005.

17. "Rebuilding of New Orleans Incredibly Big, Far From Easy: Massive Job Will Take Billions Of Dollars And Tons Of National Resolve," *Nashville Tennessean,* 5 September 2005.

18. Thomas Gabe, Gene Falk, Maggie McCarty, and Virginia W. Mason, "Hurricane Katrina: Social-Demographic Characteristics of Impacted Areas," Congressional Research Service, Report for Congress, 4 November 2005.

19. Gabe, Falk, McCarty, and Mason, "Hurricane Katrina."

20. Greater New Orleans Community Data Center, "Post-Disaster Population Estimates," *Post-Katrina Estimates and Impact Data,* 2005, http://www.gnocdc.org.

21. Donald R. Davis and David E. Weinstein, "Bones, Bombs, and Break Points: The Geography of Economic Activity," *American Economic Review* 92 (December 2002): 1269–1289.

22. Dendy Macaulay, "The Chicago Fire of 1871: An Empirical Analysis," Unpublished manuscript, University of Chicago (May 2005): 1–4.

23. Robert Baade, Robert Baumann, and Victor Matheson, "Estimating the Economic Impact of Natural and Social Disasters with an Application to Hurricane Katrina," *Urban Studies* 44 (Issue 11 2007): 2061–2076; and Robert Baade and Victor Matheson, "Race and Riots: A Note on the Economic Impact of the Rodney King Riots," *Urban Studies* 41 (Issue 13 2004): 2691–2696.

24. "Superdome upgrade completed," *ESPN,* 10 August 2011, http://www.espn.com/nfl/story/_/id/6851410/336m-post-katrina-superdome-upgrades-completed.

25. Jim Corbett, "Saints' march back to New Orleans still tempered by Katrina's harsh realities," *USA Today,* 29 June 2006, 1C.

26. Kevin J. Delaney and Rick Eckstein, *Public Dollars, Private Stadiums* (New Brunswick: Rutgers University Press, 2003).

27. New Orleans City Staff Report, *New Orleans City Business,* 14 November 2006.

28. Dan Alexander, "Billionaire Saints Owner Tom Benson to Score $400 Million Revenue Boost From Agreement With State," *Forbes,* https://www.forbes.com/sites/danalexander/2013/07/31/billionaire-saints-owner-tom-benson-to-score-400-million-revenue-boost-from-agreement-with-state/#1fa3fa955a7b, 31 July 2013.

29. John Siegfried and Andrew Zimbalist, "A Note on the Local Economic Impact of Sports Expenditures," *Journal of Sports Economics* 3 (Issue 4 2002): 361–366.

30. "Steve Gleason Statue Unveiled," *ESPN,* 28 July 2012, http://www.espn.com/nfl/story/_/id/8207214/new-orleans-saints-unveil-statue-steve-gleason-blocked-Punt.

31. "Saints Sell Out Superdome Season Tickets for First Time," *ESPN,* 20 September 2006, http://www.espn.com/nfl/news/story?id=2595126.

32. Corbett, "Saints' March Back to New Orleans Still Tempered by Katrina's Harsh Realities," 1C.

33. Alexander, "Billionaire Saints Owner Tom Benson to Score $400 Million Revenue Boost From Agreement With State."

34. "Sport Money: 2017 NFL Valuations."

35. Ken Belson and Howard Beck, "Debt Escalating, Hornets Are Purchased by NBA," *New York Times,* 7 December 2010, https://www.nytimes.com/2010/12/07/sports/basketball/07hornets.html.

36. John Henderson, "A Year After Katrina: Tulane," *Denver Post,* 26 August 2006, https://www.denverpost.com/2006/08/26/a-year-after-katrina-tulane/.

Chapter 9

1. Grantland Rice, "The Spotlight," New Orleans *Sunday Item-Tribune,* 15 December 1940. Two weeks later, on the eve of the Sugar Bowl, the *Sunday Item-Tribune* prominently featured on its editorial page an illustration, under the caption "Irresistible Interference!" that showed a grinning powerfully-built football player, rushing by four confused men, who were labeled "Private Industry," "Shipbuilding," "Defense Works," and "Tourists." Next to the football player was a road sign pointing toward New Orleans, marked "For Climate, Central Location, and Safest Seaport on Earth." Written across the football player's chest was the statement: "Sugar Bowl Nation's No. 1 Post-Season Event." New Orleans *Sunday Item-Tribune,* 30 December 1940.

2. Washington *Post,* 26 December 1936.

3. C. Vann Woodward, *Origins of the New South, 1877–1913* (Baton Rouge: Louisiana State University Press, 1951), 124–25, 154–155.

4. Michael Oriard, *King Football: Sport & Spectacle in the Golden Age of Radio & Newsreels, Movies, & Magazines, the Weekly & the Daily Press* (Chapel Hill: University of North Carolina Press, 2001), 88; and John Sayle Watterson, *College Football: History, Spectacle, Controversy* (Baltimore: Johns Hopkins, 2000), 183.

5. Fred Digby, "Looking 'Em Over," New Orleans *Sunday Item-Tribune,* 15 December 1940; Boston *Globe,* 8 December 1940; and Chicago *Tribune,* 2 January 1981.

6. Keefe cited in New York *Herald Tribune,* 15 December 1940.

7. New Orleans *Item,* 29 December 1940; and Boston *Globe,* 8 December 1940. Dallas's Cotton Bowl in December 1940, by contrast, seated only 45,000. New York *Herald Tribune,* 15 December 1940.

8. Wirt Gammon quoted in New Orleans *Sunday Item-Tribune,* 5 January 1941.

9. Mike Bynum, ed., *Pop Warner: Football's Greatest Teacher* (Langhorne, PA: Gridiron Football Properties, 1993), 280–83; New Orleans *Times-Picayune*/New Orleans *States, Dixie Roto Magazine,* week of 1 January 1956, 4; and Los Angeles *Times,* 1 January 1935.

10. New Orleans *Item,* 2 January 1935, cited in Chicago *Tribune,* 2 January 1981.

11. Blain Roberts, *Pageants, Parlors, & Pretty Women: Race and Beauty in the Twentieth-Century South* (Chapel Hill: University of North Carolina Press, 2014), 109.

12. *New York Times,* 2 January 1935.

13. Charles H. Martin, "Integrating New Year's Day: The Racial Politics of College Bowl Games in the American South" in Patrick B. Miller, ed., *The Sporting World of the Modern South* (Urbana: University of Illinois Press, 2002), 180; New York *Herald Tribune,* 27 December 1939; Baltimore *Afro-American,* 23 December 1939; and Boston *Globe,* 19 December 1939. The Cotton

Bowl had invited Boston College to play in its 1940 contest when Texas A&M turned it down for the Sugar Bowl. The Sugar Bowl's ability to land Texas A&M, a team in the Cotton Bowl's "own back yard," was seen as an indication of its superiority. Boston *Evening Transcript,* 18 December 1940; and Pittsburgh *Courier,* 23 December 1939.

14. Wells Twombly, *Shake Down the Thunder! The Official Biography of Notre Dame's Frank Leahy* (Radnor, PA: Chilton, 1974), 196–97.

15. Baltimore *Afro-American,* 23 December 1939, 31 August 1940; New York *Amsterdam News,* 21 October 1939; Chicago *Defender,* 4 November 1939; and Mabe Kountze, letter to the editor, Boston *Globe,* 8 January 1940.

16. New York *Herald Tribune,* 11 October 1938, 3 October 1940. Like the Southern white press, the African American press also used Civil War imagery in reporting on football games. The Chicago *Defender*'s article on the Boston College-Auburn game in 1939, by Mabe Kountze, was headlined "Boston College Bows to Rebels." Chicago *Defender,* 11 November 1939.

17. New Orleans *Item,* 20 December 1940.

18. Boston *Evening Transcript,* 30 December 1940; Washington *Post,* 2 December 1940; Nashville *Banner,* 24 December 1940; Boston *Globe,* 25 November, 2 December 1940; *The Heights,* 4 October 1940; and Jack Troy quoted in New Orleans *Times-Picayune,* 20 December 1940. The *Globe* reported that "it was the most horrendous whaling ever handed out to an Auburn team" during head coach Jack Meagher's reign, which began in 1934, and the worst Meagher had "ever sustained in two decades" of coaching. Auburn had been confined to its side of the field for fifty-seven minutes." Boston *Globe,* 24 November 1940.

19. Boston *Globe,* 2 December 1940; and Grantland Rice quoted in Knoxville *News-Sentinel,* 2, 13 December 1940. In early December 1940, the Eagles were awarded the August V. Lambert Memorial Trophy, given each year to the best college football team in the East. Boston College was the unanimous choice of sixty-five writers and radio commentators. New York *Herald Tribune,* 5 December 1940.

20. New Orleans *Times-Picayune,* 30 December 1940; and Murray Sperber, *Shake Down the Thunder: The Creation of Notre Dame Football* (New York: Henry Holt, 1993), 218, 442. Sperber described Leahy as an innovative coach, one of the first to use modern T-formation plays in his offense in 1940. As a coach he emulated Rockne's "model of insatiable perfectionism." Leahy achieved a phenomenal 87–11–9 record as head coach at Boston College (1939–40) and Notre Dame (1941–53). Sperber, *Shake Down,* 316, 497, 499–500.

21. Boston *Evening Transcript,* 10 December 1940; and Nashville *Banner,* 21 December 1940.

22. Boston *Globe,* 19 December 1940; Boston *Evening Transcript,* 18, 19 December 1940; and Boston *Herald,* 18 December 1940. A similar scene had developed the previous year when the Eagles left for the Cotton Bowl in Dallas. The *Evening Transcript* described the situation at South Station as "worse than bargain day at one of the department stores." Boston *Evening Transcript,* 17 December 1940.

23. Boston *Herald,* 20, 21 December 1940; and *The Heights,* 4 October 1940. *The Heights* headlined this article "Sugar Bowl Trip Triumphal March." At St. Stanislaus, several of the brothers of the Sacred Heart Order, which administered the school, came from the same Massachusetts and Rhode Island towns as members of the Boston College team. Boston *Herald,* 21 December 1940.

24. *The Heights,* 10 January 1941; and Boston *Herald,* 20 December 1940.

25. New Orleans *Times-Picayune,* 21 December 1940.

26. Boston *Herald,* 21 December 1940. The University of Tennessee football team trained for a week at Edgewater Park, Mississippi, near Gulfport on the Gulf Coast. US Senator Pat Harrison of Mississippi visited the Volunteers there. New Orleans *Times-Picayune,* 29 December 1940; and Nashville *Tennessean,* 31 December 1940.

27. Boston *Globe,* 25 December 1940; and Boston *Evening Transcript,* 14 December 1940.

28. Boston *Herald,* 28 December 1940; and Boston *Globe,* 30 December 1940. The Baton Rouge Patriots were composed of former players from Southern University and McKinley High School in that city. Louisiana *Weekly,* 28 December 1940.

29. New Orleans *Times-Picayune,* 20 December 1940; Nashville *Banner,* 20 December 1940; and Jack Troy quoted in Boston *Evening Transcript,* 28 December 1940.

30. Boston *Globe,* 29 December 1940; and Boston *Evening Transcript,* 31 December 1940. Ten of Tennessee's starters were from the South, six of them from Tennessee. Boston *Evening Transcript,* 31 December 1940.

31. Nashville *Banner,* 20, 31 December 1940. Three of Boston College's best players—Joe Zabilski, Mike Holovak, and Chet Gladchuk–upset that head coach Frank Leahy was running the Bay St. Louis training camp like "a French penal colony," began complaining to each other in Polish, which they had spoken at home. This prompted Leahy to buy a Polish-English dictionary to find out what they were saying. Twombly, *Shake Down the Thunder!,* 201.

32. Zipp Newman quoted in Boston *Evening Transcript,* 11 December 1940.

33. New Orleans *Sunday Item-Tribune,* 30 December 1940.

34. New Orleans *Times-Picayune,* 28, 29 December 1940.

35. Darden Asbury Pyron, *Southern Daughter: The Life of Margaret Mitchell* (New York: Oxford University Press, 1991), 373–76.

36. New Orleans *Item,* 31 December 1940, 1 January 1941.

37. Nashville *Tennessean,* 31 December 1940; New Orleans *Item,* 29, 31 December 1940, 2 January 1941; New Orleans *Times-Picayune,* 29 December 1940; Boston *Globe,* 31 December 1940; and *New York Times,* 31 December 1940.

38. New Orleans *Times-Picayune,* 30 December 1940; New Orleans *Item,* 2 January 1941; and Nashville *Tennessean,* 31 December 1940.

39. New Orleans *Item,* 5 January 1941; and New Orleans *Times-Picayune,* 1, 2 January 1941.

40. New Orleans *Item,* 29 December 1941.

41. New Orleans *Times-Picayune,* 2, 4 January 1941; and New Orleans *Item,* 5 January 1941.

42. Knoxville *News-Sentinel,* 31 December 1940; and New Orleans *Times-Picayune,* 31 December 1940.

43. Boston *Globe,* 3 January 1941; Boston *Herald,* 2 January 1941; and New York *Herald Tribune,* 2 January 1941.

44. Arthur Daley in *New York Times* (quotes), 2 January 1941; and Jerry Nason in Boston *Globe,* article reprinted in New Orleans *Times-Picayune,* 2 January 1941. Woodward commented that Henry Toczylowski, "an exceptionally smart quarterback," picked the right psychological moment to call the winning play. He predicted that it would probably soon become as famous as KF'79, the hidden ball play Columbia used to win the 1934 Rose Bowl against heavily favored Stanford. New York *Herald Tribune,* 3 January 1941.

45. Washington *Post,* 3 January 1941.

46. Boston *Evening Transcript,* 3 January 1941; Boston *Herald,* 5 January 1941; and New Orleans *Times-Picayune,* 4 January 1941.

47. Boston *Globe,* 10 January 1941.

48. Baltimore *Afro-American,* 28 January 1956. Montgomery had watched the 1941 Sugar Bowl from the stadium press box. Martin, "Integrating New Year's Day," in Miller, ed., *Sporting World,* 180.

49. For example, the Cotton Bowl permitted Penn State's two African American players, Wallace Triplett and Dennis Hoggard, to participate in the 1948 game when that university insisted they play. The next year the University of Oregon team, with three African Americans, played in the Cotton Bowl. The faculty of Lafayette College in Pennsylvania rejected an offer to play Texas School of Mines in the Sun Bowl scheduled for New Year's Day, 1949 in El Paso, Texas, because Sun Bowl officials informed Lafayette that its African American player, Dave Showell, would not be permitted to play. Martin, "Integrating New Year's Day," in Miller, ed., *Sporting World,* 180–84, 186–87; and New York *Herald Tribune,* 25 November 1948. In November 1947, Penn State refused the Sugar Bowl committee's invitation to send its boxing team to New Orleans for its Carnival of Sports boxing tournament because the contract specified that African Americans could not compete, even though Penn State did not have any on its boxing team. New York *Herald Tribune,* 11 November 1947.

50. New Orleans *Item,* 31 December 1954; Washington *Post,* 31 December 1954, 4 January 1955; and Jackson *Courier-Ledger,* 12 December 1955.

51. Jackson *Clarion-Ledger,* 12, 19 December 1954; Washington *Post,* 21 December 1954; and *New York Times,* 26 December 1954. Mississippi's head football coach, Johnny Vaught, preferred to recruit nearly all his players from within the state. Even five years after the 1955 Sugar Bowl, only five members of the forty-eight-member team were from out of state, and they came from Alabama, Tennessee, and Kentucky. Joe David Brown, "Babes, Brutes, and Ole Miss," *Sports Illustrated,* 19 September 1960, 126.

52. New Orleans *Item,* 30 and 31 December 1954 and 2 January 1955; Washington *Post,* 4 January 1955.

53. New Orleans *Item,* 30 December 1954; Washington *Post,* 31 December 1954; and Jackson *Clarion-Ledger,* 12 December 1954.

54. Baltimore *Afro-American,* 19 April 1941.

55. *Louisiana Weekly,* 8 January 1955; Chicago *Defender,* 15 January 1955; Pittsburgh *Courier,* 19 December 1964; and Atlanta *Daily World,* 19 May 1955.

56. New Orleans *Item,* 2 January 1955.

57. Jackson *Clarion-Ledger,* 29 December 1954.

58. *Louisiana Weekly,* 8 January 1955; Herman Hickman, "Navy 21 Mississippi 0," *Sports Illustrated,* 10 January 1955, 10–11; Chicago *Tribune,* 3 January 1955; and Chicago *Defender,* 8 January 1955.

59. Atlanta *Daily World,* 19 May 1955.

60. *Louisiana Weekly,* 9, 10, 30 April, 28 May 1955, 3 March 1956; and Chicago *Defender,* 2 June 1956.

61. Atlanta *Daily World,* 3 January 1956; and *New York Times,* 3 January 1956.

62. John Foster, "The Run That Put the Bowl in Business," *Dixie Roto Magazine* (New Orleans *Times-Picayune* and New Orleans *States*), 1 January 1956, 5.

63. Atlanta *Daily World,* 3 January 1956; and *New York Times,* 3 January 1956.

64. Atlanta *Daily World,* 7 December 1952; and Martin, "Integrating New Year's Day," in Miller, *Sporting World,* 188 – 89.

65. Adam Fairclough, *Race & Democracy: The Civil Rights Struggle in Louisiana, 1915–1972* (Baton Rouge: Louisiana State University Press, 1995), 9, 106, 172, 174, 213; *New York Times,* 1 January 1956; and Atlanta *Daily World,* 19 May 1955.

66. New Orleans *Times-Picayune,* 1, 3 January 1956; and Washington *Post,* 1 January 1956.

67. Charles H. Martin, "Racial Change and 'Big-Time' College Football in Georgia: The Age of Segregation, 1892–1957," *Georgia Historical Quarterly* 80 (Fall 1996): 552–554; and Atlanta *Constitution,* 3, 5 December 1956.

68. Martin, "Racial Change," 532, 554–55; and Atlanta *Constitution,* 6 December 1955.

69. Alfred Wright, "The Day of the Bowls is Here," *Sports Illustrated,* 26 December 1955, 26.

70. *New York Times,* 1, 3 January 1956; New Orleans *Times-Picayune,* 1 January 1956; and Martin, "Racial Change," 558.

71. New Orleans *Times-Picayune,* 3 January 1956; and Dan T. Carter, *Scottsboro: A Tragedy of the American South* (Baton Rouge: Louisiana State University Press, 1979 [1969]), 413.

72. New Orleans *Times-Picayune,* 3 January 1956; and Chicago *Tribune,* 3 January 1956. Georgia Tech head coach Bobby Dodd praised Pitt's defense as "tough, just like the pros . . . they fight you for every inch they give." Los Angeles *Times,* 3 January 1956. The attendance was 80,175. Washington *Post,* 3 January 1956.

73. New Orleans *Times-Picayune,* 3 January 1956; Los Angeles *Times,* 3 January 1956; and Pittsburgh *Courier,* 7 January 1956.

74. *New York Times,* 22 July 1956.

75. Pittsburgh *Courier,* 4 August 1956.

76. Washington *Post,* 24 January 1957; and Pittsburgh *Courier,* 17 November 1962, 19 December 1964.

77. Norfolk *Journal and Guide,* 11 August 1956.

78. Pittsburgh *Courier,* 19 December 1964; New Orleans *Times-Picayune,* 31 December 1964; Washington *Post,* 1 January 1965; and Chicago *Defender,* 21 December 1964.

79. Washington *Post,* 1, 2 January 1965, 2 January 1963, 2 January 1964.

80. New Orleans *Times-Picayune,* 6 January 1965.

81. *New York Times,* 2 January 1972.

Chapter 10

1. The current website of the Southern Association of the Amateur Athletic Union claims that the organization has been around since 1892. SAAU homepage, http://www.saau.org/, accessed June 30, 2017. However, while New Orleans' elites were no doubt planning an organization in 1892 or even earlier, it is clear from the existing record that the founding date of the official organization is 1893. A search of the *New Orleans Times Picayune* for 1892 finds only two mentions of the AAU—both to the national organization and not a New Orleans branch. "Amateur Athletic Union," *New Orleans Times Picayune,* 9 March 1892, 6; "Sporting Letter," *New Orleans Times Picayune,* 11 December 1892, 8. The archives of the SAAAU, found in the New Orleans Athletic Club Collection, do not begin until 1909. Documents in the Southern Association, Amateur Athletic Union of the United States, 1909–1939, Folder, New Orleans Athletic Club Collection, Earl K. Long Library, University of New Orleans, New Orleans, Louisiana. Hereafter NOAC Collection.

For confirmation of the 1893 date, see, "Amateur Athletic Union Meeting," New York Times, 16 November 1893, 2.; Official Handbook of the Amateur Athletic Union of the United States: Constitution, Bylaws, & General and Athletic Rules (New York: American Sports Publishing, 1896), 22–23; and Dale Somers, *The Rise of Sport in New Orleans, 1850–1900* (Baton Rouge: Louisiana State University Press, 1972), 244–245. On the domination of New Orleans in the early history of the SAAAU see, "Amateur Athletic Union Meeting," *New York Times*, 16 November 1893, 2; "To Boom Athletics in the South," *New Orleans Times-Picayune*, 21 March 1906, 10; "President MacCabe, of Amateur Athletic Union, Returns Home, But Leaves His Cause," *New Orleans Times-Picayune*, 16 April 1906, 10; "S.A.C. Comes within Lash of Landing First Honors," *New Orleans Times-Picayune*, 21 November 1906, 8; "Southern Athletes," *New Orleans Times-Picayune*, 27 March 1907, 5.; and "Athletic League Asks Audubon Park for Area," *New Orleans Times-Picayune*, 8 November 1907, 12.

2. Documents in the Southern Association, Amateur Athletic Union of the United States, 1909–1939 Folder, NOAC Collection.

3. For general cultural, political, and economic histories of New Orleans, see, Louise McKinney, *New Orleans: A Cultural History* (New York: Oxford University Press, 2006); Scott P. Marler, *The Merchants' Capital: New Orleans and the Political Economy of the Nineteenth-Century South* (New York: Cambridge University Press, 2015); Ned Sublette, *The World That Made New Orleans: From Spanish Silver to Congo Square* (Chicago: Lawrence Hill Books, 2009); and Tom Piazza, *Why New Orleans Matters* (New York: Harper Perennial, 2008). On race relations, ethnic identities, and religion, see Alecia P. Long, *The Great Southern Babylon: Sex, Race, and Respectability in New Orleans, 1865–1920* (Baton Rouge: Louisiana State University Press, 2005); John W. Blassingame, *Black New Orleans, 1860–1880* (Chicago: University of Chicago Press, 2007); Emily Ford and Barry Stiefel, *The Jews of New Orleans and the Mississippi Delta: A History of Life & Community along the Bayou* (Charleston, SC: The History Press, 2012); Donald E. DeVore, *Defying Jim Crow: African American Community Development and the Struggle for Racial Equality in New Orleans, 1900–1960* (Baton Rouge: Louisiana State University Press, 2015); R. Bentley Anderson, *Black, White, and Catholic: New Orleans Interrracialism, 1947–1956* (Nashville: Vanderbilt University Press, 2008); Rien Fertel, *Imagining the Creole City: The Rise of Literary Culture in Nineteenth-Century* (New Orleans (Baton Rouge: Louisiana State University Press, 2014); James B. Bennett, *Religion and the Rise of Jim Crow in New Orleans* (Princeton, NJ: Princeton University Press, 2016); Joseph Maselli and Dominic Candeloro, *Italians in New Orleans* (Charleston, SC: Arcadia, 2004); and Laura D. Kelley, *The Irish in New Orleans* (Lafayette: University of Louisiana at Lafayette Press, 2014).

4. For fascinating perspectives on the boycott intrigue in the United States as well as in other nations, see, Arnd Krüger and William Murray, *The Nazi Olympics Sport, Politics, and Appeasement in the 1930s* (Urbana: University of Illinois Press, 2003); and Allen Guttmann, *The Games Must Go On: Avery Brundage and the Olympic Movement* (New York: Columbia University Press, 1984).

5. "Joseph Dresner," *Southern Amateur Athlete* 4 (October 1932): 2; "Who's Who in Southern Association," *Southern Amateur Athlete* 2 (November 1930): 3; and *Southern Amateur Athlete* folder, NOAC Collection.

6. L. di Benedetto, Secretary-Treasurer, SAAAU, Annual Reports of the Officers, Committees and Minutes of the Annual Meeting of the Southern Association, A.A.U., held on September 21, 1935, at the New Orleans Athletic Club, New Orleans, Louisiana; and L. di Benedetto, Secretary-Treasurer, SAAAU, "Resolution Adopted by the Southern Association, A.A.U., Saturday, September 21, 1935, New Orleans, LA, NOAC Collection.

7. Glenn Feldman, *Politics and Religion in the White South* (Lexington: University Press of Kentucky, 2005); Eugene D Genovese, *The Southern Front: History and Politics in the Cultural War* (Columbia: University of Missouri Press, 1995); Leonard Dinnerstein and Mary Dale, *Jews in the South* (Baton Rouge: Louisiana State University Press, 1973); Mark K. Bauman, *Dixie Diaspora: An Anthology of Southern Jewish History* (Tuscaloosa: University of Alabama Press, 2006); David M. Chalmers, *Hooded Americanism: The History of the Ku Klux*

Klan (Durham: Duke University Press, 2007); and William Rawlings, *The Second Coming of the Invisible Empire: The Ku Klux Klan of the 1920s* (Macon, GA: Mercer University Press, 2016).

8. "Pioneer Sports Figure Expires," *New Orleans Times Picayune*, 11 November 1958, 1, 8.

9. "A.A.U. Backs Team in Berlin Olympics; Rejects Boycott," *New York Times*, 9 December 1935, 1, 17.

10. Krüger and Murray, *The Nazi Olympics Sport, Politics, and Appeasement in the 1930s;* and Guttmann, *The Games Must Go On.*

11. L. di Benedetto, "Greatest Field of Hurdlers Will Compete at Loyola Stadium, Dec. 28," *New Orleans Times Picayune*, 29 September 1935, 4–3.

12. "Sugar Bowl Events Off," *New York Times*, 30 December 1935, 23; and "Sugar Bowl Meet Sees Records Fall: Five Southern Marks Are Eclipsed," *New York Times*, 31 December 1935, 19.

13. "South Covers up Its Own Sports Jim Crow by Yell," *Chicago Defender*, 30 November 1935, 14.

14. Romeo L. Doughtery, "Sports Whirl: Our First Fight Is in America," *New York Amsterdam News*, 14 December 1935, 12; and Ed R. Harris, "We're All We Need," *Philadelphia Tribune*, 19 December 1935, 9.

15. For a fascinating picture of this building in the 1930s, see http://www.louisianadigitallibrary.org/cdm/ref/collection/LWP/id/7024.

16. Annual Reports of the Officers, Committees and Minutes of the Annual Meeting of the Southern Association, A.A.U., held on October 5, 1936, at the Young Men's Hebrew Association, New Orleans, Louisiana, NOAC Collection.

17. William J. Baker, *Jesse Owens: An American Life* (New York: Free Press, 1986); Mark Dyreson, "Jesse Owens: Leading Man in Modern American Tales of Racial Progress and Limits," in *Out of the Shadows: A Biographical History of the African American Athlete*, David K. Wiggins, ed. (Fayetteville: University of Arkansas Press, 2006), 111–132; and John Gleaves and Mark Dyreson, "The 'Black Auxiliaries' in American Memories: Sport, Race, and Politics in the Construction of Modern Legacies," *International Journal of the History of Sport*, 27.16–18 (November/December 2010): 2893–2924.

18. Mark Dyreson, "The Original Pan American Games? The 1937 Dallas Pan American Olympics," *International Journal of the History of Sport* 33 (January 2016): 6–28; and Mark Dyreson, "Region and Race: The Legacies of the St Louis Olympics," *International Journal of the History of Sport* 32 (August 2015): 1697–1707. I am currently working on a book manuscript with Dr. Jodella K. Dyreson on color lines in Southern track and field. Some of the work has been presented at professional meetings, including, Jodella K. Dyreson and Mark Dyreson, "The Racial Dynamics of the Forgotten Texas Centennial Olympic Games, 1936," unpublished paper presented at the 111th Annual Meeting of the Texas State Historical Association Meeting, 10 March 2007, San Antonio, Texas; Mark Dyreson, "'Everything's Bigger in Texas': Ballyhoo, Bravado, and Identity at the Texas 'Olympics' of 1936 and 1937," unpublished paper presented at the 35th Annual Conference of the North American Society for Sport History, Texas Tech University, Lubbock, Texas, 26 May 2007; Jodella K. Dyreson and Mark Dyreson, "Clearing the Color Bar: The Battles of New Orleans and the Alamo (Stadium)," unpublished paper presented at the 42nd Annual Conference of the North American Society for Sports History, Glenwood Springs, Colorado, 31 May 2014; Mark Dyreson, "Region and Race: The Legacies of the 1904 St. Louis Olympics," unpublished paper presented at the Organization for American Historians 2015 Convention, 19 April 2015, St. Louis, Missouri; Mark Dyreson, "Miami, 1969: No Black Gloves, No Racial Protests—A Major Surprise," unpublished paper presented at 43rd Annual Conference of the North

American Society for Sports History, University of Miami, Coral Gables, Florida, 24 May 2015; "Mark Dyreson, "A Farewell to Color Lines? Remembering and Forgetting at the 1996 Atlanta Olympics," unpublished paper presented at 44th Annual Conference of the North American Society for Sports History, Georgia Tech University, Atlanta, Georgia, 29 May 2016; Jodella K. Dyreson and Mark Dyreson, "The 'Lone Negro' in the Race: Recovering the Lost World of Billy Morris," unpublished paper presented at the 45th Annual Conference of the North American Society for Sports History, California State University, Fullerton, Fullerton, California, 27 May 2017; and Mark Dyreson and Jodella K. Dyreson, "Testing the AAU's Commitment to Racial Inclusion: John B. Taylor Runs in Jamestown, 1907," unpublished paper presented at 45th Annual Conference of the North American Society for Sports History, California State University, Fullerton, Fullerton, California, 27 May 2017.

While there is little published material of the subject, there is one outstanding dissertation on the subject, Gregory Bond, "Jim Crow at Play: Race, Manliness, and the Color Line in American Sports, 1876–1916" (Ph.D. diss.: University of Wisconsin-Madison, 2008).

19. "1910 National A.A.U. Meet Secured for New Orleans," *New Orleans Times Picayune,* 16 November 1909, 12; and "Progressive Union," *New Orleans Times Picayune,* 17 November 1909, 12.

20. "Mayor Behrman Seconds Move to Accept 1910 A.A.U. Games," *New Orleans Times Picayune,* 27 November 1909, 9.

21. "Twenty-One Entered for A.A.U. Championships Here," *Chicago Tribune,* 11 August 1910, 11.

22. "Fitzpatrick Balks," *New Orleans Times Picayune,* 13 August 1910, 10.

23. *Times-Picayune,* 13 August 1910, 10.

24. *Times-Picayune,* 13 August 1910, 10.

25. "Elks Indoor Baseball Team Anxious to Take on Y.M.H.A. in Series," *New Orleans Times-Picayune,* 2 September 1910, 7; and "Re-Election of Old Officers by S.A.A.A.U.," *New Orleans Times-Picayune,* 20 September 1910, 10.

26. "Negro Olympic Runner Is Ill in Hospital," *Philadelphia Inquirer,* 1 December 1908, 2; "Red and Blue Athlete Runs His Last Race," *Philadelphia Inquirer,* 3 December 1908, 10; "Negro Runner Dead: John B. Taylor, Quarter Miler, Victim of Typhoid Pneumonia," *New York Times,* 3 December 1908, 10; "Taylor, Noted Negro Athlete of Penn University Dies," *Boston Journal,* 3 December 1908, 9; and "Negro Athlete Dead in Philadelphia," *Augusta (Georgia) Chronicle,* 3 December 1908, 5.

27. *Philadelphia Inquirer,* 1 December, 1908, 2.

28. "National Amateur Athletic Meet Begins," *New Orleans Times-Picayune,* 15 October 1910, 1, 10.

29. "New Orleans on Top," *New Orleans Times-Picayune,* 16 October 1910, 1.

30. See the census figures in "African-Americans as a Percentage of the Population By Large U.S. Cities (Those With a Peak Population of 500,000 or More by 1990) Inside the Former Confederacy," http://en.wikipedia.org/wiki/Great_Migration_(African_American). See, also, DeVore, *Defying Jim Crow.*

31. Program for the 1910 National Track Meet, cover missing, NOAC Collection.

32. "New Orleans Next," *New Orleans Times Picayune,* 15 August 1911, 10.

33. Eckersall had been a quarterback, and a controversial student, earlier in the 1900s at the University of Chicago. Robin Lester, *Stagg's University: The Rise, Decline, and Fall of Big-Time Football at Chicago* (Urbana: University of Illinois Press, 1995).

34. Walter H. Eckersall, "Athlete of South Draws Color Line," *Chicago Tribune,* 9 August 1911, 10.

35. Julius N. Avendorph, "F.A. Holmes in Action," *Chicago Defender,* 12 August 1911, 1.

36. "Along the Color Line," *Crisis: A Record of the Darker Races,* 1 September 1911, 187.

37. Guttmann, *The Games Must Go On.*

38. "Star Field in Big A.A.U. Meet," *Chicago Tribune,* 10 August 1911, 12; and "Thompson Takes All Around Meet," *Chicago Tribune,* 13 August 1911, C-1.

39. "New Orleans Next," *New Orleans Times Picayune,* 15 August 1911, 10.

40. "Indian Thorpe is Best Athlete: Olympic Champion Wins All-Around Championship and Breaks," *New York Times,* 3 September 1911, 9. See also, James Edward Sullivan, compiler, *Spalding's Official Athletic Almanac for 1913* (New York: American Sports Publishing Co., 1913), 33, 71.

41. "World's Marks Go at Olympic Trials," *New York Times,* 9 June 1912, C-7–8; "Olympic 'Tryouts' Produce Surprises: Big Cambridge Meet on Saturday," *New York Times,* 10 June 1912, 10; and "How the Points May Go at the Olympics," *New York Times,* 23 June 1912, C-9.

42. "Sporting Gossip," *New Orleans Times Picayune,* 1 April 1914, 9; and "Four Have Entered for All-Around," *New Orleans Times Picayune,* 13 September 1914, 11.

43. "Brundage Captures All-Around Meet," *New Orleans Times Picayune,* 20 September 1914, 2–10; and "High Honor to Cherry Circle: Brundage of C.A.A. Wins All Round Athletic Championship," *Chicago Tribune,* 20 September 1914, B-2.

44. Guttmann, *The Games Must Go On.*

45. "Western Athletes Win A.A.U. Meet," *New York Times,* 8 August 1915, S-4; Frederick W. Rubien, "California Boys Junior Champions," *New York Times,* 7 August 1915, 5; "World's Records Broken to Beat Local Athletes," *New Orleans Times Picayune,* 7 August 1915, 11; "'Ray' for Harry Fitz," *New Orleans Times Picayune,* 7 August 1915, 11; Wood B. Expert, "Straight from the Shoulder," *New Orleans Times Picayune,* 8 August 1915, sec. real estate, classifieds, and sports, 7; "Southern Athletes are Defeated in Senior Events at Frisco," *New Orleans Times Picayune,* 8 August 1915, sec. real estate, classifieds, and sports, 11; "Doings of the Race," *Topeka Plaindealer,* 15 October 1915, 1; "Colored Boys Make Fair Showing in National Championships—Roy Mores Loses Sprint Title," *Indianapolis Freeman,* 16 September 1916, 7; *Spalding's Official Athletic Almanac for 1917* (New York: American Sports Publishing Co., 1917), 127–133; "Scott's Performance Feature of Big Meet," *New Orleans Times Picayune,* 10 September 1916, B-8; "Secretary Benny Back from Newark," *New Orleans Times Picayune,* 14 September 1916, 9; *Spalding's Official Athletic Almanac for 1918* (New York: American Sports Publishing Co., 1918), 108–111; "Glimpses of the A.A.U. Championships," *New Orleans Times Picayune,* 16 September 1917, B-11; and "Chicago Athletes Again to the Fore," *Baltimore American,* 2 September 1917, 12.

46. "A.A.U. Elects and Voices Bid for Convention," *New Orleans Times Picayune,* 30 September 1919, 20; "Will Answer Charges of Olympic Athletes at A.A.U. Meet Here," *New Orleans Times Picayune,* 7 November 1920, 15; L. di Benedetto, "National Convention of Amateur Athletic Union on Calendar for Today," *New Orleans Times Picayune,* 15 November 1920, 13; "Name Candidates for A.A.U. Head," *New York Times,* 16 November 1920, 21; L. di Benedetto, "Governor Parker Addresses A.A.U. Candidates Here," *New Orleans Times Picayune,* 16 November 1920, 17; "Insurgents Gain Control of A.A.U.," *Colorado Springs Gazette,* 17 November 1920, 9; and "A.A.U. Insurgent Ticket Victorious: Result of Election at New Orleans," *New York Times,* 17 November 1920, 21.

47. "Philadelphia Gets A.A.U. Title Games," *New York Times,* 16 November 1925, 16; "200 National Marks Approved by A.A.U.," *New York Times,* 17 November 1925, 21; and "Hulbert Reelected President of A.A.U.," *New York Times,* 18 November 1925, 19.

48. "Benedetto Goes to Cinch A.A.U. Events for N.O.," *New Orleans Times Picayune,* 7 November 1926, 6–2.; "Many Cities Seeking A.A.U. Title Fixtures," *New York Times,*

11 November 1926,33; "New Orleans Bids for Track Joust," *Salt Lake City Tribune,* 11 November 1926, 14; "New Orleans Gets 1927 Championships; Foster Boomed for Presidency," *New Orleans Times Picayune,* 16 November 1926, 10; and "New Orleans Gets A.A.U. Title Track Meet," *New York Times,* 16 November 1926, 30.

49. "Movement to Whoop Up A.A.U. Track Meet Here is Planned," *New Orleans Times Picayune,* 19 December 1926, 6–3; "Officials of A.A.U. Meet, Dine Tonight," *New Orleans Times Picayune,* 26 January 1927, 10; "$15,000 Drive for National Started," *New Orleans Times Picayune,* 20 February 1927, 6–1–2; Gene Thatcher, "City Prep Baseball League Gets Under Way Next Thursday," *New Orleans Times Picayune,* 17 March 1927, 15; "N.O. Prep School Association Goes Over Top in Fund," *New Orleans Times Picayune,* 20 March 1927, 6–2; "Drive Planned to Raise Fund for A.A.U. Meet," *New Orleans Times Picayune,* 7 April 1927, 14; and "A.A.U. Date Change Asked by Officials," *New Orleans Times Picayune,* 6 March 1927, 6–3.

50. "A.A.U. Meeting Scheduled Here is Called Off," *New Orleans Times Picayune,* 22 April 1927, 1, 6; and Wm. McG. Keefe, "Viewing the News," *New Orleans Times Picayune,* 22 April 1927, 15.

51. "H.W. Fitzpatrick Commits Suicide Over Ill-Health," *New Orleans Times Picayune,* 17 September 1926, 1.

52. "Movement to Whoop Up A.A.U. Track Meet Here is Planned," *New Orleans Times Picayune,* 19 December 1926, 6–3; "Officials of A.A.U. Meet, Dine Tonight," *New Orleans Times Picayune,* 26 January 1927, 10; "$15,000 Drive for National Started," *New Orleans Times Picayune,* 20 February 1927, 6–1–2; Gene Thatcher, "City Prep Baseball League Gets Under Way Next Thursday," *New Orleans Times Picayune,* 17 March 1927, 15; "N.O. Prep School Association Goes Over Top in Fund," *New Orleans Times Picayune,* 20 March 1927, 6–2; "Drive Planned to Raise Fund for A.A.U. Meet," *New Orleans Times Picayune,* 7 April 1927, 14; and "A.A.U. Date Change Asked by Officials," *New Orleans Times Picayune,* 6 March 1927, 6–3.

53. "Wants Fair Play for Negro Athletes," *Pittsburgh Courier,* 22 January 1927, A-5; and "In and Around New York: Square Deal," *Chicago Defender,* 17 April 1926, 8.

54. "In and Around New York: Square Deal."

55. "A.A.U. Meeting Scheduled Here is Called Off," *New Orleans Times Picayune,* 22 April 1927, 1, 6.

56. "No Bar Negroes," *Chicago Daily Tribune,* 22 April 1927, 19; and "Secretary Rubien Issues Statement," *New Orleans Times Picayune,* 22 April 1927, 6.

57. Wm. McG. Keefe, "Viewing the News," *New Orleans Times Picayune,* 22 April 1927, 15.

58. "A. A. U. National Track Meet Taken from New Orleans: Race Discrimination Sends Meet to New York," *Pittsburgh Courier,* 30 April 1927, 18; "Lily White Athletics," *Chicago Defender,* 21 May 1927, A-2; "Too Bad, New Orleans," *Chicago Broad Axe,* 21 May 1927, 3; "Too Bad, New Orleans," *Wichita Negro Star,* 17 June 1927, 1; "Draw Color Line in Athletics to Avoid Race Riot," *San Antonio Express,* 22 April 1927, 19; "New Orleans Passes N. A. A. U. Track Games," *Chicago Daily Tribune,* 22 April 1927, 19; and "Race Issue Blocks Orleans Classic," *Topeka Plaindealer,* 6 May 1927, 1.

59. The views of Gallico and Parker were reprinted in the African American press. Paul Gallico, "Sportsmanship at Low Ebb," *Pittsburgh Courier,* 30 April 1927, 18; Frank A. Young, "Keefe Pens a Few Words in New Orleans Paper but He's 'All Wet' on A.A.U. Rules," *Chicago Defender,* 30 April 1927, 9. See also, John Kieran, "Sports of the Times," *New York Times,* 31 May 1927, 30.

60. "Cutting Off its Nose," *Pittsburgh Courier,* 7 May 1927, B-8.

61. "A.A.U. Track Games for New Orleans are Cancelled, Negrophobia too Strong," *Louisiana Weekly,* 30 April 1927, 8.

62. *Louisiana Weekly,* 30 April 1927, 8.

63. "Several Cities Bid for A.A.U. Games: Decision Not to Hold Meet at New York City," *New York Times,* 23 April 1927, 11; "Lincoln, Neb., Seeking A.A.U. Championships," *New York Times,* 28 April 1927,20; "A.A.U. Favors Lincoln," *New York Times,* 29 April 1927, 18; "A.A.U. Title Games for Lincoln, Neb.: Telegraph Vote Favors Selection," *New York Times,* 17 May 1927, 37; and "National A.A.U. Meet is Awarded to Lincoln, Neb.," *New Orleans Times Picayune,* 17 May 1927, 13.

64. "A.A.U. Title Meet to Start Friday," *New York Times,* 26 June 1927, S-4; "Big New York and Newark A.C. Squads Off for National A.A.U. Meet Tomorrow," *New York Times,* 28 June 1927, 21; Bryan Field, "U.S. Track Title Won by Los Angeles A.C.," *New York Times,* 2 July 1927, 13; "Los Angeles A.C. Wins Junior A.A.U. Games," *Chicago Tribune,* 2 July 1927, 15; "I.A.C. Wins National A.A.U. Track Title; San Francisco, 2d," *Chicago Tribune,* 3 July 1927, A-1–2; Bryan Field, "440-Hurdle Record Hung Up by Gibson," *New York Times,* 3 July 1927, S-1; "Petition of 300 Workmen to See A.A.U. Games Denied," *New York Times,* 3 July 1927, S-1; "Illinois A.C. Wins Senior A.A.U. Meet," *New Orleans Times Picayune,* 3 July 1927, 5–5; "Hubbard is Again King of Jumpers," *Chicago Defender,* 9 July 1927, 9; and Chester L. Washington, "'Ches' Says," *Pittsburgh Courier,* 16 July 1927, A-4.

65. "Enter National A.A.U. Meet," *New Orleans Times Picayune,* 13 June 1927, 13.

66. Milton Bledsoe, "Hubbard Makes Great Victory Leap in National A.A.U. Meet," *Pittsburgh Courier,* 9 July 1927, A-4. See, also, "Illinois A.C. Wins Senior A.A.U. Meet," *New Orleans Times Picayune,* 3 July 1927, 5–5.

67. Mark Dyreson, "The Original Pan American Games? The 1937 Dallas Pan American Olympics," *International Journal of the History of Sport* 33 (January 2016): 6–28; Mark Dyreson, "Region and Race: The Legacies of the St Louis Olympics," *International Journal of the History of Sport* 32 (August 2015): 1697–1707; Jodella K. Dyreson and Mark Dyreson, "The Racial Dynamics of the Forgotten Texas Centennial Olympic Games, 1936," unpublished paper presented at the 111th Annual Meeting of the Texas State Historical Association Meeting, 10 March 2007, San Antonio, Texas; Mark Dyreson, "'Everything's Bigger in Texas': Ballyhoo, Bravado, and Identity at the Texas 'Olympics' of 1936 and 1937," unpublished paper presented at the 35th Annual Conference of the North American Society for Sport History, Texas Tech University, Lubbock, Texas, 26 May 2007; and Jodella K. Dyreson and Mark Dyreson, "Clearing the Color Bar: The Battles of New Orleans and the Alamo (Stadium)," unpublished paper presented at the 42nd Annual Conference of the North American Society for Sports History, Glenwood Springs, Colorado, 31 May 2014.

68. "Benedetto Back from A.A.U. Meet," *New Orleans Times Picayune,* 27 November 1927, 6–3.

69. "Charges A.A.U. with Jim-Crow Tactics," *Pittsburgh Courier,* 23 April 1932, 16.

70. "Pioneer Sports Figure Expires,"; L. diBenedetto, "Senior Track Meet Tonight," *New Orleans Times Picayune,* 23 May 1953, 15; and Bill Keefe, "Viewing the News," *New Orleans Times Picayune,* 20 December 1959, 6–2.

71. "Pioneer Sports Figure Expires."

72. Charles Martin, *Benching Jim Crow: The Rise and Fall of the Color Line in Southern College Sports, 1890–1980* (Urbana: University of Illinois Press, 2010); Charles H. Martin, "Integrating New Year's Day: The Racial Politics of College Bowl Games," *Journal of Sport History* 24 (Fall 1997): 358–377; David K. Wiggins, *Glory Bound: Black Athletes in White America* (Syracuse, N.Y.: Syracuse University Press, 1997). For great insight into the civil rights era struggles over sport in New Orleans, see, Louis Moore, "'The Power of Protest: Black Fandom in New Orleans," unpublished paper presented at 45th Annual Conference

of the North American Society for Sports History, California State University, Fullerton, Fullerton, California, 28 May 2017. I am indebted to Dr. Moore, associate professor of history at Grand Valley State University, not only for sharing his paper with me but also for sharing several *Louisiana Weekly* stories from the 1960s that I use in this essay.

73. Bill Keefe, "Viewing the News," *New Orleans Times Picayune,* 20 January 1959, 6–2; Bill Keefe, "Viewing the News," *New Orleans Times Picayune,* 20 December 1959, 6–2; Bill Keefe, "Viewing the News," *New Orleans Times Picayune,* 23 January 1959, 24; Bill Keefe, "Viewing the News," *New Orleans Times Picayune,* 4 February 1960, 2–8; "Mr. Benny's Trophy," *New Orleans Times Picayune,* 27 February 1961, 2–10; and Bill Keefe, "Viewing the News," *New Orleans Times Picayune,* 12 February 1962, 2–8.

74. N. Charles Wicker, "What's What," *New Orleans Times Picayune,* 22 September 1963, 6–7.

75. "Negro Will Run in Sugar Meet," *New Orleans Times Picayune,* 18 December 1964, 2–12; "Tan Thinclads in Sugar Meet," *Louisiana Weekly,* 26 December 1964, B-1; "Negroes in Sugar Bowl Meet," *New York Times,* 19 December 1964, 35; Jerry Pierce, "Sugar Bowl Track Meet Will Stay on the Ground This Year," *New Orleans Times Picayune,* 27 December 1964, 6–3; Nate Cohen, "Theron Lewis is Outstanding Star," *New Orleans Times Picayune,* 30 December 1964, 4–3; "Tan Cindermen A 1st I Sugar Bowl Event," *Chicago Daily Defender,* 30 December 1964, 22; "Lewis Sets Mark in the 400-Meter Run," *New York Times,* 30 December 1964, 38; Butch Curry, "Lewis Steals Show in Sugar Bowl Track Meet," *Pittsburgh Courier,* 9 January 1965, 22; and "Lewis Smashes Record in Sugar Bowl's 400-Meters," *Louisiana Weekly,* 9 January 1965, 10.

76. Jim Hall, "Time Out," *Louisiana Weekly,* 9 January 1965, 9.

77. Letter from John O. Brown, Dillard University Track Coach, to the Lee Early, President of the SAAAU, October 27, 1966; file of uncertain provenance . . . folder, n.d., 232–17; NOAC Collections.

78. "New Orleanians Off to SAAU Meeting in Honolulu," *New Orleans Times Picayune,* 1 December 1966, 6–8; "AAU Convention Leaders Named," *New Orleans Times Picayune,* 2 March 1967, 2–2; "AAU Convention Is Here Slated Here," *New Orleans Times Picayune,* 26 November 1967, 6–10; Waddell Summers, "AAU Sees US-USSR Renewal," *New Orleans Times Picayune,* 30 November 1967, 2–9; "A Women's Touch in the Sports World," *New York Times,* 3 December 1967, Sports-7; and "AAU Forwards 68 Swim Records to World Group," *New York Times,* 3 December 1967, Sports-14.

79. "NAAU Convention Opens," *Chicago Daily Defender,* 29 November 1967, 27.

80. See especially, Douglas Hartmann, *Race, Culture, and the Revolt of the Black Athlete* (Chicago: University of Chicago Press, 2003); and Amy Bass, *Not the Triumph but the Struggle: The 1968 Olympics and the Making of the Black Athlete* (Minneapolis: University of Minnesota Press, 2002). See also, John Carlos and Dave Zirin, *The John Carlos Story: The Sports Moment that Changed the World* (Chicago: Haymarket Books, 2011); Frank Evans, The Last Protest: Lee Evans in Mexico City (Kansas City, Mo.: Windsprint Press, 2006); Kevin B. Witherspoon, *Before the Eyes of the World: Mexico and the 1968 Olympic Games* (DeKalb: Northern Illinois University Press, 2008); C.D. Jackson and John Carlos, *Why?: The Biography of John Carlos* (Los Angeles: Milligan Books, 2000); Keith Brewster and Claire Brewster, *Representing the Nation: Sport, Control, Contestation, and the Mexican Olympics* (Abingdon, Oxfordshire: Taylor & Francis, 2009; and Tommie Smith and David Steele, *Silent Gesture: The Autobiography of Tommie Smith* (Philadelphia: Temple University Press, 2008).

The Mexico City Black Power protests have inspired a raft of documentaries, as well. Among the best, see, *Fists of Freedom: The Story of the '68 Summer Games,* Ross Greenburg,

George Roy, Steven Stern, Liev Schreiber (HBO, 1999); *Black Power Salute,* Natasha Dack, Geoff Small (BBC, 2008); *Salute,* Matt Norman, David Redman [Paramount Home Entertainment (Australasia), 2009]; and *Return to Mexico City,* Kiefer Sutherland, Maura Mandt, Joie Walls, David Chamberlin, Aaron Cohen, Erik Kesten (ESPN, 2009).

81. "Brundage Brands Bias Charge a Lie," *New York Times,* 16 December 1967, 59.

82. "New Orleans Athletic Club Votes To Admit Blacks," AP wire story, 4 November 1986, http://www.apnewsarchive.com/1986/New-Orleans-Athletic-Club-Votes-To-Admit-Blacks/id-93442e9487d82e66544e25e95c3480a3 (accessed 10 June 2017); Larie Tedesco, "N.O. Athletic Club Has 125th Birthday Rescuer Saved It From Demise," 2 September 1997, *New Orleans Times Picayune,* http://files.usgwarchives.net/la/orleans/newspapers/00000495.txt (accessed 10 June 2017); Joe Illuzzi, "Antonio McKay has Won Six Gold Medals of Consequence," UPI wire story, 14 February 989, http://www.upi.com/Archives/1989/02/14/Antonio-McKay-has-won-six-gold-medals-of-consequence/6141603435600/ (accessed 10 June 2017); and "McKay Becomes First Black in NYAC," *Point Pleasant* (West Virginia) *Register,* 15 February 1989, 6.

Chapter 11

1. Dan T. Carter, *The Politics of Rage: George Wallace, the Origins of the New Conservatism, and the Transformation of American Politics,* second edition (Baton Rouge: Louisiana State University Press, 2000).

2. *New York Times,* 16 November 1926, 30; *Pittsburgh Courier,* 30 April 1927, 18; and *Boston Globe,* 26 April 1927, 14. See also Mark Dyreson, "'No Room for Such a Club in Our Organization': The Southern Association of the Amateur Athletic Union's Long Fight for White Supremacy in New Orleans and the South," in this volume. For more on the machinations of the AAU in this period, see Arnold William Flath, *A History of Relations Between the National Collegiate Athletic Association and the Amateur Athletic Union of the United States, 1905–1963* (Champaign, IL: Stipes Publishing Co., 1964), 51–98.

3. New Orleans *Times-Picayune,* 28 February 1927, 9, 6 March 1927, 3. See also "Southern Association, Amateur Athletic Union," Box 6, "S" Miscellaneous, Records of Mayor Arthur "J" O'Keefe, 1926–1929, City Archives, New Orleans Public Library, New Orleans, Louisiana.

4. New Orleans *Times-Picayune,* 6 March 1927, 3.

5. New Orleans *Times-Picayune,* 20 March 1927, 5.

6. New Orleans *Times-Picayune,* 6 March 1927, 3, 27 March 1927, 3.

7. New Orleans *Times-Picayune,* 5 April 1927, 15, 6 April 1927, 15, 10 April 1927, 3, 17 April 1927, 3. For more on Paddock, see Charles William Paddock, *The Fastest Human* (New York: Thomas Nelson, 1933).

8. *Boston Globe,* 22 April 1927, 24; New York *Herald Tribune,* 22 April 1927, 1; *Pittsburgh Courier,* 30 April 1927, 18; and *Chicago Tribune,* 22 April 1927, 19. The year prior, in fact, Gustavus Kirby, former president of AAU and the International Olympic Committee spoke to a meeting of the national AAU on the value accrued to everyone who participated in amateur athletics, that universal call necessarily including black athletes, as well. See "Address of Gustavus Kirby (1926)," Folder 186 (MSSP 5000–186), Series 3: Amateur Athletic Union of the United States, Fred L. Steers Papers, Hesburgh Libraries, Department of Special Collections, University of Notre Dame, Notre Dame, Indiana.

9. New Orleans *Times-Picayune,* 22 April 1927, 15; New York *Herald Tribune,* 22 April 1927, 1; *Pittsburgh Courier,* 30 April 1927, 18; *Chicago Tribune,* 22 April 1927, 19; and Baltimore *Afro-American,* 30 April 1927, 15. For more on Hubbard, see William DeHart Hubbard Collection, Mss 1067, Cincinnati History Library and Archives, Cincinnati Museum Center, Cincinnati, Ohio.

10. New Orleans *Times-Picayune,* 22 April 1927, 15.

11. *Chicago Defender,* 30 April 1927, 9.

12. Quoted in *Chicago Defender,* 30 April 1927, 9; and New York *Amsterdam News,* 27 April 1927, 12.

13. Gallico quoted in *Pittsburgh Courier,* 30 April 1927, 18.

14. Baltimore *Afro-American,* 30 April 1927, 15.

15. Baltimore *Afro-American,* 30 April 1927, 15.

16. *Daily News* quoted in Baltimore *Afro-American,* 30 April 1927, 15.

17. The *Globe* also used New Orleans's failings to boost its own bid for the event, claiming, "There is no better track city in the good old USA." *Boston Globe,* 23 April 1927, 14, 25 April 1927, 10.

18. Nebraska's AAU delegation had originally submitted Omaha as its applicant for the games but withdrew it soon after in favor of Lincoln. New Orleans *Times-Picayune,* 17 May 1927, 13; New York *Herald Tribune,* 23 April 1927, 14, 28 April 1927, 30, 17 May 1927, 28; *Washington Post,* 15 May 1927, 21, 17 May 1927, 13; *New York Times,* 23 April 1927, 11, 28 April 1927, 20, 17 May 1927, 37; and *Boston Globe,* 28 April 1927, 17, 17 May 1927, 21.

19. New Orleans *Times-Picayune,* 10 April 1927, 5, 6 May 1927, 17, 18 May 1927, 15.

20. Chester Hingle, another New Orleanian, won the broad jump in Houston, thus qualifying for the national meet, but did not make the trip to Lincoln. New Orleans *Times-Picayune,* 7 June 1927, 13, 13 June 1927, 13, 12 July 2012, B1.

21. *Los Angeles Times,* 7 April 1927, B1; and New York *Herald Tribune,* 26 June 1927, A4.

22. *Chicago Defender,* 9 July 1927, 9; and New Orleans *Times-Picayune,* 12 July 1927, 11.

23. New Orleans *Times-Picayune,* 5 July 1927, 14, 9 July 1927, 10; and *Chicago Defender,* 9 July 1927, 9.

24. Maynard Brichford, "Avery Brundage and Racism," *Fourth International Symposium for Olympic Research,* Global and Cultural Critique: Problematizing the Olympic Games (October 1998): 132. Brundage's papers offer no evidence of his involvement in the process of the 1927 track and field championships' move to Lincoln. See Avery Brundage Collection, 1908–82, 26/20/37, University of Illinois Archives, University of Illinois at Urbana-Champaign.

25. Charles Ross, *Outside the Lines: African Americans and the Integration of the National Football League* (New York: New York University Press, 2001), 156–157, 160.

26. *Louisiana Weekly,* 2 January 1965, 5.

27. Charles Martin, "Integrating New Year's Day: The Racial Politics of College Bowl Games in the American South," in *The Sporting World of the Modern South,* ed. Patrick B. Miller (Urbana: University of Illinois Press, 2002), 178–180, 189–190.

28. *Sporting World of Modern South,* 190–192.

29. *Sporting World of Modern South,* 193.

30. Dorsey v. State Athletic Commission, 168 F. Supp. 149 (1958).

31. Dorsey v. State Athletic Commission, 151–153; and *New York Times,* 26 May 1959, 1.

32. Jeff Miller, *Going Long: The Wild 10-Year Saga of the Renegade American Football League in the Words of Those Who Lived It* (Chicago: Contemporary Books, 2003), 156.

33. New Orleans *Times-Picayune,* 5 January 1965, 5, 18.

34. Maureen Smith, "New Orleans, New Football League, and New Attitudes: The American Football League All-Star Game Boycott, January 1965" in *Sports and the Racial Divide: African American and Latino Experience in an Era of Change,* ed. Michael E. Lomax (Jackson: University Press of Mississippi, 2008), 5–6.

35. New Orleans *Times-Picayune,* 11 January 1965, 1, 5.

36. *Times-Picayune,* 11 January, 1965, 1, 5.

37. *Times-Picayune,* 11 January, 1965, 1, 5.

38. Ron Mix, "Was This Their Freedom Ride?," *Sports Illustrated,* 18 January 1965, 24–25.

39. New Orleans *Times-Picayune,* 11 January 1965, 1, 5.

40. *Louisiana Weekly,* 16 January 1965, 5.

41. *Louisiana Weekly,* 16 January 1965, 1; and New Orleans *Times-Picayune,* 12 January 1956, 1, 3. For more on Schiro, see Edward F. Haas, *Mayor Victor H. Schiro: New Orleans in Transition, 1961–1970* (Jackson: University Press of Mississippi, 2014); and Folder 56: 1966 Stadium and National Football League franchise, folder 56, Box 12, Victor H. and Margaret G. Schiro papers, 1904–1995, LaRC/Manuscripts Collection 1001, Howard-Tilton Memorial Library Special Collections, Tulane University, New Orleans, Louisiana.

42. New Orleans *Times-Picayune,* 12 January 1956, 1, 3.

43. *Times-Picayune,* 12 January 1956, 1, 3.

44. New Orleans *Times-Picayune,* 12 January 1965, 1, 13 January 1965, 25.

45. Charles K. Ross, *Mavericks, Money, and Men: The AFL, Black Players, and the Evolution of Modern Football* (Philadelphia: Temple University Press, 2016), 75.

46. *Radovich v. National Football League,* 352 U.S. 445 (1957).

47. Michael S. Martin, "New Orleans Becomes a Big-League City: The NFL-AFL Merger and the Creation of the New Orleans Saints" in *Horsehide, Pigskin, Oval Tracks and Apple Pie: Essays on Sports and American Culture,* ed. James A. Vlasich (Jefferson, NC: McFarland & Company, Inc., 2006), 119–121.

48. John Lucas, "An Analysis of an 'Over-Crowded Worried Life': General Charles Hitchcock Sherrill's Tenure on the International Olympic Committee, 1922–1936," *OLYMPIKA: The International Journal of Olympic Studies* 11 (2002): 156–157; "The United States of America and Olympism," *Olympic Review* 82–83 (September-October 1974): 451; and "Correspondence-Olympics (1929–1933)," U:137, Box 1, Ernest Lee Jahncke, Sr. Papers, Mss. 1713, 1805, Louisiana and Lower Mississippi Valley Collections, Special Collections, Hill Memorial Library, Louisiana State University, Baton Rouge, Louisiana.

Chapter 12

1. Deborah Brake, *Getting in the Game: Title IX and the Women's Sports Revolution* (New York: New York University Press, 2010), 17.

2. See Jennifer Spear, *Race, Sex, and Social Order in Early New Orleans* (Baltimore: The John Hopkins University Press, 2009); Judith Kelleher Schafer, *Brothels, Depravity, and Abandoned Women: Illegal Sex in Antebellum New Orleans* (Baton Rouge: Louisiana State University Press, 2009); and Emily Epstein Landau, *Spectacular Wickedness: Sex, Race, and Memory in Storyville, New Orleans* (Baton Rouge: Louisiana State University Press, 2013).

3. Dale A. Somers, *The Rise of Sports in New Orleans, 1850–1900* (Baton Rouge: Louisiana State University Press, 1972), 192; and Joan Paul, "Clara Gregory Baer: Catalyst for Women's

Basketball," in *Newcomb College 1886–2006: Higher Education for Women in New Orleans,* eds. Susan Tucker and Beth Willinger (Baton Rouge: Louisiana State University Press, 2012), 180. For more on the cultural history of New Orleans, see Kim Marie Vaz, *"The Baby Dolls": Breaking the Race, and Gender Barriers of the New Orleans Mardi Gras Tradition* (Baton Rouge: Louisiana State University Press, 2013); and Louise McKinney, *New Orleans: A Cultural and Literary History* (Oxford: Signal Books, 2006).

4. Karra Porter, *Mad Season: The Story of the First Women's Professional Basketball League, 1978–1981* (Lincoln: University of Nebraska Press, 2006); and Patricia Gormin, "Pride of New Orleans" *Project 8* WVUE-TV October 30, 1979, Patricia Gormin Collection, U-matic videotape 306–37, University of New Orleans. Wanda Ard also implies she knows how to play the kind of basketball expected by WBL coaches in an interview with Patricia Gormin for a feature with Project 8. See also Lissa Smith, *Nike is a Goddess: The History of Women in Sports* (New York: The Atlantic Monthly Press, 1998).

5. Porter, *Mad Seasons,* 6, 7, 11. By 1980, the NCAA would successfully created five Division I championships for women's basketball, tennis, volleyball, field hockey and swimming. See "NCAA adopts Women's Athletics" and "Thanks, But No Thanks, Women Say," *States Item,* 9 January 1980, B-1 (New Orleans); and Ray Beard, "Brown: Women's Sports to Blossom," *Times-Picayune* Sports Extra, 15 February 1980, 1.

6. Porter, *Mad Seasons,* 150.

7. Isabella, Sean Isabella, "Reliving the Origins of Lady Techster Basketball: Tech to Honor Inaugural Hoops Team from 1974–1975," *The News Star,* 19 February 2016, http://www.thenewsstar.com.

8. On the feminization of sports, see Precilla Y.L. Choi, *Femininity and the Physically Active Woman* (London: Routledge, 2000). The New Orleans NBA franchise, the Jazz, had recently left New Orleans. There were many reasons a women's team would want to differentiate itself from other New Orleans professional teams given the Saints' and Jazz's mediocre performance during the late 1970s. This is alluded to in the Project 8 feature by WVUE-TV and consistently reported in the sports pages of the metropolitan newspapers.

9. Even the founder of the WBL denied that race was an issue. Porter, *Mad Seasons,* 119.

10. Jackson, Lily Jackson, "Queen Brumfield: Imagine Getting Paid to Play Basketball," *The Times-Picayune,* 2 July 1979, 3–8.

11. For more on the focus on gender segregation in sport see, Brake, *Getting in the Game,* 29.

12. Ron Brocato, "Pride's Forest a One Girl Gang," *States Item,* 10 January 1980, D10 and Ron Brocato, "Pride GM Has Shown Dexterity in Building His Team," *States Item,* 4 March 1980, C2. The Pride acquired Hardy due of the collapse of the Washington Metros WBL franchise.

13. Ron Brocato, "Pride GM Has Shown Dexterity in Building His Team," *States Item,* 4 March 1980, C2. It seems that Brocato decided that Williams' body was of considerable note for his readership, while Ard's was not, which reinforced the definition of femininity as "petite [and] blonde."

14. Porter, *Mad Seasons,* 119.

15. Ray Beard, "Ard Enjoys Her Chance at Pro Ball with Pride," *Times-Picayune,* 23 November 1979, 2–2.

16. Bill Grady, "Pride and Prejudice," *Times-Picayune,* 2 March 1980, Dixie Magazine, 28.

17. Porter, *Mad Seasons,* 123.

18. Porter, *Mad Seasons,* 123; and Mike Strom, "Butch and the Simpsons: Both Share Blame for Demise of Pride," *Times-Picayune,* 20 March 1981, 4–5. Claudette Simpson was Dr. John Simpson's wife. The Simpsons were the majority owners of the team. At least early on, van Breda Kolff claimed he had some say in personnel choices. By the second season,

Mrs. Simpson was the general manager and exercised her opinion about draft picks, free agents, and trades. Instead of recognizing the disagreement apparently based upon a number of variables including the race of players, Mrs. Simpson cited a variety of other circumstances that led her to suspend van Breda Kolff. Strom reported that Mrs. Simpson cited Butch's choice of shoes for games ("wearing tennis shoes without socks"), his foul language, his failure to pay WBL fines in a timely manner, the team's losing streak, and "complaints of another nature" as justification for the suspension. Strom purports that van Breda Kolff and Simpson seemed to have personality differences. These differences in personality and opinion seemed to increase in number and impact over the course of the 1980–1981 season. There was also great pressure to win and to increase ticket sales and attendance. The then recent personnel trades (that Butch did not fully support) and consequential losses exacerbated an already tenuous situation. Mrs. Simpson ultimately deemed his actions worthy of suspension, even though the the season was nearing its end and the team already clinched a second postseason berth under van Breda Kolff.

19. Peter "Champ" W. Clark, "Syndrome of Sports," *Louisiana Weekly*, 10 November 1979, 2–9.

20. Peter "Champ" W. Clark, "Abernathy, one of League's Best," *Louisiana Weekly*, 10 January 1980, 2–9.

21. Peter "Champ" W. Clark, "Abernathy, one of League's Best," *Louisiana Weekly*, 10 January 1980, 2–9.

22. Peter "Champ" W. Clark, "New Orleans Wallows in Maelstrom of Racism," *Louisiana Weekly*, 21 March 1981, 2–9.

23. Peter "Champ" W. Clark, "Pride are Step-Child of Local Media," *Louisiana Weekly*, 1 November 1980, 2–11.

24. Peter "Champ" W. Clark, "Pride Contemplate Move to Kenner," *Louisiana Weekly*, 28 February 1981, 2–11.

25. Peter "Champ" W. Clark, "Pride Must Overhaul Their Roster," *Louisiana Weekly*, 5 April 1980, 2–6.

26. Peter "Champ" W. Clark, "Pride Deserve Community Support," *Louisiana Weekly*, 3 January 1981, 2–5.

27. Peter "Champ" W. Clark, "Lagniappe," *Louisiana Weekly*, 20 December 1980, 2–3.

28. Peter "Champ" W. Clark, "Pride Trade Crusoe," *Louisiana Weekly*, 10 January 1981, 2–7.

29. Peter "Champ" W. Clark, "Coretta Bloom," *Louisiana Weekly*, 15 December 1979, 2–9.

30. See Patricia Hill Collins and Sirma Bilge, *Intersectionality* (New York: Wiley, 2016); and Patricia Hill Collins, *Black Sexual Politics: African Americans, Gender, and the New Racism* (New York: Routledge, 2004), 95.

31. Peter "Champ" W. Clark, "Pride's Unsung Heroine," *Louisiana Weekly*, 14 March 1981, 2–9.

32. See Pamela Creedon, *Women, Media, and Sport: Challenging Gender Values.* (Thousand Oaks: Sage Publications, 1994); Nancy Hogshead-Makar and Andrew S. Zimbalist, *Equal Play: Title IX and Social Change* (Philadelphia: Temple University Press, 2007); and Jean O'Reilly and Susan K. Cahn, *Women and Sports in the United States: A Documentary Reader* (Boston: Northeastern University Press, 2007).

33. See Diane Heidstand, "Women and Sports in the United States, 1945–1978," in Reet Howell, *Her Story in Sport: A Historical Anthology of Women in Sports* (West Point: Leisure Press, 1982).

34. Frank Litsky, "Butch van Breda Kolff, 84, Fiery Coach, Dies," *New York Times*, 24 August 2007.

35. Brake, *Getting in the Game,* 13, 15. Academicians too position that athletics is a pie that must be shared. This is arguably accurate as far as dollars and budgets but does not translate as well into other sporting spaces. Brake argues that we will not reach parity or equality in sports until we eliminate these categorizations. No space ought to be claimed by people of certain gender or race. Instead they should be claimed by the most competent players.

36. "She Has Pride in Girls," *Times-Picayune,* 5 October 1980, 22.

37. Race was an issue that was downplayed from the first draft of the WBL. Whiteness was the goal generally and diverse racial representation was supposed to silence the discussion of race. In the inaugural season, 60% of the WBL players were white. By the third season, the percentage of white players dropped to 49% across the league. However, in New Orleans the percentage increased to 80% in the third season, further reinforcing the already pervasive racial inequities in the region and in sports more generally. Porter, *Mad Seasons,* 120–121.

38. Lily Jackson, "Queen Brumfield: Imagine Getting Paid to Play Basketball," *Times-Picayune,* 2 July 1979, 3–8.

39. For more on the biomedical model in women's sports see, Collette Dowling, *The Frailty Myth: Women Approaching Physical Equality* (New York: Random House, 2000); Choi, *Femininity and the Physically Active Woman*; and Ying Wushanley, *Playing Nice and Losing: The Struggle for Control of Women's Intercollegiate Athletics, 1960–2000* (Syracuse: Syracuse University Press, 2004).

40. Ron Brocato, "Karen Logan: A Quiet Champion of a Cause," *States Item,* 8 October 1979, C10.

41. She also said as an afterthought that it also was not good for men to be socially isolated. Her doing so does not detract from her main idea that women need to be able to do more than just play basketball. According to Logan, women needed to be prepared to build a long-term career outside of sport, which cemented her position that women were temporarily in the sports world.

42. Linda D. Williams, "Sportswomen in Black and White: Sports History from an Afro-American Perspective," in *Gender, Media, and Sport: Challenging Gender Values,* ed. Pamela J. Creedon (Thousand Oaks: Sage, 1994), 50.

43. Williams, "Sportswomen in Black and White," 47.

44. Hill Collins, *Black Sexual Politics,* 88.

45. Hill Collins, *Black Sexual Politics,* 95, 115.

46. Ron Brocato, "Pride Can't Be Ignored Anymore," *States Item,* 20 March 1980, B2.

Chapter 13

1. Originally published in *Journal of Sport and Social Issues* 38 (No. 2 2014): 148–163.

2. Michael A. Hogg, Deborah J. Terry, and Katherine M. White, "A Tale Of Two Theories: A Critical Comparison of Identity Theory With Social Identity Theory," *Social Psychology Quarterly* 58 (December 1995): 255–269.

3. Owen Hargie, David Dickson, John Mallett, and Maurice Stringer, "Communicating Social Identity: A Study of Catholics and Protestants in Northern Ireland," *Communication Research* 35 (No. 6 2008): 792–821.

4. Amelie Mummendey, Thomas Kessler, Andreas Klink, and Rosemary Mielke, "Strategies to Cope With Negative Social Identity: Predictions By Social Identity Theory and Relative Deprivation Theory," *Journal of Personality and Social Psychology* 76 (February 1999): 229–245.

5. Hargie et al., "Communicating Social Identity"; and Mummendey et al., "Strategies to Cope With Negative Social Identity."

6. Hargie et al., "Communicating Social Identity," 792.

7. Ziona Austrian, and Mark S. Rosentraub, "Cities, Sports, and Economic Change: A Retrospective Assessment," *Journal of Urban Affairs* 24 (December 2002): 549–563.

8. Robert A. Baade, "Professional Sports as Catalysts for Metropolitan Economic Development," *Journal of Urban Affairs* 18 (March 1996): 1–17.

9. Robert A. Baade and Richard F. Dye, "The Impact of Stadiums and Professional Sports on Metropolitan Area Development," *Growth and Change* 21 (April 1990): 1–14.

10. Dennis Coates and Brad R. Humphreys, "The Growth Effects of Sport Franchises, Stadia, and Arenas," *Journal of Policy Analysis and Management* 18 (September 1999): 601–625.

11. Baade and Dye, "The Impact of Stadiums and Professional Sports on Metropolitan Area Development"; Dean V. Baim, *Sports Stadiums as Wise Investments: An Evaluation* (Chicago: Heartland Institute Policy Study No. 32, November 1990); and Charles C. Euchner, *Playing the Field: Why Sports Teams Move and Cities Fight to Keep Them* (Baltimore: Johns Hopkins University Press, 1994).

12. Coates and Humphreys, "The Growth Effects of Sport Franchises, Stadia, and Arenas."

13. Mark S. Rosentraub, "Does the Emperor Have New Clothes? A Reply to Robert A. Baade," *Journal of Urban Affairs* 18 (March 1996): 23–31.

14. Rosentraub, "Does the Emperor Have New Clothes?" 27.

15. Daniel L. Wann, S. Inman, C.L. Ensor, R.D. Gates, and D.S. Caldwell, "Assessing the Psychological Well-Being of Sport Fans Using the Profile of Mood States: The Importance of Team Identification," *International Sports Journal* 3 (Winter 1999): 81–90.

16. Edward R. Hirt, Dolf Zillman, Grant A. Erickson, and Chris Kennedy, "Costs and Benefits of Allegiance: Changes in Fans' Self-Ascribed Competencies After Team Victory Versus Team Defeat," *Journal of Personality and Social Psychology* 63 (No. 5 1992): 724–738.

17. Michael C. Davis and Christian M. End, "A Winning Proposition: The Economic Impact of Successful National Football League Franchises," *Economic Inquiry* 48 (January 2010): 39–50.

18. N. Schwarz, F. Starck, D. Kommer, and D. Wagner, "Soccer, Rooms, and The Quality of Life: Mood Effects on Judgments of Satisfaction With Life In General and With Specific Domains," *European Journal of Social Psychology* 17 (No. 1 1987): 69–79.

19. Timothy A. Judge and Shinichiro Watanabe, "Another Look at the Job Satisfaction-Life Satisfaction Relationship," *Journal of Applied Psychology* 78 (No. 6 1993): 939–948.

20. Marianne Tait, Margaret Y. Padgett, and Timothy T. Baldwin, "Job and Life Satisfaction: A Reevaluation of The Strength of The Relationship and Gender Effects as A Function of The Date Of The Study," *Journal of Applied Psychology* 74 (No. 3 1989): 502–507.

21. Davis and End, "A Winning Proposition."

22. Alice M. Isen, "Some Ways in Which Affect Influences Cognitive Processes: Implications For Advertising And Consumer Behavior," in *Cognitive and Affective Responses to Advertising*, ed. Patricia Cafferata and Alice M. Tybout (Lanham, MD: Lexington Books, 1989), 91–117.

23. Austrian and Rosentraub, "Cities, Sports, and Economic Change," 550.

24. MJ Platow, M. Durante, N. Williams, M. Garrett, J. Walshe, S. Cincotta, and A. Brautchu, "The Contributions of Sport Fan Social Identity to the Production of Prosocial Behavior," *Group Dynamics: Theory, Research, and Practice* 3 (No. 2 1999): 161–169.

25. Robert S. Brown, "Sport and Healing America," *Society* 42 (November/December 2004): 37–41. Quote from p. 41.

26. Stefan Fatsis, "Football's Saints Ponder Whether to Relocate," *Wall Street Journal,* 8 September 2005, B1, B5.

27. Tim Layden, "Marching In," *Sports Illustrated,* 22 January 2007, 38.

28. Peter Finney, "Win Was a Long Time Coming," *Times-Picayune,* 25 January 2010, A01.

29. Tim Layden, "March of History," *Sports Illustrated,* 11 February 2010, 72.

30. John Pope, and Bruce Nolan, "All Over New Orleans, People Shared the Euphoria From a Stunning Victory," *Times-Picayune,* 9 February 2010, A01.

31. Nakia Hogan, "The *Times-Picayune* Picks South Louisiana's 25 Most Influential People in Sports," *Times-Picayune,* 19 July 2009, C01.

32. Layden, "March of History."

33. Finney, "Win Was a Long Time Coming."

34. Robert A. Baade and Victor A. Matheson, "Professional Sports, Hurricane Katrina, and the Economic Redevelopment of New Orleans," *Contemporary Economic Policy* 25 (No. 4 2007): 594.

35. Baade and Matheson, "Professional Sports, Hurricane Katrina, and the Economic Redevelopment of New Orleans," 594.

36. Tim Layden, "Faithful, Joyful, Triumphant," *Sports Illustrated,* 11 February 2010, 10.

37. Baade and Matheson, "Professional Sports, Hurricane Katrina, and the Economic Redevelopment of New Orleans," 591–592.

38. Layden, "Faithful, Joyful, Triumphant," 10.

39. Baade and Matheson, "Professional Sports, Hurricane Katrina, and the Economic Redevelopment of New Orleans."

40. Baade and Matheson, "Professional Sports, Hurricane Katrina, and the Economic Redevelopment of New Orleans."

41. Fatsis, "Football's Saints Ponder Whether to Relocate," B1, B5; and Layden, "Marching In," 38.

42. Fatsis, "Football's Saints Ponder Whether to Relocate," B1.

43. Layden, "Marching In," 38; and Peter King, "The Future is Now," 8 May 2006, *Sports Illustrated,* 38.

44. Sally Jenkins, "A City's Biggest Moment. Easy," *Washington Post,* 25 January 2010, D01; and Paul Schwartz, "The Big Brees-y-Saints QB, and City, Each Rose From Ruin," *New York Post,* 25 January 2010, 72.

45. John DeShazier, "A Magical Mix; The Saints' Return to the Superdome In 2006 Against The Falcons Stands as the Franchise's Iconic Moment at the Facility, But All the Ingredients Are Present For That to Be Topped Sunday," *Times-Picayune,* 23 January 2010, S03.

46. Layden, "Marching In," 38.

47. Peter King, "Patron Saint," *Sports Illustrated,* 11 February 2010, 58.

48. Quoted in Lee Jenkins, "Super Bowl XLIV For You, New Orleans," *Sports Illustrated,* 15 February 2010, 30.

49. Layden, "Marching In," 38; Baade and Matheson, "Professional Sports, Hurricane Katrina, and the Economic Redevelopment of New Orleans"; Alexander Wolff, "Two Years After Katrina," *Sports Illustrated,* 27 August 2007, 80; and Hogan, "The *Times-Picayune* Picks South Louisiana's 25 Most Influential People in Sports," C01.

50. Mark Lorando, "The Crying Game; Win or Lose Today, Many Who Dats Won't Be Able to Hold Back the Tears," *Times-Picayune,* 24 January 2010, D1.

51. Brent St. Germain, "Who Dat Nation Shows National Pride," *Houma Today,* 16 January 2010, available from www.houmatoday.com.

52. Dave Walker, "The Chant Is Older Than We Think," *Times-Picayune,* 13 January 2010, A01.

53. Dave Walker, "Super Bowl Smashes TV Record: More People Viewed the Saints-Colts Game Than Any Program in History," *Times-Picayune*, 9 February 2010, A01.

54. Dave Walker, "Media Magnet: Attracted by the Alluring Success of the Saints, the TV World Has Focused Dozens of Camera Lenses on New Orleans," *Times-Picayune*, 8 February 2010, D16.

55. Rebecca Mowbray, "State Eager to Ride Saints' Coattails: Team's Success Mirrors La.'s Rise Officials Say," *Times-Picayune*, 6 February 2010, C11.

56. Hogan, "The *Times-Picayune* Picks South Louisiana's 25 Most Influential People in Sports," C01; and Wolff, "Two Years After Katrina," 80.

57. David L. Altheide, *Qualitative Media Analysis* (Thousand Oaks, CA: Sage Publishing, 1996); and Thomas R. Lindlof and Bryan C. Taylor, *Qualitative Communication Research Methods*, 2nd ed. (Thousand Oaks, CA: Sage Publishing, 2002).

58. Emeril Lagasse, "A Team to Savor," *Sports Illustrated*, 11 February 2010, 80.

59. Mark Maske, "A City and Its Team Enjoy a Magical Run; The People of New Orleans Revel in the Saints' 11–0 Start," *Washington Post*, 4 December 2009, D01.

60. Mike Vaccaro, "Super Dreams: They're Aints And Dolts No More," *New York Post*, 8 February 2010, 78.

61. LeCharles Bentley, "It's the People of New Orleans That Make the Place So Special," *Times-Picayune*, 6 February 2010, S73.

62. S. Burtt, "We Can Learn A Lot From Our Heroes, NO Saints," *Mobile Register*, 15 February 2010, C01.

63. David Hammer, "Color Blind Bond; Racial Harmony Stands Out in Who Dat Nation," *Times-Picayune*, 2 February 2010, A01.

64. Jenkins, "A City's Biggest Moment. Easy," D01.

65. Jenkins, "A City's Biggest Moment. Easy," D01.

66. Peter King, "Super Saints," *Sports Illustrated*, 11 February 2010, 41.

67. Mummendey, Kessler, Klink, and Mielke, "Strategies to Cope with Negative Social Identity."

68. Andrew Canulette, "Community Savors Magical Moment," *Times-Picayune*, 11 February 2010, H01.

69. John Pope and Bruce Nolan, "All Over New Orleans, People Shared the Euphoria From a Stunning Victory," *Times-Picayune*, 9 February 2010, A01.

70. John DeShazier, "Saints Carried New Orleans Banner High," *Mobile Register*, 9 February 2010, B03.

71. Mark Cannizzaro, "No Freeney Pass for Indy Defense: Manning and Company Favorites in Name Only," *New York Post*, 6 February 2010, 54.

72. Mark Maske, "Saints' Brees, Payton in Disbelief a Day After Win; New Orleans's QB, Coach Say Super Bowl Triumph Will Take Time to Sink In," *Washington Post*, 9 February 2010, D03.

73. Ted Griggs, "Experts: Win Will Help Productivity," *Baton Rouge Advocate*, 9 February 2010, B04.

74. Ted Griggs, "Experts: Win Will Help Productivity," B04.

75. Mark Ballard, "Are Saints Really a Winner?" *Baton Rouge Advocate*, 24 January 2010, B07.

76. "Jazz and razz; Worthy of Praise. And Not," *Times-Picayune*, 11 February 2010, B06.

77. Baade and Matheson, "Professional Sports, Hurricane Katrina, and the Economic Redevelopment of New Orleans."

78. Wolff, "Two Years After Katrina," 7.

Contributors

Thomas Aiello is associate professor of history and African American studies at Valdosta State University. He is the author of *The Grapevine of the Black South: The Scott Newspaper Syndicate in the Generation Before the Civil Rights Movement* (Georgia, 2018), and *Dixieball: Race and Professional Basketball in the Deep South, 1947–1979* (Tennessee, 2019). His books on Louisiana sports include *The Kings of Casino Park: Black Baseball In the Lost Season of 1932* (Alabama, 2011), *Paul Morphy: The Pride and Sorrow of Chess* (Louisiana, 2010), and *Bayou Classic: The Grambling-Southern Football Rivalry* (LSU, 2010).

Robert A. Baade is the Ernest A. Johnson Professor of Economics at Lake Forest College in Lake Forest, Illinois. He earned his PhD in economics from the University of Wisconsin. He is widely acknowledged as one of the leading experts on the economic impact of sports teams, infrastructure, and events, and his work has appeared, among others places, in *Regional Studies, Journal of Urban Affairs,* and *Oxford Review of Economic Policy.* He also has served as the President of the International Association of Sports Economists.

Kasey Britt (MS—Louisiana State University) is an operations manager at LA Fitness in the area of Tampa/St. Petersburg, Florida and a graduate of the LSU Sport Management program.

Elizabeth Booksh Burns is the Associate Director of New Student Orientation at the University of Alabama at Birmingham (UAB) and holds an MA in Communication Management from UAB. She is an Adjunct Professor at UAB and Troy University.

Mark Dyreson is professor of kinesiology, affiliate professor of history, and the director of research and educational programs for the Center for the Study of Sports in Society at Pennsylvania State University. A fellow in the National Academy of Kinesiology, a former president of the North American Society for Sport History, the managing editor of the *International Journal of the History of*

Sport, and the coeditor of the Sport in Global Society: Historical Perspectives book series from Routledge Press, he has published several books and articles on the history of modern sport.

Samantha Gonzales (MS—Louisiana State University) is a Coordinator for Facility Operations at LSU in University Recreation and a graduate of the LSU Sport Management program.

Callan N. Hendershott is double major in economics and math at the College of the Holy Cross in Worcester, Massachusetts. She has worked as a research assistant in the Weiss Summer Research Program in Economics at Holy Cross and has also studied at the University of Melbourne in Australia.

Michael S. Martin holds the Cheryl Courrégé Burguières/Board of Regents Professorship in History at the University of Louisiana at Lafayette. His research and teaching interests focus on Louisiana history, public history, and the history of the South. Martin's most recent publications include *The Louisiana Experience* (as co-author, 2017); *Creolization in the French Americas* (as co-editor, 2015); *Russell Long: A Life in Politics* (2014); *Louisiana Legacies: Readings in the History of the Pelican State* (as co-editor, 2013); *Louisiana Beyond Black and White: Recent Interpretations of Twentieth-Century Race and Race Relations* (as editor, 2011); and *Historic Lafayette* (2007). He also is managing editor of the journal *Louisiana History,* the state's historical journal published quarterly by the Louisiana Historical Association.

Victor A. Matheson is a professor in the Department of Economics and Accounting at the College of the Holy Cross in Worcester, Massachusetts. He earned his PhD in economics from the University of Minnesota. He has published extensively in the field of the economics of collegiate and professional sports and is the President of the North American Association of Sports Economists as well as the editor of the *Journal of Sports Economics.* He also has worked as an intercollegiate and professional soccer referee.

Richard V. McGehee is retired professor of physical education at Southeastern Louisiana University and currently a research fellow in Latin American studies at the University of Texas at Austin.

Katherine C. Mooney is assistant professor of history at Florida State University and the author of *Race Horse Men: How Slavery and Freedom Were Made at the Racetrack.*

Stephen H. Norwood is professor of history at the University of Oklahoma. Most recently, he is the editor of *New York Sports: Glamour and Grit in the Empire City* (2018). He is the author of five books, including *Antisemitism and the American Far Left* (Cambridge University Press, 2013) and *The Third Reich in the Ivory Tower: Complicity and Conflict on American Campuses* (Cambridge University Press, 2009), which was a Finalist for the National Jewish Book Award for Holocaust Studies. His book *Labor's Flaming Youth* won the Herbert G. Gutman Award for American Social History. Norwood coedited (with Eunice G. Pollack) the prize-winning two-volume *Encyclopedia of American Jewish History* (ABC-CLIO, 2008). He has published numerous scholarly articles in American social, labor, sport, gender, Jewish and African-American history. In addition to *New York Sports,* his sport history publications include *Real Football: Conversations on America's Game* and articles in several anthologies, the *Journal of Sport History,* and *Modern Judaism.* He was co-winner of the Macmillan/SABR Award in Baseball History.

Gregory L. Richard is director of the Legal Studies Program, codirector of the Law & Society Program, and associate professor of history at Winona State University. He attended the University of Louisiana at Lafayette and the Paul M. Hebert Law Center at Louisiana State University in Baton Rouge, where he earned a Juris Doctor and a Bachelor of Civil Law in 2004, and did his doctoral work at the University of Mississippi. He clerked for the Louisiana Department of Justice and worked with the Innocence Project–New Orleans. His research interests include United States constitutional and legal history United States history after the Civil War, Modern US history, the civil rights movement, the history of the carceral state in the United States, prison reform and corrections history in general, and the federal courts' work during the civil rights movement.

Randy Roberts is 150th Anniversary Professor and Distinguished Professor of History at Purdue University and was the 2015–2016 Charles Boal Ewing Chair of Military History at West Point. In addition to winning the Charles B. Murphy

Outstanding Teaching Award at Purdue University and twice receiving Teacher of the Year in the School of Liberal Arts, he won the Carnegie Foundation for the Advancement of Teaching Indiana Professor of the Year. He has won several national book awards. His book, coauthored with Johnny Smith, *Blood Brothers: The Fatal Friendship Between Muhammad Ali and Malcolm X,* received featured reviews in the *Los Angeles Times,* the *Wall Street Journal,* the *New York Times,* the *London Times,* the *National Review,* and other newspapers and magazines. His most recent book coauthored with Johnny Smith is *A Season In the Sun: The Rise of Mickey Mantle.*

Chad S. Seifried (PhD—The Ohio State University) is the L. M. "Pat" and Mildred Harrison Endowed Professor in sport management at the Louisiana State University. His research interests embrace the use of historical methods to review the management history associated with organizations, individuals, and sport facilities to highlight the contribution of history within contemporary management settings.

Dale A. Somers was only thirty-two when he died of cancer just after Louisiana State University Press published *The Rise of Sports in New Orleans, 1850–1900* in 1972. It was his first book, but Somers had already published several significant articles and had held his Tulane PhD for six years. The Galveston native was on the faculty of Georgia State University, a popular professor and president of the school's AAUP chapter, who returned home to Texas to die. His tragic early death was a loss for both Louisiana history and sports history, and it seemed to presage the young burial of comprehensive sports histories of New Orleans and the state. *The Rise of Sports in New Orleans* has stood for decades as the seminal text on its subject and a paragon of early urban sports histories that helped demonstrate the value of such treatments to the rise of social history as a discipline.

Stacy Lynn Tanner was born and raised in Florida. She earned her MA in history and her PhD in interdisciplinary humanities from Florida State University. She is professor of humanities at Seminole State College in Sanford, Florida where she teaches humanities, history, and cultural studies. Her primary research areas include WGSS, media studies, and sports studies.

Alexa Webb (MS—Louisiana State University) is an Athletic Academic Coordinator with the University of Virginia and graduate of the LSU sport management program.

Index